Human
Physical Growth
and Maturation
Methodologies and Factors

NATO ADVANCED STUDY INSTITUTES SERIES

A series of edited volumes comprising multifaceted studies of contemporary scientific issues by some of the best scientific minds in the world, assembled in cooperation with NATO Scientific Affairs Division.

Series A: Life Sciences

Recent Volumes in this Series

The series is published by an international board of publishers in conjunction with NATO Scientific Affairs Division

A Life Sciences	Plenum Publishing Corporation
B Physics	New York and London
C Mathematical and Physical Sciences	D. Reidel Publishing Company Dordrecht and Boston
D Behavioral and Social Sciences	Sijthoff International Publishing Company Leiden
E Applied Sciences	Noordhoff International Publishing Leiden

Human Physical Growth and Maturation

Methodologies and Factors

Edited by

Francis E. Johnston

University of Pennsylvania
Philadelphia, Pennsylvania

Alex F. Roche

Fels Research Institute
Wright State University School of Medicine
Yellow Springs, Ohio

and

Charles Susanne

Free University of Brussels
Brussels, Belgium

PLENUM PRESS ● NEW YORK AND LONDON
Published in cooperation with NATO Scientific Affairs Division

Library of Congress Cataloging in Publication Data

Nato Advanced Study Institute on Human Physical Growth and Maturation: Methodologies
and factors, Sogesta Conference Centre, Italy, 1979.
Human physical growth and maturation.

(NATO advanced study institutes series: Series A, Life sciences; v. 30)
"Proceedings of the NATO Advanced Study Institute on Human Physical Growth and
Maturation: Methodologies and Factors, held at the Sogesta Conference Centre, Urbino,
Italy, May 28–June 7, 1979."
Includes index.
1. Human growth–Congresses. 2. Aging–Congresses. 3. Maturation (Psychology)–Con-
gresses. I. Johnston, Francis E., 1931-   II. Roche, Alex F., 1921-   III. Susanne,
Charles. IV. Title. V. Series.
QP84.N32 1979   612'.6   79-27633
ISBN 0-306-40420-6

Proceedings of the NATO Advanced Study Institute on Human Physical Growth
and Maturation: Methodologies and Factors, held at the Sogesta Conference Centre,
Urbino, Italy, May 28–June 7, 1979.

© 1980 Plenum Press, New York
A Division of Plenum Publishing Corporation
227 West 17th Street, New York, N.Y. 10011

Printed in the United States of America

PREFACE

The present volume grew out of a NATO Advanced Study Institute
held at Sogesta, Italy, during the summer of 1979. We are most
grateful for the generous financial support of NATO and for the
provision of travel funds by The National Science Foundation
(Washington, D.C., U.S.A.) and Ross Laboratories (Columbus, Ohio,
U.S.A.). The Institute could not have been held in a more suitable
place nor could the staff at Sogesta have been more helpful. The
efforts of all concerned contributed to the success of this Institute, which was attended by 97 scientists from 23 countries.

It is hoped the present volume will be useful to those who
were unable to attend the Institute although it will be an incomplete substitute for the Institute itself. Necessarily, it lacks
the formal and informal discussions that followed the lectures,
the interchanges that occurred at group meetings, and, of course,
the instruction given in the practicums. Nevertheless, we hope it
will be useful to a wide range of professionals interested in growth
and development.

F. E. J.

A. F. R.

C. S.

CONTENTS

CONTRIBUTORS

R. Darrell Bock, University of Chicago, Chicago, Illinois 60637, U.S.A.

Ingeborg Brandt, University Children's Hospital Bonn, 5300 Bonn 1, Germany, F. R.

Arto Demirjian, Centre de Recherches sur la Croissance, Université de Montréal, Case Postale H3T1J6, Montréal 101, Canada

Roland Hauspie, Belgian National Science Foundation, Free University Brussels, Pleinlaan 2, 1050 Brussels, Belgium

Francis E. Johnston, Department of Anthropology, University of Pennsylvania, Philadelphia, Pennsylvania 19104, U.S.A.

Robert M. Malina, Department of Anthropology, University of Texas, Austin, Texas 78712, U.S.A.

Violetta de Martino, Institute of Psychiatry, University of Rome, Rome, Italy

Ettore Marubini, Instituto de Statistica Medica e Biometria, Universita degli Studi di Milano, Via Venezian 1, 20133, Milano, Italy

Paolo Parisi, Department of Medical Genetics, University of Rome and The Mendel Institute, Rome, Italy

Alex F. Roche, Fels Research Institute and Department of Pediatrics, Wright State University School of Medicine, Yellow Springs, Ohio 45387, U.S.A.

Charles Susanne, Free University Brussels, Pleinlaan 2, 1050 Brussels, Belgium

David Thissen, University of Kansas, Lawrence, Kansas 66045, U.S.A.

INTRODUCTION

En qualité de membre du Groupe "Facteurs Humains" il m'est très agréable de vous saluer au nom de la Division des Affaires Scientifiques de l'OTAN.

Je sais, par expérience, quels efforts et quelles difficultés doivent affronter les collègues désireux d'organiser une rencontre comme celle-ci. C'est la raison pour laquelle je tiens à leur exprimer la reconnaissance et les félicitations de la Division des Affaires Scientifiques, pour les avoir surmontés.

Il n'entre pas dans mes intentions de vous infliger un grand discours sur le rôle éminent de la Division des Affaires Scientifiques de l'OTAN, mais je souhaite néanmoins vous rappeler les grandes lignes sur son activité.

L'objectif essentiel, du programme scientifique consiste à renforcer, par tous les moyens connus, la coopération entre les scientifiques appartenant à des pays membres de l'Alliance. Cette action est menée de manière totalement indépendante des programmes militaires, sans concertation avec les responsables de ces programmes et sans que leur avis soit même sollicité sur d'éventuelles orientations à donner aux activités de la Division. La plus grande partie de l'effort financier, environ 55% du budget de la Division, est consacré à de jeunes chercheurs, en vue de leur permettre de compléter leurs études pour obtenir un doctorat ou une formation post-doctorale.

Le programme de l'Institut des Sciences Avancées, 20% du budget, est destiné à fournir à de jeunes scientifiques maitrisant déjà parfaitement une discipline, l'opportunité d'entendre et de prendre contact avec les plus grands savants existant au monde dans leur discipline et à se connaître entre eux.

Les bourses de recherches, 14% du budget, sont destinées à promouvoir des coopérations internationales, dans toutes les disciplines scientifiques, sur des programmes élaborés par les chercheurs eux-mêmes.

Un second type d'activité du Comité Scientifique consiste à créer un groupe spécial destiné à développer les recherches et la coopération dans des domaines très précis. Actuellement six groupes existent : Science des Systèmes, Inter action air-mer, Facteurs humains, Science de la mer, Matériel scientifique, Sciences écologiques. Chaque groupe est composé d'un certain nombre d'experts nommés en principe pour trois ans et appartenant aux différents pays de l'Alliance.

L'action de ces groupes se développe de maintes façons : organisation de colloques et de symposiums, prise en charge de visites d'étude ou de cycles de conférences, échanges de personnels scientifiques entre laboratoires, financement de voyages de conseillers de haut niveau, bourses de recherches etc ...

Ainsi que vous pouvez le constater, l'intervention de la Division se fait dans de nombreuses directions, ce qui lui permet de répondre à la mission qui lui a été confiée.

Avant de terminer je voudrais revenir sur l'Institut des Sciences Avancées, puisque notre réunion se rapporte plus précisément à son activité. Il constitue à mon sens un outil d'une efficacité considérable à condition que les règles élémentaires citées plus haut soient respectées. Il faut absolument que les auditeurs possèdent déjà un très haut niveau dans la discipline retenue pour bénéficier des exposés des plus grands Maîtres de la Recherche en la matière. S'il n'en était pas ainsi, les savants que l'on prie de venir exposer les idées les plus récentes dans leur domaine, n'auraient pas en face d'eux les interlocuteurs qu'ils sont en droit d'espérer. Les auditeurs doivent réellement constituer la génération montante des savants dans la discipline, pour retirer un réel profit de leur rencontre. S'il n'en était pas ainsi la réunion ne présenterait qu'un intérêt anecdotique ou touristique.

Je suis persuadé que cette réunion respecte ces règles élémentaires.

La liste des conférenciers réunit bon nombre des plus éminents spécialistes mondiaux de la Croissance Humaine. Nul doute que les auditeurs montreront par leurs interventions, le niveau de leurs questions, l'élévation des discussions, qu'ils constituent bien l'élite de la prochaine génération de chercheurs dans ce domaine encore si mal connu.

Professeur Alex COBLENTZ

Université René Descartes - PARIS -

INTRODUCTION

The scientific study of human physical growth and maturation has a long illustrious history involving leading scientists from many countries. Although much has been learned, much remains to be achieved. Future progress is dependent upon the standardization of procedures, use of sophisticated methods and the involvement of many disciplines. Also, it is dependent upon the recruitment of young scientists and the successful implementation of new studies, particularly in developing countries where the growth and maturation of many children are retarded due to environmental factors.

Physical growth and maturation are important partly because they are normal physiological processes that are essential for the well-being of the human organism. Aspects of growth and maturation can be used as "indicators" of genetically determined variation, environmental factors or pathological processes. Physical growth and maturation are important, however, in their own right because the physiological competence of the growing organism and of the adult organism may be compromised if these processes are abnormal. This is particularly obvious in the central nervous, locomotor, and reproductive systems.

The chapters in the present volume are arranged into three sections. The methodological aspects of the study of human growth and development have received considerable attention in the first section. Size was perhaps one of the first human attributes to be measured in a way that is still regarded as valid. But even for well-known aspects of size such as weight, there is a need for a standardization of methods, including equipment. The methodology of a growth study must begin with statement of a question and then selection of a research design. Between these steps and the final data analysis many intermediate matters must be addressed, including the selection of appropriate variables and the use of the best methods for recording the relevant data. There has been considerable recent progress in all these areas; this progress is reviewed critically in the present volume.

1

Some excellent studies of physical growth and maturation are considered in the second section. This section includes reviews of the physical changes observed in adolescents and adults and the factors responsible for them. Attention is given also to the prediction of adult stature, craniofacial growth and age at menarche.

Any account of growth and maturation would be incomplete without reference to present knowledge of the environmental influences known to control these processes. These environmental factors are considered in Section III of this volume where particular attention is given to nutrition, physical activity, socioeconomic factors and psychosocial factors. There are many new findings and exciting new methods. Of course, genetic mechanisms also are important in the regulation of growth and maturation. The literature in this area and the methodology that has recently become available, particularly in relation to analyses of data from twins and path analysis, are reviewed.

Finally, it must be stressed that growth is dynamic. This is stated repetitively in the literature and by lecturers but, alas, all too often growth data are analysed in a cross-sectional fashion. Appropriate analyses of growth depend upon the utilization of serial data. These data can be used in many ways, e.g., to calculate increments or correlations from one age to the next. The ultimate aim is to describe and understand the patterns of growth in individuals. This can be done only after fitting mathematically defined curves to sets of serial data for individuals. These procedures have been improved greatly in recent years and have become much more readily available through the application of computer technology. What has been achieved provides the hope that data recorded at a single age will allow reasonably accurate predictions of the patterns of growth for individuals. This major new step would have seemed impossible a few years ago.

It is hoped this volume will be a beginning rather than an end for the reader. Each chapter concludes with a selective bibliography which the reader is encouraged to consult for more detailed and extensive information.

F.E.J.
A.F.R.
C.S.

I. METHODOLOGY

1. RESEARCH DESIGN AND SAMPLE SELECTION

IN STUDIES OF GROWTH AND DEVELOPMENT

Francis E. Johnston

Department of Anthropology
University of Pennsylvania
Philadelphia, Pa.   19104

The study of human growth and development is an integral part
of the scientific study of human biological structure, function and
diversity. Consequently, the research upon which our knowledge is
based must be firmly established in the methodology of science and
must reflect that set of attitudes and approaches which has come to
be known as the scientific method. Just as with any research, the
success or failure of a growth study depends ultimately upon the
quality of the research design. As used here, research design involves all steps which lead from the formulation of an initial question, through the development of a series of procedures which will
provide an appropriate data base and the analysis of that base, to
the interpretation of the analysis and the extension of the interpretation from the immediate to the general. Each step is crucial
and none can be ignored or treated lightly. Good research requires
detailed planning, careful consideration of alternatives, and strict
attention to the rules of both logic and objectivity.

ALTERNATE STRATEGIES IN GROWTH RESEARCH

There is no one research strategy to be used in growth research.
The design adopted by any investigator must be appropriate to answer
the question which has been asked. A number of alternate strategies
have been utilized and in this section the more important are covered, with a brief discussion of the strengths and weaknesses of each.

Descriptive and Correlative Studies

The most common type of research into growth and development is

5

descriptive. An investigator sets out to describe some aspect of growth which was hitherto unknown, in order to add to our knowledge of the process and the way in which it varies under different conditions. The purpose is not to answer questions about how something is regulated or what factors act to create variation. Instead, descriptive research seeks only to present data on growth and development.

In a descriptive study there are two aspects of research design which are especially important. The first aspect concerns the careful description and delineation of the unit, or units, of study. The particular feature of growth which is being described must be identified as completely as is possible. It is of little, if any, value merely to describe the changes with age of some anthropometric dimension, if that dimension has no underlying basis within the process of growth. It is not sufficient justification to describe age changes in something which is measured only because it is convenient.

It is also important to describe and delineate the population which has been sampled. The population must be defined biologically and demographically so as to give specificity to the research. Given for example the historical complexities of the movements of Africans to the New World, and of their descendants within the Americas, the term "American Negro" has very little biological or demographic meaning. One should provide more precise delineation.

The second aspect of research design important in a descriptive study involves the development of techniques of measurement which will generate appropriate data objectively, with errors which are within acceptable limits. The unit of measurement must be described in such a way that, if warranted, the study can be replicated.

Even though descriptive studies are rather low on the scale of research prestige, they should not be disparaged. We are constantly reminded that we lack simple, though essential, basic data on growth and its variability. At the same time, we must acknowledge that far too many descriptive studies are repetitive and unnecessary, providing us with no new information but only validating over and over what is well-established.

Correlative studies attempt to identify factors which are related to the changes of growth and development. In some instances, the factors identified may be related causally to growth; i.e., they are responsible for the observed changes. While causality is not so easy to establish, it can be done if the following criteria are satisfied: 1) A and B are statistically associated; 2) A is causally prior to B; and 3) the association does not disappear when the effects of other causally prior variables are removed. When these criteria are met, A is said to cause B (Hirschi and Selvin, 1973).

If the above criteria cannot be satisfied, then the relationship observed is a correlation, or association. Establishing a correlation between growth and some external variable may indicate the existence of some prior factor. This in itself may be of interest and very well could stimulate additional research.

Experimental and Observational Studies

In the tradition of the scientific method, the experimental study stands as the classic design. The investigator introduces a change by manipulating the conditions within which the study is carried out and observes the result. The manipulation, or treatment, is held responsible for the change, thereby establishing a causal link.

Central to the experimental design is the concept of control. By this is meant that the investigator regulates the external conditions so that he or she can be certain that only the treatment has exerted an influence on the outcome of the experiment. The investigator exerts control over the experiment in three ways.

First, a control group is utilized. The control group is similar in every way to the group undergoing the experiment except that no treatment is applied to the controls. This provides a baseline against which the change induced by the treatment may be evaluated.

Second, external conditions would could affect both treatment and control groups are fixed so as not to vary. These conditions are chosen in advance by the investigator, based upon existing knowledge and might include such variables as temperature, diet, or genotype. By fixing them, these extraneous variables are prevented from exerting a confounding effect and obfuscating the results.

Third, variables which are not controlled are randomized between treatment and control groups. This is usually accomplished by the random assignment of subjects to the treatment or the control group. By doing this, uncontrolled variables are equalized in the two groups so that they do not exert an influence upon either one. Randomization of subjects is an important consideration which is too-often overlooked in research. Though it is not always possible to do so, it should be considered by every investigator.

An observational study is one in which the investigator does not manipulate the external conditions. Instead, measurements are made and related to variations which are measured in those external variables which are hypothesized to be significantly associated. In many instances a control group will be utilized. Usually, such a group is comprised of subjects who live under a different set of conditions. For example, a researcher might wish to investigate the effects of malnutrition upon growth and might select for study a group of children whose diets are clearly deficient in particular nutrients. The growth of these children might then be compared to a control group of children of the same ages, sex distribution, and ethnic background whose diets were not deficient in those nutrients.

Traditionally, an experimental study is conducted in a laboratory where conditions are more easily controlled. In some instances it is possible to carry out experimental studies in a natural setting, though invariably it is impossible to exert complete control. Likewise, observational studies are done in a natural setting, though on occasion a researcher will wish to observe in a laboratory, and not impose a change upon the conditions.

By controlling extraneous variables, an investigator making an experimental study may focus attention upon the direct relationship between the experimental alteration and the resulting change. Causality is usually quite straightforward. On the other hand, investigators conducting observational studies are unable to control other variables. Instead, such variables are themselves studied and their effects upon the growth process recorded. This results in observational studies usually being multivariate, with the effects of a number of variables determined. These effects may then be sequentially removed, using appropriate statistical techniques, so that the main effect being examined may be determined. Or the effects of the primary and secondary variables may be compared in order to determine their absolute and relative magnitudes.

The experimental study is the classic research design of science. The essence of its strength lies in the exercise of control over confounding variables. Such a design is the final arbiter of scientific questions and, when properly executed, is difficult to criticize.

However, the experimental design is not always sufficient by itself. By its nature, experimental research constrains variation and reduces the complexity of the natural world to the simplicity of the laboratory design. In some instances this constraint is necessary and desirable. But, if the purpose of the research is ultimately to determine interrelationships and causality in the natural setting, where variables do not always act in splendid isolation from each other, an experimental approach may not provide a complete answer. Experiments can reveal the effects of malnutrition upon growth, by controlling all other factors. But they cannot reveal the relative magnitude of the effects of malnutrition in a community in which diet, disease, demography, and socioeconomic deprivation are all acting simultaneously and usually jointly.

The observational study, by its nature, is suited to the complexities noted above, since it permits the analysis of various factors simultaneously. However, in a natural environment not everything can be measured. The possibility that uncontrolled variation may produce confounding effects is real.

In addition observational studies require sophisticated statistical techniques. While there have been many recent developments in multivariate statistics, these developments have often led to the use of mathematical models which exceed the training of many scientists. In addition, these models may make a priori assumptions about the nature of the data which cannot always be met. Failure to meet those assumptions can lead to erroneous conclusions.

THE IMPORTANCE IN RESEARCH OF REPLICATION

The preceding section should indicate that there is no single

research strategy which is optimal for every situation. Every strategy has those situations in which it is applicable, yet, in every
application, there remains an element of uncertainty. After formu-
lating the question to be investigated, every researcher must select
the strategy most appropriate to answer that question from the range
of strategies which are available. The conclusions which are drawn
will be limited by the strength of the design, once the strategy is
selected. But, even with the best design, no single study can be
accepted as conclusive beyond doubt. The complexities of the processes of growth and development, and of the factors which are related to them, are such that any study may be confounded by extraneous and uncontrolled variables.

      For these reasons, the replication of scientific research is
essential. This may mean repeating a study using a similar design.
Or it may involve changing a design slightly, or even totally, in
order to take a different approach to the solution of the same problem. Replications establish the correctness of a relationship, or
modify, even reject, a proposed causality. Eventually the pattern
will emerge and further replications are unnecessary.

THE SELECTION OF A CONTROL GROUP

      In studies of growth and development it is common for an inves-
tigator to utilize an external control group. A data set is selected
from the literature to serve as a comparison for the sample which is
studied. This approach is especially common in observational studies.
The data selected may have been provided by someone else to serve
specifically as a control, in which case they are referred to as reference data, or reference standards.

      In recent years, a number of reference standards have been deve-
loped for use in growth studies. These standards have been based
upon samples of adequate size and drawn using sophisticated techniques. In particular, the reference standards developed by the
U.S.A. National Center For Health Statistics (Hamill et al, 1977)
are particularly useful since they represent statistically that seg-
ment of the American population between birth and 18 years and are
widely recommended for use as an international reference (e.g., see
Waterlow et al, 1977).

      In experimental studies, the sample may serve as its own control.
The pattern of growth may be established by measurements made before
the application of the treatment. The comparison of pre-treatment
to post-treatment growth allows the determination of the effects of
the treatment.

      In yet another approach, a sample may be subdivided into two
groups, one serving as the control for another. Consider, for example, a study of the effects of chronic undernutrition on growth
(Scholl et al, 1979). All children born in a Latin American community over a 12-month period were studied for the next 6 years. This

cohort was subdivided into those children who had experienced chronic
undernutrition and those who had not. These two groups were then
compared in various ways.

The above approaches are ones that are commonly used both in experimental and observational research. The detection of a difference due to some effect depends upon the comparison of one group to
the other, usually involving an appropriate statistical test of the
differences between the means. While useful results may emerge, the
sensitivity of such a procedure may be reduced if the variation within the two groups is large. In such a case, a significant effect may
go undetected unless large sample sizes are utilized, something often
not possible.

As an alternative to the above, investigators may utilize a
design referred to as the matched pair, or case control, method.
Using this method, the investigator matches an individual from the
experimental group to another individual, who is assigned to the control group. Matching is accomplished on the basis of whatever variables are deemed necessary to control. Differences are determined
within each pair for the variable under study, and then summed. The
statistical test then employed evaluates the null hypothesis that the
mean within-pair difference is zero, a more powerful test than one
which evaluated the differences between the means of two samples.
An example of a matched pair analysis of growth is shown in Table 1.

Table 1. An example of a matched pair analysis. The comparison of periosteal, endosteal, and compact bone
breadths of children with thalassemia, maintained
at high hemoglobin levels, to normal children.
See text for matching criteria. Data from Johnston
and Roseman (1967); n = 23 pairs.

	Periosteal Breadth	Endosteal Breadth	Compact Bone Breadth
Mean[a]	-0.19	-0.99	+0.70
S.D.[b]	0.21	0.18	0.12
t	0.90	5.50	5.83
p	NS[c]	<0.001	<0.001

[a] Mean within-pair difference, in millimeters
[b] Standard deviation of differences
[c] Not significant

The Table shows the results of a study of the growth of compact bone in children with thalassemia who had been maintained at hemoglobin levels in excess of 9 g/100 cc by blood transfusions. Each child with thalassemia was matched with a normal control, the criteria for matching being age and sex. It was not necessary to match for country of origin, although all children were of European ancestry. It was not possible to match for height or weight since children with thalassemia are slowed drastically in their growth and these variables are greatly affected.

The study was conducted to evaluate the effectiveness of maintaining children with thalassemia at a high hemoglobin level, in terms of the maintenance of bone. The data were obtained from measurements of the second metacarpal on hand-wrist x-rays and a matched pair design was selected as appropriate. The results indicate that the children with thalassemia, maintained at high hemoglobin levels, add bone at the periosteal surface at a normal rate, as indicated by the absence of significant differences between the subjects and their controls. However, the differences in endosteal breadth indicate that this bone is not maintained, but is lost through resorption. The significant difference in thickness of the compact layer of bone, obtained from the subtraction of the endosteal from the periosteal breadth, indicates that children with thalassemia have less bone than do children without the disease, even though they might have near normal hemoglobin levels, maintained by transfusion.

A matched pair design is an efficient one from the standpoint of statistical analysis. However, the success of such a design rests upon the criteria used for matching. If significant variables are not utilized, then the two groups may differ on those variables and the matched pair design may produce erroneous results.

ERROR OF MEASUREMENT

The basis of scientific research is measurement. Observations must be made in a careful, objective, and well-defined manner so as to permit the most powerful analysis possible of the variable being studied. Unless careful attention is paid to the techniques of measurement, the resulting data will be useless.

Unfortunately, despite the most careful attention to detail, there will always be an error of measurement. The extent of any error depends upon the state of the observer, the state of the instruments used, the state of the conditions in which the measurements are made, and the state of the subject. A basic principle of research design is that each of these determinants is considered so as to reduce the error to a tolerable minimum and the residual error is quantified so that its contribution to the variance in the trait or dimension under study will be known.

Error of measurement may be either random or systematic. Random error occurs when, in the case of a replication of a measurement, the probability of the replicate being the larger of the two is equal to the probability of the original being larger. The sum of the difference between the original and replicate measurements, over a given number of trials, will be zero. Increased random error will be reflected in an increased variance of the difference.

Random error usually arises when the factor responsible for the error affects the original measurement and the replicate equally. In the case of the research itself, when measurements are not being replicated, random error will increase the between-subject variance and reduce the power of a statistical test of significance.

Systematic error results from the factor responsible for the error affecting the original measurement and the replicate differentially. In growth studies, systematic error may arise if more than one observer collects data and the observers employ different methodologies. If, for example, one observer measures the treatment group and another measures the control group, and if the techniques of the observers vary, then the error of measurement could either eliminate a significant difference or create one when there is none.

Unfortunately, growth studies devote little time to the quality control necessary to limit measurement error, and only occasionally is the error actually quantified. A notable exception is the Health Examination Survey of the U.S. Public Health Service. This survey examined a national probability sample (n > 15,000) of 6- to 17-year-olds and employed, over an 8 year period, more than 10 observers. The techniques of quality control and the quantification of the error of measurement have been presented in as detailed a manner as is available anywhere in the growth literature (see, e.g., Hamill et al, 1973, Johnston et al, 1974, and Roche et al, 1976).

LONGITUDINAL, CROSS-SECTIONAL, AND MIXED DESIGNS

A growth study is a study of growth. While such a statement is circular in the extreme, it points out that the focus of a growth study is not the examination of a subject at one moment in time, but the analysis of change in individuals as they grow and develop. The problems of designing a growth study so as to allow the analysis of growth are often difficult ones and central to any consideration of research design. While they have been discussed by several authors (Tanner, 1962, Jelliffe, 1974, Johnston, 1974, Van't Hof et al, 1977, Marubini, 1978), the major points warrant discussion in this paper.

Cross-Sectional Design

In a cross-sectional design subjects are examined but once. If the subjects are of different ages, growth is inferred from an analysis of differences between the measurements of individuals, or between the age-group means.

The advantages of a cross-sectional design are obvious. Since each subject is examined but once a research project may be conducted quickly. Furthermore, such a design makes possible the drawing of a large sample, numbering if desired in the tens of thousands. Under such conditions, standard errors of the means will be low and confidence intervals narrow.

Cross-sectional designs are highly cost-efficient and, wherever possible and appropriate, should be utilized. The speed with which an analysis may be completed adds significantly to this efficiency. Many longitudinal studies, in which data collected over 50 years ago form their bases, are still being analyzed. Since no study can be isolated from the times in which it was carried out, the interpretation of the analyses of the older longitudinal studies may be more of historic than scientific interest.

But cross-sectional studies are severely constrained by a single methodological problem which cannot be overcome. Since each subject is examined but once, a cross-sectional study does not measure the growth of any single individual. Any description of growth over time is a composite one derived from the entire sample. Individual variation in the growth rate cannot be calculated so that there is no estimate of within-group variance in that parameter.

Furthermore, individuals do not grow parallel to the 50th percentile values of the group. Instead they display significant shifts in their growth rates and, if only cross-sectional data are available, such shifts cannot be analyzed.

Longitudinal Design

In a longitudinal design, a sample of subjects is measured repeatedly at specific times and over pre-determined intervals. Growth is calculated as the increment between successive examinations and, if desired, converted to an annual rate by dividing the increment of growth by the increment of time expressed in decimals of a year.

The strengths of a longitudinal design are well-known. Put simply, if one wishes to know about the growth of individuals, one must measure individual growth. Only serial measurements provide the data. Wherever there are significant inflections in rates of growth, as in infancy or adolescence, longitudinal data are needed to estimate the inflections precisely. Without question, the longitudinal design is the hallmark of a growth study.

At the same time, a longitudinal design will not insure a good growth study, or an adequate or appropriate data base. Such an approach is not the one of choice for every study.

Longitudinal studies generate enormous amounts of data. While, on the surface, this would not seem to be a problem, it can be serious unless the investigator is prepared to deal with the data. It is one thing to calculate the descriptive statistics in a cross-sectional study. But it is something else to analyze incremental data and to deal successfully with the many subtle aspects they present. All too often, investigators unprepared for the complexities of longitudinal data analysis seem paralyzed by what they have produced. They carry out only simple analysis more appropriate for a cross-sectional study and not only fail to exploit the advantages of the longitudinal design, but also wrongly treat the data as if they were cross-sectional.

Since a longitudinal study examines a single sample repeatedly, it is not always clear how comparable the sample is to another sample. Since the different age groups contain the same individuals, any sampling bias is carried throughout the age groups. Since the groups are not independent of each other, many conventional statistical analyses are inappropriate.

The intensity of a longitudinal design usually precludes its being carried out on a large sample. Standard errors of the mean are larger and confidence intervals wider. Since an increment involves two measurements, measuring error has twice the impact that it does in a cross-sectional design.

A longitudinal study may be devastated by subject attrition. The only way to maintain adequate sample sizes is to generate a high level of involvement among the subjects and their parents. Unfortunately, the greater the involvement the more likely it is to affect the growth of the children comprising the sample. Known as the Hawthorne Effect, this results from subjects knowing that they are part of a study (Blalock, 1970) and unconsciously manipulating other variables. Thus, parents whose children are part of a longitudinal sample may become more aware of growth and of the need for a proper environment. As a result, they may change their children's diets so that the subjects no longer represent the population from which they were originally drawn as a sample.

The above may seem like a harsh indictment of the longitudinal design. If so, it is not because such a design is not basic to the study of growth. Rather, the above comments are intended to emphasize that a longitudinal study is not to be begun lightly, but only after careful consideration of all aspects of the design, including the hypotheses being tested and the analyses used in testing.

Mixed Design

In practice, a pure longitudinal study is rare, unless it covers only a short time period. The cost of a longitudinal study and the necessary time involvement make it virtually impossible to follow a complete sample for the entire period of the study. Consequently, most investigators combine the longitudinal and cross-sectional designs in order to take advantage of the strengths of both without necessarily fally prey to the traps of either.

In a simple example of a mixed design, an investigator follows a large sample of children from the target population, examining the group on schedule and recording measurements and observations from those participants available at the time of examination. Subjects may drop out of the study, others may enter the study. The design involves a series of cross-sectional samples providing both a longitudinal and a cross-sectional component. The one component may be analyzed by examining the appropriate sub-set, while the other component may be analyzed in a similar fashion. Such a design is not usually developed by careful planning, but usually arises as a matter of convenience.

A more elegant form of a mixed design is known as the mixed longitudinal study, one which is designed to provide a series of longitudinal data sets in a relatively short period of time. The sets are then linked to permit the analysis of growth over a much longer age range. An example of such a design in presented in Table 2. The ex-

Table 2. An example of a mixed longitudinal design. Four cohorts are examined successively for 4 years, the examination of each beginning at a different age.

Year of Study	Age At Each Examination			
	Cohort 1	Cohort 2	Cohort 3	Cohort 4
1	Birth	3	6	9
2	1	4	7	10
3	2	5	8	11
4	3	6	9	12

simulates a design in which 4 cohorts of children are selected and examined annually for 4 years. The age at first examination differs for each cohort, that of Cohort 1 being birth, with each successive one being 3 years older than the preceding. After the 4th year of the study, longitudinal data are available from birth through 12 years of age. Furthermore, because the design is such that the cohort ages overlap by one year, the comparison of, for example, the 4-year examination of Cohort 1 to the first year examination of Cohort 2 permits the investigator to analyze and to correct for Cohort effects. Mixed longitudinal designs are becoming more widely used in growth studies, though their potential is only now being realized.

SELECTION OF SUBJECTS

As scientists our interests go beyond the subjects from whom we collect data to the larger universe, or aggregate. This is a part of the principle of generalization, in which the results of a study are extended beyond the immediate to the more general.

Normally, the aggregate is referred to as the population and the subjects examined comprise the sample. In a sound research design, the first consideration is to identify the population to be studied and then to draw from that population a sample of individuals who will provide the data. The sample selected will be small enough in size to be handled by the resources of the investigator, yet large enough to provide acceptable answers to the questions asked. This means determining just how much error can be tolerated in the study and adjusting sample size so that it will be large enough to yield errors less than what is decided to be the minimum. Specific procedures for doing this are covered by various authors (e.g., Snedecor and Cochran, 1967).

There are various strategies for drawing the appropriate sample, again covered by a number of authors (e.g., Som, 1973, Goldstein, 1978). Most of them rely upon the laws of probability to insure that the sample does in fact represent the population from which it has been drawn.

The simplest approach to sampling, at least from the conceptual point of view, involves drawing a random sample. This is defined by Som (1973) as one in which "the sample selected has the same _a priori_ chance of selection as any other sample of the same size." This means that any individual in the population must have the same chance of being selected as any other individual and usually requires the use of a table of random numbers to assure equality of probability.

Though simple in principle, a random sample is virtually impossible in practice, since humans may exercise whatever choices they have and decide not to participate in a study. Even when the sample is selected by acceptable techniques, it is necessary to determine whether or not there is any bias due to subject non-participation.

Another approach frequently employed is known as stratified sampling. The universe, or population, is divided into strata and each is sampled separately to provide a sample of known composition. In such an approach, it is still important to adhere as close as possible to random sampling within each stratum.

When the study is an experimental one, it is important to assign subjects randomly to treatment and control groups. As noted above, randomization is a procedure which relies upon the laws of probability to produce similar distributions of existing factors in the two groups and, though it requires somewhat larger numbers of subjects, is nore efficient than attempting to hold those variables constant (Blalock, 1970).

GROWTH STUDIES AND SAMPLES OF CONVENIENCE

Frequently an investigator conducting a growth study will use no particular criteria for selecting a sample other than the availability of a group of children. While this will not necessarily introduce a bias, it very well can do so if the children and youth of different ages differ in other characteristics. For example, consider a common design used in studying the growth of children from a developing country, or from a lower socioeconomic class in a stratified society. An investigator will examine the children attending one or more schools, taking appropriate measurements as data are collected. The measurements are grouped by age and sex and analyzed by conventional statistical methods.

The examination of the characteristics of the different age groups may often reveal significant differences among them. For example, if it is required that a child complete primary school but not secondary school, the children from poorer families are likely to leave school at the completion of the primary grades in order to assist in providing income. In such a case, the socioeconomic status of the younger children will be lower than that of older children who remain in school. Conclusions based upon such data may be in error, in view of the well-known association of socioeconomic status with growth and development.

There are other examples of problems introduced by utilizing samples of convenience. Studies of physical activity of children often utilize subjects from physical education classes, all-too-often ignoring the self-selection that occurs. Studies which draw their subjects from health care centers include only those who are conscious enough of their health to come to such a center.

Growth studies should take full advantage of the many ways to draw a sample. But one should be wary of utilizing groups just because it is handy to do so. The lack of population delineation and the failure to exercise acceptable techniques for drawing a sample are valid criticisms of much of the published research in growth. Anyone who is reading such a publication is well-advised to examine carefully the research design and especially the criteria used for selecting a sample.

CONCLUSIONS

There is no magic to research design. It represents a logical and straightforward approach to solving a relevant scientific problem. But there are no shortcuts. It is the responsibility of any investigator to exercise careful planning, from the initial formulation of the problem through all steps leading to its solution. All of us are plagued by inappropriate research strategies, the collection of inadequate data, and the failure to apply basic principles of sample selection to the process of enlisting subjects. Above all, researchers should resist the temptation to rush headlong into the collection of data without exercising careful judgment based upon the principles of the scientific method so as to insure the best possible research design.

REFERENCES

Blalock, H. M., 1970, "An Introduction to Social Research," Prentice-Hall, Englewood Cliffs, N. J.

Goldstein, H., 1978, Sampling for growth studies, in: "Human Growth, 1, Principles and Prenatal Growth," F. Falkner and J. M. Tanner, ed., Plenum, New York.

Hamill, P. V. V., Johnston, F. E., and Lemeshow, S., 1973, "Height and Weight of Youths, 12-17 Years, United States," DHEW Publ. No. (HSM) 73-1606, U. S. Govt. Print. Off., Washington, D. C.

Hamill, P. V. V., Johnson, C. L., Reed, R. B., and Roche, A. F. 1977, "NCHS Growth Curves For Children, Birth-18 Years, United States," DHEW Publ. No. (PHS) 78-1650, U. S. Govt. Print. Off., Washington, D. C.

Hirschi, T. and Selvin, H. C., 1973, "Principles of Survey Analysis," Free Press, New York.

Jelliffe, D. B., 1974, Relative values of longitudinal, cross-sectional, and mixed data collection in community studies, in: "Nutrition and Malnutrition," A. F. Roche and F. Falkner, ed., Plenum, New York.

Johnston, F. E., 1974, Cross-sectional versus longitudinal studies, in: "Nutrition and Malnutrition," A. F. Roche and F. Falkner, ed., Plenum, New York.

Johnston, F. E. and Roseman, J. M., 1967, The effects of more frequent transfusions upon bone loss in thalassemia major, Pediat. Res., 1:479.

Johnston, F. E., Hamill, P. V. V., and Lemeshow, S., 1974, "Skinfold Thickness of Youths, 12-17 Years, United States," DHEW Publ. No. (HRA) 74-1614, U. S. Govt. Print. Off., Washington, D. C.

Marubini, E., 1978, The mathematical handling of long-term longitudinal data, in: "Human Growth, 1, Principles and Prenatal Growth," F. Falkner and J. M. Tanner, ed., Plenum, New York.

Roche, A. F., Roberts, J., and Hamill, P. V. V., 1976, "Skeletal Maturity of Youths, 12-17 Years, United States," DHEW Publ. No. (HRA) 77-1642, U. S. Govt. Print. Off., Washington, D. C.

Scholl, T. O., Johnston, F. E., Cravioto, J., DeLicardie, E. R., and Lurie, D. S., 1979, The relationship of growth failure (chronic undernutrition) to the prevalence of clinically-severe protein energy malnutrition and to growth retardation in PEM, Amer. J. Clin. Nutr., 32:872.

Snedecor, G. W. and Cochran, W. G., 1967, "Statistical Methods," Sixth Edition, Iowa State Univ. Press, Ames.

Som, R. K., 1973, "A Manual of Sampling Techniques," Heinemann, London.

Tanner, J. M., 1962, "Growth At Adolescence," Second Edition, Blackwell, Oxford.

Van't Hof, M. A., Roede, M. J., and Kowalski, C. J., 1977, A mixed longitudinal data analysis model. Human Biol., 49:165.

Waterlow, J. C., Buzina, R., Keller, W., Lane, J. M., Nichaman, M. Z., and Tanner, J. M., 1977, The presentation and use of height and weight data for comparing the nutritional status of groups of children under the age of 10 years. Bull. World Health. Org., 55:489.

2. SURVEYS OF PHYSICAL GROWTH AND MATURATION

J. C. van Wieringen

University Children's Hospital Het Wilhelmina
Kinderziekenhuis
Nieuwe Gracht 137, 3512 LK Utrecht

MOTIVATION

Scientific interest in growth may have its origin in anthro-pology and medico-biology. Anthropometry as part of human biology has no restrictions concerning the anatomical parts or regions of the human body. Measurements as such, relationships between dif-ferent parts of body, and proportional aspects can be established and compared for different races and ethnic groups. These measure-ments may be related to physiological and psychological character-istics of populations, may give insight into pre-historic events (i.e., origin and evolution of mankind), and may be used for ergo-nomic purposes in labour and sport.

Anthropometry in medico-biological research may be separated to investigations on: anatomic and chemical body composition, physiology and patho-physiology of growth and maturation, relation-ships between growth and environment, between body build and physical capacity, between body composition and risk factors for specified diseases, and between growth pattern and health status of a population.

There are three reasons for repeated surveys of height, weight and sex characteristics:

1. Height, weight and stages of sexual development are important
   parameters for the physician who wishes to control individual
   growth and physical development. To establish a medical judgment of an individual's state of health, one has to compare his
   or her measurements with reference data or standard values.
   Suitable standards must be based on surveys of height, weight,

and sex characteristics of the population to which the child belongs. Since growth standards may change over time, surveys must be repeated periodically at intervals of about 10 years.

2. Secular changes in growth patterns are important indicators of the health status of a population. Influenced by hygienic, cultural, and economic conditions, they are related to changes in morbidity and mortality, the other two major health indicators. Because secular changes are clearly perceptible in variables such as height, weight and sexual maturity, these characteristics provide the biometric data for studies of secular growth shifts.

3. Secular changes in growth and maturation have important social implications. A logical concomitant of changes in stature is, for example, that clothing, furniture, and tools have to be redesigned, and that the architecture of homes, schools, and workshops has to be adapted. An earlier development of maturation characteristics, accompanied by an earlier onset of biological adulthood, will undoubtedly affect legislation, jurisdiction, and education.

Because there is a strong relationship between a secular increase in height and a decrease in morbidity and mortality, increasing height is given the adjective "positive", and decreasing height "negative". In the light of ongoing positive secular changes in rich industrialized countries like Norway and The Netherlands, where the median height of young male adults exceeds 180 cm, a cessation of the trend should be considered negative rather than neutral.

It must be emphasized that genetically determined differences in growth and maturation exist (Tanner and Eveleth, 1975). But one may conclude that a difference in mean height is genetic only if different ethnic groups have been living in exactly the same conditions for several generations. There are convincing arguments for the statement that too often living conditions are considered "equal" while seriously studied socio-economic, cultural and demographical data are not presented.

In the (shorter) populations of southeast Europe menarche occurs earlier than in the (taller) populations of northwest Europe. One is inclined to assume genetic causes for these differences in menarcheal age, but Johnston (1974) points out that many factors control this maturational characteristic.

DESIGN OF A CROSS-SECTIONAL SURVEY

To provide the medical profession with reference data, and
(or) to study the process of secular growth changes, one has to
make a choice among three methods of gathering the data: longitudinal, semi-longitudinal, and cross-sectional.

Longitudinal studies may provide important knowledge concerning
growth velocity (including, for example, individual values for the
adolescent growth spurt: beginning, peak height velocity, end,
magnitude), and interrelationships between variables such as height,
weight, maturity, etc. But to compile contemporary growth diagrams
and to study secular growth changes, this approach takes too long
and can include only small samples. Other disadvantages are the
loss of individuals from the sample and changes among the
investigators.

Cross-sectional surveys may be performed in a rather short
period and provide enough regional or nation-wide biometric data
to compute the distributions of the variables investigated. By
comparing former and recent data per age-group, secular growth
changes can be discovered and studied. By plotting in a diagram
the computed data of the subsequent age-groups "artifical growth
curves" may be compiled. Nearly all individual curves will
deviate from these curves due to individual fluctuations in growth
velocity, especially during the first two years and during adolescence. Moreover, in the presence of a positive secular shift,
theoretically most individual curves will deviate upwards from the
standard curves. If, for example, the positive secular trend of
adolescents is 2 cm per decade, a child who measured exactly the
median height at the age of 8 years will be 2 cm taller than the
10-years-old median standard value at the age of 18 years.

Semi-longitudinal investigations meet most of the disadvantages of longitudinal projects, but the work-load is heavy. Consequently, in The Netherlands we concluded periodic cross-sectional
surveys are the method of choice for the two purposes mentioned
above (van Wieringen et al., 1971).

Sampling

Theoretically, the best way to sample is to acquire the
individuals from the Registrar's Office by a mathematically determined selection procedure. In that case about 100 examined individuals per age-group should be sufficient to calculate mean
(median) and standard deviation (and selected centiles) for attained
height and weight. However, it is hardly possible to examine 100
children for every year-group of 170,000-250,000 individuals,

scattered over about 840 municipalities, as is the situation in
The Netherlands. Therefore, a stratified method of sampling has to
be chosen: one or two municipalities per province per degree of
urbanization and, in a particular municipality, those attending one
or two welfare clinics and some of the pupils at one or two schools.
Preference for a particular municipality can be influenced by the
degree of co-operation of the staff of maternal and school health
services.

The total number of individuals in the sample depends on
several factors:

- The number of age-groups. At infancy the class-intervals
  of the age-groups are 1 week until the age of 3 months, 2
  weeks until 3 to 6 months, and 3 weeks from 6 to 12 months
  of age. During the pre-school period, the class-intervals
  are 3 months, and during the school-age and adolescent
  periods they are 6 months.

- The analysis of data for attained height and weight needs
  at least 100 examinations per age-group, but it is preferable to base the computation of centiles on 200-300
  examinations.

- The distribution of weight for height, especially in infancy
  and at adolescence when this relationship is age-dependent,
  needs several hundreds of examinations to obtain enough
  data per height-class of 2 cm.

- Other analyses, for example, the influence of environmental
  factors on growth and maturation, require considerable
  enlargement of the sample.

Pupils of schools for special education should not be included
in the sample because, among this category, pathological disturbances are more common than among pupils of the regular primary
schools. If many immigrants of ethnic minority-groups are living
in certain areas, it has to be considered whether or not these
groups belong to the population for which the reference data will
be established. If immigration happened rather recently, these
groups have to be excluded from the study of secular changes.

The youngest age-group in the sample for the study of sex
characteristics is 8 years old for girls and 9 years old for boys.

Co-operating Doctors and Nurses in the Field

A network of welfare clinics and school health services exists
in The Netherlands. Welfare clinics cover 90% of the children aged

from birth to 3 years, and school health services cover 100% of
the pupils of all levels of education aged 4 to 16 years.

Although the doctors and nurses in these institutions are
familiar with biometric examinations, all of them should be trained
personally in measuring height and weight, and in the accuracy of
registration. In the current survey, the staff of each well baby
clinic is trained in measuring head circumference. As far as the
school doctors are asked to examine adolescents, they have to be
instructed in estimating the stage of development of sex characteristics. Preceding personal instruction, the co-operating teams
are sent a detailed protocol of the survey.

In general, cooperation in a scientific research project lays
a burden on the doctors and the nurses in the field. To avoid too
much interference with their daily work, to promote enthusiasm and
to maintain the standard of examinations on a high level, they
should not be asked to participate for too long a period.

Tools and Methods

The measures and scales as used by the co-operating teams must
be tested before the survey. Medical scales are not manufactured
for commercial purposes; therefore, they may not meet the requirements of the weights and measures office. Any inaccuracy greater
than 1% of the load is sufficient reason to reject the scales.
However, for baby scales the permissible maximum margin of error
is 50 gm, and for upright scales, 300 gm. The sensitivity (i.e.,
minimum load causing deflection of the indicator) permitted for
empty baby scales is 15 gm, and 100 gm for upright scales.

Height. Until their second birthday, children are measured
supine, and after that, standing. A flat measuring board is used
to measure infants at the health centres, with a vertical plank at
the head and a yardstick calibrated in millimeters along the side.
By using a right-angled triangle, the base of which can be slid
along the yardstick, the children's length can be perpendicularly
projected onto the yardstick.

Measuring is performed by two people as follows: The child
lies down on the measuring board. The person helping the nurse
(mother or assistant) sees that the crown of the child's head
reaches the plank at the head of the board. The line from the
upper edge of the attachment of the ear to the lateral corner of
the eye should be vertical. The nurse straightens the child's
legs by pressing the knees down with the left hand. If the child's
head loses contact with the plank through this manoeuvre, the mother
or assistant pushes the head back against the plank. The nurse
pushes the triangle against the soles of the child's feet with her

right hand. The child's length is noted in millimeters.

From the age of two years onwards, height is measured using
one of two types of apparatus depending on the possibilities of the
room where the child is examined. One type is a metal yardstick,
vertically attached to the wall, along which a right-angled triangle
can be moved. The horizontal edge of the triangle projects the top-
most point of the head onto the yardstick. A second type of apparatus is known by the registered name of "Microtoise". This is simple
to nail to the wall and readily portable if one has to perform
measurements in several places. To measure persons taller than the
investigator, a stool is used to avoid errors due to parallax.

In measuring, the child stands barefoot with heels, buttocks
and back touching the wall or the yardstick. The heels are kept
together, the feet forming an angle of 45°. In the case of genua
valga, the feet may be placed sufficiently apart that the child
need not bend one knee in front of the other. The head is held so
that the line from the upper edge of the attachment of the ear to
the lateral corner of the eye is horizontal. Then the child
actively stretches as much as possible, without traction being
exercised, and the height is read in mm.

Weight. Infants are weighed nude, older children and (young)
men stripped to their drawers, older girls also retaining vest or
brassière. The weight is recorded in gm for infants and in hgm for
older children.

Head circumference. A narrow measuring tape, calibrated in
mm, is applied around the head at its greatest circumference: over
the glabella and the os occipitale. An infant should be held
sitting upright.

Sexual maturation. The beginning of adolescence coincides
with the first sign of development of one or more sex characteristics. The end of adolescence is indistinct. For example, a school-
girl of 11 years of age, who has just reached menarche (age at first
menstruation), can scarcely be considered physically and mentally
adult although in many cultures girls marry very soon after menarche.
On the other hand, many people who are physically adult may show
adolescent-like behaviour for many years.

There are many physical and physiological changes related to
adolescence (Marshall, 1978). Nearly all organs are involved in
maturation: the central nervous system, the endocrine regulation
system, the locomotor system. In addition there are changes in
body composition and proportions and in secondary sex characteristics. There is an increase in strength and exercise tolerance
and in performance on pulmonary function tests. Sexual maturation
is not the result of one simple process, but of a complex of

processes in the central nervous system and in the endocrine regulation system. To compile reference data for sexual development,
observations are made of testis volume, penis and scrotum, and
pubic hair in males, and of pubic hair, breast, age at menarche in
females.

Secondary sex characteristics that are not suitable for this
purpose include axillary hair in males. Generally, this appears
when the development of the genitalia is well advanced but its
appearance is very variable in timing in relation to the development of pubic hair. First facial hair may appear about one year
later than axillary hair. It develops rather slowly and is seldom
present before the genitalia and pubic hair are completely developed.
The breaking of the voice is very hard to examine objectively, and
the process shows far too great a variation to be useful. Oigarche,
or the age at first ejaculation, is very difficult to record and
there is possible confusion between performance and potential. In
females there are changes in the ovaries, uterus, and vagina but
these cannot be observed in surveys.

The manifestation of some developmental items occurs as an
"event", occurring at an age in each individual, while for other
items it is a situation that lasts for several weeks, months, or
even years. An example of the first category is the first menstruation. The age at which it happens is "menarche", but in medical
parlance the term "menarche" is sometimes used for the first menstruation rather than the age at which this occurs. The developmental stages for pubic hair, genitalia and breasts are examples
of the second category. A child will arrive at PH_3 or PH_4, or
may be in stages PH_3, or PH_4, etc. The development from a stage
into the next one is rather gradual. Nevertheless, in a survey
the observer should not score between the stages, for example $3\frac{1}{2}$,
or "over three but not yet four".

Penis, scrotum. The development of these organs is divided
into five stages:

G_1 - testis, scrotum, and penis are the same size and shape as
in the young child.

G_2 - enlargement of scrotum and testis. The skin of the scrotum
becomes redder, thinner and wrinkled. Penis no larger or
scarcely so.

G_3 - Enlargement of the penis, especially in length; descent of
scrotum.

G_4 - Continued enlargement of the penis and sculpturing of the
glans. Increased pigmentation of scrotum. This stage is
sometimes best described as "not quite adult".

G_5 - Adult stage. Scrotum ample, penis reaching nearly to bottom
of scrotum.

Testis volume. The volume is determined partly visually, partly by means of palpation. The investigator extends the scrotum, isolates each testis in turn with one hand, takes the testis model (orchidometer) in the other, looks for the appropriate bead and reads the stated volume.

The school doctor and the clinician are of course interested in the first sign of maturation of the testis, that is, when the volume exceeds 3-4 ml. Because in 10% of adult men the testis volume is greater than 27 ml, the orchidometer used in a survey should have a range from 1 ml to at least 40 ml (Wafelbakker). The largest bead of the Prader orchidometer is 25 ml. This is adequate for the pediatrician and the endocrinologist, because generally the difference between an average and a large volume is of no clinical importance. The shape of the models may be either ellipsoid (Prader, 1966; Zachmann et al., 1974), or between ellipsoid and somewhat rectangular on transverse section (Wafelbakker, cited by van Wieringen et al., 1971).

Pubic hair. In girls and boys six stages of pubic hair development can be distinguished.

girls: PH_1 - no growth of pubic hair.

PH_2 - initial, scarcely pigmented hair, especially along the labia.

PH_3 - sparse dark, visibly pigmented, curly pubic hair on labia.

PH_4 - hair "adult" in type, but not in extent.

PH_5 - lateral spreading; type and spread of hair adult.

PH_6 - further extension laterally, upwards, or disperse (apparently occurs in only 10% of women).

boys: PH_1 - no growth of pubic hair. The hair in the pubic area does not differ from that on the rest of the abdomen.

PH_2 - slightly pigmented, longer, straight hair, often still downy; usually at base of penis, sometimes on scrotum. It is difficult to observe stage 2 in photographs.

PH_3 - dark, definitely pigmented, curly pubic hair around the base of the penis. Stage 3 can be observed in photographs.

PH_4 - pubic hair definitely adult in type, but not in extent (no further than inguinal fold).

PH_5 - spread to medial surface of thighs, but not upwards.

PH_6 - hair spreads along linea alba. This occurs in 80% of men.

Good lighting is essential for a correct appraisal of the first pigmented hairs, i.e., beginning of stage PH_2. If pubic hair stages are graded from photographs PH_2 is recorded at too old an age.

Breast. The development of the mammae is divided into five stages.

M_1 - only the nipple is raised above the level of the breast, as in the child.

M_2 - budding stage: bud-shaped elevation of the areola. On palpation, a fairly hard "button" can be felt, disc- or cherry-shaped. Areola increased in diameter and surrounding area slightly elevated.

M_3 - further elevation of the mamma. Diameter of areola increased further. Shape of mamma now visibly feminine.

M_4 - increasing fat deposits. The areola forms a secondary elevation above that of the breast. This secondary mound apparently occurs in about half of all girls, and in some cases persists in adulthood.

M_5 - adult stage. The areola (usually) subsides to the level of the breast and is strongly pigmented.

The diameter of the areola increases slightly during pubescence in boys. Many boys will experience, almost always temporarily, some enlargement of breast tissue. This may develop up to stage 3 and may cause discomfort and embarrassment.

Menarche. The method of choice for establishing the distribution of the age of menarche is the "status quo" method. By means of the question, "Have you started your periods yet?" or in the colloquial speech of the region or the particular population concerned, for each age-group the percentage of girls giving the answer, "yes", should be calculated.

Recording of Data

In a laboratory it is possible to store the recorded data automatically in a computer. One disadvantage is that the observer does not have the opportunity to notice incorrect inputs when methods are applied incorrectly. In the field, one has to write the data on special record cards. It must be emphasized that rounding off by the observers has to be avoided. This may lead to systematic errors.

In the present survey, we have asked the examiner to give his personal (subjective) impression in terms of tall, small, lean,

stout or "nothing particular". Unusual data have to be accepted
if they match the impression of the observer.

Data Processing

One has to decide to what extent one will use a computer.
In 1965, we obtained the frequency distributions of height and
weight according to sex and age by sorting them. Nowadays, there
are computer programs for calculating the median (P50) and the
other centiles. Means and standard deviations should be calculated
only if the distributions are Gaussian.

Biometric standard values should be based on examinations of
"normal" individuals. When compiling standards, one should eliminate data that are influenced by pathological disturbances. A
difficult problem is the elimination of erroneous raw data and
outliers. Extremes in height, weight and developmental levels may
occur in healthy individuals. Values exceeding 3 standard deviations are found in less than 1 in 1000 people. In 270,000 Dutch
conscripts of the combined 1974, 1975 and 1976 drafts, heights
smaller than -3 s.d. below the mean were found for about 600
individuals while 4 among 1000 young adult men had heights exceeding 200 cm. In the light of the positive secular shift, one is
inclined to consider very short heights as more likely than very
tall ones to be artefacts.

Age-groups. Age-grouping should be based on the difference
between date of birth and date of examination, both coded in days.
For determining the class-intervals of the age-groups, the increment of the variable between the class-limits should be taken into
account. Because of this increment, the s.d. for the group is
somewhat greater than at the class-mark, which is an age-point,
not an age range or interval. To avoid the influence of this
increment on the observed variance, the age-classes have to be
restricted to 1, 2 and 3 weeks during infancy, to a quarter of a
year during the preschool period, and to half a year at older ages.
An adjustment can be made to convert the variance within an age-
group to that at an age-point using the formula given by Healy
(1962):

$$Sp = \sqrt{Sg^2 - \frac{k^2}{12}}$$

Sp = standard deviation at an age-point (class-mark),

Sg = standard deviation for the age-group, and

 k = mean increment between class-intervals.

Too often in publications on biometric data, it is difficult to determine whether the figures given in tables and graphs are related to age-points or to age-groups, and in the latter case, what are the class-limits.

Fitting curves to numerical variables. The data recorded from the 1965 Dutch survey resulted in smooth curves for median heights and weights, based on the computed values for age-groups. The greater the distance between the other centiles and the median (P50), the greater was the irregularity of the curves when the plotted values were connected. There are computer programs to smooth curves but fitting by eye is acceptable also. Both methods have to fulfill the same conditions: the subsequent values of a centile must increase (eventually decrease) gradually; in other words, the increments per interval must change slightly and regularly and the differences between the centiles must change regularly and gradually. The smoothed centiles at a given age depend largely on the data of several preceding and subsequent age-groups.

At suitable age-points, the smoothed curves must be read off and noted in tables as standard values. When curves are fitted by eye, the P50 (median) should be drawn as a straight line in a diagram. The often subtle changes in the other centiles can be visualized by plotting them at both sides of the straight P50.

Fitting the curves of developmental items. Sigmoid curves reflect the increasing proportion of a population that has passed developmental characteristics in relation to increasing age. Best fit sigmoid curves may be computed by the probit-analysis or log-method. If the size of the sample is sufficient, also eye-fitted smoothing may be used. Most developmental items, for instance those concerning psychomotor development in infancy and the pre-school period, show a skewed age distribution but age at menarche has practically a Gaussian distribution.

Weight for height. Nutritional status should not be described simply in terms of weight-for-age. Secular changes in height make it clear that attained height is of primary importance for the assessment of a population's nutritional status. Weight for height represents a second important indicator, while body composition (derived from anatomical and bio-chemical data) is an essential part of the measurement of nutritional status.

Weight for height is a first step in the assessment of body composition. Many attempts have been made to establish mathematical formulae (indices) that relate weight to height. The best should be the index in which the influence of height is eliminated, but such an index does not exist. One of the best indices in this respect is that of Quételet (W/H2), but this index varies

considerably during growth. If standard values for age are available, plotting attained (median or mean) weight against the attained
(median or mean) height in one diagram appears to be the method of
choice in order to compare the weight-height relationships of
various populations. However, if there are large differences in
adult height, for the populations concerned, this method of comparison is inadequate near the end of the growth period.

The best insight into the weight-height relationship is
gained if enough data permit the establishment of the distribution
of weight for relatively small height-classes (1-2 cm interval).
The distribution of weight for height is practically age-independent
during the age-periods from about 1 to 12 years of age (girls) and
1 to 13 years of age (boys). During infancy and adolescence,
weight for height is age-dependent: at the same height older
children are heavier than younger ones. In the Dutch 1965 survey
over 60,000 observations were made. This number permitted us to
compile standard values for the distribution of weight for height
(van Wieringen, 1972). Standards for the distribution of weight
for height cannot be calculated in cross-sectional studies on
height and weight with small samples.

GROWTH AND MATURATION DIAGRAMS FOR PRACTICAL USE

Growth and maturation diagrams are used to develop curves
fitted by eye to the computed raw data. Tabulated standard values
are read from the smoothed curves. In research on growth and
maturation, it is necessary to study and compare the tabulated
figures, but it is often very useful to visualize them also. By
doing so, it sometimes becomes obvious that the published data are
not as reliable as they seemed to be in the tables. If only
standard values for age are available for specified populations,
the best method of comparison is to plot height in a height-for-
age diagram, and mean (or median) weight and height in a weight-
for-height diagram. Tabulated results of repeated measures of a
child's height and weight, including the age of examination, hardly
give a suitable impression of growth. Regularity, velocity,
unexpected deviations, maintenance of the "growth canal" may be
detected only on the basis of visualized data in a growth diagram.
Therefore, a growth chart forms an essential part of every medical
record for children, in the hospital as well as in a maternal and
child health center and a school health program.

Using a growth and maturation diagram in the observation of
an individual child, one has to keep in mind several points.
Growth and development data are only part of the medical examination and can never take the place of it. Subsequent data of a
child should be plotted on the chart and compared with cross-
sectional standard values. The standard values represent what is

"usual" at a given time and for a particular population. So they
represent what may be "acceptable", not what is "normal or optimal".
Extreme individual values are not by definition unacceptable or
pathological, but may indicate the need for a clinical examination.
The mid-parent height is an important variable in judging the growth
of a child. Drawing a curve in a two-dimensional grid is rather
difficult and must always be checked.

For each secondary sex characteristic, the range from +2 to
-2 s.d. of the distribution of age is about 4 years. The interval
between "acceptable" extremes is about 6 years. The individual
duration of a particular stage varies considerably: some boys
pass from G_2 to G_5 in less time than others need to pass from stage
G_2 to G_3.

An individual takes about 2 to 5 years to pass through all
stages of the maturation of one organ. There is no correlation
between the duration of the maturation process and the age at which
it starts.

The first sign of sexual maturation in most boys is the
increase in testicular volume, and in most girls the "bud" stage
(M_2) of the breasts.

In boys, there is not a strong relationship between the
stages of the different sex characters, for example, testicular
volume varies considerably in every genital stage. In girls, the
strongest relationship is found between menarche and stage M_4 of
breast development.

In girls, the age at peak height velocity (midpoint of the
year with the maximum increment in height) coincides mostly with
M_3. Practically always menarche occurs after peak height velocity.
While peak height velocity occurs about two years earlier in girls
than boys, the beginning of sexual maturation is only a few months
earlier in girls than boys, and complete sexual maturity is reached
at approximately the same time in both girls and boys.

In growth and maturation diagrams the variables on the
ordinate and the abscissa should be well-described and the sex of
the children distinctly indicated. The grid should be adapted to
practical use so that plotting by assistants and nurses is reliable.
Interpolation is permitted. The incline of the curve should be
about 45°. A steeper incline increases the differences while a
more horizontal curve lessens them. The lines of grid and curves
should be as thin as possible. There is no need to make the
median (P50) thicker than the other centiles. Rather, the normal
range should be emphasized.

The diagrams should include P_3, P_{10}, P_{25}, P_{50}, P_{75}, P_{90} and P_{97} of height for age and P_{10} and P_{90} of weight for height. Those for ages at stages of secondary sex development should include P_{10}, P_{50} and P_{90}. There should be a place to record the height and weight of the father and mother and head circumference in infants. A separate sheet is needed to record the many items of psycho-motor development in infancy and the pre-school period. Special diagrams must be available with height, weight, and head circumference according to conceptual age for the assessment of the newly-born. All the text should be printed horizontally.

REFERENCES

Healy, M. J. R., 1962, The effect of age-grouping on the distribu-
        tion of a measurement affected by growth, Am. J. Phys.
        Anthropol., 20:49.
Johnston, F. E., 1974, Control of age at menarche, Hum. Biol.,
        46:159.
Marshall, W. A., 1978, Puberty, in: "Human Growth, 2. Postnatal
        Growth," F. Falkner and J. M. Tanner, eds., Plenum Press,
        New York.
Prader, A., 1966, Testicular size: assessment and clinical
        importance, Triangle, 7:240.
Tanner, J. M., and Eveleth, P. B., 1975, Variability between
        populations in growth and development at puberty, in:
        "Puberty; Biologic and Psychosocial Components," S. R.
        Berenberg, ed., Stenfert Kroese Publishers, Leiden.
Wafelbakker, F., de Wijn, J. F., and de Haas, J. H., in press
        (cited by van Wieringen et al., 1971).
Wieringen, J. C. van, 1972, "Secular Changes of Growth, 1964-1966
        Height and Weight Surveys in the Netherlands in Historical
        Perspective," thesis, University of Leiden.
Wieringen, J. C. van, Wafelbakker, F., Verbrugge, H. P., and de
        Haas, J. H., 1971, "Growth Diagrams 1965, Netherlands,"
        Wolters-Noordhoof, Groningen.
Zachmann, M., Prader, A., Kind, H. P., Häfliger, H., and Budliger,
        H., 1974, Testicular volume during adolescence; cross-
        sectional and longitudinal studies, Helv. Pediatr. Acta,
        29:61.

3. THE MEASUREMENT OF BODY COMPOSITION

Robert M. Malina

Department of Anthropology
University of Texas
Austin, Texas 78712

Measurement of the body's composition is more complex than the measurement of body size. Although studies of height and weight provide valuable information in understanding growth processes, both provide only dimensional data. Height is a linear measurement, while weight is a measure of body mass; as such they provide limited information about body composition. Hence, much effort has been expended in quantifying the body's composition in vivo (Brožek and Henschel, 1961; Brožek, 1963a, 1965; Garn, 1961, 1963; National Academy of Sciences, 1968; Bergner and Lushbaugh, 1967; Malina, 1969; Forbes, 1978). This report offers an overview of selected methods for measuring body composition, with specific emphasis on those used in growth studies.

DIRECT CHEMICAL ANALYSIS

The human body is composed of four basic chemical constituents, water, protein, mineral and fat (Brožek, 1966). Data derived from biochemical analyses of cadavers are limited and statistically inadequate. Nevertheless, these data provide the framework for estimating body composition in vivo, since all other methods for estimating body composition are indirect. Thus, these limited data are the reference upon which computations for estimates of body composition in vivo are based.

Direct chemical analyses of the human body in conjunction with indirect measurements of body composition have led to the development of the concept of a "reference man", i.e., an average individual free of disease. The most widely used reference body is that

of the young adult reference male (Brožek et al., 1963), while the
composition of an infant reference male at birth and during the
first year of life is available also (Fomon, 1967). More recently,
composition of a reference fetus from 24 through 40 weeks gestational age has been described (Ziegler et al., 1976). Composition
of a reference female is not available, nor is information about
the chemical composition of the body for the years between infancy
and adulthood.

INDIRECT METHODS: MODELS AND APPROACHES

A two compartment model is most commonly used in assessing
body composition in vivo. Body weight is partitioned into fat and
fat-free components (Brožek, 1966). One component is measured indirectly, while the other is derived by subtraction. Definition of
the fat-free or lean component, however, varies. It may be referred
to as lean body mass (LBM) or lean body weight (LBW); or fat-free
body (FFB), fat-free mass (FFM) or fat-free weight(FFW). These
labels are often treated as if they were synonymous, but there is a
basic difference between the two more commonly used terms, LBM and
FFB. LBM as introduced by Behnke is an in vivo concept (Behnke,
1961, see also Behnke and Wilmore, 1974). Weight of the LBM is considered to be divided into constant proportions of water (70-72%),
mineral (7%), and organic matter including an undetermined amount
of essential lipids (2-5%). This constancy or fixed composition of
LBM throughout adult life has been questioned (see Wedgwood, 1963;
Womersley et al., 1976; Brown and Jones, 1977). FFB, on the other
hand, is an in vitro concept applied to carcass analysis. It is
defined as body weight minus total fat, sometimes called chemical
fat, as determined by a specific technique, e.g., ether extraction.
FFB and LBM thus differ in the amount of essential lipids, variously
estimated from 2 to 10% of the fat-free weight (Behnke, 1961). Although LBM and FFB are often interpreted as synonymous, this difference should be noted. LBM is a more "elastic" (Brožek, 1961) or
more "delicate" (Forbes, 1978) concept because the quantity of
essential lipids is not known with precision.

Other approaches for in vivo assessment of body composition
include three component models. Anderson's (1963) model partitions
weight into muscle-free lean, skeletal muscle, and fat, while
Moore et al. (1963) divide body weight into body cell mass (skeletal muscle and visceral parenchyma), fat and the remainder (extra-
cellular water, red cells, and the skeleton).

The preceding models approach the body's composition in an
holistic or gross manner. Except for fat, they provide little information about specific tissue components. For example, LBM fails to
distinguish between bone, muscle, and various viscera. The whole

body models also provide little information about the regional distribution or development of the components. The latter is important
relative to specific compositional changes, sites of change, and
genesis of sex differences during growth.

Body composition methods focusing on specific tissues and on
areas of the body are available. They focus primarily upon fat,
muscle and bone. Fat is one of the basic components built into all
models of body composition. Also, fat has also received much emphasis for three reasons: 1) it is the most variable component of the
body's composition, 2) concern for overweight and obesity, and
disease-mortality correlates of excess fatness, and 3) the availability of calipers to measure subcutaneous tissue (external in
contrast to internal fat). In contrast, muscle and bone are not
amenable to relatively simple measurement with calipers. Presently
there is no satisfactory indirect method to measure the weight of
the skeleton or bone mineral in vivo, with the possible exception
of neutron activation determination of total body calcium and phos-
phorus (Cohn et al., 1977). Measurement of muscle mass in vivo has
similar problems, but estimates are possible from potassium determination and creatinine excretion (see below). These measure of
bone and muscle are basically whole-body estimates, giving little
information about regional development or patterning. Other methods,
however, provide reasonable estimates at specific body sites (see
below).

WEIGHT = LBM + FAT

Densitometry, gamma ray spectrometry, and hydrometry are the
three most commonly used methods for estimating body composition
within the two compartment model. Other methods are available, but
have been used less often.

Densitometry

Body density (mass/unit volume) is determined by underwater
weighing, or air, helium or water displacement. Underwater weighing
is probably the more widely used method (Buskirk, 1961). Residual
volume and the volume of gas in the gastrointestinal tract influence
body density. The former is measured, while the latter is usually
estimated at 100 ml for adults (Buskirk, 1961). Variation in measuring body density based on replicate determinations and expressed
as the standard deviation of the difference distribution, ranges
from 0.0004 to 0.0027 gm/cc for 11 studies, including two of children (Buskirk, 1961; Durnin and Rahaman, 1967; Piechaczek, 1975;
Harsha et al., 1978; Lohman et al., 1978; Zavaleta and Malina, unpublished).

Body density measurements may be converted to a percentage of body weight that is fat. Formulae vary, and "...no universally valid formulas for densitometric estimation of the fat content can be offered..." (Brožek et al., 1963, p. 138). Two formulae for estimating fat from density appear most frequently in the literature:

(1) % Fat = $\dfrac{4.570}{\text{Density}}$ - 4.142 (Brožek et al., 1963)

(2) % Fat = $\dfrac{4.950}{\text{Density}}$ - 4.500 (Siri, 1956).

These formulae and assumptions underlying them are based upon adults. Validity of fat estimates is based upon the assumption that (1) the densities of fat (0.90 gm/cc) and lean (1.10 gm/cc) components are known and are constant; and (2) adults are identical in composition except for variability in the proportion of fatness (Siri, 1961). It should be emphasized that the assumptions are essentially based on the young adult reference male, so that application of formulae to children may give elevated fat estimates. Density differences between children and adults may be due also to hydration differences and lower bone densities in children.

Gamma Ray Spectrometry

The radioisotope ^{40}K comprises 0.012% of the naturally occurring potassium in man (Anderson and Langham, 1959). The concentration of ^{40}K is measured via a gamma ray detector or whole body counter. There are three types of counters: sodium iodide crystal, and liquid and plastic scintillation. The former has a low efficiency, while the latter have a higher efficiency (Forbes, 1978). Reproducibility of ^{40}K counts from day to day and over several months or years give coefficients of variation between 1.2% and 5% (Forbes et al., 1968; Flynn et al., 1972; Pierson et al., 1974; Forbes, 1978). Since potassium occurs mostly in cells and especially in muscle tissue, ^{40}K counts are used to estimate LBM as follows:

$$\text{LBM} = \frac{\text{mEq K}}{68.1} \quad \text{(Forbes and Hursh, 1963).}$$

This equation assumes a constant proportion of potassium in the LBM (68.1 mEq/kg). This value is an average of chemical analyses of three cadavers and a fourth value derived from a survey of the earlier literature (Forbes and Hursh, 1963; Burkinshaw and Cotes, 1973). Since a sex difference in potassium content of the LBM is suggested (Forbes et al., 1968; Womersley et al., 1972, 1976; Burkinshaw and Cotes, 1973), formulae to estimate LBM vary with sex and age:

(1) for males and females under 13 years, as above;

(2) for females 18 years and older,

$$LBM = \frac{mEq\ K}{64.2} \quad (Forbes,\ 1978).$$

A graduated value of the potassium content of the LBM for females 13 to 18 years of age is recommended (Forbes, 1978), the constant in the equation decreasing from 68.1 to 64.2 mEq/kg. It is not known when adult concentrations of potassium in lean tissue are attained. Potassium concentrations are lower in newborn infants, and it is assumed that the transition to adult values occurs in infancy or early childhood (Forbes and Hursh, 1963; Garrow et al., 1965; Maresh and Groome, 1966; Novak et al., 1970).

Hydrometry

Deuterium and tritium oxides, isotopes of water, are used to measure total body water (TBW), which is the largest compositional compartment in the body. It is assumed that water comprises about 72 to 73% of the FFB in normally hydrated individuals (Siri, 1956; Moore et al., 1963; Novak, 1967), although the water content of the FFB has been estimated to vary from 67 to 74% (Siri, 1961). More recently, Sheng and Huggins (1979) summarized the results of eight direct estimates of TBW in adult humans.

Assuming that water content of the FFB is relatively constant, LBM is estimated from TBW as follows:

$$LBM = \frac{TBW}{0.732} \quad .$$

There has been some discussion of the denominator in this equation, Keys and Brožek (1953) and Siri (1956) recommending 0.718 and 0.72 respectively. Sheng and Huggins (1979) comment that the commonly used denominator, 0.732, gives at best, a gross approximation, and suggest a value of 0.716. This value is the mean of five direct estimates of TBW. When 0.716 is used in the equation to derive LBM and then fat, it results in a difference of only -0.2 kg between directly measured and calculated fat, or 2% of total fat. In contrast, use of 0.732 results in a difference of +0.9 kg, or 8% of total fat (Sheng and Huggins, 1979). In addition to questions concerning the water content of the FFB, there is a methodological problem with tritium and deuterium oxides. Hydrogen exchange with organic compounds of the body results in an overestimate of TBW by 0.5 to 2% (Sheng and Huggins, 1979). Reproducibility of TBW estimates give coefficients of variation from 1.8 to 9% (Forbes, 1978). Estimates of body composition from TBW during growth are only approximations for it is not certain when adult hydration of LBM is attained, i.e., in early childhood (Novak, 1966), or adolescence (Heald et al., 1963; Hunt et al., 1963).

Overview

     Density is used to estimate fatness, and LBM is derived by sub-
traction, while ^{40}K and TBW are used to estimate LBM, and fatness
is derived by subtraction. The methods vary logistically. Densitometry by underwater weighing and water displacement require no chemical analysis and the basic equipment is perhaps the least expensive. Further, it can, with modifications, be applied to a field
situation where electrical power might not be available. On the
other hand, the densitometric procedure is somewhat slow, and
requires subject training, so that a lower age limit for its use
is probably 6 or 7 years. The measurement of ^{40}K is non-invasive,
but the equipment is expensive and sensitive (calibration errors,
instability). Precision of counts also varies (see Cohn and Dombrowski, 1970). Time taken to measure ^{40}K, 5 to 30+ minutes, varies
with the counter and size of the subject. Other problems which may
limit the applicability to children under 5 or 6 years are claus-
trophobia and the ability of the child to sit still. Measurement
of TBW requires about 2 to 3 hours for mixing of the isotopes prior
to chemical analysis with special equipment. The method can be in-
vasive if plasma samples are used.

     Methods of estimating body composition within the two-compart-
ment model are suffiently different so that one can inquire whether
the three methods considered provide similar estimates. Among prepubertal boys, Cureton et al. (1975) found that estimates of percentage fat from density, ^{40}K and skinfolds (see below) were, on the
average, similar. However, the range of differences for individuals
was large, 0 to 12%, and there was a systematic tendency for estimates based on density to exceed those based on ^{40}K in leaner subjects. Among 16 year old youth, Hampton et al. (1966) compared LBM
estimates from density, ^{40}K and anthropometry (see below). The
three estimates agreed closely in White males, but density and ^{40}K
gave higher estimates of LBM than anthropometry in Blacks, probably
reflecting skeletal differences (see Malina, 1969, 1973). Among
females, anthropometric estimates were consistently higher than
density and ^{40}K estimates of LBM. Behnke (1969, p. 28) relates the
differences in females to sex differences in essential lipids and
proposes the concept of "minimal weight": "...in the female weight
that incorporates about 14 per cent 'essential' fat is equivalent
to lean body weight in the male that incorporates about 3 per cent
'essential' fat..." Essential fat in the breasts, omentum, and other
tissues accounts for the difference.

     Among adult male and female military personnel, Krzywicki et
al. (1974) compared estimates of fat derived from density, ^{40}K and
TBW. Mean estimates of fatness in females did not differ by the
three methods, but differed significantly in males. ^{40}K gave the
highest estimates and TBW the lowest. The range of individual var-

iation in estimated fatness was also considerably greater in males than females. Myhre and Kessler (1966) showed higher estimates of fat with ^{40}K than density, the differences increasing with age. Finally, in a small sample of adult males and females, Womersley et al. (1972) reported similar LBM estimates with density and a modified ^{40}K method (Boddy et al., 1971), but lower estimates based on ^{40}K as generally calculated (Forbes and Hursh, 1963). The latter difference was especially larger in females by 5.1 and 7.3 kg.

There are thus differences among the estimates of body composition derived from density, ^{40}K and TBW, the most consistent being an overestimate of fat from ^{40}K in adults. Comparative methodological studies of children and youths are limited. Estimates of body composition with the "whole body" approaches are adequate for grouped data, but there is considerable variation between techniques on an individual basis.

Anthropometric Estimates of LBM and Fat

For a long time anthropometric methods have been used to quantify body composition, for example, the early effort of Matiegka (1921). The ready availability of tapes, calipers and anthropometers, the relative ease of measurement procedures suitable for field conditions and large scale surveys, the relative lack of cultural restrictions against external and non-invasive measurements have encouraged the development of anthropometric methods for estimating body composition. Skinfolds (see below) are perhaps the most widely used measurements in anthropometric estimates (Stitt, 1962; Brožek, 1963b), while more elaborate systems including skeletal widths, and trunk and limb circumferences are also available (e.g., Behnke et al., 1959; Behnke, 1963; Behnke and Wilmore, 1974; von Döbeln, 1959; Steinkamp et al., 1965; Crenier, 1966). One of Behnke's methods, for example, estimates LBW from 6 or 8 skeletal diameters and height in children (5+ years), adolescents and adults:

(1) $LBW = D(LBW)^2 \times h^{0.7} \times 0.263$ (males)

(2) $LBW = D(LBW)^2 \times h^{0.7} \times 0.255$ (females),

D(LBW) is the sum of six or eight diameters divided by the sum of their respective constants and h is height. Constants for each diameter are determined from the group mean for the diameter, height, and LBW estimated for the group. Constants are available from reference data, but should be derived specifically for the group under study (Behnke and Wilmore, 1974).

A variety of equations for predicting fat or LBM from anthropometric dimensions are available. The equations, however, are pop-

ulation specific, and must be validated across several samples.
Their general applicability cannot be assumed without testing on
other subjects (Damon and Goldman, 1964; Wilmore and Behnke, 1969,
1970). Selected examples of available prediction equations for
children and youth include those predicting density from skinfolds
(Pařízková, 1961; Durnin and Rahaman, 1967; Nagamine et al., 1967,
1968); density from skinfolds, girths and diameters (Michaels and
Katch, 1968; Young et al., 1968); LBM from skinfolds and weight
(Lohman et al., 1975); TBW from height and weight (Mellits and Cheek,
1970); and percentage fat from height, weight and the triceps skinfold (Frerichs et al., 1979). Prediction equations generally assume
a linear relationship among variables. Some evidence, however,
suggests a curvilinear relationship between skinfolds and body density (Allen et al., 1956; Durnin and Womersley, 1974; Chien et al.,
1975). Equations from skinfolds might also be influenced by individual differences in fat patterning (Garn, 1955, 1961, 1963). When
selection of an equation is necessary, careful attention should be
given to the sample, the correlation between predicted and measured
composition values, the standard error of estimate, and the number
of measurements. Errors inherent in anthropometric techniques and
original body composition procedures must be considered also.

TISSUE-SPECIFIC AND/OR REGIONAL APPROACHES

Whole body estimates of composition provide important data,
but they indicate little about the relative distribution or regional development of major tissue components. As such, it is difficult
to assess sites of changes and specific tissue changes during growth,
areas of the body involved in sex differences, etc. To this end, a
number of approaches have been used, with a primary emphasis on
body fatness.

Skinfolds

In many areas of the body, subcutaneous tissue is loosely
attached to the underlying structure. It can easily be pulled up
between the thumb and forefinger into a double fold of skin and
subcutaneous tissue, which can be satisfactorily measured by
applying a "constant-pressure" caliper. The measurement of skinfolds
is the most commonly used indicator of fatness. Skinfolds can be
measured at many sites on the body, with the triceps, subscapular and
suprailiac being perhaps the most common. Skinfold thicknesses are
used to describe subcutaneous fat distribution and change per se,
and to predict total body fatness. In addition to variation among
skinfold calipers available, sources of variation in skinfold
measurement include location of the site, manner of grasping the
fold, placement of the caliper (i.e., depth), differences in skin

texture, and differences in skinfold compressibility (Brožek and Kinzey, 1960; Clegg and Kent, 1967; Ruiz et al., 1971; Burkinshaw et al., 1973). Measurement experience is a significant factor, as is variation within and among technicians. Coefficients of variation for five skinfolds within technicians of the U.S. Health Examination Survey (Johnston et al., 1974) varied from 15.4% (triceps) to 17.7% (suprailiac), while those between technicians varied between 6.5% (triceps) and 24.5% (mid-axillary).

Ultrasound

Since bone, muscle and fat vary in density and acoustical properties, high frequency sound waves can be used to differentiate the tissues (Stouffer, 1963). Ultrasonic methods have been used primarily in the study of subcutaneous fat, relating the measurements to skinfold thicknesses. It must be noted that skinfold measurements include a double fold, while ultrasound measures only a single layer. The latter ordinarily gives thicknesses which are about 60 to 65% of the former (Bullen et al., 1965; Maaser, 1972). Correlations between ultrasonic and skinfold measurements range from 0.6 to 0.9 (Bullen et al., 1965; Booth et al., 1966; Sloan, 1967; Haymes et al., 1976). Correlations, however, vary with site, and are generally higher in women; results, however, are not consistent across studies (e.g., Bullen et al., 1965, and Haymes et al., 1976). Correlations between ultrasonic measures of fat and body density, however, are moderate, ranging from -0.54 to -0.79 for seven sites. Except for measurements of the thigh, correlations between ultrasonic fat and density are consistently lower than those for corresponding skinfolds and density (Sloan, 1967), so that ultrasonic measurements have no greater accuracy of prediction than cheaper and perhaps simpler skinfold caliper measurements.

Ultrasound has not been used extensively in the study of muscle and bone. Ikai and Fukunaga (1968, 1970) used ultrasonic methods to estimate the cross-sectional area of muscle relative to strength in Japanese adults.

Methodological aspects of the ultrasonic technique include operator error in applying the instrument (e.g., variable pressure of probe on skin) and interpreting impulses on the monitor. Repeated measurements, however, correlate highly (Bullen et al., 1965; Haymes et al., 1976). A portable device is presently available (Sanchez and Jacobson, 1978) which may enhance field application of the method.

Creatinine Excretion

Creatinine excretion provides an estimate of muscle mass. Although creatinine is not solely a by-product of muscle metabolism,

the volume excreted in the urine is a function of skeletal mass
(Cheek, 1968; Malina, 1969, 1978; Forbes, 1978). The amount excreted
over a 24-hour period is used to estimate muscle mass on the assumption that: 1 g excreted per 24 hours is derived from 20 kg of muscle
mass (Cheek, 1968). Estimates of muscle mass from urinary creatinine
excretion are subject to dietary (pre-formed creatinine), physical
activity and age effects (Garn, 1963). Technical considerations
require that the timing of 24-hour urine collection be carefully
controlled, as a 15 minute error in collection is 1% of the 24-hour
period (Forbes, 1978). Correlations between creatinine excretion
and LBM (^{40}K, TBW, density, and exchangeable potassium) are moderate
to high, +0.56 to +0.99 (Boileau et al., 1972; Forbes and Bruining,
1976). The correlation between creatinine excretion and LBM is
affected by physical conditioning, decreasing from +0.73 before
training to +0.57 after training (Boileau et al., 1972).

Radiography

Radiographic studies of body composition began long before
the advent of more sophisticated indirect approaches (Stuart et al.,
1940; Stuart and Dwinell, 1942; Stuart and Sobel, 1946; Reynolds,
1944, 1948, 1950; Reynolds and Grote, 1948; Garn, 1961, 1963).
Radiographic methods were used widely in normative studies of body
composition during growth and adulthood, but are less common at
present.

The radiographic approach assesses fat, muscle and bone at
selected sites. The technique requires precise and standardized
positioning, tube to film distance, and object to film distance
to minimize distortion, magnification and parallax (Tanner, 1962).
The arm and calf are the areas most commonly used for soft tissue
radiography, with the thigh and forearm used less often. Because
of the application of x-rays for skeletal maturity assessment,
the hand-wrist area is commonly used to study cortical bone changes
of the second metacarpal (Garn, 1970). Chest radiographs are occasionally used to assess lower thoracic fat (Garn and Haskell, 1959;
Comstock and Livesay, 1963).

Widths of fat, muscle and bone are measured at specified levels
or sites. The earlier observations of Reynolds and Stuart (see
above) were limited to the widest part of the calf. Data from the
Child Research Council in Denver (Maresh, 1966, 1970) were measured
at maximum width of the forearm and calf, and the lateral half of
the thigh at mid-length of the femur. Tissue widths in the Harpenden Growth Study (Tanner, 1962, 1965, 1968) were measured at mid-
arm (half way between acromion and the head of the radius), at
maximum calf, and on the lateral half of the thigh at the junction
of the middle and distal thirds. Philadelphia data (Johnston and

Malina, 1966; Malina and Johnston, 1967) were measured at the widest breadth of the arm and at maximum calf width. Thus, although names of the sites are used interchangeably, measurement sites vary. Also, focal distances vary between studies. Measurements of tissue widths are quite accurate, but methods of taking and deriving measurements differ. In the calf, for example, the fibula may be included as muscle, or the interosseous space may be excluded. On the other hand, some measurements are derived by subtraction, e.g., total width of the arm, anterior and posterior fat widths, and humerus width are measured; muscle width is obtained by subtraction.

Tissue measurements are commonly reported as widths, but are also reported as cross-sectional areas, assuming the limb is a cylinder. Data are reported for specific sites, e.g., arm or calf, and for areas combined, e.g., arm plus calf plus thigh. The implication is obvious. It is difficult to compare radiographic measurements of fat, muscle and bone across studies; the data from different studies, however, show qualitatively similar patterns of growth in the three tissues for specific areas and areas combined. The pattern of change in fat is most variable, and combining fat data for different sites, especially extremity and trunk, may be misleading. Combining fat measurements even at the same site may limit the information. During adolescence, for example, females show relatively greater medial calf fat loss; in contrast, lateral calf fat changes are less (Malina and Johnston, 1967). The preceding illustrates the genesis of the sexual dimorphism in placement of calf fat in adults (Garn and Saalberg, 1953).

Correlations among fat, muscle and bone measurements within an extremity are rather low (generally 0.5), suggesting tissue independence, while those between corresponding tissues in the arm, thigh and calf are moderate to high for fat (0.5 to 0.9) and low to moderate for muscle and bone (0.3 to 0.7; Malina, 1969). A comparison of 12 radiographic fat sites in young adult males indicates higher inter-relationships among more centrally located sites (i.e., deltoid, thoracic, iliac, trochanteric) than among more peripheral or extremity sites (Garn, 1957).

Earlier studies of bone included only periosteal widths, while more recent efforts consider cortical bone and the medullary cavity, with more emphasis on the former. Some efforts have been made to estimate skeletal mass from cortical bone measurements (Garn, 1970), but intercorrelations among cortical widths in different bones are generally low, circa 0.3 (Johnston and Malina, 1970). This would suggest that a measurement of a single bone cannot be confidently used as an indicator of cortical width in other areas of the skeleton or of skeletal mass.

Correlations between radiographic muscle widths and creatinine excretion are moderate, circa 0.7 (Reynolds and Clark, 1947; Garn, 1961). Dietary variation may influence the correlations (Garn, 1961), but the presence of variable amounts of fat between muscles may be a contributing factor (Forbes, 1978). Correlations between radiographic fat widths and body density are low to moderate, ranging from -0.58 to -0.76 for four sites in adult men (Brožek et al., 1958), and from -0.08 to -0.71 for 13 fat sites in adult women (Young et al., 1963a, 1963b). Among women, correlations are generally lower for fat measures on the calf, except for medial calf fat. Correlations between skinfold thickness and radiographic fat width at corresponding sites range from 0.48 to 0.93, with most values >0.8 (Hammond, 1955; Clarke et al., 1956; Garn, 1956; Garn and Gorman, 1956; Brožek and Mori, 1958; Young et al., 1963a; Singh, 1967). The lowest correlation was for the thigh in young adult women (Young et al., 1963a), while corresponding values for boys and girls were 0.82 and 0.89 respectively (Hammond, 1955).

Photon Absorptiometry

Estimates of bone mineral are provided by photon absorption procedures, in which a collimated photon beam from a low energy radionuclide source scans a transverse section of bone, usually the radius or ulna (Cameron et al., 1968; Mazess et al., 1973). Photons are then measured by a scintillation detector, thus providing an estimate of bone mineral. The technique is rather precise and accurate. Correlations among scans of the same bone are high (0.90 to 0.95), while those between scans of different extremity bones are lower (0.8 to 0.9; Mazess, 1968). The correlation between radiographic measures of cortical area of the radius and photon absorption estimates at the same site in vivo is 0.84 (Mazess and Cameron, 1972), while correlations of cortical measurements of excised ulnae and radii, and photon absorption estimates of mineral at several sites range from 0.60 to 0.92 (Mazess et al., 1970). This would suggest that radiographic measures of cortical bone may not accurately portray bone mineral as measured by photon absorption. The usefulness of photon scanning to estimate total skeletal mass thus needs further evaluation.

Arm Anthropometry

Arm circumference and triceps skinfold are widely used in nutritional anthropometry and surveillance. Both measurements are taken at the same level, and arm circumference is corrected for the thickness of the triceps skinfold to give an estimate of mid-arm muscle, or more correctly, muscle-bone diameter, circumference or area (Jelliffe and Jelliffe, 1969). Correlations between estimated mid-arm muscle circumference and diameter with radiographic muscle widths in adult males are moderately high, circa 0.85 (Singh, 1967). Anthropometric estimates of mid-arm muscle area are highly related (0.92) with computerized axial tomographic scans in adults, but the former consistently overestimate muscle area by about 10% (Heymsfield et al., 1979). Correlations between estimated mid-arm muscle circumference and densitometrically estimated LBM are also moderatately high, circa 0.75 to 0.85 in young males (Johnston, 1979; Zavaleta and Malina, unpublished), but somewhat lower, circa 0.60 in young females (Johnston, 1979).

Selected formulae (Gurney, 1969; Jelliffe and Jelliffe, 1969; Gurney and Jelliffe, 1973; Frisancho, 1974; Martorell et al., 1976) for converting arm circumference (C_a) and the triceps skinfold (S_t) in centimeters are summarized below:

(1) Arm area (cm^2) = $\dfrac{C_a^2}{4\pi}$

(2) Arm muscle diameter (cm) = $\dfrac{C_a}{\pi} - S_t$

(3) Arm muscle circumference (cm) = $C_a - (\pi \times S_t)$

(4) Arm muscle area (cm^2) = $\dfrac{(C_a - \pi S_t)^2}{4\pi}$

(5) Arm fat area (cm^2) = (1) - (4) or $\dfrac{S_t \times C_a}{2} - \dfrac{\pi S_t^2}{4}$

Corrected arm circumference, though widely used, has several limitations. The procedure assumes that the arm is a cylinder and that subcutaneous fat is evenly distributed. Also, the size of the humerus is not considered. Variation in skinfold compressibility, the use of different skinfold calipers, and errors in measurement are other important factors. To adjust for the uneven distribution of arm fat, Bouterline-Young (1969) and Forbes (1978) suggest the use of both the biceps (S_b) and triceps (S_t) skinfolds in correcting arm circumference:

(1) Arm muscle circumference (cm) = $C_a - \dfrac{\pi}{2}(S_t + S_b)$

(2) Arm muscle area (cm^2) = $\dfrac{1}{4\pi}\left[C_a - \dfrac{\pi}{2}(S_t + S_b)\right]^2$

(Forbes, 1978).

Biopsy Studies of Muscle and Fat

   A biopsy is a technique in which a sample of muscle or adipose
tissue is taken in vivo, generally under a local anesthetic. The
technique is "blind" in the sense that, in the present context, it
is assumed that the sample taken is representative of a muscle as a
whole or of a fat depot. A sample of muscle tissue is removed with
a percutaneous biopsy needle (Bergstrom, 1962 , 1975; Nichols et al.,
1968) or by surgical excision (Nichols et al., 1968; Talbert and
Haller, 1968). The amount of tissue removed varies between 20 and
100 mg (Bergstrom, 1975), although larger samples (e.g., 1 gm, Talbert and Haller, 1968) may be taken, depending on the purpose of
the study. Samples of adipose tissue are taken from a subcutaneous
fat depot by needle aspiration, or from both subcutaneous and deeper
sites at surgery (Hirsch et al., 1960; Hirsch and Gallian, 1968).

   Although skeletal muscle biopsies have been used rather widely
in studies of athletes and activity effects (Hoppeler et al., 1973;
Costill et al., 1976; Prince et al., 1976; Thorstensson, 1976; Burke
et al., 1977; Bylund et al., 1977; Green et al., 1979; see also Malina, this volume), application to growth studies is limited largely
to the work of Cheek and colleagues (Cheek, 1968, 1974, 1975; Cheek
and Hill, 1970; Cheek et al., 1971). The amount of DNA per nucleus
is relatively constant at 6.2 pg/diploid nucleus; hence, the number
of nuclei in a muscle tissue sample is estimated by dividing the
total DNA in the tissue by 6.2. Cheek and colleagues have referred
to this estimate of nuclear number as muscle "cell" number, and to
the ratio of protein (cell mass) to DNA (nucleus) in the sample as
an index of "muscle cell size." Assuming that a gluteal biopsy
sample is representative of skeletal muscle in general, and using
creatinine excretion as an estimate of skeletal muscle mass, Cheek
and colleagues have generalized estimates of number and size to total
muscle mass. Aside from sampling problems, both in terms of muscle
group and number of subjects (Malina, 1978), there are other limitations. Problems associated with creatinine excretion have been mentioned earlier. Methodological concerns relative to estimates of
"cell" or more specifically nuclear number are apparent. Muscle
fibers are multinucleate, and the amount of DNA in a muscle indicates
nothing about the fibers in it. The amount of protein per unit DNA
also reveals nothing about the size of the muscle fiber; rather, it
simply shows the amount of cytoplasm associated with each nucleus
(Widdowson, 1970).

   In contrast to biopsy studies of muscle tissue during growth,
there has been more interest in adipose tissue from a developmental
perspective (Brook, 1972; Knittle, 1972, 1978; Bonnet et al., 1976;
Knittle et al., 1977, 1979; Hager, 1977; Hager et al., 1977; Kirtland and Gurr, 1979). Average fat cell size, i.e., average lipid
per cell, is estimated by dividing the total lipid in a tissue sample

by the number of cells in the sample. Fat cells are counted elec-
tronically after osmium fixation (Hirsch and Gallian, 1968), or
microscopically in an isoosmotic solution after freeze-cutting
(Sjöström et al., 1971). The counting of fat cells may be limited
in that only fat cells with a certain amount of lipid are identified, and preadipocytes or small fat cells may be omitted (Häger,
1977). The total number of fat cells in the body is, in turn,
estimated by dividing total body fat by the average fat cell size.
The latter may be for a single site or averaged over several sites.
Estimated size of fat cells varies with the site sampled, and cells
from deeper sites tend to be smaller than those from superficial
sites (Brook, 1971; Salans et al., 1971; Krotkiewski et al., 1975;
Bonnet et al., 1976; Gurr and Kirtland, 1978). The assumption
that a single sample is representative of total body fat is thus
questionable. There may be greater variation in fat cell size
between sites than between individuals.

Total body fat is estimated from measures of density, ^{40}K or
TBW, or by prediction from skinfold thicknesses (Salans et al.,
1971; Brook et al., 1972; Bonnet et al., 1976; Häger et al., 1977;
Knittle et al., 1977). Limitations and errors in the indirect
methods for estimating total body fat and in predictions from
regression equations have been discussed earlier.

SUMMARY

Methods for estimating body composition in a living person are
many, complex, and at times disparate. They range from traditional
anthropometry to more complicated biopsy or neutron-activation
techniques. Those methods applied in a growth and developmental
perspective have been reviewed. Emphasis is placed upon the
methods per se and interrelationships among methods, and not on
the quantification of body composition nor on age trends and sex
differences. Although the literature on body composition is
extensive and many methods have been applied to children and youth,
there is a need to validate many of the techniques on the growing
organism. There is also a need to apply several methods to the
same individual as well as a need to apply the techniques to more
children.

REFERENCES

Allen, T.H., Peng, M.T., Chen, K.P., Huang, T.F., Chang, C., and
    Fang, H.S., 1956, Prediction of total adiposity from skinfolds
    and the curvilinear relationship between external and internal
    viscosity, Metabolism, 5:346.
Anderson, E.C., 1963, Three-component body composition analysis
    based upon potassium and water determinations, Ann. N.Y. Acad.
    Sci., 110:189.
Anderson, E.C., and Langham, W.H., 1959, Average potassium concen-
    tration of the human body as a function of age, Science, 130:713.
Behnke, A.R., 1961, Comment on the determination of whole body
    density and a resume of body composition data, in: "Techniques
    for Measuring Body Composition," Brožek, J., and Henschel, A.
    (eds.), Nat. Acad. Sci.-Nat. Res. Council, Washington, p. 118.
Behnke, A.R., 1963, Anthropometric evaluation of body composition
    throughout life, Ann. N.Y. Acad. Sci., 110:450.
Behnke, A.R., 1969, New concepts of height-weight relationships,
    in: "Obesity," N.L. Wilson (ed.), F.A. Davis, Philadelphia,
    p. 25.
Behnke, A.R., and Wilmore, J.H., 1974, "Evaluation and Regulation
    of Body Build and Composition," Prentice-Hall, Englewood Cliffs,
    New Jersey.
Behnke, A.R., Guttentag, O.E., and Brodsky, C., 1959, Quantification
    of body weight and configuration from anthropometric measure-
    ments, Human Biol., 31:213.
Bergner, P.E., and Lushbaugh, C.C. (eds.), 1967, "Compartments, Pools,
    and Spaces in Medical Physiology," U.S. Atomic Energy Commission,
    Washington.
Bergstrom, J., 1962, Muscle electrolyes in man, Scand. J. Clin. Lab.
    Invest., 14, Suppl. 68.
Bergstrom, J., 1975, Percutaneous needle biopsy of skeletal muscle
    in physiological and clinical research, Scand. J. Clin. Lab.
    Invest., 35:609.
Boddy, K., King, P.C., Tothill, P., and Strong, J.A., 1971, Measure-
    ment of total body potassium with a shadow shield whole-body
    counter: calibration and errors, Phys. Med. Biol., 16:275.
Boileau, R.A., Horstman, D.H., Buskirk, E.R., and Mendez, J., 1972,
    The usefulness of urinary creatinine excretion in estimating
    body composition, Med. Sci. Sports, 4:85.
Bonnet, F.P., Duckerts, M., and Heuskin, A., 1976, Subcutaneous
    adipose tissue growth in normal and obese children: methodol-
    ogical problems, in: "The Adipose Child," Z. Laron (ed.),
    Karger, Basel, p. 104.
Booth, R.A.D., Goddard, B.A., and Paton, A., 1966, Measurement of
    fat thickness in man: a comparison of ultrasound, calipers
    and electrical conductivity, Br. J. Nutr., 20:719.
Bouterline-Young, H., 1969, Arm measurements as indicators of body
    composition in Tunisian children, J. Trop. Pediat., 15:222.

Brook, C.G.D., 1971, Composition of human adipose tissue from deep and subcutaneous sites, Br. J. Nutr., 25:377.

Brook, C.G.D., 1972, Evidence for a sensitive period in adipose-cell replication in man, Lancet, 2:624.

Brook, C.G.D., Lloyd, J.K., and Wolf, O.H., 1972, Relation between age of onset of obesity and size and number of adipose cells, Br. Med. J., 2:25.

Brown, W.J., and Jones, P.R.M., 1977, The distribution of body fat in relation to habitual activity, Ann. Human Biol., 4:537.

Brožek, J., 1961, Editor's comment, in: "Techniques for Measuring Body Composition," J. Brožek and A. Henschel (eds.), Nat. Acad. Sci.-Nat. Res. Council, Washington D.C., p. 120.

Brožek, J. (ed.), 1963a, Body composition, Ann. N.Y. Acad. Sci., 110:1.

Brožek, J., 1963b, Quantitative description of body composition: Physical anthopology's "fourth" dimension, Current Anthrop., 4:3.

Brožek, J. (ed.), 1965, Human body composition, Symp. Soc. Human Biol., 7:1.

Brožek, J., 1966, Body composition: models and estimation equations, Amer. J. Phys. Anthrop., 24:239.

Brožek, J., and Henschel, A., (eds.), 1961, "Techniques for Measuring Body Composition," Nat. Acad. Sci.-Nat. Res. Council, Washington D.C.

Brožek, J., and Kinzey, W., 1960, Age changes in skinfold compressibility, J. Gerontol., 15:45.

Brožek, J., and Mori, H., 1958, Some interrelations between somatic, roentgenographic and densitometric criteria of fatness, Human Biol., 30:322.

Brožek, J., Grande, F., Anderson, J.T., and Keys, A., 1963, Densitometric analysis of body composition: revision of some quantitative assumptions, Ann. N.Y. Acad. Sci., 110:113.

Brožek, J., Mori, H., and Keys, A., 1958, Estimation of total body fat from roentgenograms, Science, 128:901.

Bullen, B.A., Quaade, F., Olesen, E., and Lund, S.A., 1965, Ultrasonic reflections used for measuring subcutaneous fat in humans, Human Biol., 37:375.

Burke, E.R., Cerný, F., Costill, D., and Fink, W., 1977, Characteristics of skeletal muscle in competitive cyclists, Med. Sci. Sports, 9:109.

Burkinshaw, L., and Cotes, J.E., 1973, Body potassium and fat-free mass, Clin. Sci., 44:621.

Burkinshaw, L., Jones, P.R.M., and Krupowicz, D.W., 1973, Observer error in skinfold thickness measurements, Human Biol., 45:273.

Buskirk, E.R., 1961, Underwater weighing and body density: A review of procedures, in: "Techniques for Measuring Body Composition," Brožek, J., and Henschel, A. (eds.), Nat. Acad. Sci.-Nat. Res. Council, p. 90.

Bylund, A.-C., Bjurö, T., Cederblad, G., Holm, J., Lundholm, K., Sjöström, M., Angquist, K.A., and Schersten, T., 1977, Physical training in man: Skeletal muscle metabolism in relation to muscle morphology and running ability, Europ. J. Appl. Physiol. 36:151.

Cameron, J.R., Mazess, R.B., and Sorenson, J.A., 1968, Precision and accuracy of bone mineral determination by direct photon absorptiometry, Invest. Radiol., 3:141.

Cheek, D.B., (ed.), 1968, "Human Growth," Lea and Febiger, Philadelphia.

Cheek, D.B., 1974, Body composition, hormones, nutrition, and adolescent growth, in: "Control of the Onset of Puberty," M.M. Grumbach, G.D. Grave, and F.E. Mayer (eds.), Wiley, New York, p. 424.

Cheek, D.B., 1975, Growth and body composition, in: "Fetal and Postnatal Cellular Growth: Hormones and Nutrition," D.B. Cheek, (ed.), Wiley, New York, p. 389.

Cheek, D.B., and Hill, D.E., 1970, Muscle and liver cell growth: role of hormones and nutritional factors, Fed. Proc., 29:1503.

Cheek, D.B., Holt, A.B., Hill, D.E., and Talbert, J.L., 1971, Skeletal muscle cell mass and growth: the concept of the deoxyribonucleic acid unit, Pediat. Res., 5:312.

Chien, S., Peng, M.T., Chen, K.P., Huang, T.F., Chang, C., and Fang, H.S., 1975, Longitudinal studies on adipose tissue and its distribution in human subjects, J. Appl. Physiol., 39:825.

Clarke, H.H., Geser, L.R., and Hunsdon, S.B., 1956, Comparison of upper arm measurements by use of roentgenogram and anthropometric techniques, Res. Quart., 27:379.

Clegg, E.J., and Kent, C., 1967, Skinfold compressibility in young adults, Human Biol., 39:418.

Cohn, S.H., and Dombrowski, C.S., 1970, Absolute measurement of whole-body potassium by gamma-ray spectrometry, J. Nucl. Med., 11:239.

Cohn, S.H., Abesamis, C., Zanzi, I., Aloia, J.F., Yasumura, S., and Ellis, K.J., 1977, Body elemental composition: comparison between black and white adults, Amer. J. Physiol., 232:E419.

Comstock, G.W., and Livesay, V.T., 1963, Subcutaneous fat determinations from a community-wide chest x-ray survey in Muscogee County, Georgia, Ann. N.Y. Acad. Sci., 110:475.

Costill, D.L., Daniels, J., Evans, W., Fink, W., Krahenbuhl, G., and Saltin, B., 1976, Skeletal muscle enzymes and fiber composition in male and female track athletes, J. Appl. Physiol., 40:149.

Crenier, E.J., 1966, La prédiction du poids corporel normal, Biométr. Hum., 1:10.

Cureton, K.J., Boileau, R.A., and Lohman, T.G., 1975, A comparison of densitometric, potassium-40 and skinfold estimates of body composition in prepubescent boys, Human Biol., 47:321.

Damon, A., and Goldman, R.F., 1964, Predicting fat from body measurements: densitometric validations of ten anthropometric equations, Human Biol., 36:32.

Durnin, J.V.G.A., and Rahaman, M.M., 1967, The assessment of the
    amount of fat in the human body from measurements of skinfold
    thickness, Br. J. Nutr., 21:681.
Durnin, J.V.G.A., and Womersley, J., 1974, Body fat assessed from
    total body density and its estimation from skinfold thickness:
    measurements on 481 men and women aged from 16 to 72 years,
    Br. J. Nutr., 32:77.
Flynn, M.A., Woodruff, C., Clark, J., and Chase, G., 1972, Total
    body potassium in normal children, Pediat. Res., 6:239.
Fomon, S.J., 1967, Body composition of the male reference infant
    during the first year of life, Pediatrics, 40:863.
Forbes, G.B., 1978, Body composition in adolescence, in: "Human
    Growth, Volume 2," F. Falkner and J.M. Tanner (eds.), Plenum,
    New York, p. 239.
Forbes, G.B., and Bruining, G.J., 1976, Urinary creatinine excretion
    and lean body mass, Amer. J. Clin. Nutr., 29:1359.
Forbes, G.B., and Hursh, J.B., 1963, Age and sex trends in lean
    body mass calculated from K^{40} measurements, with a note on the
    theoretical basis for the procedure, Ann. N.Y. Acad. Sci.,
    110:255.
Forbes, G.B., Schultz, F., Cafarelli, C., and Amirhakimi, G.H., 1968,
    Effects of body size on potassium-40 measurement in the whole
    body counter (tilt-chair technique), Health Phys., 15:435.
Frisancho, A.R., 1974, Triceps skin fold and upper arm muscle size
    norms for assessment of nutritional status, Amer. J. Clin.
    Nutr., 27:1052.
Frerichs, R.F., Harsha, D.W., and Berenson, G.S., 1979, Equations
    for estimating percentage of body fat in children 10-14 years,
    Pediat. Res., 13:170.
Garn, S.M., 1955, Relative fat patterning: An individual character-
    istic, Human Biol., 27:75.
Garn, S.M., 1956, Comparison of pinch-caliper and x-ray measurements
    of skin plus subcutaneous fat, Science, 124:178.
Garn, S.M., 1957, Selection of body sites for fat measurement,
    Science, 125:550.
Garn, S.M., 1961, Radiographic analysis of body composition, in:
    "Techniques for Measuring Body Composition," J. Brožek and A.
    Henschel (eds.), Nat. Acad. Sci.-Nat. Res. Council, Washington
    D.C., p. 36.
Garn, S.M., 1963, Human biology and research in body composition,
    Ann. N.Y. Acad. Sci., 110:429.
Garn, S.M., 1970, "The Earlier Gain and the Later Loss of Cortical
    Bone in Nutritional Perspective," C C Thomas, Springfield,
    Illinois.
Garn, S.M., and Gorman, E.L., 1956, Comparison of pinch-caliper and
    teleroentgenogrammetric measurements of subcutaneous fat,
    Human Biol., 28:407.
Garn, S.M., and Haskell, J.A., 1959, Fat changes during adolescence,
    Science, 129:1615.

Garn, S.M., and Saalberg, J.H., 1953, Sex and age differences in the composition of the adult leg, Human Biol., 25:144.

Garrow, J.S., Fletcher, K., and Halliday, D., 1965, Body composition in severe infantile malnutrition, J. Clin. Invest., 44:417.

Green, H.J., Thomson, J.A., Daub, W.D., Houston, M.E., and Ranney, D.A., 1979, Fiber composition, fiber size and enzyme activities in vastus lateralis of elite athletes involved in high intensity exercise, Europ. J. Appl. Physiol., 41:109.

Gurney, J.M., 1969, Field experience in Abeokuta, Nigeria (with special reference to differentiating protein and calorie reserves), J. Trop. Pediat., 15:225.

Gurney, J.M., and Jelliffe, D.B., 1973, Arm anthropometry in nutritional assessments: nomogram for rapid calculation of muscle circumference and cross-sectional muscle and fat areas, Amer. J. Clin. Nutr., 26:912.

Gurr, M.I., and Kirtland, J., 1978, Adipose tissue cellularity: a review, 1, Techniques for studying cellularity, Int. J. Obesity, 2:401.

Häger, A., 1977, Adipose cell size and number in relation to obesity, Postgrad. Med. J., 53 (suppl. 2):101.

Häger, A., Sjöström, L., Arvidsson, B., Björntorp, P., and Smith, U., 1977, Body fat and adipose tissue cellularity in infants: a longitudinal study, Metabolism, 26:607.

Hammond, W.H., 1955, Measurement and interpretation of subcutaneous fat, with norms for children and young adult males, Br. J. Prev. Soc. Med., 9:201.

Hampton, M.C., Huenemann, R.L., Shapiro, L.R., Mitchell, B.W., and Behnke, A.R., 1966, A longitudinal study of gross body composition and body conformation and their association with food and activity in a teen-age population: anthropometric estimation of body build, Amer. J. Clin. Nutr., 19:422.

Harsha, D.W., Frerichs, R.R., and Berenson, G.S., 1978, Densitometry and anthropometry of black and white children, Human Biol., 50:261.

Haymes, E.M., Lundegren, H.M., Loomis, J.L., and Buskirk, E.R., 1976, Validity of the ultrasonic technique as a method of measuring subcutaneous adipose tissue, Ann. Human Biol., 3:245.

Heald, F.P., Hunt, E.E., Jr., Schwartz, R., Cook, C.D., Elliot, O., and Vajda, B., 1963, Measures of body fat and hydration in adolescent boys, Pediatrics, 31:226.

Heymsfield, S.B., Olafson, R.P., Kutner, M.H., and Nixon, D.W., 1979, A radiographic method of quantifying protein-calorie undernutrition, Amer. J. Clin. Nutr., 32:693.

Hirsch, J., and Gallian, E., 1968, Methods for the determination of adipose cell size in man and animals, J. Lipid Res., 9:110.

Hirsch, J., Farquhar, J.W., Ahrens, E.H., Peterson, M.L., and Stoffel, W., 1960, Studies of adipose tissue in man, Amer. J. Clin. Nutr., 8:499.

Hoppeler, H., Luthi, P., Claasen, H., Weibel, E.R., and Howald, H., 1973, The ultrastructure of the normal human skeletal muscle, Pflugers Arch., 344:217.

Hunt, E.E., Jr., and Heald, F.P., 1963, Physique, body composition, and sexual maturation in adolescent boys, Ann. N.Y. Acad. Sci., 110:532.

Ikai, M., and Fukunaga, T., 1968, Calculation of muscle strength per unit cross-sectional area of human muscle by means of ultrasonic measurement, Int. Z. Angew. Physiol., 26:26.

Ikai, M., and Fukunaga, T., 1970, A study on training effect on strength per unit cross-sectional area of muscle by means of ultrasonic measurement, Int. Z. Angew. Physiol., 28:173.

Jelliffe, E.P.P., and Jelliffe, D.B. (eds.), 1969, The arm circumference as a public health index of protein-calorie malnutrition of early childhood, J. Trop. Pediat., 15: Mgh. 8, p. 177.

Johnston, F.E., 1979, Anthropometry and nutritional status, Paper prepared for Workshop on Nutrition and Health Status Indicators, La Jolla, Ca., unpublished.

Johnston, F.E., and Malina, R.M., 1966, Age changes in the composition of the upper arm in Philadelphia children, Human Biol., 38:1.

Johnston, F.E., and Malina, R.M., 1970, Correlations of midshaft breadths and compact bone thickness among bones of the upper and lower extremities of children aged 6 to 16 years, Amer. J. Phys. Anthrop., 32:323.

Johnston, F.E., Hamill, P.V.V., and Lemeshow, S., 1974, Skinfold thickness of youths 12-17 years, United States, "Vital and Health Statistics, Series 11, Number 132," National Center for Health Statistics, Washington D.C.

Keys, A., and Brožek, J., 1953, Body fat in adult man, Physiol Rev., 33:245.

Kirtland, J., and Gurr, M.I., 1979, Adipose tissue cellularity: a review, 2, The relationship between cellularity and obesity, Int. J. Obesity, 3:15.

Knittle, J.L., 1972, Obesity in childhood: a problem in adipose tissue cellular development, J. Pediat., 81:1048.

Knittle, J.L., 1978, Adipose tissue development in man, in: "Human Growth, Volume 2," F. Falkner and J.M. Tanner (eds.), Plenum, New York, p. 295.

Knittle, J.L., Ginsberg-Fellner, F., and Brown, R.E., 1977, Adipose tissue development in man, Amer. J. Clin. Nutr., 30:762.

Knittle, J.L., Timmers, K., Ginsberg-Fellner, F., Brown, R.E., and Katz, D.P., 1979, The growth of adipose tissue in children and adolescents, J. Clin. Invest., 63:239.

Krotkiewski, M., Sjöström, L., Björntorp, P. and Smith, U., 1975, Regional adipose tissue cellularity in relation to metabolism in young and middle-aged women, Metabolism, 24:703.

Krzywicki, H.J., Ward, G.M., Rahman, D.P., Nelson, R.A., and Consolazio, C.F., 1974, A comparison of methods for estimating human body composition, Amer. J. Clin. Nutr., 27:1380.

Lohman, T.G., Bioleau, R.A., and Massey, B.H., 1975, Prediction of lean body mass in young boys from skinfold thickness and body weight, Human Biol., 47:245.

Lohman, T.G., Slaughter, M.H., Selinger, A., and Boileau, R.A., 1978, Relationship of body composition to somatotype in college men, Ann. Human Biol., 5:147.

Maaser, R., 1972, Die Ultraschallmessung der subcutanen Fettgeweb-sdicke zur Beurteilung des Ernahrungszustandes von Kindern, Z. Kinderheilk., 112:321.

Malina, R.M., 1969, Quantification of fat, muscle and bone in man, Clin. Orthop., 65:9.

Malina, R.M., 1973, Biological substrata, in: "Comparative Studies of Blacks and Whites in the United States," K.S. Miller and R.M. Dreger (eds.), Seminar Press, New York, p. 53.

Malina, R.M., 1978, Growth of muscle tissue and muscle mass, in: "Human Growth, Volume 2," F. Falkner and J.M. Tanner (eds.), Plenum, New York, p. 273.

Malina, R.M., and Johnston, F.E., 1967, Relations between bone, muscle and fat widths in the upper arms and calves of boys and girls studied cross-sectionally at ages 6 to 16 years, Human Biol., 39:211.

Maresh, M., 1966, Changes in tissue widths during growth, Amer. J. Dis. Child., 111:142.

Maresh, M.M., 1970, Measurements from roentgenograms, heart size, long bone lengths, bone, muscle and fat widths, skeletal mat-uration, in: "Human Growth and Development," R.W. McCammon (ed.), C.C. Thomas, Springfield, Illinois, p. 155.

Maresh, M., and Groome, D.S., 1966, Potassium-40 serial determin-ations in infants, Pediatrics, 38:642.

Martorell, R., Yarbrough, C., Lechtig, A., Delgado, H., and Klein, R.E., 1976, Upper arm anthropometric indicators of nutritional status, Amer. J. Clin. Nutr., 29:46.

Matiegka, J., 1921, The testing of physical efficiency, Amer. J. Phys. Anthrop., 4:223.

Mazess, R.B., 1968, Estimation of bone and skeletal weight by the direct photon absorptiometric method, Paper presented at the Symposium on Skeletal Mineralization, American Association of Physical Anthropologists, Annual meeting, Detroit.

Mazess, R.B., and Cameron, J.R., 1972, Growth of bone in school children: comparison of radiographic morphometry and photon absorptiometry, Growth, 36:77.

Mazess, R.B., Cameron, J.R., and Sorenson, J.A., 1970, A comparison of methods for determining bone mineral content, in: "Progress in Methods of Bone Mineral Measurement," G.D. Whedon and J.R. Cameron (eds.), U.S. Dept. HEW, Washington D.C., p. 455.

Mazess, R.B., Judy, P.F., Wilson, C.R., and Cameron, J.R., 1973, Progress in clinical use of photon absorptiometry, in: "Clin-ical Aspects of Metabolic Bone Disease," B. Frame, A.M. Par-fitt and H.M. Duncan (eds.), Excerpta Medica, Amsterdam, p. 37.

Mellits, E.D., and Cheek, D.B., 1970, The assessment of body water
    and fatness from infancy to adulthood, Mon. Soc. Res. Child.
    Dev., 35 (serial no. 140):12.
Michael, E.D., and Katch, F.I., 1968, Prediction of body density
    from skin-fold and girth measurements of 17-year-old boys,
    J. Appl. Physiol., 25:747.
Moore, F.D., Olesen, K.H., McMurrey, J.D., Parker, H.V., Ball, M.R.,
    and Boyden, C.M., 1963, "The Body Cell Mass and Its Supporting
    Environment," Saunders, Philadelphia.
Myhre, L.G., and Kessler, W.V., 1966, Body density and potassium 40
    measurements of body composition as related to age, J. Appl.
    Physiol., 21:1251.
Nagamine, S., Yamakawa, K., Isobe, S., Ichinose, Y., and Kaga, A.,
    1967, Body composition in adolescence, in: "Annual Report of
    the National Institute of Nutrition," Tokyo, p. 57.
Nagamine, S., Yamakawa, K., Oshima, S., Ichonise, Y., Isobe, S.,
    Tsuji, E., and Suzuki, S., 1968, Body composition of Japanese
    school children, in: "Annual Report of the National Institute
    of Nutrition," Tokyo, p. 37.
National Academy of Sciences, 1968, "Body composition in Animals
    and Man," National Academy of Sciences, Washington D.C.
Nichols, B.L., Hazlewood, C.F., and Barnes, D.J., 1968, Percutaneous
    needle biopsy of quadriceps muscle: potassium analysis in normal
    children, J. Pediat., 72:840.
Novak, L.P., 1966, Total body water and solids in six- to seven-
    year-old children: differences between the sexes, Pediatrics,
    38:483.
Novak, L.P., 1967, Total body water in man, in: "Compartments, Pools,
    and Spaces in Medical Physiology," P.E. Bergner and C.C. Lush-
    baugh (eds.), U.S. Atomic Energy Commission, Washington, p. 197.
Novak, L.P., Hammamoto, K., Orvis, A.L., Burke, E.C., 1970, Total
    body potassium in infants, Amer. J. Dis. Child., 119:419.
Parízková, J., 1961, Total body fat and skinfold thickness in child-
    ren, Metabolism, 10:794.
Piechaczek, H., 1975, Oznaczanie całkowitego tłuszczu ciała metodami
    densytometryczną i antropometryczną, Mat. Prac. Antrop.
    (Wrocław), 89:3.
Pierson, R.N., Lin, D.H.Y., and Phillips, R.A., 1974, Total-body
    potassium in health: effects of age, sex, height, and fat,
    Amer. J. Physiol., 226:206.
Prince, F.P., Hikida, R.S., and Hagerman, F.C., 1976, Human muscle
    fiber types in power lifters, distance runners and untrained
    subjects, Pflugers Arch., 363:19.
Reynolds, E.L., 1944, Differential tissue growth in the leg during
    childhood, Child Dev., 15:181.
Reynolds, E.L., 1948, Distribution of tissue components in the fe-
    male leg from birth to maturity, Anat. Rec., 100:621.
Reynolds, E.L., 1950, The distribution of subcutaneous fat in child-
    hood and adolescence, Mon. Soc. Res. Child Dev., 15, no.2

Reynolds, E.L., and Clark, L.C., 1947, Creatinine excretion, growth
    progress and body structure in normal children, Child Dev.,
    18:155.
Reynolds, E.L., and Grote, P., 1948, Sex differences in the distri-
    bution of tissue components in the human leg from birth to mat-
    urity, Anat. Rec., 102:45.
Ruiz, L., Colley, J.R.T., and Hamilton, P.J.S., 1971, Measurement of
    triceps skinfold thickness, Brit. J. Prev. Soc. Med., 25:165.
Salans, L.B., Horton, E.D., and Sims, E.A.H., 1971, Experimental
    obesity in man: cellular character of the adipose tissue, J.
    Clin. Invest., 50:1005.
Sanchez, C.L., and Jacobson, H.N., 1978, Anthropometry measurements,
    a new type, Amer. J. Clin. Nutr., 31:1116.
Sheng, H-P., and Huggins, R.A., 1979, A review of body composition
    studies with emphasis on total body water and fat, Amer. J.
    Clin. Nutr., 32:630.
Singh, R., 1967, A study of fat, muscle, bone, and comparison bet-
    ween roentgenogrammetric and somatometric methods for assessing
    subcutaneous fat and muscle thickness in the upper arm of adult
    males, Z. Morph. Anthrop., 58:308.
Siri, W.E., 1956, The gross composition of the body, Adv. Biol. Med.
    Physics, 4:239.
Siri, W.E., 1961, Body composition from fluid spaces and density:
    Analysis of methods, in: "Techniques for Measuring Body Compo-
    sition," J. Brožek and A. Henschel (eds.), Nat. Acad. Sci.-
    Nat. Res. Council, Washington, p. 223.
Sjöström, L., Björntorp, B., and Vrana, J., 1971, Microscopic fat
    cell size measurements on frozen-cut adipose tissue in compar-
    ison with automatic determinations of osmium-fixed fat cells,
    J. Lipid Res., 12:521.
Sloan, A.W., 1967, Estimation of body fat in young men, J. Appl.
    Physiol., 23:311.
Steinkamp, R.C., Cohen, N.L., Gaffey, W.R., McKey, T., Bron, G.,
    Siri, W.E., Sargent, T.W., and Isaacs, E., 1965, Measures of
    body fat and related factors in normal adults, II, A simple
    clinical method to estimate body fat and lean body mass, J.
    Chron. Dis., 18:1291.
Stitt, K.R., 1962, "Skinfold Measurement; A Method of Determining
    Subcutaneous Fat: An Annotated Bibliography," Department of
    Foods and Nutrition, University of Alabama, Tuscaloosa.
Stouffer, J.R., 1963, Relationship of ultrasonic measurements and
    x-rays to body composition, Ann. N.Y. Acad. Sci., 110:31.
Stuart, H.C., and Dwinell, P.H., 1942, The growth of bone, muscle
    and overlying tissues in children six to ten years of age as
    revealed by studies of roentgenograms of the leg area, Child
    Dev., 13:195.
Stuart, H.C., and Sobel, E.H., 1946, The thickness of the skin and
    subcutaneous tissue by age and sex in childhood, J. Pediat.,
    28:637.

Stuart, H.C., Hill, P., and Shaw, C., 1940, The growth of bone, muscle and overlying tissues as revealed by studies of roent-genograms of the leg area, Mon. Soc. Res. Child Dev., 5, no.3
Talbert, J.L., and Haller, J.A., 1968, Muscle biopsy technique in infants and children, in: "Human Growth," D.B. Cheek (ed.), Lea and Febiger, Philadelphia, p. 649.
Tanner, J.M., 1962, "Growth at Adolescence," (2nd. ed.), Blackwell Scientific Publications, Oxford.
Tanner, J.M., 1965, Radiographic studies of body composition in children and adults, Symp. Soc. Human Biol., 7:211.
Tanner, J.M., 1968, Growth of bone, muscle and fat during childhood and adolescence, in: "Growth and Development of Mammals," G.A. Lodge and G.E. Lamming (eds.), Plenum, New York, p. 3.
Thorstensson, A., 1976, Muscle strength, fibre types and enzyme activities in man, Acta Physiol. Scand., Suppl. 443.
Von Döbeln, W., 1959, Anthropometric determination of fat-free body weight, Acta Med. Scand., 165:37.
Wedgwood, R.J., 1963, Inconstancy of the lean body mass, Ann. N.Y. Acad. Sci., 110:141.
Widdowson, E.M., 1970, Harmony of growth, Lancet, 1:901.
Wilmore, J.H., and Behnke, A.R., 1969, An anthropometric estimation of body density and lean body weight in young men, J. Appl. Physiol., 27:25.
Wilmore, J.H., and Behnke, A.R., 1970. An anthropometric estimation of body density and lean body weight in young women, Amer. J. Clin. Nutr., 23:267.
Womersley, J., Boddy, K., King, P.C., and Durnin, J.V.G.A., 1972, A comparison of the fat-free mass of young adults estimated by anthropometry, body density and total body potassium content, Clin. Sci., 43:469.
Womersley, K., Durnin, J.V.G.A., Boddy, K., and Mahaffy, M., 1976, Influence of muscular development, obesity, and age on the fat-free mass of adults, J. Appl. Physiol., 41:223.
Young, C.M., Blondin, J., Tensuan, R., and Fryer, J.H., 1963b, Body composition studies of "older" women, thirty to seventy years of age, Ann. N.Y. Acad. Sci., 110:589.
Young, C.M., Sipin, S.S., and Roe, D.A., 1968, Body composition studies of pre-adolescent and adolescent girls, III, Predicting specific gravity, J. Amer. Diet. Assoc., 53:469.
Young, C.M., Tensuan, R.S., Sault, F., and Holmes, F., 1963a, Estimating body fat of normal young women, Visualizing fat pads of soft-tissue x-rays, J. Amer. Diet. Assoc., 42:409.
Zavaleta, A.N., and Malina, R.M., unpublished, Densitometric estimates of body composition in Mexican-American boys.
Ziegler, E.E., O'Donnell, A.M., Nelson, S.E., and Fomon, S.J., 1976, Body composition of the reference fetus, Growth, 40:329.

4. THE MEASUREMENT OF SKELETAL MATURATION

Alex F. Roche

Fels Research Institute
and Department of Pediatrics
Wright State University School of Medicine
Yellow Springs, Ohio   45387

Human biologists usually apply the term "maturity" to level of maturity; that is, the extent to which an individual, or a group of individuals, has proceeded towards adulthood. Therefore, maturation is a particular type of development: development that proceeds to the same end point in all individuals. In this sense, measures relative to adult size for the same individual, for example, present stature as a percentage of actual or predicted adult stature, are measures of maturity. The measurement of skeletal maturity is based on the recognition of maturity indicators; these are visible changes or stages that occur during maturation.

For several centuries, there has been interest in the anatomical differences, other than size, between the skeletons of children and adults. The general sequence of changes observed in a bone are shown in Figure 1.

NUMBER OF CENTERS

Soon after the introduction of radiography, attempts were made to use maturational features visible in radiographs to classify individuals. The first method was based on onset of ossification of the carpals or the whole hand-wrist (Pryor, 1907; Rotch, 1908, 1909); later the hemiskeleton was used (Åkerlund, 1918; Pyle and Sontag, 1943; Elgenmark, 1946; Harding, 1952). With these methods, radiographic positioning can vary within comparatively wide limits, assessors require little training, and the method is quick. The measurements are reliable (Garn and Rohmann, 1959) although it is difficult to distinguish between early ossification

and calcification, particularly in cervical vertebral bodies
(Hadley, 1956). The first definitive radiographic sign that bone
is present is the observation of trabeculae.

The sequence of onset of ossification is relatively fixed
within the hand-wrist (Yarbrough et al., 1973; Low et al., 1975).
Therefore, the actual centers can be determined with an average
error of identification of one center per radiograph from the number of centers ossified (Yarbrough et al., 1973). Either Greulich-

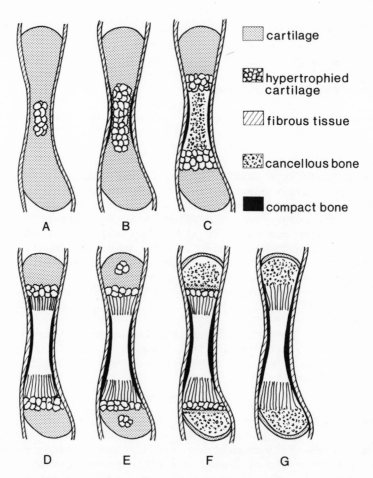

Fig. 1. A diagram of the maturation of a long bone in which the
         length of the bone has been kept constant. The approxi-
         mate age scale is: A, 6th prenatal week; B, 7th prenatal
         week; C, 12th prenatal week; D, 16th prenatal week to 2
         years; E, 2 to 6 years; F, 6 to 16 years and G, adulthood.
         The clear area in D-G represents the marrow cavity.

Pyle (1959) or Tanner-Whitehouse (1975) area skeletal ages for the hand-wrist are slightly less effective in identifying the centers ossified than using the number of centers only. Yarbrough and his associates (1973) showed that the number of centers ossified method and the Greulich-Pyle and Tanner-Whitehouse skeletal age methods measure the same phenomenon.

The number of centers method is applicable only to preschool children if restricted to the hand-wrist. The age range could be extended if the hemiskeleton were assessed but the method would be of little value after 7 years because few centers ossify after this age. Furthermore, radiation hazards and financial costs prohibit examination of the hemiskeleton.

METHODS BASED ON MEASUREMENTS

Methods based on size alone are inappropriate for the assessment of maturity but those based on relationships between measurements can be used. The most widely investigated of the latter is the carpal ossification ratio which was introduced by Carter (1923, 1926) and employed in many studies (Prescott, 1923; Freeman and Carter, 1924; Gates, 1924; Baldwin et al., 1928; Flory, 1936; Kelly and Reynolds, 1947). Although the technique differed slightly from study to study, the essential aim was to measure the total carpal area, defined as a quadrilateral, and the part of this area occupied by bone. The method is inaccurate when centers are small and towards the end of maturation when the carpal outlines overlap.

The ratio between the width of an epiphysis and the width of the corresponding metaphysis has been studied in a wide range of bones. This is a very useful maturity indicator in normal individuals but it is not applicable in many pathological conditions that grossly affect the ends of the bones.

ATLAS METHODS

The basic concept of the atlas method is that each child passes through the same sequence of changes in bone shape during maturation. It is considered individual variations in shape are so slight that a single set of standards for each sex, or in some cases a single set for both sexes, can provide a scale by which the maturity level of a child can be judged. Use of the atlases depends upon the recognition of maturity indicators. Many such indicators have been described but few have determined whether these "indicators" are useful. In fact, many unsatisfactory indicators are included in the atlases.

The sequence of maturity indicators is variable within areas
that include numerous bones, such as the foot (Todd, 1937; Abbott
et al., 1950; Garn and Rohmann, 1960). It has been claimed the
sequence is fixed for each bone (Acheson, 1957; Tanner, 1958, 1962;
Helm et al., 1971) but this is not so. The sequence may vary between the two ends of a bone. For example, in one Fels participant
the relative widths of the epiphyses of the proximal phalanges indicate a skeletal age of 9.5 years (Greulich-Pyle) but the widths
of the epiphyseal zones of these bones indicate a skeletal age of
14 years. Also, differences in maturity level occur between the
medial and lateral condyles of the femur (Roche and French, 1970).

The claim that the sequence of maturity indicators is fixed
has been challenged in regard to onset of ossification and
epiphyseo-diaphyseal fusion (Moss and Noback, 1958; Garn and
Rohmann, 1960; Garn et al., 1961). Few relevant studies of intermediate maturity indicators have been reported but the large reported ranges of bone-specific skeletal ages (least mature to most
mature) within individual hand-wrists (Figure 2, Roche et al.,
1976) show sequence variation for intermediate maturity indicators
is common. These data show the need for bone-specific assessments
when atlas methods are used. In comparison with area assessments,
they are more accurate and they are systematically more advanced
(Johnson et al., 1973; Low et al., 1975). The need to assign bone-
specific skeletal ages is shown also by the essential independence
of epiphyseal bone scores and carpal scores in both the Tanner-
Whitehouse and Taranger methods that are described later (Taranger
et al., 1976). Many atlas standards include bones at markedly
different levels of maturity; this reduces the replicability of
assessments unless these are made bone by bone (Acheson et al.,
1963; Roche et al., 1970).

When the atlas method is applied, a radiograph is compared
with the standards until one is found that is at the same maturity
level as the radiograph. The skeletal age recorded for the radiograph is that of the standard it matches. Often it is desirable
to interpolate between standards. The procedure should be applied
to individual bones and bone-specific skeletal ages should be
recorded.

Little is known of the best method for combining bone-specific
skeletal ages to obtain the skeletal age of an area. The flat
response surface found on analysis of the structure of bone-
specific hand-wrist skeletal ages indicates the median is the most
useful appropriate value (Roche et al., 1975a). Bones that are
not radiopaque can be rated only as "less than x years"; those
that are adult can be rated only as "more than y years," where x
and y respectively are the mean ages at which the bone becomes
radiopaque and adult. These ratings cannot be used to calculate
means; if mean skeletal ages were derived only from the remaining

bones, some illogical changes could occur in serial area skeletal ages for individuals. However, a median can be calculated if fewer than half the bones are "adult."

The most carefully prepared atlases were published by the Cleveland group (Greulich and Pyle, 1950, 1959; Pyle and Hoerr, 1955, 1969; Hoerr et al., 1962). Using mixed longitudinal radiographs from a large sample and relying on their knowledge of maturational processes in the skeleton and the earlier work of Todd (1937), they selected preliminary standards, working backwards from the oldest to the youngest. During this process, they established approximate ages for the appearance of particular maturity indicators in each sex. When the listing of maturity indicators was considered complete for a bone, standard radiographs were selected for each sex that represented best the central tendency of maturity for each bone when 100 radiographs, at each six months of age, were arrayed in order of maturity level. Later, radiographs were selected that were representative of the central tendencies for all bones.

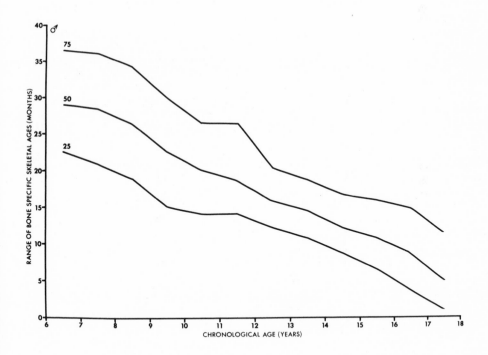

Fig. 2.   Selected percentiles of the range of bone-specific skeletal ages (Greulich-Pyle) within the hand-wrists of individual boys (Roche et al., 1976).

Recent atlases for the knee and the hand-wrist present a single series of standards in which male and female skeletal age equivalents are assigned to each standard (Pyle and Hoerr, 1969; Pyle et al., 1971) despite the sex-associated differences in patterns of maturation (Abbott et al., 1950; Moss and Noback, 1958; Scheller, 1960; Garn and Rohmann, 1960; Hewitt and Acheson, 1961; Pyle et al., 1961; Garn et al., 1966, 1967, 1975; Thompson et al., 1973; Roche et al., 1975b).

Throughout the atlases there are problems in regard to the language used. Standard anatomical terminology is not always employed and many descriptions of indicators are difficult to interpret. This reduces the reliability of assessments. Also, these atlases do not include precise instructions for the user; this has led many to apply the Greulich-Pyle atlas in a "personal" fashion. Workers differ in the order in which they assess bones when using the Greulich-Pyle atlas. The ages assigned to bones rated early in the sequence influence the rating of bones assessed later.

There are other difficulties with these atlases. Size is not a maturity indicator but this is the only difference between successive standards for some bones. Furthermore, progressive skeletal ages have been assigned to the distal end of the ulna although the epiphysis has not ossified and this bone cannot be assessed reliably in its absence. The reproduction and positioning of some standards is unsatisfactory, particularly in the knee and foot-ankle atlases (Hoerr et al., 1962; Pyle and Hoerr, 1969). Finally, some changes between successive standards reflect different patterns of maturation rather than differences in level of maturity.

In measuring the maturity level of the hand-wrist, it has been claimed carpal skeletal ages should be disregarded if they differ from the skeletal ages of the short bones of the hand-wrist (Acheson et al., 1963); when they agree there is no point in their inclusion. Others have suggested the carpals be excluded or receive low weightings because they are so variable in rates of maturation (Baldwin et al., 1928; Wallis, 1931; Todd, 1937; Bayer and Newell, 1940; Garn and Rohmann, 1959, 1960; Johnston and Jahina, 1965; Acheson, 1966). Variability is an advantage if it assists meaningful discrimination among individuals, but it causes difficulties in applying the single set of standards in the Greulich and Pyle atlas.

The Applicability of the Atlas Standards

Data have been reported from large national probability samples of non-institutionalized United States children aged 6 to 17 years (Roche et al., 1974, 1976). The data from each individual were weighted to obtain estimates that closely approximate those that

would have been obtained had all United States children and youths
within this age range been examined. Particularly from 9 to 13
years, the skeletal maturity standards in the Greulich-Pyle atlas
are markedly in advance of the mean levels of maturity in these
national probability samples (Figure 3).

All assessments were made against male standards without the
chronological age or the sex being known. Consequently, the means
of the skeletal ages assigned to girls are in advance of the corresponding chronological ages (Figure 3). The skeletal ages assigned to the girls were modified to what it was considered they
would have been had these radiographs been assessed against female
standards using the bone-specific sex differences published by
Pyle and others (1971). The means of these female-equivalent ages
("FE" in Figure 3) are less than the chronological ages but the
differences are smaller than those for the boys. These findings
for the general population of United States children are most important in the interpretation of Greulich-Pyle skeletal ages.

The unusual protocol for the assessment of radiographs in
these national surveys provide a totally unbiased estimate of sex-
associated differences in skeletal maturity levels (Figure 4).
These differences are generally similar to those reported by Pyle
and others (1971) until 13 years after which those obtained from
the national surveys are much smaller.

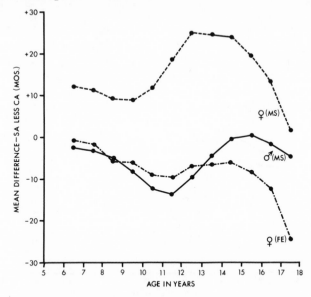

Fig. 3.   Mean differences between skeletal age (Greulich-Pyle) and
          chronological age in a nationally representative sample
          of U.S. children (From Roche et al., 1976). MS = male
          standard; FE = female equivalent ages.

CHOICE OF AN AREA FOR ASSESSMENT

An area for assessment must be chosen that can be radiographed
with minimal radiation, as few radiograph views as possible should
be used, and all useful relevant information should be obtained
from each radiograph.

However, there are limitations to the accuracy with which one
can generalize to the whole skeleton from the assessment of only
one part. The positive correlations between ages at onset of ossification and skeletal maturity levels are too low for accurate estimation of the maturity of one area from the assessment of another
(Crampton, 1908; Reynolds and Asakawa, 1951; Garn et al., 1964,
1966, 1967, 1967a; Roche and French, 1970). Assessment of one
joint area, rather than bilateral corresponding areas, is recommended. Although lateral differences are common (e.g., Long and
Caldwell, 1911; Flecker, 1932; Flory, 1936; Torgersen, 1951;
Dreizen et al., 1957; Baer and Durkatz, 1957; Greulich and Pyle,
1959; Christ, 1961; Roche, 1963), those reporting such differences
agree they are not of practical importance.

The hand-wrist is assessed more commonly than the other areas,
partly because it was the first for which atlases of standards were
available. Some prefer the hand-wrist because many bones are

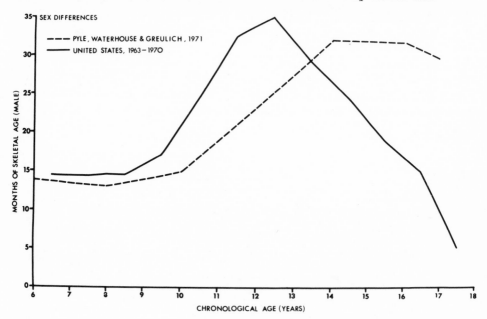

Fig. 4.   Sex-associated differences in skeletal maturity levels.
The United States data are from nationally representative
samples (Roche et al., 1974, 1976).

present in a relatively small area. However, some bones in the
hand-wrist, e.g., proximal phalanges, provide redundant information
(Tanner et al., 1962, 1975; Clarke and Hayman, 1962; Roche, 1970;
Sproul and Peritz, 1971). Assessing all of them will lead to more
accurate measurements of maturity but the gain is likely to be
small.

The hand-wrist is easy to position for radiography and little
irradiation is involved. More important is the disadvantage that
long age ranges occur, particularly 11 to 16 years in boys and 9
to 14.5 years in girls, during which few maturational changes are
apparent in the hand-wrist (Sauvegrain et al., 1962). Also, its
usefulness is limited before 4 years of age and towards the end of
maturation because some bones in this area, e.g., distal phalanges,
reach adult levels at about 15 years in boys and 13.5 years in
girls.

The area to be assessed should be determined partly by the
reason for the assessment. For example, the knee should be assessed if a measure of skeletal maturity is required to estimate
the potentials for leg elongation or growth in stature (Roche et
al., 1975b), while the vertebral column should be assessed if there
is concern about the timing of an operation to correct scoliosis
(Anderson et al., 1963; Bailey, 1971). However, a satisfactory
method for measuring the maturity level of the vertebral column is
unavailable.

SCORING METHODS

The first scoring method was introduced by Acheson (1954) who
summed scores (1, 2 or 3) arbitrarily allocated to stages. Modifications of this approach, without statistical analyses, have
been reported by Wetherington (1961) and Sempé (1972).

A major advance occurred when Tanner and his colleagues (1962,
1975) improved and extended the method of Acheson. Their method
uses approximately 9 "stages" for each of 20 hand-wrist bones. The
bones of the second and fourth "rays"[1] are omitted because their
skeletal maturity levels are correlated highly with those of corresponding bones in other rays (Hewitt, 1963; Roche, 1970; Sproul
and Peritz, 1971).

The scores assigned to all stages by Tanner and his associates
were derived by assuming all the stages observed within a hand-

---

[1]Each ray of the hand includes a metacarpal with its associated
phalanges, e.g., metacarpal III, proximal phalanx III, middle
phalanx III and distal phalanx III.

wrist radiograph reflect the same underlying quantity, the level of
skeletal maturity for the hand-wrist, although the bones are usually
at different stages. Scores corresponding to stages were selected
to minimize the disparity among the bone-specific scores for the
individual, summed over all individuals in the standardizing group.
The scores for each stage were derived objectively but later a subjective factor was introduced to balance the contributions of types
of bones. There was concern that the many metacarpal and phalan-
geal bones would mask the contribution of the carpals, radius and
ulna to the total score. Consequently the authors devised one
score for the carpals and one for the radius, ulna and short bones
(RUS). Furthermore, in the RUS total score, the scores for the
bones in the rays were weighted lightly so that their total contribution, for the group, equalled the combined scores of the radius
and ulna. The scores are usually transformed to skeletal ages
(years) from tables or graphs. There are problems at the upper
end of the scale where a difference of one stage for a bone can
alter the skeletal age for the hand-wrist by as much as 0.8 years.

Tanner-Whitehouse skeletal ages are systematically higher
than those obtained using the Greulich-Pyle atlas (Roche et al.,
1974, 1976) due to differences between the standardizing populations. Also these skeletal ages differ in their associations with
pubertal events (Himes and Roche, in preparation) indicating these
skeletal ages differ in their biological meaning.

The Tanner-Whitehouse method has been modified by Sempé (1972),
Medicus and others (1971), and Marti-Henneberg and others (1974).
There is no objection to such modifications if their scientific
basis is established as carefully as that of the original method.

ROCHE-WAINER-THISSEN METHOD

The Roche-Wainer-Thissen method is for the measurement of the
maturity of the knee (Roche et al., 1975b). The authors listed
reported maturity indicators, made the descriptions anatomically
correct, and developed grading methods that are as objective as
possible. Some indicators are graded by comparison with photographs and drawings, some by fitting standard curves to margins,
and the remainder by measuring ratios between distances.

The indicators retained were shown to be reliable and they
discriminated; i.e., they were present in some but not all children
during a particular age range. In addition, the indicators retained had the quality of universality. By definition, each grade
of an indicator must occur during maturation. Consequently, there
are ages when either the least mature or the most mature grade is
universal although, because children mature at different rates,

there may be no age when a particular intermediate grade is present in all children. When this occurred, serial radiographs were reviewed to determine that the intermediate grade occurred in the sequence of changes in each child. The criterion of universality was applied to the ratios by determining whether they became approximately constant at older ages.

The indicators finally chosen were valid; this refers to the quality by which a radiographic feature indicates skeletal maturity. A priori, the bones of a child become more mature with increasing chronological age. Therefore, the prevalence of grades of valid maturity indicators must change systematically with age until the most mature grade is universal. Group prevalence data provide only a general guide to validity because in almost all serial studies some children miss visits. A better measure is obtained from the prevalence of "reversals" in serially organized data; i.e., changes in indicators with increasing age in the reverse directions to those expected from group trends. Finally, useful maturity indicators must have the quality of completeness; this refers to the extent to which the indicator can be graded in a group of radiographs.

The parameters used to construct the Roche-Wainer-Thissen scale were the chronological age at which each indicator grade is present in 50% of children (threshold) and the rate of change in the prevalence of each indicator with age (slope). Indicator grades may have different slopes but reach their thresholds at the

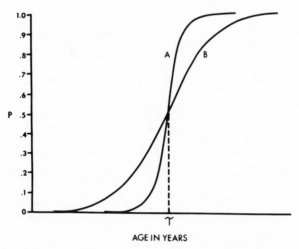

AGE IN YEARS

Fig. 5. An example of two indicators that have the same threshold but different slopes. B is less discriminatory than A and so is less useful as a maturity indicator.

same age (Figure 5). The slope is closely associated with the use-fulness of an indicator; the steeper the slope, i.e., the more rapid the change in prevalence with age, the more informative the indicator. However, indicator grades may have the same slope but reach their thresholds at different ages. These indicators are equally informative but they differ in their ages of maximum use-fulness (Figure 6). The slope and the threshold for each indicator grade were combined to a single continuous index using latent trait analysis (Birnbaum, 1968; Samejima, 1969, 1972). This index was scaled so that the mean and variance of skeletal age in the standardizing group were equal to the mean and variance of chronological age.

This method separates the within-age variance to two compon-ents: one attributable to real variations in maturity level, the other to the error (provided as the standard error of the individ-ual measurement) inherent in any scheme. Only the Roche-Wainer-Thissen method separates these errors. The standard error of the individual measurement is small when many highly informative indicator grades are assessed with thresholds near the chronologi-cal age of the child. The standard error is large in contrary circumstances and when unusual combinations of indicator grades are observed. The errors are larger at some ages than others as shown by the total information curve (Figure 7). The information available from a knee radiograph is relatively great until 2 years, decreases to 6 years and then remains approximately constant.

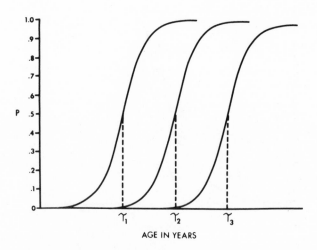

Fig. 6. An example of three indicators (1, 2 and 3) having the same slope (discriminating ability) but different thresholds (T_1, T_2 and T_3).

The Roche-Wainer-Thissen method is based on 34 maturity indicators but at any one age only about eight must be graded because there are limits to the age ranges during which each indicator is useful. A measurement requires little time but the recorded grades must be transferred to a computer; a small microcomputer will suffice. Published programs provide the skeletal age appropriate for the radiograph with the standard error of the particular estimate. Unlike the Tanner-Whitehouse method, the RWT method allows for missing values which is important if part of an area cannot be measured.

A corresponding method is being developed for the hand-wrist. Preliminary data indicate the hand-wrist will be more useful than the knee after about 8 years of age. The mathematical basis of the method makes it easy to obtain a combined estimate for the hand-wrist and knee with a consequent reduction in the standard error.

TARANGER METHOD

Taranger and his associates (Taranger et al., 1970, 1972, 1976) recorded the raw data needed for Tanner-Whitehouse measurements and calculated the mean age of appearance of each stage. This led to the development of a "bone stage chart." The zones on this chart for each stage begin with the mean age of appearance of

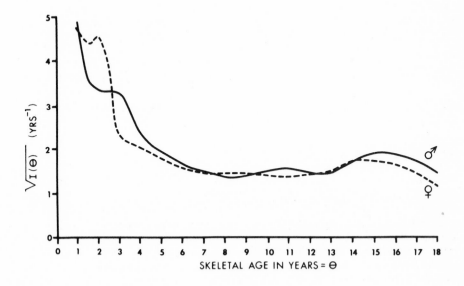

Fig. 7.   The total system information curves for the RWT method at all ages for both sexes.

the stage and end with the mean age of appearance for the subsequent
stage.

The chart is used by encircling the letters corresponding to
the stages observed in a radiograph and comparing the position of
these circles with chronological age. This visual profile shows
the variations among bones in maturity levels. Skeletal age is
obtained by summing the maturity scores for the stages. Each
maturity score is the average of the mean appearance time and the
mean disappearance time of the stage, with age expressed as (log
conceptional age) 1000. The maturity scores are combined without
weighting and transformed to a skeletal age equivalent using
published graphs.

SKELETAL AGE SCALE

All maturity scales are divided to "skeletal age years,"
except in the Tanner-Whitehouse and Taranger methods where the
maturity level can be described either in skeletal age years or
scores. "Skeletal age years" are not units. Typically, girls
achieve adult levels of skeletal maturity before boys. Therefore,
more maturation occurs during a typical female skeletal age year
than during a male skeletal age year. Similar considerations apply
to scores. Furthermore, bones differ in the chronological ages at
which they reach adult maturity levels (Roche et al., 1974); therefore, the amount of maturity achieved per skeletal age year differs
among bones.

The nature of the scale makes it difficult to monitor individual progress. Consider, for example, a 10-year-old boy with a
skeletal age of 6 years. During the first year of treatment, he
may advance 2 "years" in skeletal maturity and then be an 11-year-
old boy with a skeletal age of 8 years. It appears he has had
considerable catch-up in maturity level but this cannot be proven.
His early deficit (4 "years" at chronological age 10 years) may be
no greater than his later one (3 "years" at chronological age 11
years).

CRANIOFACIAL AREA AND VERTEBRAL COLUMN

There are no useful methods for the measurement of maturity
for important areas of the skeleton. The first is the craniofacial
area. It may be possible to develop a method to measure craniofacial maturity levels based on changes in the ossification and
shape of the cranial base (e.g., Ortiz and Brodie, 1949; Moss and
Greenberg, 1955; Irwin, 1960; Shapiro and Janzen, 1960; Konie,
1964; Kier, 1968; Schopfner et al., 1968; Latham, 1972; Invergall
and Thilander, 1972; Melsen, 1972; Lewis and Roche, 1977).

The vertebral column is another area for which a method of measurement is needed. Recently, maturity indicators for cervical vertebral bodies from 10 to 15 years have been described by Lamparski (1972, 1975). He had a small sample (144 children aged 10 to 15 years) and described too few indicators for each vertebra to allow accurate measurement. Although much remains to be done, this was important pioneering work.

SKELETAL MATURITY IN THE NEWLY-BORN

In all methods for the measurement of maturity, the data are normed against chronological age. In effect, the aim is to determine the chronological age at which the observed set of maturity levels is most likely to be present. This causes difficulties when maturity is to be measured at birth because of possible errors in gestational ages calculated from last menstrual periods. There is no alternative but it is essential that prevalence data be derived only from mothers in whom gestational ages are likely to be accurate. Interesting data relative to the epiphyses for the head of the humerus and the coracoid process have been reported (Kuhns et al., 1973) but a method based on these findings has not been developed.

RECOMMENDATIONS

Considering the various methods currently available for the measurement of skeletal maturity, it is desirable to make recommendations. The Greulich-Pyle and Pyle-Hoerr atlases for the hand-wrist and knee respectively should be used for teaching purposes because the successive standards provide excellent descriptions of what is seen radiographically. When a close check on the rate of skeletal maturation is required, another method should be used. That of Taranger has advantages over the Tanner-Whitehouse method for the hand-wrist if there is particular interest in the pattern of maturation. More commonly, interest is centered on the general level and for this the Tanner-Whitehouse method is the best of those currently available. If there is interest in stature or inequality of leg lengths, then the knee should be assessed using the method of Roche, Wainer and Thissen; also, this is the method of choice at ages up to 4 years when the hand-wrist provides little information.

CONCLUSION

There has been considerable progress in the methodology of measuring skeletal maturity during recent decades. Many useful indicators have been described but further studies of indicators

and of relationships between them are needed. A clear conceptual
framework and an appropriate statistical methodology are now available that should be applied to various areas of the skeleton and
other organ systems.

REFERENCES

Abbott, O. D., Townsend, R. O., French, R. B., and Ahmann, C. F.,
        1950, Carpal and epiphysial development. Another index of
        nutritional status of rural school children, Am. J. Dis.
        Child., 79:69.
Acheson, R. M., 1954, A method of assessing skeletal maturity from
        radiographs. A report from the Oxford Child Health Survey,
        J. Anat. (London), 88:498.
Acheson, R. M., 1957, The Oxford method of assessing skeletal
        maturity, Clin. Orthop., 10:19.
Acheson, R. M., 1966, Maturation of the skeleton, in: "Human
        Development," F. Falkner, ed., W. B. Saunders Co., Phila-
        delphia.
Acheson, R. M., Fowler, G., Fry, E. I., Janes, M., Koski, K.,
        Urbano, P., and Van der Werff Ten Bosch, J. J., 1963,
        Studies in the reliability of assessing skeletal maturity
        from X-rays. Greulich-Pyle Atlas, Part I, Hum. Biol.,
        35:317.
Åkerlund, Å., 1918, Entwicklungsreihen in Röntgenbildern von Hand,
        Fuss und Ellenbogen in Mädchenund Knabenalter, Fortschr.
        auf dem Gebiete der Roentgenstrahlen, 33:1.
Anderson, M., Green, W. T., and Messner, M. B., 1963, Growth and
        predictions of growth in the lower extremities, J. Bone
        Joint Surg., 45A:1.
Baer, M. J., and Durkatz, J., 1957, Bilateral asymmetry in skele-
        tal maturation of hand and wrist: roentgenographic
        analysis, Am. J. Phys. Anthropol., 15:181.
Bailey, J. A., 1971, Forms of dwarfism recognizable at birth,
        Clin. Orthop., 76:150.
Baldwin, B. T., Busby, L. M., and Garside, H. V., 1928, "Anatomic
        Growth of Children. A Study of Some Bones of the Hand,
        Wrist and Lower Forearm by Means of Roentgenograms,"
        University of Iowa Studies in Child Welfare, No. 40.
Bayer, L. M., and Newell, R. R., 1940, The assessment of skeletal
        development of the hand and knee between the ages of 8 and
        14 years, Endocrinology, 26:779.
Birnbaum, A., 1968, Some latent trait models and their use in infer-
        ring an examinee's ability, in: "Statistical Theories of
        Mental Test Scores," F. M. Lord and M. R. Novick, eds.,
        Addison-Wesley, Reading, Mass.
Carter, T. M., 1923, "A study of radiographs of the bones of the
        wrist as a means of determining anatomical age," unpublished
        doctoral dissertation, Dept. Educ., University of Chicago.

Carter, T. M., 1926, Technique and devices used in radiographic study of the wrist bones of children, J. Educ. Psychol., 17:237.

Christ, H. H., 1961, A discussion of causes of error in the determination of chronological age in children by means of x-ray studies of carpal-bone development, South Afr. Med. J., 35:854.

Clarke, H. H., and Hayman, N. R., 1962, Reduction of bone assessments necessary for the skeletal age determination of boys, Res. Quar., 33:202.

Crampton, C. W., 1908, Physiological age--a fundamental principle, Am. Phys. Educ. Rev., 13, reprinted in Child Dev., 1944, 15:3.

Dreizen, S., Snodgrasse, R. M., Webb-Peploe, H., Parker, G. S., and Spies, T. D., 1957, Bilateral symmetry of skeletal maturation in human hand and wrist, Am. J. Dis. Child., 93:122.

Elgenmark, O., 1946, The normal development of the ossific centres during infancy and childhood. A clinical roentgenologic and statistical study, Acta Paed., 33: Suppl. 1.

Flecker, H., 1932, Roentgenographic observations of the times of appearance of epiphyses and their fusion with the diaphyses, J. Anat., 67:118.

Flory, C. D., 1936, Osseous development in the hand as an index of skeletal development, Monogr. Soc. Res. Child Dev., 1(3):1.

Freeman, F. N., and Carter, T. M., 1924, A new measure of the development of the carpal bones and its relation to physical and mental development, J. Educ. Psychol., 15:257.

Garn, S. M., and Rohmann, C. G., 1959, Communalities of the ossification centers of the hand and wrist, Am. J. Phys. Anthropol., 17:319.

Garn, S. M., and Rohmann, C. G., 1960, Variability in the order of ossification of the bony centers of the hand and wrist, Am. J. Phys. Anthropol., 18:219.

Garn, S. M., Rohmann, C. G., and Robinow, M., 1961, Increments in hand-wrist ossification, Am. J. Phys. Anthropol., 19:45.

Garn, S. M., Silverman, F. N., and Rohmann, C. G., 1964, A rational approach to the assessment of skeletal maturation, Ann. Radiol., 7:297.

Garn, S. M., Rohmann, C. G., and Blumenthal, T., 1966, Ossification sequence polymorphism and sexual dimorphism in skeletal development, Am. J. Phys. Anthropol., 24:101.

Garn, S. M., Rohmann, C. G., and Silverman, F. N., 1967, Radiographic standards for postnatal ossification and tooth calcification, Med. Radiogr. Photogr., 43:45.

Garn, S. M., Rohmann, C. G., Blumenthal, T., and Silverman, F. N., 1967a, Ossification communalities of the hand and other body parts: Their implication to skeletal assessment, Am. J. Phys. Anthropol., 27:75.

Garn, S. M., Poznanski, A. K., and Larson, K. E., 1975, Magnitude
    of sex differences in dichotomous ossification sequences of
    the hand and wrist, Am. J. Phys. Anthropol., 42:85.
Gates, A. I., 1924, The nature and educational significance of
    physical status and of mental, physiological, social and
    emotional maturity, J. Educ. Psychol., 15:329.
Greulich, W., and Pyle, S. I., 1950, "Radiographic Atlas of Skele-
    tal Development of the Hand and Wrist," Stanford University
    Press, Stanford, Calif.
Greulich, W., and Pyle, S. I., 1959, "Radiographic Atlas of Skele-
    tal Development of the Hand and Wrist," 2nd. ed., Stanford
    University Press, Stanford, Calif.
Hadley, L. A., 1956, "The Spine. Anatomico-Radiographic Studies:
    Development and the Cervical Region," Charles C Thomas,
    Springfield, Ill.
Harding, V. S. V., 1952, A method of evaluating osseous development
    from birth to 14 years, Child Dev., 23:247.
Helm, S., Siersbaek-Nielsen, S., Skieller, V., and Björk, A., 1971,
    Skeletal maturation of the hand in relation to maximum
    puberal growth in body weight, Tandlaegebladet, 75:1223.
Hewitt, D., 1963, Pattern of correlations in the skeleton of the
    growing hand, Ann. Hum. Genet., 27:157.
Hewitt, D., and Acheson, R. M., 1961, Some aspects of skeletal de-
    velopment through adolescence. I. Variations in the rate
    and pattern of skeletal maturation at puberty, Am. J. Phys.
    Anthropol., 19:321.
Hoerr, N. L., Pyle, S. I., and Francis, C. C., 1962, "Radiographic
    Atlas of Skeletal Development of the Foot and Ankle. A
    Standard of Reference," Charles C Thomas, Springfield, Ill.
Invergall, B., and Thilander, B., 1972, The human spheno-occipital
    synchondrosis. I. The time of closure appraised macro-
    scopically, Acta Odontol. Scand., 30:349.
Irwin, G. L., 1960, Roentgen determination of the time of closure
    of the spheno-occipital synchondrosis, Radiology, 75:450.
Johnson, G. F., Dorst, J. P., Kuhn, J. P., Roche, A. F., and Davila,
    G. H., 1973, Reliability of skeletal age assessments,
    Am. J. Roentgenol., 118:320.
Johnston, F. E., and Jahina, S. B., 1965, The contribution of the
    carpal bones to the assessment of skeletal age, Am. J.
    Phys. Anthropol., 23:349.
Kelly, H. J., and Reynolds, L., 1947, Appearance and growth of
    ossification centers and increases in the body dimensions
    of White and Negro infants, Am. J. Roentgenol., 57:477.
Kier, E. L., 1968, The infantile sella turcica; new roentgenologic
    and anatomic concepts based on a developmental study of the
    sphenoid bone, Am. J. Roentgenol., 102:747.
Konie, J. C., 1964, Comparative value of x-rays of the spheno-
    occipital synchondrosis and of the wrist for skeletal age
    assessment, Angle Orthod., 34:303.

Kuhns, L. R., Sherman, M. P., Poznanski, A. K., and Holt, J. F., 1973, Humeral-head and coracoid ossification in the newborn, Radiology, 107:145.

Lamparski, D. G., 1972, "Skeletal Age Assessment Utilizing Cervical Vertebrae," Master's thesis, Department of Dental Science, University of Pittsburgh.

Lamparski, D. G., 1975, Skeletal age assessment utilizing cervical vertebrae, Am. J. Orthod., 67:458.

Latham, R. A., 1972, The sella point and postnatal growth of the human cranial base, Am. J. Orthod., 61:156.

Lewis, A. B., and Roche, A. F., 1977, The saddle angle: constancy or change?, Angle Orthod., 47:46.

Long, E., and Caldwell, E. W., 1911, Some investigations concerning the relation between carpal ossification and physical and mental development, Am. J. Dis. Child., 1:113.

Low, W. D., Fung, S. H., and Cerny, E. E., 1975, "Biological Age of Southern Chinese Boys," paper presented at Tenth International Congress of Anatomists, Tokyo, Japan.

Marti-Henneberg, C., Patois, E., Niiranen, A., Roy, M. P., and Masse, N. P., Bone maturation velocity, Compte-Rendu de la XIIe Réunion des Equipes Chargées des Etudes sur la Croissance et le Développement de l'Enfant Normal, Centre International de l'Enfance, Paris.

Medicus, H., Grøn, A.-M., and Moorrees, C. F. A., 1971, Reproducibility of rating stages of osseous development (Tanner-Whitehouse system), Am. J. Phys. Anthropol., 35:359.

Melsen, B., 1972, Time and mode of closure of the spheno-occipital synchondrosis determined on human autopsy material, Acta Anat., 83:112.

Moss, M. L., and Greenberg, S. N., 1955, Postnatal growth of the human skull base, Angle Orthod., 25:77.

Moss, M. L., and Noback, C. R., 1958, A longitudinal study of digital epiphyseal fusion in adolescence, Anat. Rec., 131:19.

Ortiz, M. H., and Brodie, A. G., 1949, On the growth of the human head from birth to the third month of life, Anat. Rec., 103:311.

Prescott, D. A., 1923, The determination of anatomical age in school children and its relation to mental development, in: "Studies in Educational Psychology and Educational Measurement," W. F. Dearborn, ed., Harvard Monographs in Education, Series 1, No. 5, Graduate School of Education, Harvard University, Cambridge.

Pryor, J. W., 1907, The hereditary nature of variation in the ossification of bones, Anat. Rec., 1:84.

Pyle, S. I., and Hoerr, N. L., 1955, "Radiographic Atlas of Skeletal Development of the Knee. A Standard of Reference," Charles C Thomas, Springfield, Ill.

Pyle, S. I., and Hoerr, N. L., 1969, "A Radiographic Standard of Reference for the Growing Knee," Charles C Thomas, Springfield, Ill.

Pyle, S. I., and Sontag, L. W., 1943, Variability in onset of ossi-
    fication in epiphyses and short bones of the extremities,
    Am. J. Roentgenol. Rad. Ther., 49:795.
Pyle, S. I., Stuart, H. C., Cornoni, J., and Reed, R. B., 1961,
    Onsets, completions, and spans of the osseous stage of de-
    velopment in representative bone growth centers of the
    extremities, Monogr. Soc. Res. Child Dev., 26(1):1.
Pyle, S. I., Waterhouse, A. M., and Greulich, W. W., 1971, "A
    Radiographic Standard of Reference for the Growing Hand
    and Wrist; Prepared for the United States National Health
    Examination Survey," Case Western Reserve University Press,
    Cleveland.
Reynolds, E. L., and Asakawa, T., 1951, Skeletal development in
    infancy; standards for clinical use, Am. J. Roentgenol.,
    65:403.
Roche, A. F., 1963, Lateral comparisons of the skeletal maturity
    of the human hand and wrist, Am. J. Roentgenol., 89:1272.
Roche, A. F., 1970, Associations between the rates of maturation
    of the bones of the hand-wrist, Am. J. Phys. Anthropol.,
    33:341.
Roche, A. F., and French, N. Y., 1970, Differences in skeletal
    maturity levels between the knee and hand, Am. J. Roent-
    genol., 109:307.
Roche, A. F., Rohmann, C. G., French, N. Y., and Davila, G. H.,
    1970, Effect of training on replicability of assessments of
    skeletal maturity, Am. J. Roentgenol., 108:511.
Roche, A. F., Roberts, J., and Hamill, P. V. V., 1974, "Skeletal
    Maturity of Children 6-11 Years, United States," Vital and
    Health Statistics, Series 11, No. 140, DHEW Pub. No. (HRA)
    75-1622, U.S. Government Printing Office, Washington, D.C.
Roche, A. F., Wainer, H., and Thissen, D., 1975a, "Predicting Adult
    Stature for Individuals," Monogr. Pediatr. 3, Karger, Basel.
Roche, A. F., Wainer, H., and Thissen, D., 1975b, "Skeletal
    Maturity. The Knee Joint as a Biological Indicator,"
    Plenum Publishing Corp., New York.
Roche, A. F., Roberts, J., and Hamill, P. V. V., 1976, "Skeletal
    Maturity of Youths 12-17 Years, United States," Vital and
    Health Statistics, Series 11, No. 160, DHEW Pub. No. (HRA)
    77-1642, U.S. Government Printing Office, Washington, D.C.
Rotch, T. M., 1908, Chronologic and anatomic age in early life,
    JAMA, 51:1197.
Rotch, T. M., 1909, The development of the bones in childhood
    studied by the roentgen method with the view of establish-
    ing a developmental index for the grading of and the pro-
    tection of early life, Trans. Am. Assoc. Physicians, 24:
    603.
Samejima, F., 1969, Estimation of latent ability using a response
    pattern of graded scores, Psychometrika, 34:Monogr. Suppl.

Samejima, F., 1972, General model for free response data, Psychometrika, 37:Monogr. Suppl. 18.

Sauvegrain, J., Nahum, H., and Bronstein, H., 1962, Etude de la maturation osseuse du coude, Ann. Radiol., 5:542.

Scheller, S., 1960, Roentgenographic studies on epiphysial growth and ossification in the knee, Acta Radiol.Suppl., 195.

Schopfner, C. E., Wolfe, T. W., and O'Kell, R. T., 1968, The intersphenoid synchondrosis, Am. J. Roentgenol., 104:183.

Sempé, M., 1972, Accroissements et maturation squelettiques: Analyse numérique de la maturation osseuse du poignet et de la main. Paper presented at meeting of Co-ordinated Growth Teams, Institute of Child Health, London, February 7-11, 1972.

Shapiro, R., and Janzen, A. H., 1960, "The Normal Skull: A Roentgen Study," Hoeber, New York.

Sproul, A., and Peritz, E., 1971, Assessment of skeletal age in short and tall children, Am. J. Phys. Anthropol., 35:433.

Tanner, J. M., 1958, Growth and the prediction of abnormality, Dent. Pract., 8:220.

Tanner, J. M., 1962, "Growth at Adolescence," 2nd ed., Blackwell, Oxford.

Tanner, J. M., Whitehouse, R. H., and Healy, M. J. R., 1962, "A New System for Estimating Skeletal Maturity from the Hand and Wrist, with Standards Derived from a Study of 2,600 Healthy British Children," International Children's Centre, Paris.

Tanner, J. M., Whitehouse, R. H., Marshall, W. A., Healy, M. J. R., and Goldstein, H., 1975, "Assessment of Skeletal Maturity and Prediction of Adult Height: TW2 Method," Academic Press, New York.

Taranger, J., Karlberg, P., Lichtenstein, H., and Bruning, B., 1970, Some aspects on methods for evaluation of skeletal maturation, Compte-Rendu de la Xe Réunion des Equipes Chargées des Etudes sur la Croissance et le Développement de l'Enfant Normal, Centre International de l'Enfance, Davos.

Taranger, J., Karlberg, P., Lichtenstein, H., and Bruning, B., 1972, Estimation of skeletal maturity, Compte-Rendu de la XIe Réunion des Equipes Chargées des Etudes sur la Croissance et le Développement de l'Enfant Normal, Centre International de l'Enfance, Londres.

Taranger, J., Lichtenstein, H., and Svennberg-Redegren, I., 1976, Somatic pubertal development, in: "The Somatic Development of Children in a Swedish Urban Community. A Prospective Longitudinal Study," Gotab, Kungälv, Sweden.

Thompson, G. W., Popovich, F., and Luks, E., 1973, Sexual dimorphism in hand and wrist ossification, Growth, 37:1.

Todd, T. W., 1937, "Atlas of Skeletal Maturation," C. V. Mosby, St. Louis.

Torgersen, J., 1951, Asymmetry and skeletal maturation, Acta Radiol., 36:521.

Wallis, R. S., 1931, "How Children Grow: An Anthropometric Study
        of Private School Children from Two to Eight Years of Age,"
        University of Iowa Studies in Child Welfare, No. 208.
Wetherington, R. K., 1961, An alternate method of assessing skele-
        tal maturity from the hand and wrist, Papers of the Michi-
        gan Acad. Sci., Arts & Letters, 19:419.
Yarbrough, C., Habicht, J.-P., Klein, R. E., and Roche, A. F.,
        1973, Determining the biological age of the preschool
        child from a hand-wrist radiograph, Invest. Radiol., 8:233.

5.   DENTAL DEVELOPMENT: A MEASURE OF PHYSICAL MATURITY

Arto Demirjian

Université de Montréal
Montréal, Québec, Canada

Dental development is a measure of physical maturity, which can be used from birth to adolescence, in parallel with skeletal maturity (bone age) and pubertal maturity, as indicated by the secondary sex characteristics and menarche.

Dental maturation can be studied in both dentitions: deciduous and permanent.   Two different approaches can be used: clinical (emergence) and radiographic (calcification).   Furthermore, the resorption of the deciduous teeth can be assessed.   Even though this latter approach has not yet been fully investigated, it can add some valuable information to the study of dental maturity.

Dental emergence, which has wrongly been called "eruption", has been extensively investigated in the literature.   The word eruption denotes the <u>continuous</u> elevation of the tooth bud from inside the maxillary bones, towards the alveolar ridge, and up to the occlusal plane;   while the word "emergence" should be reserved for a fleeting and <u>temporary</u> event of a very short duration which is the piercing of the gum and the first appearance of the tooth in the oral cavity.   This continuous maturational process of the tooth--in other words, the elevation of the tooth toward the occlusal plane, its development, or calcification--can only be studied by radiography.

Dental emergence (both deciduous and permanent) has been thoroughly investigated as to its relations to racial origin, sex, socioeconomic status, nutrition, etc.   While the emergence of the deciduous dentition is delayed in Asiatic and African children compared with Americans and Europeans (McGregor et al., 1968;

83

Mukherjee, 1973; Billewicz et al., 1973; Bambach et al., 1973),
the opposite is true for the permanent dentition where Asiatics
and Africans are ahead of Americans and Europeans (Voors and
Metselaar, 1958; Lee et al., 1965; Brook and Barker, 1972; Garn et
al., 1973). Lavelle (1976) found a high degree of variation in
dental emergence, between samples derived from four regions in
England, and claims that "further evidence is required before the
physiological value of the timing of tooth emergence into the oral
cavity can be ascertained." Socioeconomic status and nutrition do
not seem to affect dental emergence to the same degree as skeletal
maturity (Bambach et al., 1973; Infante and Owen, 1973; Trupkin,
1974; Delgado et al., 1975; Garn et al., 1973; Mukherjee, 1973;
Billewicz and McGregor, 1975).

While sexual differences in the emergence of the permanent
dentition are well established, girls being 1 to 6 months ahead of
boys (Hurme, 1949; Garn et al., 1959; Fanning, 1961; Robinow, 1973;
Helm and Seidler, 1974), the question is still controversial for the
deciduous dentition. Some authors report no difference between
boys and girls (Falkner, 1957; Roche et al., 1964; Billewicz et al.,
1973; El Lozy et al., 1975), others found an earlier emergence
pattern in boys (Meredith, 1946; MacKay and Martin, 1952; Ferguson
et al., 1957), while still others (Bambach et al., 1973) reported a
delayed emergence among boys.

Before the use of X-rays in dentistry, clinical emergence was
the only criterion of dental maturity. In England (Saunders, 1837),
the emergence of the second molar was accepted as a proof of age in
the "Factory Act". Later, dental emergence was again used as a
measure of maturity for school entrance purposes (Beik, 1913; Bean,
1914; Cattell, 1928). This latter author was the first to assess
dental maturity by the number of emerged teeth in the mouth. Since
then, due to the relative facility and clinical practicability of
this approach, it has been and is still used by several investigators as a dental maturity measure (Voors and Metselaar, 1958;
McGregor et al., 1968; Filipsson, 1975; Brown, 1978; Moorrees and
Kent, 1978). Attempts have even been made to predict adult height
by the number of emerged teeth (Malcolm and Bue, 1970; Filipsson
and Hall, 1975).

As for the ossification centers, counting the number of emerged
teeth disregards useful information about the rate of change with
age, while the radiographic assessment of the dentition adds valuable information on maturity indicators either before or after
emergence. Furthermore, as previously stated, individual variations
in emergence introduce a high probability of inaccuracy to its use
as an indicator of dental age for the individual child.

Dental age has also been determined by the use of developmental
stages assessed from dental radiographs. Gleiser and Hunt (1955)

were the first to point out that dental calcification is a better
criterion of maturation than emergence. Since then, several
authors have investigated this approach and its advantages over
the use of dental emergence, and made it a refined tool for the
study of dental maturity. What are these advantages? As mentioned
previously, the calcification of a tooth can be followed longitudinally from radiographs through continuous sequences of developmental stages as opposed to emergence which is a fleeting event of
short duration (the tooth can be "absent" at time of examination
but present a week later). Furthermore, X-rays constitute permanent records for further investigations in the clinical assessment of the child.

    While the emergence of a tooth is subject to several exogen-
ous factors such as crowding, infection, premature extraction of
the deciduous predecessor, the maturational process of the dental
bud is not altered by any of these factors (Fanning, 1961; Brook
and Barker, 1973; Johnsen, 1977).

    The use of emergence as a maturity measure is limited to
certain ages. For example, the emerging period of the deciduous
teeth is approximately from the 6th to the 30th month; while the
permanent dentition emerges between the 6th and 12th years of age.
For boys, the mean age of emergence for the first group of teeth
(I_1, I_2, M_1) is between 6 and 7 years and for the second group

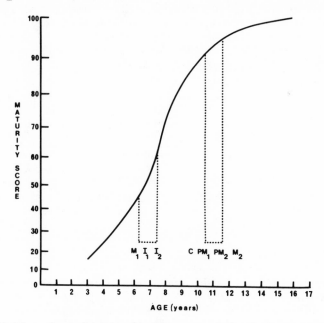

Fig. 1.   Median dental maturity curve and period of emergence of
          7 permanent teeth in boys.

(C, Pm_1, Pm_2, M_2) between 10.5 and 11.5 years (Figure 1). Emergence activity outside these age intervals is limited to advanced or retarded cases.

Figure 1 compares clearly the periods of life when dental development and dental emergence can be used as a maturity measure. With a slight advancement, the situation is similar for girls. Here, the emergence of the third molar is not taken into consideration because of the inconsistency of its emergence between the 16th and the 20th year. Sometimes it does not emerge at all due to its impaction in the mandibular bone. The advantage of the use of radiographs for the study of dental maturity is obvious: these give a complete picture of the developmental life span of the dentition (both deciduous and permanent) from the third month of intrauterine life when the calcification of the deciduous teeth starts, until the end of adolescence when third molar development is complete. Furthermore, radiographic assessment of the root resorption of the deciduous teeth can shed more light on our understanding of dental maturity.

Finally, another argument favoring the use of dental calcification as a measure of maturity is that it offers the possibility of an overall picture of the dentition as a system (as the skeletal system) rather than dealing with individual teeth. This latter point is mostly useful in human biology. For all these reasons, dental formation or calcification should be considered a more convenient and efficient measure of physical maturity than dental emergence.

Each tooth undergoes the same sequence of developmental stages during maturation as do the bones of the hand-wrist area. The first stage starts with the calcification of the cusp tip while the final stage is the closure of the apical end, which is the end of dental maturation. During this maturational process there is a continuous change in the size as well as the shape of the maturing tooth. In order to study the entire process, different stages should be selected arbitrarily and described in detail. The description of the stages should take into account (a) major developmental milestones of the tooth, (b) biological changes in the dental structure, (c) objectivity and reproducibility of the assessment.

Mandible vs maxilla. It is well known that there are differences in the chronology of the development of some mandibular and maxillary teeth, but as there is no clear overall tendency of advancement or retardation for either the mandibular or the maxillary teeth, the mandibular dentition has been generally chosen as being representative of the development of the whole dental system (Gleiser and Hunt, 1955; Demisch and Wartmann, 1956; Fanning, 1961;

Moorrees et al., 1963; Demirjian et al., 1973). This is similar to the choice of the hand-wrist region as representative of the skeletal system. Furthermore, the picture of the mandibular teeth is clearer and not hidden by bony structures, as is the case for the maxillary teeth.

A high degree of correlation has been found in the development of the right and left mandibular teeth (Knott and Meredith, 1966; Demirjian et al., 1973), so, for purposes of simplicity and practicality, the left mandibular teeth have been chosen as the basis for the assessment of dental development. A complete review of the techniques, sample sizes and approaches used in the previously mentioned studies is given by Demirjian (1978). All methods use the length of the tooth, either the crown or the root, as a criterion of maturity. In dental maturity, as in skeletal maturity, the relationship between measurements (crown/root) is more important than size alone. It might be quite difficult to distinguish between 1/4 and 1/3 or 2/3 of the root length, especially in a cross-sectional sample. Moreover, absolute lengths of teeth vary greatly from individual to individual.

There are two approaches to the assessment of skeletal maturation by means of X-rays: the atlas method and the scoring method. The atlas method is based upon the description of maturity indicators at different stages during the process of maturation. In the age range studied a typical "profile" is chosen at each series of ages. There is, as yet, no atlas designed for dental maturity assessment comparable to the widely used Greulich and Pyle (1959) atlas for the hand-wrist area. The results of the atlas method are less accurate for area assessment than for bone-specific assessment.

Another bone specific maturity assessment approach is the scoring method introduced by Acheson (1954) and improved by Tanner et al. (1972, 1975) which gives a score to each bone according to its stage of development. Scores corresponding to stages were selected to minimize the disparity among the bone-specific scores for the individual. Each stage is given a numerical score, from 0 for the absence of any calcified bone or immaturity, to 100 for the final stage of total maturity. The scoring technique for skeletal age assessment of Tanner et al. (1975) has been applied to the evaluation of dental maturity by Demirjian et al. (1973). In this system, seven mandibular teeth of the left side have been utilized; later, a simplified system based on four teeth (M_2, M_1, Pm_2, Pm_1) or (M_2, Pm_2, Pm_1, I_1) was described by Demirjian and Goldstein (1976). The purpose of these simplified systems is to reduce the time required for the assessment, to enable human biologists to use the existing oblique head plates, and, in cases where M_1 is extracted, to assess the dental maturity of the child from the remaining teeth. In all three systems equal "biological" weights have been given to each tooth. The correlation coefficient between the three systems is 0.7 to 0.9 for each age group between 6 and 16 years. This could be anticipated since most of the same teeth are involved in the three scoring systems. A detailed description of the mathematical approach for these scoring systems is given by Healy and Goldstein (1976).

In the first description of the scoring system for practical purposes, the use of panoramic X-rays was advised but the periapical films (regular dental film) can also be used for rating purposes; 3-4 films of the hemimandible suffice. The X-ray machines used for periapical films are simpler and more practical for studies in the field, and no detail is lost even if the image is distorted because the shape of the tooth is assessed and not the absolute length. An example of periapical films is shown in Figure 2.

Figure 3 illustrates the eight developmental stages of the seven mandibular teeth as seen on a periapical or panoramic radiograph. The self-weighted scores for seven mandibular teeth corresponding to these stages (Table 1) are given along the centile curves for boys (Figure 4) and girls (Figure 5). The centile curves enable one to assess the centile position of an individual's

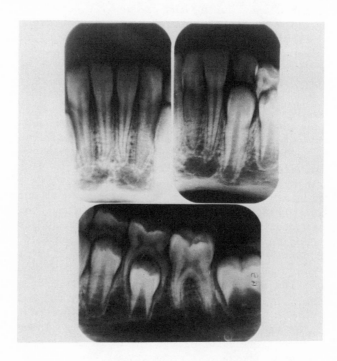

Fig. 2.   Periapical films of the 7 left mandibular teeth.

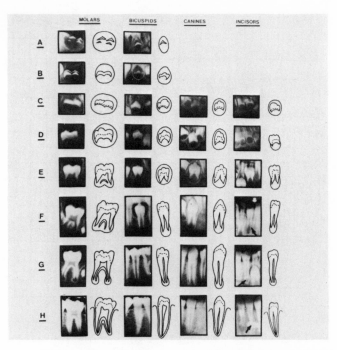

Fig. 3.   Developmental stages of the permanent dentition.

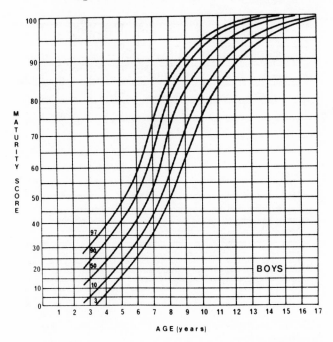

Fig. 4.   Dental maturity percentiles of scores for boys from 3 to
          17 years of age (based on seven left mandibular teeth).

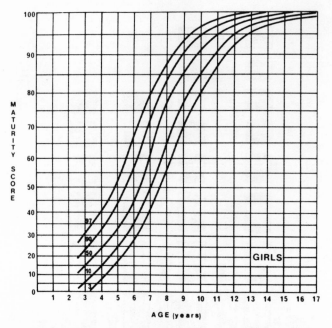

Fig. 5.   Dental maturity percentiles of scores for girls from 3 to
          17 years of age (based on seven left mandibular teeth).

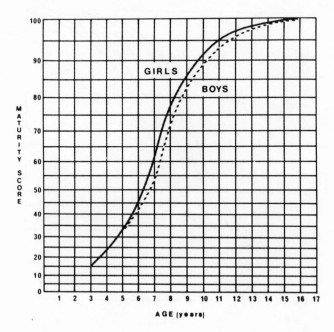

Fig. 6.   Comparative curves (median) of dental development scores
          for boys and girls.

Table 1. Self Weighted Scores for Dental Stages of the Seven Left
          Mandibular Teeth

Tooth	O	A	B	STAGE (BOYS) C	D	E	F	G	H
M$_2$	0.0	1.7	3.1	5.4	8.6	11.4	12.4	12.8	13.6
M$_1$				0.0	5.3	7.5	10.3	13.9	16.8
PM$_2$	0.0	1.5	2.7	5.2	8.0	10.8	12.0	12.5	13.2
PM$_1$			0.0	4.0	6.3	9.4	13.2	14.9	15.5	16.1
C				0.0	4.0	7.8	10.1	11.4	12.0
I$_2$				0.0	2.8	5.4	7.7	10.5	13.2
I$_1$				0.0	4.3	6.3	8.2	11.2	15.1

Tooth	O	A	B	STAGE (GIRLS) C	D	E	F	G	H
M$_2$	0.0	1.8	3.1	5.4	9.0	11.7	12.8	13.2	13.8
M$_1$				0.0	3.5	5.6	8.4	12.5	15.4
PM$_2$	0.0	1.7	2.9	5.4	8.6	11.1	12.3	12.8	13.3
PM$_1$			0.0	3.1	5.2	8.8	12.6	14.3	14.9	15.5
C				0.0	3.7	7.3	10.0	11.8	12.5
I$_2$				0.0	2.8	5.3	8.1	11.2	13.8
I$_1$				0.0	4.4	6.3	8.5	12.0	15.8

maturity score. If required, the maturity score can be converted
to "dental age", by finding the age at which the 50th centile value
equals the maturity score. However, since dental development is a
maturational process and the scores reflect this maturation, we
feel it more appropriate to use maturity scores than dental age
when comparing the development of individuals or tracing the progress of a particular child.

Sexual dimorphism in dental development. Figure 6 illustrates
the median dental maturity curves of boys and girls between the
ages of 3 and 17 years. It can be seen that the curves for boys
and girls coincide up to age 5, but from this age on, girls are
ahead of boys until about age 14, when the final plateau is reached.

The analysis of the developmental curves of individual teeth
shows a common pattern, that is to say similarity in timing between
sexes, for the early stages of development. From the earlier stages
(A, B, C and D) of development of most teeth, there is no difference

between boys and girls in the chronology of dental calcification.
In this respect, our results agree with those of Garn et al. (1958),
Fanning (1961) and Moorrees et al. (1963). The mean difference for
all teeth is 0.4 years, the largest difference being with the
canine, 0.9 years, girls being more precocious than boys in their
dental development. To illustrate the maturational process of an
individual tooth, the developmental curves of the second molar are
traced for each stage óf its development for both boys and girls
(Figure 7).

    These curves show no difference in the median ages between
boys and girls for the first stage "A", which represents the beginning of the calcification of the cusps. This corresponds to 3.4
years in chronological age, for both boys and girls. Up to age 5,
and stage "C", the sex difference in timing is no more than 0.1
years for the median age which is not considered significant; but
the difference is already clearly evident at age 6.0 years, when
more than 90% of both boys and girls have reached the latter stage.
At the same age, almost 50% of the girls and 30% of the boys have
reached the next stage, "D". At the median age of attainment of
stage "D", girls are already in advance over boys by 0.3 years,
that is, 6.2 years of age for girls and 6.5 years for boys. This
difference of 0.3 years remains almost unchanged until the last
stage, "H", of apical closure, except for stage "G", where girls
are 0.6 years ahead of boys. It is not before age 18 that 100% of

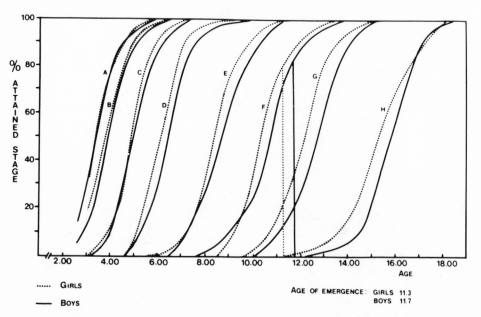

Fig. 7. The attained maturational stages at each age of the second
         molar for boys and girls.

girls have reached the last stage, while for boys of the same age
there is still a residual 2% who have not reached this stage.

On the same diagrams, the vertical lines drawn at age 11.6
years for boys and 11.3 years for girls represent the mean age of
emergence of the second mandibular molar of the same population.
At these ages, about 20% of boys and girls have already reached
stage "G", which is the completion of distal root elongation (apex
still open); 80% of the children of both sexes, at the same emergence ages, are still at the previous stage "F", which approximately
represents the completion of 3/4 of root length. For boys and girls,
the emergence of the mandibular second molar occurs between the
formation of 3/4 of the root, and its completion.

Similar to the second molar, we calculated for each individual
tooth the proportion of children who had attained each stage for
each six-month age group. The curves have been smoothed by hand.
They all show a common pattern for all teeth, namely a close similarity in the chronology of dental development in boys and girls up
to and including stage "C". At this stage, the enamel formation
of the occlusal surface is completed and dentinal formation has
begun; approximately half the crown is formed. After stage "D",
girls are consistently ahead of boys for all stages of development;
for closure of the apex for the canine the difference is as much
as 1.4 years. Also we have calculated the median age of attainment of each stage for each tooth, as well as the average time required per stage for each tooth in both sexes (Demirjian and
Levesque, unpublished data).

The Prediction of Emergence Based on Developmental Stages

All the individual curves of the mandibular teeth, besides
their similarity in the developmental pattern, have another common
point. Without distinction, clinical emergence of all teeth occurs
when 70 to 90% of the population has reached stage "F" of formation,
which is approximately 3/4 of the root formation. This is in
accordance with Grøn's (1962) findings. The remaining 10 to 30%
have already reached the next stage "G" of root completion. In a
delayed case of emergence, for example in the case of the second
molar, if the X-ray picture shows a developmental stage "E", on
the average, the tooth will emerge about 1.8 years later. But if
the root development has already reached stage "F", emergence is
imminent. Figure 8 illustrates the curves of developmental stage
"F" for all mandibular teeth as well as the chronology of their
emergence.

Correlations between Teeth

Kendall's rank correlation coefficient was calculated

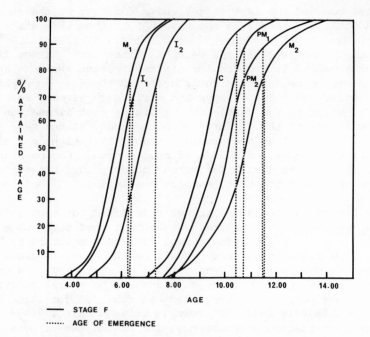

Fig. 8. The attained maturational stage (%) of stage F for each
        mandibular tooth and their emergence at selected ages.

separately for boys and girls (Table 2), and for each pair of
teeth, at all ages in the sample: The effect of age was then par-
tialled out to give the corrected rank correlation coefficient.

    The correlations are substantially similar for boys and girls.
Within each sex, higher correlations are obtained for the first
molar with the lateral incisor; between the two incisors; between
the two pre-molars and between the canine and the first pre-molar.
It is noticeable that they all involve teeth passing through similar stages at similar times, while inversely, the lowest correlations are recorded between teeth with markedly different patterns
of development. These differences between different groups of
teeth could be used to choose the best replacement when a tooth is
missing and must be replaced by another to estimate dental maturity.

The Reliability of Assessments from Dental X-rays

    Several approaches have been used to assess dental development
from X-rays (Gleiser and Hunt, 1955; Garn et al., 1958; Nolla, 1960;
Fanning, 1961; Moorrees et al., 1963; Nanda and Chawla, 1966;

Table 2. Kendall's Partial Correlation Coefficients (age constant)
for all Pairs of Teeth for Girls and Boys (in parentheses)

GIRLS (BOYS)	M_2	M_1	PM_2	PM_1	C	I_2	I_1
M_2	1(1)						
M_1	.42(.43)	1(1)					
PM_2	.56(.58)	.41(.41)	1(1)				
PM_1	.53(.52)	.48(.45)	.61(.64)	1(1)			
C	.50(.47)	.50(.43)	.50(.52)	.63(.62)	1(1)		
I_2	.40(.40)	.80(.76)	.39(.40)	.45(.45)	.51(.45)	1(1)	
I_1	.34(.34)	.65(.63)	.34(.36)	.40(.38)	.43(.37)	.74(.70)	1(1)

Demirjian et al., 1973). These systems divide the developmental
period of the teeth into arbitrarily selected stages. Although
very diversified, they present a common difficulty: the reproducibility of the ratings, either intra- or inter-examiner. This leads
to the question of the reliability of the assessment of dental
development from radiographs.

To date, a specific study has not been done to evaluate the
reliability of the ratings from X-rays. However, some investigators (Demisch and Wartmann, 1956; Hotz, 1959; Fanning, 1961; Grøn,
1962; Sapoka and Demirjian, 1971) have reported intra- and inter-
examiner reliability. In these studies, the percentage of the
discrepancies is given along with the maximum difference in the
assigned stages. Because the discrepancies are higher in inter-
than intra-examiner evaluations, we investigated reliability in
both situations (Levesque and Demirjian, unpublished data). Two
samples were studied: a cross-sectional and a longitudinal, and
four different age groups: 6, 8, 10 and 12 years. These age
groups cover the most active period of dental development. Six
examiners independently evaluated 191 radiographs, according to the
system devised by Demirjian et al. (1973). Two examiners had already mastered the technique, whereas the remaining four were
trained by rating about 100 radiographs, cross-sectionally and
longitudinally. Five examiners rated the X-rays cross-sectionally
and the sixth rated them longitudinally. The longitudinal evaluation tended to underestimate the attained stage. The percentage
of discrepancies between two cross-sectional evaluations was between
15 and 25%. The difficulty lay mostly in the rating of the 6-year-
old group where the examiners had insufficient training to distinguish the change from stage C to D. On the other hand, the description of stage "E" was not precise and complete enough for the

uniradicular teeth. This stage has been redefined as follows:
stage "E" b) "The root length reaches at least 1/3 of the crown
height." Nearly all the discrepancies encountered were of one
stage; these occurred at all ages and with all examiners. Our
results emphasize the necessity of verifying the evaluations of two
or more examiners involved in a study; also they show the need for
such cross-checking when comparing populations evaluated by different persons using the same system. One suggested procedure is to
circulate a standardized series of reference radiographs among
researchers studying population groups.

Correlation between Different Maturity Measures

     For a long time, it has been believed that a correlation
exists between dental maturity and other maturational parameters,
such as skeletal maturity, menarche, etc. This is true when the
number of emerged teeth is compared with the skeletal maturity of
children of different age groups. Later, when a larger number of
children in each age group was investigated, and the assessment
techniques of either skeletal or dental maturity refined, the
existing correlation between the maturation of these two systems
(skeletal and dental) was found to be quite low (Hotz, 1959; Green,
1961; Lewis and Garn, 1960; Steel, 1965; Gyulavari, 1966; Lacey,
1973; Demirjian, 1978). Also this has been proven true with
children with different hormonal or other systemic diseases (Edler,
1977; Myllärniemi et al., 1978; Sears et al., 1979). The evidence
indicates that dental and skeletal maturation, with possible
differences in genetic control, are quite independent of each other.
The same environmental factors affect both processes but to
different degrees.

REFERENCES

Acheson, R. M., 1954, A method of assessing skeletal maturity from
        radiographs: a report from The Oxford Child Health Survey,
        J. Anat., 88:498.
Bambach, M., Saracci, R., and Young, H. B., 1973, Emergence of
        deciduous teeth in Tunisian children in relation to sex
        and social class, Hum. Biol., 45:435.
Bean, R. B., 1914, Eruption of teeth as physiological standard for
        testing development, Pedagog. Sem., 21:596.
Beik, A. K., 1913, Physiological age and school entrance, Pedagog.
        Sem., 20:283.
Billewicz, W. Z., Thomson, A. M., Baber, F. M., and Field, C. E.,
        1973, The development of primary teeth in Chinese (Hong
        Kong) children, Hum. Biol., 45:229.

Billewicz, W. Z., and McGregor, I. A., 1975, Eruption of permanent teeth in West African (Gambian) children in relation to age, sex and physique, Ann. Hum. Biol., 2:117.

Brook, A. H., and Barker, D. K., 1972, Eruption of teeth among the racial groups of Eastern New Guinea: A correlation of tooth eruption with calendar age, Arch. Oral Biol., 17:751.

Brook, A. H., and Barker, D. K., 1973, The use of deciduous tooth eruption for the estimation of unknown chronological age, J. Trop. Pediatr. Environ. Child Health, 19:234 (monogr. no. 28).

Brown, T., 1978, Tooth emergence in Australian Aboriginals, Ann. Hum. Biol., 5:41.

Cattell, P., 1928, "Dentition as a Measure of Maturity," Harvard Monographs in Education, No. 9, Harvard University Press, Cambridge.

Delgado, H., Habicht, J.-P., Yarbrough, C., Lechtig, A., Martorell, R., Malina, R. M., and Klein, R. E., 1975, Nutritional status and the timing of deciduous tooth eruption, Am. J. Clin. Nutr., 28:216.

Demirjian, A., Goldstein, H., and Tanner, J. M., 1973, A new system of dental age assessment, Hum. Biol., 45:211.

Demirjian, A., and Goldstein, H., 1976, New systems for dental maturity based on seven and four teeth, Ann. Hum. Biol., 3:411.

Demirjian, A., 1978, Dentition, in: "Human Growth," vol. 2, F. Falkner and J. M. Tanner, eds., Plenum Press, New York.

Demisch, A., and Wartmann, P., 1956, Calcification of the mandibular third molar and its relation to skeletal and chronological age in children, Child Dev., 27:459.

Edler, R. J., 1977, Dental and skeletal ages in hypopituitary patients, J. Dent. Res., 56:1145.

El Lozy, M., Reed, R. B., Kerr, G. R., Boutourline, E., Tesi, G., Ghamry, M. T., Stare, F. J., Kallal, Z., Turki, M., and Hemaidan, N., 1975, Nutritional correlates of child development in southern Tunisia. IV. The relation of deciduous dental eruption to somatic development, Growth, 39:209.

Falkner, F., 1957, Deciduous tooth eruption, Arch. Dis. Child., 32:386.

Fanning, E. A., 1961, A longitudinal study of tooth formation and root resorption, N. Z. Dent. J., 57:202.

Ferguson, A. D., Scott, R. B., and Bakwin, H., 1957, Growth and development of Negro infants, J. Pediatr., 50:327.

Filipsson, R., 1975, A new method for assessment of dental maturity using the individual curve of number of erupted permanent teeth, Ann. Hum. Biol., 2:13.

Filipsson, R., and Hall, K., 1975, Prediction of adult height of girls from height and dental maturity at ages 6-10 years, Ann. Hum. Biol., 2:355.

Garn, S. M., Lewis, A. B., Koski, P. K., and Polacheck, D. L.,
     1958, The sex difference in tooth calcification, J. Dent.
     Res., 37:561.
Garn, S. M., Lewis, A. B., and Polacheck, D. L., 1959, Variability
     of tooth formation, J. Dent. Res., 38:135.
Garn, S. M., Sandusky, S. T., Nagy, J. M., and Trowbridge, F. L.,
     1973, Negro-Caucasoid differences in permanent tooth
     emergence at a constant income level, Arch. Oral Biol.,
     18:609.
Gleiser, I., and Hunt, E. E., Jr., 1955, The permanent mandibular
     first molar: its calcification, eruption and decay, Am. J.
     Phys. Anthropol., 13:253.
Green, L. J., 1961, The interrelationships among height, weight, and
     chronological, dental and skeletal ages, Angle Orthod., 31:
     189.
Greulich, W. W., and Pyle, S. I., 1959, "Radiographic Atlas of
     Skeletal Development of the Hand and Wrist,", 2nd ed.,
     Stanford University Press, Stanford.
Grøn, A. M., 1962, Prediction of tooth emergence, J. Dent. Res.,
     41:573.
Gyulavari, O., 1966, Dental and skeletal development of children
     with low birth weight, Acta Paediatr. Acad. Sci. Hung., 7:
     301.
Healy, M. J. R., and Goldstein, H., 1976, An approach to the
     scaling of categorized attributes, Biometrika, 63:219.
Helm, S., and Seidler, B., 1974, Timing of permanent tooth emergence
     in Danish children, Community Dent. Oral Epidemiol., 2:212.
Hotz, R., 1959, The relation of dental calcification to chronologi-
     cal and skeletal age, Europ. Orthod. Soc., 1959:140.
Hurme, V. O., 1949, Ranges of normalcy in the eruption of permanent
     teeth, J. Dent. Child., 16:11.
Infante, P. F., and Owen, G. M., 1973, Relation of chronology of
     deciduous tooth emergence to height, weight, and head cir-
     cumference in children, Arch. Oral Biol., 18:1411.
Johnsen, D. C., 1977, Prevalence of delayed emergence of permanent
     teeth as a result of local factors, J.A.D.A., 94:100.
Knott, V. B., and Meredith, H. V., 1966, Statistics on eruption of
     the permanent dentition from serial data for North American
     white children, Angle Orthod., 36:68.
Lacey, K. A., 1973, Relationship between bone age and dental devel-
     opment, Lancet, 2:736.
Lavelle, C. L. B., 1976, The timing of tooth emergence in four pop-
     ulation samples, J. Dent., 4:231.
Lee, M. M. C., Chan, S. T., Low, W. D., and Chang, K. S. F., 1965,
     Eruption of the permanent dentition of southern Chinese
     children in Hong Kong, Arch. Oral Biol., 10:849.
Lewis, A. B., and Garn, S. M., 1960, The relationship between tooth
     formation and other maturational factors, Angle Orthod.,
     30:70.

MacKay, D. H., and Martin, W. J., 1952, Dentition and physique of
    Bantu children, J. Trop. Med. Hyg., 55:265.
Malcolm, L. A., and Bue, B., 1970, Eruption times of permanent
    teeth and the determination of age in New Guinean children,
    Trop. Geog. Med., 22:307.
McGregor, I. A., Thomson, A. M., and Billewicz, W. Z., 1968, The
    development of primary teeth in children from a group of
    Gambian villages, and critical examination of its use for
    estimating age, Br. J. Nutr., 22:307.
Meredith, H. V., 1946, Order and age of eruption for the deciduous
    dentition, J. Dent. Res., 25:43.
Moorrees, C. F. A., Fanning, E. A., and Hunt, E. E., Jr., 1963, Age
    variation of formation stages for ten permanent teeth, J.
    Dent. Res., 42:1490.
Moorrees, C. F. A., and Kent, R. L., Jr., 1978, A step function
    model using tooth counts to assess the developmental timing
    of the dentition, Ann. Hum. Biol., 5:55.
Mukherjee, D. K., 1973, Deciduous dental eruption in low income
    group Bengali Hindu children, J. Trop. Pediatr. Environ.
    Child Health, 19:207.
Myllärniemi, S., Lenko, H. L., and Perheentupa, J., 1978, Dental
    maturity in hypopituitarism, and dental response to substi-
    tution treatment, Scand. J. Dent. Res., 86:307.
Nanda, R. S., and Chawla, T. N., 1966, Growth and development of
    dentitions in Indian children. I. Development of permanent
    teeth, Am. J. Orthod., 52:837.
Nolla, C. M., 1960, The development of the permanent teeth. J. Dent.
    Child., 27:254.
Prahl-Andersen, B., and Van't Hof, M. A., 1979, Dental skeletal
    disharmony and malocclusion, J. Dent. Res., 58:366.
Robinow, M., 1973, The eruption of the deciduous teeth (factors
    involved in timing), J. Trop. Pediatr. Environ. Child Health,
    19:200 (monograph no. 28).
Roche, A. F., Barkla, D. H., and Maritz, J. S., 1964, Deciduous
    eruption in Melbourne children, Aust. Dent. J., 9:106.
Sapoka, A. A. M., and Demirjian, A., 1971, Dental development of
    the French-Canadian child, J. Can. Dent. Assoc., 37:100.
Saunders, E., 1837, "The Teeth a Test of Age, Considered with
    Reference to the Factory Children," H. Renshaw, London.
Sears, R., Nazif, M., Zullo, T., 1979, Effects of sickle cell
    disease on dental and skeletal maturation, J. Dent. Res.,
    58:270.
Steel, G. H., 1965, The relation between dental maturation and
    physiological maturity, Dent. Pract., 16:23.
Tanner, J. M., Whitehouse, R. H., Healy, M. J. R., and Goldstein,
    H., 1972, "Standards for Skeletal Age," Centre International
    de l'Enfance, Paris.

Tanner, J. M., Whitehouse, R. M., Marshall, W. A., Healy, M. J. R.,
    and Goldstein, H., 1975, "Assessment of Skeletal Maturity
    and Prediction of Adult Height: TW2 Method," Academic Press,
    London.
Trupkin, D. P., 1974, Eruption patterns of the first primary tooth
    in infants who were underweight at birth, J. Dent. Child.,
    41:279.
Voors, A. W., and Metselaar, 1958, The reliability of dental age as
    a yardstick to assess the unknown calendar age, Trop. Geogr.
    Med., 10:175.

6. GENERAL STATISTICAL CONSIDERATIONS IN ANALYSIS

Ettore Marubini

Instituto di Statistica Medica e Biometria
Università degli Studi di Milano
Via Venezian 1   20133   Milano, Italy

The feature of any standard of whatever sort is to enable the pediatrician to give at least a tentative answer to the question: "Is this child normal?" with respect to the aspect of growth being studied. This question is not quite as simple as may appear at first sight and one must begin by realizing that the term normal commonly entails two different meanings, namely:

i) "conforming to an ideal standard": in this sense the "norm" is considered a target value, quite possibly an unattainable one, and the opposite of normal is "subnormal";

ii) "usual" or "typical" of a standardizing population of healthy subjects: in this sense the "norm" is considered a set of values that occur very frequently and the opposite of normal is now "abnormal" (Healy, 1978).

In clinical practice normality refers to the second of the above definitions. The conventional solution to assess the meaning of a quantitative characteristic consists in laying down arbitrary "limits of normality". These are two figures interpreted as including the values of a given percentage (say 95%) of normal healthy individuals. These individuals should be ascertained through careful, large-scale surveys that allow the researchers to study in detail the percentage distribution of the characteristic being investigated. With an extra layer of convention, the "limits of normality" are computed by taking the sample average of the findings plus and minus twice the standard deviation (SD) without taking into account the shape of the distribution. Owing to the fact that the property of 95% of a distribution being contained within the arithmetic mean ±2SD applies only to a Normal (Gaussian) distribution, and that several distributions of clinical variables do not follow or even approximate Normality, rather often this calculation provides misleading limits.

As far as growth is concerned, pediatricians have, for some time, become accustomed to a more advanced approach. Rather than only determining whether an individual's value is or is not within the range of normality, the standards most widely used aim at allotting a centile score to the individual for a particular char-acteristic. This shows the user what proportion of the reference group has values smaller than the observed one. The usual method of constructing such standards is to estimate centiles at a number of ages, for instance at every year of age, and then to pass smooth curves through these points to cover the whole age range. Thus, from a statistical viewpoint, the basic problems are those of estimating the centiles of a population from a sample.

THE GAUSSIAN DISTRIBUTION

The Gaussian distribution is the most important continuous probability distribution not so much because it is suitable to fit a wide range of observed frequency distributions but because of the central place it occupies in sampling theory.

The probability density, $f(x)$, of a Gaussian random variable (x) is given by the expression:

$$f(x) = \frac{1}{\sigma\sqrt{2\pi}} \exp\left\{\frac{-(x-\mu)^2}{2\sigma^2}\right\} \left| -\infty < x < \infty \right| \tag{1}$$

where: e = base of natural logarithms
  π = mathematical constant = 3.14159 ...
  μ = mean of x
  σ = standard deviation of x

As is known, μ is estimated by the sample mean;

$$m = \sum_{i=1}^{n} x/n$$

and σ^2 is estimated by the sample variance (mean square)

$$s^2 = \left[\frac{\sum_{i=1}^{n} x/n(x_i-m)^2}{n-1}\right]$$

(the subscript i=1,2, ... n identifies the n units belonging to the sample).

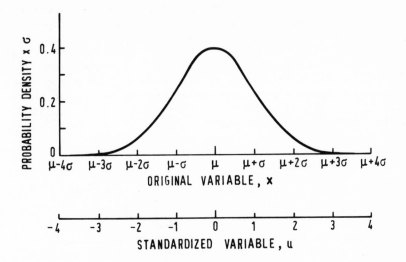

Fig. 1.   The probability density function of a Gaussian
distribution showing the scales of the original and the
standardized variable.

The curve (1) is shown in Figure 1.   On the horizontal axis
are marked the positions of the mean μ and the values of × which
differ from μ by ±σ, ±2σ and ±3σ.

The Gaussian distribution is unimodal, bell-shaped and
symmetrical about × = μ so that a given deviation below the mean
(center of symmetry) is as common as the corresponding deviation
above the mean.   Clearly, most of the values lie fairly close to
the center and a relatively small proportion of the area under the
curve lies outside the values × = μ + 2σ and × = μ - 2σ: approximately 5%.   Of course, it follows from (1) that the area under the
entire curve is unity but for the purposes of statistical inference, one can ascertain areas under any part of a Gaussian distribution.   To this end, fortunately, it is not necessary to integrate
the expression (1) but it is enough to resort to pertinent tables
and read from them the tail areas corresponding to any given
multiple of σ (or vice versa).   In fact, the tables are entered
by the standardized deviate:

$$u = \frac{× - μ}{σ} \tag{2}$$

The scale of the standardized variable is shown at the bottom
of Figure 1; the correspondence between the × (original variable)
- scale and the u-scale is easily understood.

Figure 2 shows the roles of the two constants (parameters) of the Gaussian distribution. In the upper part: changing μ alone shifts the entire curve along the abscissa. In the lower part: changing σ alone changes the spread of the distribution. Figure 3 shows the relationship among three Gaussian distributions with different standard deviations; by centering the origin of the variable at the common mean and by taking the scales of the abscissa proportional to the standard deviation, the areas under the three curves appear the same.

ESTIMATING GAUSSIAN CENTILES

Quantitative Variables

It is well known that several measurements, namely height, sitting height and limb lengths, closely follow a Gaussian distribution; others, such as skinfold thicknesses, many circumferential or girth measurements and many biochemical variables, are positively skewed.

Weight is peculiar: in fact, at birth the distribution can be fitted by the Gaussian density function (De Scrilli et al., 1978) while it appears positively skewed at all successive ages. Therefore, the shape of the distribution of the anthropometric variable should be studied preliminary to any processing of the data. This study has two goals: to test whether the Gaussian distribution really fits these sample data and to search for a suitable (usually logarithmic) transformation of the original measurement scale to Normalise the skewed distributions. To fulfill these aims, a four-stage plotting technique should play a major role. These stages are:

i)   draw two orthogonal axes and scale the abscissa according to the measurement units of the anthropometric variable studied (for example: cm for stature, Kg for weight) and the ordinate according to the standardized deviate scale (u-scale of Figure 1). The lowest point on the ordinate is -3 and the highest point is +3.

ii)   arrange the n sample values in ascending order and call the i-th value from the minimum $x^{(i)}$;

iii) for i = 1, 2, ... n, compute the proportion $p_i = (i-1/2)/n$ and read from a table of the Gaussian distribution the corresponding deviates $u^{(i)}$;

iv)   plot the $u^{(i)}$ against the corresponding $x^{(i)}$.

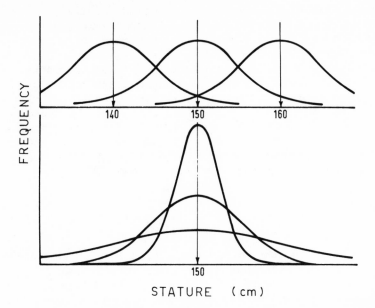

Fig. 2. The roles of the two constants of the Gaussian distribution. Upper part: the curves have different means but the same S.D. Lower part: the curves have the same means but different S.D.

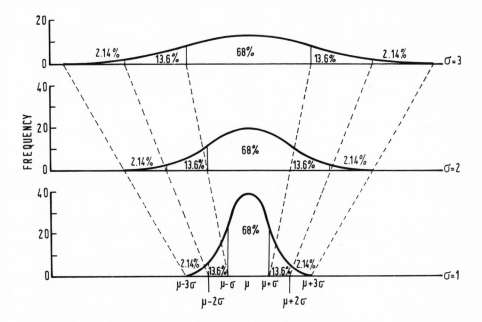

Fig. 3. Relationship among three Gaussians with different S.D.

If the sample is drawn from a Gaussian population the points lie fairly close to a straight line. If the distribution is positively skewed the points tend to lie on a curve that is concave downwards. In such a case, the original data should be replaced by their logarithms and plotted again: if the plot is still a curve, concave downwards (upwards), one can subtract from (add to) each original figure a constant, that can be found by trial and error, to make the scatter plot linear. For a detailed discussion on transformations and their uses, see Thöni (1973). If one is now confident the standardizing population reasonably approximates the Gaussian distribution, the centiles ($\hat{Y}_{100p}$) can be estimated using the sample mean and standard deviations, namely:

$$\hat{Y}_{100p} = m - u_p s$$
$$\hat{Y}_{100p} = m + u_p s \tag{3}$$

where u_p is given by the Gaussian distribution tables for the preselected p level of probability. For example, to compute the 10th and 90th centiles, u_p is equal to -1.282 and +1.282 respectively. Owing to the fact that the centile is a linear combination of two sample estimates (m and s) which, as such, are subject to sampling error, it is worth investigating the effect of this on the estimated centile.

It can be shown easily that the sampling error of the centile is approximately:

$$\sigma(\hat{Y}_{100p}) = \sigma(\hat{Y}_{100(1-p)}) \cong \sigma\sqrt{(1+u_p^2/2)/n} \tag{4}$$

For girls 6 years old, Tanner et al. (1966) give:

$$m = 113.4 \quad \text{and} \quad s = 5.14$$

Thus:

$$\hat{Y}_{10} = 106.8 \quad \text{and} \quad \hat{Y}_{90} = 120.0$$

It follows from (4):

$$s(\hat{Y}_{100p}) = s(\hat{Y}_{100(1-p)}) = 6.94/\sqrt{n}$$

The above mentioned authors have the sample size n = 1000 and therefore $s(\hat{Y}_{100p}) = \pm 0.22$ cm and the 95% confidence range of the centile is: $2 \cdot 1.96 \cdot 0.22 = 0.86$ cm.

Suppose n = 150; it follows: $s(\hat{Y}_{100p}) = \pm 0.57$ cm with a 95% confidence range approximately equal to 2.5 cm. These results stress the relevance of the sample size to the reliability of the estimates of centiles.

By following an alternative approach one can assess that the actual proportion (P = 0.8) of the population contained between two estimated centiles is subject to sampling error. The standard deviation of the percentage (100 P) is approximately (Wilks, 1941):

$$\sigma[100(1-2_p)]=\sigma[100\ P]\cong u_p \exp\ \{-u_p\}/\sqrt{\pi n} \tag{5}$$

With u_p = 1.282 (5) gives: $\sigma(80)$ = 0.32/$\sqrt{n}$. Thus: for n = 1000, $\sigma(80)$ = 1.01% and for n = 150, $\sigma(80)$ = 2.61%. In the latter case, the 95% confidence limits of the percentage of the population contained between the sample centiles m±1.28 s are: 80%±(1.96· 2.61) ≅75% ——— 85%. These results suggest the possibility of substituting the range defined by two centiles with another range that contains at least a given percentage of the population with a predetermined γ level of confidence. Such an interval is called tolerance interval and its borderline values are called tolerance limits. These limits also are computed by adding to and subtracting from the sample mean the sample standard deviation multiplied by an appropriate coefficient k. Howe (1969) shows that for n > 30; k can be approximated fairly well by the following:

$$k = \lambda z \tag{6}$$

where:

$$\lambda = u_{(1+P)/2}(1+ \frac{1}{n})^{\frac{1}{2}} \tag{7}$$

$$z = \left[\frac{n - 1}{\chi^2_{n-1;\ 1-\gamma}} \right] \tag{8}$$

For n > 30, χ^2 can be approximated by (Hald, 1952):

$$\chi^2_{n-1;\ 1-\gamma} = \frac{1}{2}\left[(2n-1)^{\frac{1}{2}} + u_{1-\gamma}\right]^2 \tag{9}$$

Suppose γ = 0.95 and n = 150:

(9) gives: $\chi^2_{149,0.05} = \frac{1}{2}(2\cdot150-1)^{\frac{1}{2}}-1.645 = 122.408$

(8) gives: $z = \left[\frac{150-1}{122.408}\right]^{\frac{1}{2}} = 1.21724$

when P = 0.80 (7) gives $\lambda=1.282(1+1/150)^{\frac{1}{2}} = 1.28627$ and thus: k=1.28627 · 1.21724 = 1.56050.

Expressions (6), (7) and (8) show that, for n → ∞, k → $u_{(1+P)/2}$, i.e. the tolerance limits, converge in probability to two constants which fix the boundaries of an interval containing the true percentage P of the population.

It is now time to consider the estimate of the standard deviation. As an example, consider children 7 years old: what is
required is the standard deviation of a population of children all
aged exactly 7 years whilst the available sample provides data for
children whose ages range from 6.5 to 7.5 years. Because the
measurement is increasing during this interval, the sample standard
deviation is larger than the "instantaneous" figure required.
Healy (1962), after showing that the mean age-grouped sample
estimates the mean of the center of the interval, suggests application of an appropriate correction to the variance. This consists in reducing the usual estimate of the variance by $b^2/12$,
where b is the mean increment in growth over the above interval.

An alternative approach allows the user to compute centiles
and their confidence limits without taking into account the form
of the distribution, i.e., by means of distribution-free methods.
These simply assume that the density function is continuous.
After arraying the n sample data in ascending order, the p-th
centile (Y_{100p}) is estimated by the order statistic whose number
is (n+1) p/100. The α-level confidence interval of the p-th
centile is provided by the two order statistics $\hat{Y}^r$ and $\hat{Y}^v$ where
(when n>20):

$$r = np + u_{\alpha/2}\sqrt{np(1-p)} \tag{10}$$

$$v = np + u_{1-\alpha/2}\sqrt{np(1-p)} \tag{11}$$

Usually the two figures given by (10) and (11) are not
integers; they are rounded to the highest nearest integer.

It can be shown (Conover, 1971) that the above interval is
such as:

$$\text{Probability } \{\hat{Y}^{(r)} \leq Y_{100p} \leq \hat{Y}^{(v)}\} = 1 - \alpha \tag{12}$$

Distribution-free methods can be utilized also to compute
tolerance intervals although they will not be considered here.
For a detailed discussion of the technique the reader is referred
to the already-mentioned book by Conover (1971) and to the mono-
graph by Guenther (1977). In this context, it is worth considering the loss of information that results from resorting to distribution-free methods when the parent population is in fact
Gaussian. This loss is quite substantial; in fact, according to
Tanner (1952), the distribution-free approach needs, in a Gaussian
distribution, just four times as many to estimate the 95th centile
with the same accuracy as the 1.645 σ level, and 14 times as many
to estimate the 97.5 centile with the same accuracy as its
corresponding 2σ level.

This consideration could suggest that the research worker compute the sample mean and standard deviation and use them to estimate centiles by means of expression (3) even when the parent distribution differs slightly from a Gaussian one. One can evaluate the extent to which this approach is advisable by studying the effect of the lack of Normality on the population percentage included between two centiles. Taking into account that the distribution resulting from the combination of two Gaussian distributions is not Gaussian, one can consider combining two distributions with the same mean but different standard deviations.

The result will be a symmetrical but long-tailed distribution of non-Gaussian shape. To fulfill the aims, one has now to calculate the proportion of this distribution contained between the limits given by expression (3). For sake of simplicity one can put $\mu=0$. Furthermore, let $\sigma_1=1$ and $\sigma_2=2.5$ (the standard deviations of the two parent Gaussian distributions) and $\pi=0.80$ and $1-\pi=0.20$ (the proportions in which they appear in the mixture). The standard deviation of the combined distribution is:

$$\sigma=\sqrt{0.8\cdot1+0.20\cdot2.5^2} = 1.43178$$

The 10th and 90th centiles of the mixed distribution are: −1.835 and 1.835 respectively. Using the tables of the Gaussian distribution, it is found that the proportions included between the two above values are:

in the first distribution,

$(\sigma_1=1):P_1\{-1.835 \leq u \leq 1.835\} = 0.93349$

in the second distribution,

$(\sigma_2=2.5):P_2\{-1.835/\sigma_2 < u < 1.835/\sigma_2\} = 0.53582$

Thus the P corresponding to the mixture is:

$$P = 0.80 \cdot 0.93349 +$$
$$\underline{\quad 0.20 \cdot 0.53582 \quad}$$

$$= 0.85396$$

Table 1 reports the percentage (100P) of the mixture included between the 10th and 90th centiles, between the 2.5th and 97.5th centiles and between the 0.5th and 99.5th centiles when $\sigma_1=1$, for different values of σ_2 as well as of π.

The findings show that the first of the three above intervals, particularly when $\sigma_2=2.5$ and $\sigma_2=3.0$, tends to include a percentage rather larger than 80% whereas the other two agree quite well with the expected 95% and 99% respectively. Therefore, before resorting to distribution-free methods, it is necessary to investigate the

Table 1. Percentage of Population Included by Limits $\mu \pm z_p \sigma$. The Population is a Mixture, in the Ratio $\pi/(1-\pi)$, of Two Gaussian Populations with Means μ and Standard Deviation 1 and σ_2 respectively.

u_{1-p} and u_p	values of 100P when $\sigma = 1$	π	σ_2			
			1.5	2.0	2.5	3.0
±2.576	99.0	0.95	98.9	98.6	98.4	98.2
		0.90	98.8	98.3	97.8	97.5
		0.85	98.7	98.0	97.4	96.9
		0.80	98.6	97.8	97.2	97.0
±1.960	95.0	0.95	95.0	95.2	95.5	95.8
		0.90	95.0	95.1	95.3	95.4
		0.85	94.9	94.9	94.8	94.7
		0.80	94.8	94.7	94.4	94.4
±1.282	80.0	0.95	80.4	81.5	83.0	84.7
		0.90	80.7	82.4	84.5	86.6
		0.85	80.9	83.0	85.3	87.2
		0.80	81.1	83.3	85.4	87.1

lack of Normality with a thorough evaluation of asymmetry and kurtosis.

Quantal Variables

The status of growth and development of a child is often assessed in terms of the age at which a selected event, regarded as a "maturity indicator", is attained. Typical events commonly used in clinical practice include eruption of deciduous or permanent teeth, fusion of epiphyses, and the occurrence of menarche. Therefore, standards are required to evaluate whether the age of attainment is normal. The procedure adopted to construct these standards differs from the one previously discussed because the event itself (and the expected age at which it occurs) is observable only if the child is followed longitudinally and observed many times. More usually, the researcher knows that the event has or has not occurred; in the first case subjects can be asked to recall the age at which they attained the indicator but, unfortunately, it has been shown that recall data are subject to error and bias even for a fairly important event like menarche. The alternative approach, that avoids the biasing effect of recollection, consists in selecting a suitable sample and asking each subject his or her age and simply whether or not he or she has attained the appropriate indicator. At any given age, the proportion of the group in which the event has occurred is computed; plotting these proportions against age, an S shaped curve is drawn increasing from 0% to 100%.

The S curve in the left part of Figure 4 is derived from data for age at menarche in Carrara girls (Marubini and Barghini, 1969); in the right part of this figure the curve has been linearized by transforming the percentages to <u>probits</u>, i.e. $u_p + 5$, to avoid the negative sign (see: Finney, 1971). This transformation is based on the hypothesis that the ages at which menarche occurred followed a Gaussian distribution in this population. Once a straight line has been fitted to the transformed points, one can read the ages pertinent to any required centile directly from it. Unfortunately, the numerical method for fitting, although straightforward, is much more tedious than it may appear at first sight, because it has to take into account the fact that the plotted points are not equally precise. In fact, they are commonly based on different numbers of cases and moreover the distortion of the scale of the ordinate in passing from the left to the right part of Figure 4 greatly decreases the precision of points relative to proportions near 0 or 1. This method is not described here; the interested reader is referred for details to the already-mentioned book by Finney (1971).

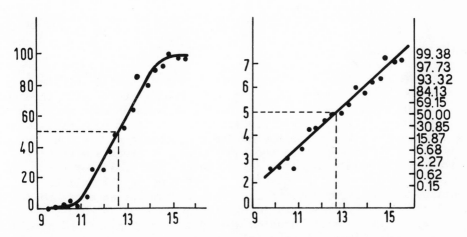

Fig. 4. Cumulative distribution functions of age at menarche of Carrara's girls (Marubini and Barghini, 1969). Horizontal axis: age in years. Vertical axis: left graph, percentage; right graph, probit on the left side and percentage on the right one.

The equation of the straight line drawn in Figure 4 is:

$$\hat{Y} = -6.09 + 0.88t \tag{13}$$

(where Y = percentage in probits and t = age in years and decimals of a year) and it allows computation of the following estimates of three centiles:

$\hat{t}_{10}$= 11.15 years

$\hat{t}_{50}$= median = 12.60 years

$\hat{t}_{90}$= 14.06 years

These estimates obtained by probit analysis suffer from the same age-grouping effect previously discussed with regard to the construction of standards for quantitative variables. In fact, in processing quantal data too, each subject is assigned the age corresponding to the mid-point of his age group. This tends to underestimate the slope of the probit line and thereby give ages that are too extreme for outlying percentiles. It has been shown by Tocker (1949) that, to avoid the above bias, both the intercept and the slope of equation (13) should be multiplied by a factor $(1 + b^2h^2/24)$ where h is the width of the grouping interval. In the previous example the value of this factor:

$$[1 + (0.88 \cdot 0.34)^2 /24]$$

is practically negligible.

VELOCITY STANDARDS

The data suitable for constructing standards dealt with till now are usually collected by "cross-sectional" studies that involve the measurement of individuals of different ages at each point on the time scale. Alternatively, "longitudinal" studies entail the measurement of subjects on successive occasions over a given number of years. In between these two basic types of study are the so-called "mixed-longitudinal" ones, in which some or all of the children are measured at least twice, but some or all fail to continue in the study for its entire span from age at entry to complete maturity. Most studies initially planned as longitudinal effectively become mixed studies when some children fail to attend as a result of illness, change of address, etc. Such studies with a "longitudinal" component are essential to construct velocity standards that allow a pediatrician to answer questions such as: "Is the child's rate of growth in stature during the past year normal for his age and sex?"

When children are studied during a definite long period of growth, say during adolescence, a suitable curve, for example, the logistic curve (Marubini et al., 1972), can be fitted to the plot of Y vs. age and the corresponding velocity curve obtained by differentiation. When only few measurements on the same subjects are available, the alternative to this strategy is the so-called increment method of estimating velocities that correspond to simply computing the growth increments. As a matter of fact, the difference between a pair of measurements is readily interpretable and pertinent standards for it can be constructed easily. Once differences for all children have been computed, the standards can be obtained by the procedure outlined on pages 104-110.

It is worth noting that two measurement errors are involved in calculating the value of any increment; this implies that the standard error of the difference between successive observations is $\sqrt{2}$ times that of the individual measurements. This drawback can be partly avoided by using the approach suggested by van't Hof et al. (1976). Furthermore, it may be shown that the increment method averages the velocity over the time interval; thus it tends to underestimate the peak velocity for a given child. As far as mixed-longitudinal data are concerned, the cross-sectional component cannot assist the computation of the standard deviation of growth rate but it can contribute to the estimation of mean growth velocity. The statistical methods suitable for dealing with mixed-longitudinal data are rather complicated and the interested reader is referred to the papers by Tanner (1951) and by Rao and Rao (1966).

REGRESSION STANDARDS

In the previous section it is pointed out that standards or norms for growth are devices appropriate for representing the frequency distributions of a measurement (distance standards) or of combinations of measurements (velocity standards) for a given population at a particular historical time. Because use of these standards implies a comparison between the child being investigated and a standardizing population, it follows that the suitability of the population sampled to compute standards is of basic importance if the procedure is to be accurate. Particularly, it should be noted that a homogeneous group can allow the production of standards whose centiles are closer together, i.e., more sensitive standards. Leaving aside considerations concerning sampling design that are outside the scope of this paper, one could construct standards for a given anthropometric variable by making allowance for a concomitant variable. For example, everybody knows tall parents in general have tall children and short parents have short children. Therefore, it is reasonable to use parental height as a covariate. Following this approach, Tanner et al.

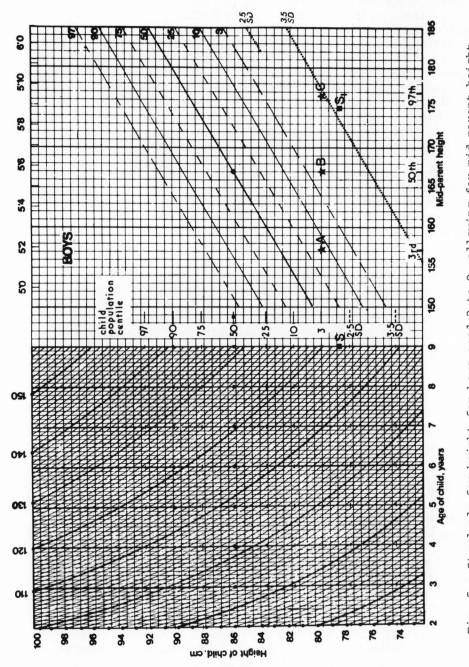

Fig. 5.   Standards for height for boys aged 2 to 9, allowing for mid-parent height.

(1970) published standards for children's height at ages 2 to 9
years.   These workers considered their "norms" more powerful than
"parent-unknown" standards in the sense of being able to detect
cases of pathological short stature where this might not have
been suspected and in giving a more solid basis to the diagnosis
"genetic small stature".   In theory, further refinements could be
made by allowing additionally for the heights of siblings, uncles,
aunts and grandparents.   In the approach of Tanner et al., the
covariate is equal to the average of mother's and father's heights.
At each age, the linear equation: $Y=\beta_0+\beta_1 X$ (where: Y=child's
height and X=mid-parent height) was fitted using pooled data from
studies conducted in London, Brussels, Stockholm and Zurich under
the supervision of the International Children's Centre, Paris.
They examined the shape of the distributions of residuals (not of
Y as on page 103) around the linear regression and found they
approximated a Gaussian distribution with approximately constant
variance.   The chart used to obtain parent-specific centiles for
boys is shown in Figure 5.

   The simplest way to use the chart is to find first the
child's height, interpolating where necessary, and follow the

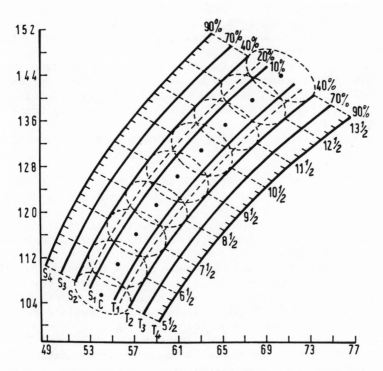

Fig. 6.   Correnti's (1949) height-for-chest auxogram.

curve till the correct age is reached. Place a ruler from this
point along the horizontal lines across to the right hand portion
of the chart; then the point where this crosses the vertical line
corresponding to the mid-parent height is the one required. The
centile position of this point is read (Tanner et al., 1970).
Thirty years ago, Correnti (1949) published a height-for-chest-
circumference auxogram (Figure 6). At each year of age, the
averages of height and chest circumference are plotted and an
ellipse is drawn around them. This includes 40% of the total
children of that age. Similar height-for-weight auxograms were
published also (Correnti, 1953). The ellipses are computed by
assuming that the joint distribution of the two variables is
Gaussian for each age. Although the auxogram has a much firmer
biometrical foundation than some grids used after World War II,
particularly the Wetzel grid (1941), the above assumption is
questionable and certainly not tenable for many ages.

REFERENCES

Conover, W. J., 1971, "Practical Nonparametric Statistics," John
        Wiley and Sons, New York.
Correnti, V., 1949, Sulle variazioni della statura e del perimetro
        toracico nell'accrescimento. Atti dell'Accademia Nazionale
        dei Lincei, Rendiconti, 7:177.
Correnti, V., 1953, Il metodo degli auxogrammi e le sue applica-
        zioni, Pediatria Internazionale, 4:169.
De Scrilli, A. M., Marubini, E., Milani, S., and Rainisio, M.,
        1978, Birth weight distributions: First report of an
        Italian multi-centric survey, Acta Med. Auxol., 10:5.
Finney, D. J., 1971, "Probit Analysis," The University Press,
        Cambridge.
Guenther, W. C., 1977, "Sampling Inspection in Statistical Quality
        Control," Charles Griffin's Monographs and Courses, No. 37,
        London.
Healy, M. J. R., 1962, The effect of age-grouping on the distribu-
        tion of a measurement affected by growth, Am. J. Phys.
        Anthropol., 20:49.
Healy, M. J. R., 1978, Statistics of growth standards, in: "Human
        Growth, 1. Principles and Perinatal Growth," F. Falkner
        and J. M. Tanner, eds., Plenum, New York.
Howe, W. G., 1969, Two sided tolerance limits for normal popula-
        tion: Some improvements, J. Am. Stat. Assoc., 64:610.
Marubini, E., and Barghini, G., 1969, Richerche sull'età media di
        comparsa della pubertà nella popolazione scolare femminile
        di Carrara, Minerva Pediatrica, 21:281.
Marubini, E., Resele, L. F., and Barghini, G., 1972, The fit of
        Gompertz and logistic curves to longitudinal data during
        adolescence, Hum. Biol., 44:511.

Rao, M. N., and Rao, C. R., 1966, Linked cross-sectional study for
     determining norms and growth rates. A pilot survey on
     Indian school-going boys, Sankyā, B28:237.
Tanner, J. M., 1951, Some notes on the reporting of growth data,
     Hum. Biol., 23:93.
Tanner, J. M., 1952, Assessing growth and development, Arch. Dis.
     Childh., 27:10.
Tanner, J. M., Goldstein, H., and Whitehouse, R. H., 1970,
     Standards for children's height at ages 2-9 years allowing
     for height of parents, Arch. Dis. Childh., 45:755.
Tanner, J. M., Whitehouse, R. H., and Takaishi, M., 1966,
     Standards from birth to maturity for height, weight, height
     velocity and weight velocity: British children, 1965,
     Arch. Dis. Childh., 41:454 and 613.
Thöni, H., 1973, Trasformazione di variabili usate nell'analisi
     dei dati sperimentali, Applicazioni Biomediche del calcolo
     electronico, 8:159.
Tocher, K. D., 1949, A note on the analysis of grouped probit
     data, Biometrika, 36:9.
Van't Hof, M. A., Roede, M. J., and Kowalski, C., 1976, Estimation
     of growth velocities from individual longitudinal data,
     Growth, 40:217.
Wetzel, N. C., 1941, Physical fitness in terms of physique develop-
     ment and basal metabolism, J. Am. Med. Assoc., 116:1187.
Wilks, S., 1941, On the determination of sample sizes for setting
     tolerance limits, Ann. Math. Stat., 12:91.

7. QUANTITATIVE GENETIC ANALYSIS OF VARIATION IN ADULT STATURE:

THE CONTRIBUTION OF PATH ANALYSIS[1]

R. Darrell Bock

The University of Chicago

Chicago, IL   60637

In textbook discussions of quantitative inheritance, human adult stature is invariably cited as an example of a highly multifactorial trait, normally distributed in given breeding groups, showing substantial genetic determination, and presenting no evidence of X-linked influence or other major gene effects (see Cavalli-Sforza and Bodmer, 1971). Although continuing research adds more detail to this picture, especially in revealing the contribution of nutrition and other environmental effects, the essential outline remains valid at the present time. In particular, attempts to detect somatic and X-linked major gene influence on adult stature have thus far yielded negative results (Fain, 1978).

For genetic studies, the methodological implication of this view of human stature (given that there is no possibility of experimental studies in this area) is that quantitative analysis of the inheritance of stature must depend almost exclusively upon such statistics as the means, standard deviations and correlations obtained from samples of persons sharing varying degrees of biological and environmental relationship (Falconer, 1963). In asymmetric relationships, such as parent-offspring, the Pearson-product-moment correlation coefficient is an appropriate descriptive statistic; but for symmetric relationships such as same sex twins, or as an index of common relationship between three or more persons, Fisher's intraclass correlation coefficient is required. Applied to measurements of mature stature assumed to be multifactorial and normally distributed in human populations, these coefficients are in fact the

---

[1]Supported in part by NSF Grant BNS 76-22943-A02 to the Center for Advanced Study in the Behavioral Sciences, Stanford, California.

maximum likelihood estimates of parameters of the multivariate distribution that describes the variation in stature among related persons. A complete description of the multivariate normal distribution requires also, of course, specification of the means and standar deviations, but for populations in Hardy-Weinberg equilibrium, they are often assumed constant and are arbitrarily set to zero and one, respectively. Only the pairwise correlations among distinct variable are required to specify the multivariate normal distribution of these standardized variables.

In biometrical studies, the correlations for relatives of various degrees are estimated in large samples assumed randomly drawn from a defined population. Stature, which is relatively simple to measure in adults, is readily investigated in this way, and numerous studies of familial correlations in height can be found in the biometric and anthropological literature (Mueller, 1976). The earliest example, that of Pearson and Lee (1903), was collected originally to illustrate the old theory of blending inheritance, but it can also be employed to test the modern theory of multifactorial inheritance. In his classic paper, "The correlation between relatives on the supposition of Mendelian inheritance," R.A. Fisher (1918) used these data in computations illustrating his theory. His result demonstrates, however, the pitfalls of such analyses when the critical assumptions are not exposed to scrutiny. The genetic theory indicates that, if the influence of the common family environment is assumed the same between offspring as between parent and offspring, some degree of excess of the offspring-offspring correlation over the parent-offspring correlation can be attributed to the effects of dominance, i.e., the interaction of genes at the same locus. Making this assumption, Fisher found evidence of dominance but no evidence for any effect of common family environment on siblings.

He was, of course, unaware of the secular increase in stature that modern genetical analysis shows cannot be attributed wholly to selection or reduced inbreeding and must be due in part to changing environment (Cavalli-Sforza and Bodmer, 1971; Meredith, 1976). If he were, he might not have eliminated secular trend from the analysis by taking correlations about generation means, and he would have been more critical of the gratuitous assumption of a common family environment. With the wisdom of hindsight, we can now see that the environment, nutritional and otherwise, that affects the mature stature of offspring can be substantially different than that which affected the stature of parents in the previous generation. When the correlations are analyzed under this more general assumption, the role of environment in determining adult stature (which pediatric and physical anthropological studies have amply confirmed) is clearly revealed in the analysis of familial correlations (Rao, et al., 1975). (See Section 4 of the present paper).

It was precisely to expose the critical assumptions to scrutiny, and also to relieve quantitative geneticists of the mental labor that characterizes Fisher's algebraic methods for calculating expected correlations among relatives, that Sewall Wright developed the method of path coefficients (Wright, 1934). Path analysis is useful not only for deriving expected familial correlations, but also for interpreting the results obtained by Fisher and others by algebraic methods (Li, 1968). Because it represents relationships between measures in schematic form (the path diagram), path analysis enables the investigator to grasp a complex system of relationships and to examine its implications. The diagram represents a linear structural model connecting the putative causal variables with the response variables. When suitable data are available, the plausibility of the model can be tested by a goodness of fit statistic comparing the observed correlations with those deduced from the model. Parameters of the model can also be estimated (Jöreskog, 1970; Rao, Morton and Yee, 1974). By providing criteria for rejecting inappropriate models, this type of analysis implements a theory of plausible causal inference which, although never as secure as experimental inference, is nevertheless the only basis for progress in a purely observational science.

Part of the appeal of path analysis is that its simple and elegant principles can be learned and applied accurately in a very short time. The novice will find the text, Path Analysis--A Primer, by C.C. Li (1975) an excellent introduction to the subject. The present paper makes use of some of Li's examples to illustrate the principles of path analysis before applying them to the problem of accounting for genetic and non-genetic sources of variation in adult stature. The account is intended merely to introduce the main ideas of path analysis: the reader is encouraged to pursue the subject further in the references cited.

1   DEFINITIONS, PRINCIPLES AND EXAMPLES

Path analysis is a method of computing correlations between variables connected by specified causal linear relationships. It is based on parameters called "path coefficients," which express the putative causal relationships between variables. A path coefficient between a causal variable and a response variable (or independent and dependent variable) is simply the standardized regression coefficient of the latter on the former:

$$p_{YX} = \beta_{YX} = b_{YX} \frac{\sigma_X}{\sigma_Y} \tag{1}$$

where p_{YX}, a path coefficient, is equal to the standardized partial regression coefficient β_{YX} (beta-weight), which in turn is the un-standardized regression weight multiplied by the standard deviation of the distribution of X and divided by the standard deviation of the distribution of Y. Note that all variables, both observed and unobserved in path analysis, must be assumed to have a distribution. Values of the independent variable cannot be selected arbitrarily as they are in experiments and prediction studies. For statistical tests of path analytic models, the variables are usually assumed to have a joint multivariate normal distribution. This assumption is not necessary, however, when path analysis is used to compute correlations or used descriptively.

1.1 Simple Regression

A path analysis is expressed in a path diagram, as, for example, the diagram for simple regression shown in Figure 1. This diagram expresses the fact that variation in Y is caused by a variable X, which is observable, and an uncorrelated residual U, which is unobservable.

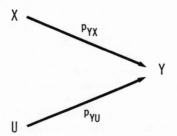

Fig. 1. Simple regression. Uncorrelated causes totally
determining the variation in Y.

For uncorrelated causes, the path coefficients are simply correlation coefficients:

$$p_{YX} = r_{YX}$$
$$p_{UX} = r_{UX} \tag{2}$$

Because X and U are uncorrelated and comprise all variables causing variation in Y,

$$p_{YX}^2 + p_{YU}^2 = 1 \tag{3}$$

Equation (3) expresses the correlation of Y with itself, which is 1. It may be calculated from the path diagram in Figure 1 by tracing all paths from Y to itself, first backwards (i.e., against the direction of the arrow), multiplying together the path coefficients found along each separate path, and adding the result. The total is a correlation between the variables in which each term of the sum represents the contribution of a separate path. In simple regression there are two such paths:

Path	Contribution
Y,X,Y	$R^2 = p^2_{YX}$
Y,U,Y	$U^2 = p^2_{YU}$

$$R^2 + U^2 = 1$$

1.2 Multiple Regression

The path diagram in Figure 2 represents the multiple correlation between Y and two correlated independent variables X_1 and X_2, plus an uncorrelated residual, U.

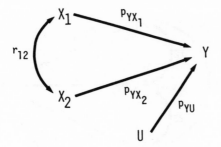

Fig. 2. Multiple regression with two correlated causes and an uncorrelated residual.

This diagram includes possible correlation between causes. Correlation between causes is represented by a two-headed arrow, and the value associated with such links is a correlation and not a path coefficient. (It is important to understand that, unlike the case of simple regression, path coefficients, or β-weights, in multiple regression are not correlations and may be greater than 1 when there are negative path coefficients or negative correlations between variables.)

When computing correlations between observable variables, one may trace a double-headed arrow in either direction. In each direction of the trace, the path coefficients are multiplied by the coefficient of the correlational link. Thus, the total determination of Y in Figure 2 is

Path	Contribution
Y, X_1, Y	$R^2 = p^2_{YX}$
Y, X_2, Y	$+ p^2_{YX_2}$
Y, X_1, X_2, Y	$+ p_{YX_1} \cdot r_{X_1 X_2} \cdot p_{YX_2}$
Y, X_2, X_1, Y	$+ p_{YX_2} \cdot r_{X_1 X_2} \cdot p_{YX_1}$
$Y, U, Y,$	$U^2 = 2_{YU}$

$$R^2 + U^2 = 1$$

The path diagram in Figure 3 illustrates multiple regression with three correlated courses and an uncorrelated residual. This diagram illustrates the further rule that, in calculating correlations, a traced path may include only <u>one</u> correlational link.

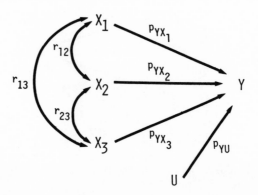

Fig. 3.   Multiple regression with three pairwise correlated causes and an uncorrelated residual.

In Figure 3, there are ten paths that contribute to the total determination of Y.

Path	Contribution
Y, X_1, Y	$R^2 = p_{YX_1}^2$
Y, X_2, Y	$+ p_{YX_2}^2$
Y, X_3, Y	$+ p_{YX_3}^2$
Y, X_1, X_2, Y	$+ p_{YX_1} \cdot r_{X_1 X_2} \cdot p_{YX_2}$
Y, X_2, X_1, Y	$+ p_{YX_2} \cdot r_{X_1 X_2} \cdot p_{YX_1}$
Y, X_1, X_3, Y	$+ p_{YX_1} \cdot r_{X_1 X_3} \cdot p_{YX_3}$
Y, X_3, X_1, Y	$+ p_{YX_3} \cdot r_{X_1 X_3} \cdot p_{YX_1}$
Y, X_2, X_3, Y	$+ p_{YX_2} \cdot r_{X_2 X_3} \cdot p_{YX_3}$
Y, X_3, X_2, Y	$+ p_{YX_3} \cdot r_{X_2 X_3} \cdot p_{Y_2}$
Y, U, Y	$U^2 = p_{YU}^2$

$$R^2 + U^2 = 1$$

1.3 The Backward-forward Rule

The final rule for tracing paths in complex diagrams is that a path may not contain a step in which a forward path is followed by a backward path (excluding the correlational links that may be regarded either as forward or backward). Li (1975) illustrates the plausibility of this rule by the diagram in Figure 4 which represents three offspring of four uncorrelated parents from a random mating population. The half sibs X and Y are genetically related

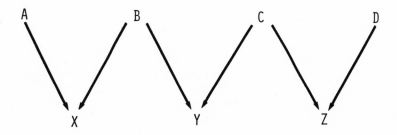

Fig. 4. Offspring of uncorrelated parents.

(correlated) through the common parent B and are connected by a backward-forward path. Similarly, the related half sibs Y and Z are connected by a backward-forward path. X and Z, on the other hand, are unrelated, and the path between them contains the forbidden forward-backward step B, Y, C.

2 CORRELATION BETWEEN PARENT AND OFFSPRING, AND OFFSPRING AND OFFSPRING

With the preceding brief introduction to path analysis, we have assembled enough machinery to deduce parent-offspring and offspring-offspring correlations under realistic assumptions. The classical, or Fisherian, model assuming one generation of assortative mating and no epistacy (interaction of genes at different loci) is contained in the path diagram in Figure 5. (This diagram is an elaboration of Figure 6 in Kolakowski, 1970.) Formulas for the correlations between phenotypes may be computed by assigning values to the coefficients of paths and correlational links and by tracing all possible paths connecting genotypes. Multiplying coefficients along the way and adding the results for each path gives the required correlation.

The paths most central to the diagram are those with coefficients a, b and a', b' (for father and mother, respectively) which represent the determined part of the variation due to the chance processes of miosis and fertilization. For somatic loci in diploid organisms, these coefficients have the value $1/\sqrt{2}$ irrespective of the sex of parent or offspring. But for X-linked loci, the value of the father's coefficient b is 0 for sons and 1 for daughters, while the mother's is b' = $1/\sqrt{2}$ for offspring of both sexes.

Strictly speaking, the diagram in Figure 5 represents correlation due to one genetic locus, but in the absence of epistacy, correlations computed from the diagram are valid for the average effect of n loci. Moreover, a path diagram cannot strictly represent nonlinear relationships such as the effects of gene interaction at a locus, i.e., dominance. But by partitioning variance due to such interaction into linear and dominance components in the manner introduced by Fisher, we may represent the portion due to the separate genes (and hence capable of heritable transmission to offspring) by the linear component, and represent the portion due to interaction of the two genes at the locus by an uncorrelated dominance component. In the diagram, the corresponding path coefficients are labeled g and d, respectively (with subscripts or primes as appropriate). Thus, the total genotypic variance is $g^2 + d^2 = 1$.

Similarly, the phenotypic variation is partitioned into portions representing uncorrelated genotypic and environmental determination, with respective path coefficients h and e. The total phenotypic variance is therefore $h^2 + e^2 = 1$.

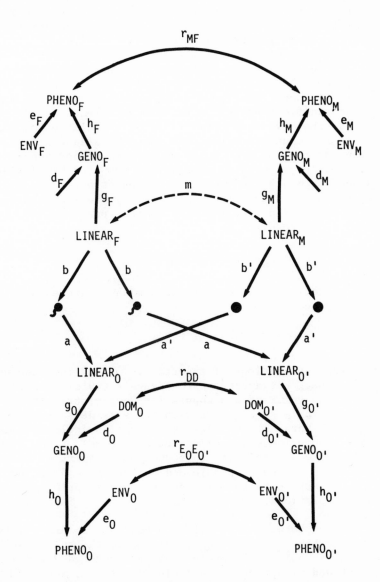

Fig. 5 Causal paths and correlational links connecting parents (top), parental gametes (middle) and two offspring (bottom)

2.1 Parent-offspring Correlation

For many behavioral and physical traits, including adult
stature, it must be assumed in general that the phenotype influences
mate selection and thus introduces some degree of assortative mating.
Correlation in adult stature of mates is of the order .3 to .4 in
Western countries, but is virtually absent in less developed societies (e.g., the Mandinko of Gambia; see Roberts, Billewicz and
McGregor, 1978). The effect of assortative mating, which acts on
individual loci much like a very weak form of inbreeding, is to
introduce an additional causal path between parent and offspring.
The effect of phenotypic assortment on the correlation of parental
genotypes is represented by the link shown on a dashed line with
correlation coefficient m. On the assumption of one generation of
assortative mating, the value of m may be computed by viewing the
causal scheme from a parental linear component upward in reverse,
i.e., regarding the phenotype as determining the linear variation
and reversing the direction of paths in this part of the diagram.
This leads to the result

$$m = 2g_F h_F g_M h_M r_{MF}$$

or, if the effects of environment and dominance are assumed the
same in mother and father

$$m = 2g^2 h^2 r_{MF}$$

Additional generations of assortative mating increase the correlation somewhat, but according to Fisher's (1918) analysis, the
first generation value of m accounts for most of the effect. Fisher
gives a result for n generations with the same degree of assortment
(see Crow and Kimura, 1970), but the derivation includes many
problematic assumptions, including that of no selection. Since extremes of stature are believed to reduce probability of mating,
Fisher's results are questionable and perhaps should not be used in
a first approximation to the expected parent-offspring and offspring-
offspring correlations.

If the link between parental genotypes due to assortative mating
is included in the diagram, then according to the rule that a causal
path may contain only one correlation, the expected correlation between parent and offspring for somatic loci (i.e., setting M = F = P
and not distinguishing between path coefficients with and without
primes) proves to be

$$r_{PO} = \tfrac{1}{2}h_O g_O h_P g_P + \tfrac{1}{2}h_O g_O h_P g_P m$$

or, if effects of dominance and heritability are the same in the parental and offspring generations,

$$r_{PO} = \tfrac{1}{2}h^2 g^2 (1+m) \quad ,$$

which is Fisher's result.

2.2 Offspring-offspring Correlation

Unlike the phenotypic correlation between parent and offspring, the correlation between phenotypes of two offspring of the same parents (full sibs) may include a contribution due to correlation of the dominance effects. Because full sibs have a probability of $\tfrac{1}{4}$ of having the same genes in common by descent (i.e., genes descended from the same ancestral gene), they tend to share the same inter-action effects at each locus of a multifactorial trait. As a result, some phenotypic correlation arises from this source. In the path diagram, the correlation coefficient of the link connecting the off-spring dominance is, in the case of full sibs, $r_{DD} = \tfrac{1}{4}$. Including this link and ignoring primes leads to Fisher's result of offspring-offspring correlation:

$$r_{OO} = \tfrac{1}{4}g_O^2 h_O^2 + \tfrac{1}{4}g_O^2 h_O^2 + \tfrac{1}{4}d_O^2 h_O^2 + \tfrac{1}{4}g_O^2 h_O^2 m + \tfrac{1}{4}g_O^2 h_O^2 m$$

$$= h_O^2(\tfrac{1}{2}g_O^2 + \tfrac{1}{4}d_O^2) + \tfrac{1}{2}g_O^2 h_O^2 m$$

But as pointed out in Section 1, Fisher ignored the possibility of correlation between the environments of sibs. If that link is added, with correlation coefficients $r_{E_O E_O'}$, say, the expected off-spring-offspring correlation includes the additional term

$$e_O^2 r_{E_O E_O'}$$

3   CULTURAL TRANSMISSION

In a recent paper, Rao, Morton and Yee (1978) have argued that the Fisherian treatment of a correlation between relatives omits potentially important cultural sources of correlation and thus biases the analysis toward genetic causes. (See also corrections by Goldberger, 1978, Rao, Morton and Yee, 1978; see Rice, Cloninger and Reich, 1978.) They have therefore included the additional causal paths and correlational links shown in Figure 6. The coefficients of these paths and correlations are identified as follows:

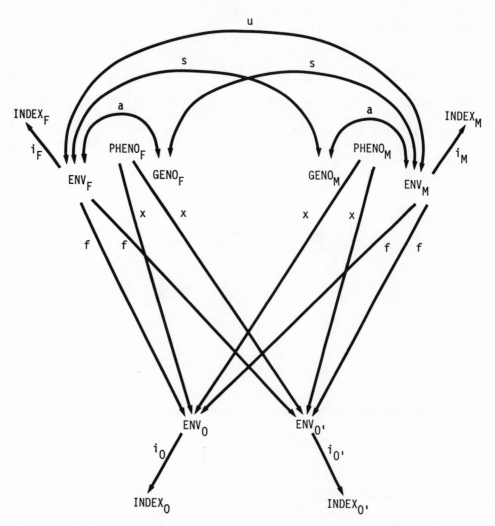

Fig. 6. Additional causal paths and correlations connecting parental
         genotypes, phenotypes and environments (top) with offspring
         environments (bottom)

s = correlation between the (childhood) family environment of an adult and the genotype of his or her spouse.

u = correlation between (childhood) family environments of spouses.

f = effect of parent's (childhood) family environment on the environment of offspring.

x = effect of parent's (adult) phenotype on environment of offspring.

i_p = effect of parent's (childhood) family environment on an index of that environment (e.g., an index of socio-economic status).

i_0 = effect of offspring's environment on an index of environment.

a = correlation between parental genotype and (childhood) family environment of parent. (Like m, a may be evaluated by reversing paths.)

In order to obtain actual numerical estimates of these additional coefficients, it is necessary to have data on other types of relations and to have measured indices of environments. Rao, Morton and Yee (1978) therefore include many additional types of relationships, such as parent and offspring living apart, offspring and foster parent, half sibs reared together and apart, cognate and affine uncle-niece, first cousins, parental exclusion (misattributed paternity), etc. Specializing coefficients in Figure 6 for each of these cases, the corresponding expected correlations can be computed. If the number of observed correlations from these relationships equals or exceeds the number of coefficients to be estimated, and if the resulting system of nonlinear equations is "identified," that is, if there are as many functionally independent equations as there are independent unknowns, then the coefficients can in principle be estimated. If there are more such equations than unknowns, the coefficients can be estimated and the goodness-of-fit of the model can also be tested. Computer programs which test identifiability and goodness of fit, and estimate coefficients and standard errors have been devised. (Rao, Morton and Yee, 1976, report the availability of a program called NUVAR.)

The additional paths in Figure 6 each contributes a term for environmental effects to the parent-offspring correlation. Assuming possible dominance effects as shown in Figure 5 (Rao, et al. assume no dominance) and using the subscript P to represent contributions of either parent, one finds by tracing all possible paths from one offspring to one parent, the correlation

$$r_{PO} = h_P^2 g_P^2 (1+m)/2 + e_O xmg_P^2 h_P^2 + h_P se_O (f+e_P x) + h_P ae_O f + e_O x$$
$$+ e_O e_P uf + e_P h_O g_O g_P (a+s)/2 + h_P xe_O e_P s + e_O e_P u(f+e_P x)$$

Actually to evaluate all of these path coefficients requires other information than that contained in the measures of stature of parents and full siblings. Particularly valuable are persons of the same degree of biological relatedness living in more and less similar environments. Data for the latter reduce the confounding of biological and environmental similarity that is typical of most human biometrical genetic studies. A fair test of environmental effects may then be possible.

4   ALTERNATIVE ESTIMATES OF COMPONENTS OF VARIATION IN STATURE

Variance components, expressed as fractions of the total variance, are given for the Fisherian model by Crow and Kimura (1970, p.161). Their results, reproduced in the top section of Table 1, are based on the data of Pearson and Lee (1903), which were obtained by self-reports of English subjects. Similar estimates, but based on a model that explicitly includes cultural transmission, are shown in the bottom section of Table 1. These results, taken from Rao, MacLean, Morton and Yee (1975), are based on field measurements of 1,618 sib pairs and 1,340 parent-offspring pairs collected in northeastern Brazil.

The analysis of the Pearson and Lee data, which assumes without justification that the nutritional environment of parent as a child and offspring as a child is as similar as that of two offspring reared together, attributes all of the excess of offspring-offspring correlation to dominance. As a result, all variation can be accounted for without assigning any to environmental effects. When these environments are assumed possibly dissimilar and a corresponding path coefficient evaluated, on the other hand, 16 percent of the variation is attributed to the common environment of sibs. In addition, an even larger amount (44%) remains unaccounted for by genetic and common environmental causes and is presumably due to other unassignable environmental effects. Although more variation of the nutritional environment would be expected in the Brazilian sample than in the English sample, the results of the analysis under the cultural transmission model are more consistent with the well-established effects of diet on stature than is the Fisherian analysis.

Table 1.   Variance Components for Total Determination of
Standing Height Under Alternative Models

1.   Fisherian model with dominance and assortative mating
but without cultural transmission[a]

Source of Variation	Estimated Variance Component
Linear effect of genotype	.62
Dominance	.21
Assortative mating	.17
Environment	.00
TOTAL	1.00

2.   Model with genetic and cultural transmission and
assortative mating[b]

Source of Variation	Estimated Variance Component
Genotype	.40
Common environment	.16
Random environment	.44
TOTAL	1.00

[a]Crow and Kimura (1975)
[b]Rao, et al. (1975)

5.   DISCUSSION

In the past, biometrical genetic studies of multifactorial
traits have not been productive of any very satisfactory account of
human variation. The fault seems to be in the oversimplified models
that were assumed in order to make data analysis tractable. With
the advent of path analysis and modern statistical methods for its
implementation, biometrical methods for identifying genetic, environmental and cultural sources of quantitative variation take on new
interest and relevance. Initially, complex models comprehending
all possible sources will have to be assumed. The model represented
by Figure 6 is an example. But as data accumulate for measures such
as standing height, it may become apparent that some of these
potential sources are unimportant and can be ignored. Hopefully,
the path diagram will have the right balance between quantitative
detail and conceptual simplicity so as to constitute a satisfactory
theory of the determinants of variation in mature stature. It must
be emphasized that such a theory, being based on observational data

and having no practical application, cannot be proven by experimental
or pragmatic tests. But like successful theories in other observational sciences, it may have sufficient quantitative accuracy and
detail to be intellectually satisfying to knowledgeable persons.

REFERENCES

Cavalli-Sforza, L.L., and Bodmer, W.F., 1971, "The Genetics of Human
    Populations," Freeman, San Francisco.
Crow, J.F., and Kimura, M., 1970, Correlation between relatives and
    assortative mating, Chapter 4, in: "An Introduction to Popula-
    tion Genetics Theory," Holt, Rinehart and Winston, New York.
Fain, P.R., 1978, Characteristics of simple sibship variance tests
    for the detection of major loci and application to height,
    weight and spatial performance. Ann. Human Genet., London,
    42:109-120.
Falconer, D.S., 1963, Quantitative inheritance, in: "Methodology
    of Human Genetics," W.J. Burdette, ed., Holden-Day, San
    Francisco, pp.193-216.
Fisher, R.A., 1918, The correlation between relatives on the
    supposition of Mendelian inheritance. Transactions of the
    Royal Society, Edinburgh, 52:399-433.
Goldberger, A.S., 1978, The nonresolution of IQ inheritance by path
    analysis, Amer. J. Human Genet., 30:442-445.
Jöreskog, K.G., 1970, A general method for analysis of covariance
    structures. Biometrika, 57:239-251.
Kolakowski, D.A., 1970, A behavior-genetic analysis of spatial
    ability utilizing latent-trait estimation, unpublished Ph.D.
    dissertation, Department of Education, University of Chicago.
Li, C.C., 1968, Fisher, Wright and path coefficients, Biometrics,
    24:471-483.
Li, C.C., 1975, "Path Analysis--A Primer," Boxwood Press, Pacific
    Grove (California).
Meredith, H.V., 1976, Findings from Asia, Australia, Europe and
    North America on secular change in mean height of children,
    youths and young adults, Amer. J. Phy. Anthro., 44:315-326.
Mueller, W.H., 1976, Parent-child correlations for stature and
    weight among school-aged children: A review of 24 studies,
    Human Biol., 48:379-397.
Pearson, K., and Lee, A., 1903, On the laws of inheritance in man.
    I. Inheritance of physical characters, Biometrika, 2:357-462.
Rao, D.C., MacLean, C.J., Morton, N.E., and Yee, S., 1975, Analysis
    of family resemblance. V. Height and weight in northeastern
    Brazil, Amer. J. Human Genet., 27:509-520.
Rao, D.C., Morton, N.E., and Yee, S., 1974, Analysis of family
    resemblance. II. A linear model for familial correlation,
    Amer. J. Human Genet., 26:331-359.

Rao, D.C., Morton, N.E., and Yee, S., 1976, Resolution of cultural
    and biological inheritance by path analysis, Amer. J. Human
    Genet., 28:228-242.
Rao, D.C., Morton, N.E., and Yee, S., 1978, Resolution of cultural
    and biological inheritance by path analysis: Corrigenda and
    reply to Goldberger letter, Am. J. Human Genet., 30:445-448.
Rice, J., Cloninger, C.R., and Reich, T., 1978, Multifactorial
    inheritance with cultural transmission and assortative mating.
    I. Description and basic properties of the unitary models,
    Amer. J. Human Genet., 30:618-643.
Roberts, D.F., Billewicz, W.Z., and McGregor, I.A., 1978, Herit-
    ability of stature in a West African population, Ann. Human
    Genet., London, 42:15-24.
Wright, S., 1934, The method of path coefficients, Ann. Math. Stat.,
    5:161-215.

II.   GROWTH AND AGEING

8 . POSTNATAL GROWTH OF PRETERM AND FULL-TERM INFANTS

Ingeborg Brandt

University Children's Hospital Bonn
5300 Bonn 1
Germany, F.R.

The characteristic of growth in infancy is its high velocity. It can be assessed properly only by repeated measurements at regular intervals in longitudinal studies. In this paper stress is laid on the growth in head circumference because of its close correlation with brain development during the first 2 years of life and because of its small variability among different ethnic groups or geographic regions (Nellhaus, 1975). In addition to general growth patterns, catch-up growth in the head circumference of small for gestational age (SGA) preterm infants will be discussed.

Some of the data to be described relate to "intrauterine" or "fetal" growth curves. These are based on single measurements after birth of infants born at different postmenstrual ages. Postmenstrual age is the period from the first day of the mother's last menstrual period prior to the pregnancy. Inaccuracies are introduced, for example, when the apparent last menstrual period was not actually a period but withdrawal bleeding after the cessation of a hormonal contraceptive. Furthermore, some women have occasional bleedings for one or two months after the start of pregnancy. The confusing use of "conceptional age" for the time from the first day of the mother's last menstrual period until birth plus postnatal age is to be avoided. Conceptional age, which may vary by 8 to 17 days from postmenstrual age, should be used only for the time from conception to birth.

The assessment of postmenstrual age is a prerequisite for the proper evaluation of newborn infants, i.e., to differentiate between small for gestational age (SGA) infants with a birth weight below the 10th percentile of "intrauterine curves" and appropriate

139

for gestational age (AGA) infants with a birth weight between the
10th and 90th percentiles. Infants of the same weight but of different postmenstrual ages differ in risks and neurological development during the newborn period. The following methods can be used
for postmenstrual age assessment: (1) obstetric history, (2) ultrasound measurements in early pregnancy, (3) clinical external characteristics, and (4) neurological examination (Brandt, 1979a). A
correction for postmenstrual age has to be made to evaluate the
growth of preterm infants; that is, discounting the extent of
prematurity from chronological age. The period during which this
age correction is necessary depends on the specific growth velocity.
This will be discussed with the different growth variables.

GROWTH VELOCITY

    Growth velocity is calculated from two measurements a certain
distance apart in time; usually the increment is plotted midway
between the two ages at which the measurements were made. Reference data for velocity can be obtained only from repeated measurements of the same individuals at regular intervals. Growth
velocity values are small compared with distance values; therefore,
the measurements on which such standards are based must be obtained
meticulously. Measuring errors are potentially doubled when calculating velocity from two measurements. Further, it is essential
to measure all infants at the same ages or to correct the individual measurements to such set ages. During a period of very rapid
growth and of weekly measurements, as in preterm infants before the
expected date of delivery, variations of 2-3 days in ages at examinations will distort the growth curves. Therefore, the actual
examination ages must be corrected to the exact target ages; linear
interpolation can be used for this purpose. If data for varying
intervals are combined, the velocity curves tend to be flattened.

    The starting point of the growth curves should be postmenstrual
age at birth for preterm infants and the expected date of delivery
for full-term infants (40 weeks of gestation) irrespective of its
actual duration, for example, 39 to 41 weeks. According to
Hosemann (1949), the mean duration of gestation is 281-282 days
after the first day of the mother's last menstrual period. This
is in agreement with recent findings from Norway of Bjerkedal et
al. (1973) and of Hohenauer (1973).

THE SAMPLE

    The growth patterns presented here are based on a longitudinal
study from birth to the sixth year of age. The final sample consists of (a) 84 low risk full-term infants chosen at random; and
(b) 108 preterm infants with birthweights of 1500 g, admitted to

the Bonn University Children's Hospital between 1967 and 1975, and
some of higher birthweight, chosen at random.   In Bonn, the small
preterm infants of the surrounding obstetric departments are cared
for at the University Children's Hospital.   Infants with malformations and with severe neurologic handicaps have been excluded.
Using the criteria of postmenstrual age and birthweight, the preterm infants are classified to 64 AGA infants and 44 SGA infants.
Each of the latter had a birthweight below the 10th percentile of
Lubchenco et al. (1963).

The preterm infants were examined at intervals of one to two
weeks until their expected date of delivery.   All infants were
examined monthly during the first year, three-monthly in the second
year and six-monthly thereafter.

GENERAL GROWTH PATTERNS

Weight

Before the expected date of delivery, the extrauterine weight
gain of the preterm infants is smaller than that suggested for the
intrauterine fetus during the corresponding period.   Between 32 and
40 postmenstrual weeks, the mean weight curve of the preterm infants
follows approximately the 10th percentile of cross-sectional "intrauterine curves" from different sources (Brandt, 1978).

At term and at one month, the weight of the preterm infants
(Fig. 1, dotted lines) is still low and significantly less than
that of the full-term control infants (p < 0.01).   At 2 months the
weight curve (median, 10th and 90th percentiles) of the preterm
infants has reached that of the full-term control infants and from
then on there is no significant difference between the groups.
Therefore, the percentiles from 2 to 18 months in Fig. 1 are based
on preterm and full-term infants combined.

When considering weight, the age should be corrected for
prematurity from birth to 21 months; during this period there are
significant differences in weight amounting to 0.4-1.3 kg depending
on whether the ages of the preterm infants have been corrected.
From 24 months onwards this difference is between 100 and 200 g and
is no longer significant (p > 0.05), so that it is not necessary
to correct the ages.

Comparison between data from different countries for the age
range one month to 5 years shows the Bonn preterm and full-term
infants' weights are similar to those of full-term infants in other
studies in Europe (Tanner et al., 1966; Karlberg et al., 1976;
Prader and Budliger, 1977) and the U.S.A. (Hamill et al., 1977),

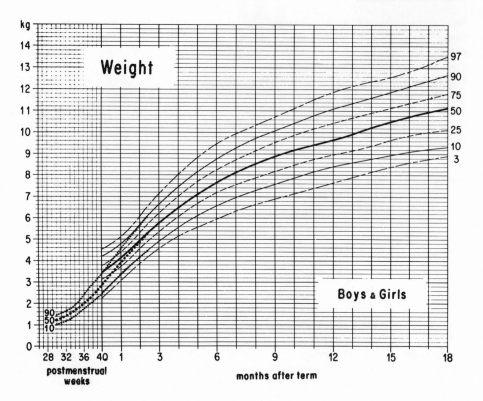

Fig. 1. Percentile curves for weight development, longitudinal;
•••• from 30 postmenstrual weeks to 2 months after term
AGA preterm infants, N = 64; ---- from 0 to 1 month full-
term infants, N = 84, and from 2 to 18 months for AGA
preterm and full-term infants combined, N = 148.

but the Bonn infants tend to be less heavy for their length. For
instance, at ages 3 through 24 months the median weights of the
Bonn full-term boys agree within 100 g with the results from the
U.S.A., but they are 1.0 to 1.5 cm longer (Brandt, 1978, 1979c).

The mean birthweight doubling time of the Bonn full-term
infants is 4.5 months in boys and 5 months in girls, which agrees
with the report of Lenz (1954) that birthweight is doubled within
the first 5 months on average. Neumann and Alpaugh (1976) reported
mean values of 3.6 months for boys and 4.1 months for girls in
California. The lower the birthweight of preterm infants, the
sooner it is doubled; for example, in a boy born at 31 postmenstrual
weeks with a birthweight of 1100 g, doubling occurred within 7 weeks.

Velocity curves of intrauterine or extrauterine growth in
weight in the perinatal period, derived from longitudinal data,

have not been available until recently. If mean weight velocities
are derived from the distance data of "intrauterine curves" from
different authors, there is a spurt between 32.5 and 36.5 postmenstrual weeks with a maximum velocity of about 1000 g per month
from 32.5 to 34.5 weeks; thereafter the velocity decreases to about
500 g per month at 39.5 postmenstrual weeks (Brandt, 1978).

The extrauterine mean weight velocity of the preterm infants
before term ranges from 380 g to 890 g per month and is significantly slower (p < 0.005) than in the first and second month after
term, when it amounts to 1000 g per month (Fig. 2, upper part).
The early postnatal retardation is caught up by the preterm infants
in the first month after term, when they gain significantly more
weight than full-term control infants (1000 g versus 640 g, Fig. 2,
lower part). The weight velocity of the preterm infants during
the second month is slightly, but not significantly, more rapid
than that of full-term infants (1000 g versus 950 g); thereafter
up to 5 years of age the weight velocity of the preterm infants
corresponds to that of the full-term control infants (p > 0.20).
In general, weight velocity slows from its peak of 950 g at 1.5
months, to 200 g at 19.5 months. Subsequently until 5 years,
weight velocity remains relatively constant, ranging between 170
and 200 g per month, with little or no sex difference.

As expected, weight velocity is the growth indicator that is
most dependent on caloric intake. The introduction of early and
high-caloric feeding of preterm infants according to the Tizard
scheme (Weber et al., 1976) has led to an extrauterine weight
velocity similar to that suggested for the fetus in the third
trimester. Most of the preterm infants in the Bonn study were
born before this change in postnatal nutrition.

Supine Length/Stature

The postnatal growth in length of the preterm infants before
expected date of delivery is slow, like that of weight. The 50th
percentile is markedly lower than the medians of "intrauterine
curves" from different authors (Brandt, 1978).

Between the expected date of delivery and 18 months of age
the preterm infants are significantly shorter (p < 0.01) than full-
term control infants; the difference decreases from 2.5 cm (term)
to 1.2 cm (18 months). After 21 months the difference decreases
to 0.9 cm and is no longer significant. In Figure 3, the 3rd,
50th and 97th percentiles of the preterm infants (boys above,
girls below) from 32 postmenstrual weeks to 4 months after term
(line of dots, shaded area) are compared with the percentiles for
full-term control infants. At the expected date of delivery, for
example, the 50th percentile of the preterm infants corresponds to
the 10th percentile of the full-term infants.

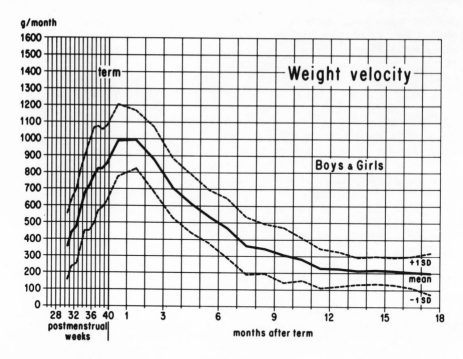

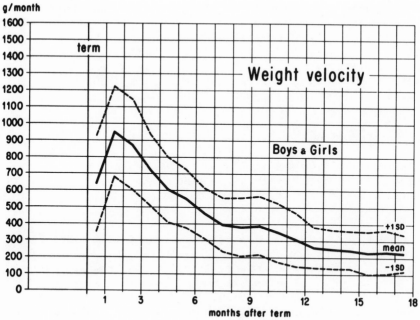

Fig. 2.   Velocity curves of weight from 30.5 postmenstrual weeks to
          17.5 months after expected date of delivery, mean and one
          standard deviation, unsmoothed values; above AGA preterm
          infants, N = 64; below full-term infants, N = 84.

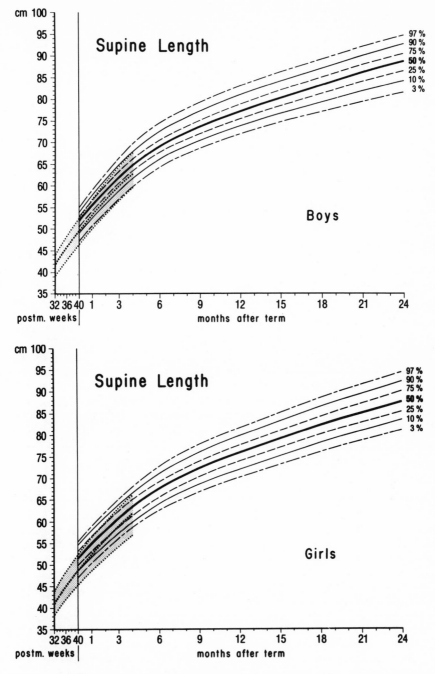

Fig. 3.   Supine length, percentiles, boys (above) and girls (below):
          32 postmenstrual weeks to 4 months (3, 50, 97, line of
          dots, shaded area) AGA preterm infants; 0 to 18 months (3
          to 97) full-term infants.

From 2 to 5 years of age, the median lengths of the preterm
infants tend to be 0.3-1.2 cm less than those of the full-term
infants, but the difference is not statistically significant.
Because the midparent stature for the preterm infants of 168.3 cm
is 1.5 cm less than of the full-term infants (169.8 cm), the small
difference in recumbent length between the groups may be attributed
to genetic factors rather than to preterm birth. Most other studies
report a tendency for preterm infants to remain shorter than full-
term infants during the first years after birth.

The necessary period for age adjustment to values for supine
length in premature infants is from birth to 3 years. There are
significant differences in recumbent length between corrected and
uncorrected ages for preterm infants that decrease from 7.7 cm at
birth to 1.4 cm at 3 years. From 3.5 to 5 years the difference
decreases to 0.9-1.0 cm and is nonsignificant. From 3.5 years
onwards, it is not necessary to correct for age.

Comparisons among data from various countries from one month
to 5 years of age show that the full-term infants of the Bonn study
are longer than the children of other European studies (Falkner,
1958; Sempé et al., 1964; Tanner et al., 1966; Spranger et al.,
1968; Bäckström and Kantero, 1971; Karlberg et al., 1976; Prader
and Budliger, 1977), and of the U.S.A. (Hamill et al., 1977). They
are of the same supine length/stature, or somewhat taller, as Dutch
infants (van Wieringen et al., 1971) who are among the tallest in
the world (Brandt, 1978).

The Bonn preterm infants' supine length after the age of 18
months, when they have surmounted their initial postnatal growth
retardation, is also similar to that of full-term infants in other
European studies. At 36 months, for example, the preterm boys and
girls are longer than full-term infants from Hamburg (Spranger et
al., 1968), London (Falkner, 1958; Tanner et al., 1966), Paris
(Sempé et al., 1964), and the U.S.A. (Hamill et al., 1977). They
agree well with the results from Stockholm (Karlberg et al., 1976);
the preterm girls are only 0.3 cm shorter than the Dutch girls (van
Wieringen et al., 1971). When a comparison is made with the growth
charts of Tanner et al. (1966), the median of the Bonn study
corresponds with the 75th percentile from the London study up to 5
years. There is a similar correspondence for German children of
older ages (Maaser, 1974; Kunze, 1974).

The mean extrauterine growth velocity in supine length of the
preterm infants from 30 to 40 postmenstrual weeks (Fig. 4, upper
part) is relatively constant, ranging from 3.3 to 4.0 cm per month.
It is similar to that during the first month after term of 3.8 cm
per month, which is the same in AGA preterm and full-term infants.

Supine length velocity has its peak much earlier in fetal life than weight and head circumference as demonstrated by Thompson (1942) who plotted the data from His (1874) calculated in cm per lunar month, i.e., 4 weeks. Between 4 and 5 lunar months, i.e., 16 and 20 weeks, there is a peak increment of 10 to 11 cm. Thereafter the velocity decreases to be about 4 cm per month at the age of 8 lunar months which is similar to the rate in the Bonn preterm infants (Fig. 4, upper part).

Recently this period of very rapid growth has been documented by repeated ultrasound measurements of fetal crown-rump length during early pregnancy using the technique introduced by Robinson (1973). Between the 9th and 15th week of gestation, the fetus grows in length at a high velocity, i.e., 1.6 mm per day on average according to Hackeloer and Hansmann (1976). Hansmann et al. (in press) have calculated a growth velocity for crown-rump length of 10-12 mm per week between 11 and 18 postmenstrual weeks. During this period, an estimation of gestational age, based on only one measurement of crown-rump length, is possible to ± 4.7 days, and by three independent measurements to ± 2.7 days with a reliability of 95% (Robinson and Fleming, 1975).

From the second to the eighth month, preterm infants (Fig. 4, upper part) grow significantly faster than full-term infants (Fig. 4, lower part; p < 0.05). Subsequently, up to 5 years, the growth velocity of preterm and full-term infants is either identical or the preterm infants grow a little faster but without a significant difference. The data suggest a protracted but complete "catch-up" of the initial postnatal retardation of growth in supine length of preterm infants.

In general, supine length velocity, calculated in cm per month, slows from its peak of 3.7 cm at 0.5 month, to 0.9 cm at 22.5 months, i.e., to about one-fourth. Subsequently until 5 years, supine length velocity decreases to 0.5 cm per month.

Ponderal Index of Rohrer

The ponderal index $\left(I = \dfrac{100 \times \text{weight in g}}{\text{supine length in cm}^3} \right)$

or weight-supine length ratio was introduced by Rohrer (1921) for assessment of nutritional status and for comparisons among groups of infants. This index has been used to judge the nutritional status of newborn infants (Lubchenco et al., 1966; Miller and Hassanein, 1971).

Between 30 and 40 postmenstrual weeks, the Rohrer index (50th percentile) increases from 2.33 to 2.62 (Lubchenco et al., 1966),

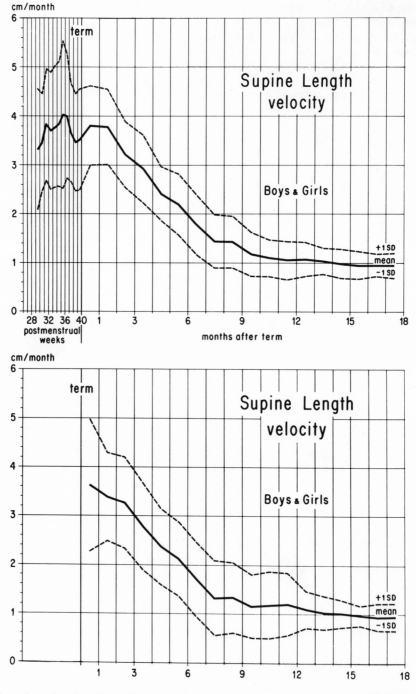

Fig. 4. Supine length velocity, calculated in cm per month, AGA
         preterm infants above and full-term infants below.

showing that the intrauterine fetus becomes heavier for supine
length during the last trimester of pregnancy. A corresponding
change does not occur during the extrauterine development of preterm infants. In these infants, between 30 and 40 postmenstrual
weeks, the 50th percentile of the Rohrer index ranges from 1.98 to
2.37, corresponding to the 10th percentile of Lubchenco et al.
(1966); thus the preterm infants are light for their supine length.
In SGA infants, the Rohrer index demonstrates clearly the growth
retardation in weight and the risk of hypoglycemia because of the
lack of energy reserves (Brandt, in press). Therefore a calculation of the Rohrer index is recommended in newborns with intrauterine malnutrition.

Head Circumference

     Growth in head circumference is closely related to brain size
in the first year as has been shown in many studies. Recently Buda
et al. (1975) reported a "strong linear relation between occipito-
frontal head circumference and calculated skull volume in infants
with normally shaped skulls" with a correlation coefficient of
0.97. Regular postnatal measurements of head circumference are of
prognostic value, because growth is very rapid in the first 6 to 9
months, and easily disturbed by illness or malnutrition. This
danger exists not only in the developing countries but also in the
industrialized nations.

     Head circumference is measured horizontally around the great-
est occipito-frontal diameter, exerting light pressure with a
fibreglass tape. For accuracy, it is advisable to do this measurement in a sitting or standing position, because many infants resist
being put in a supine position. Usually the zero point on the tape
is located over the glabella.

     The postnatal growth of head circumference of the preterm
infants before expected date of delivery is similar to that for the
intrauterine fetus (Brandt, 1978). The mean growth curve of preterm
infants corresponds with "intrauterine curves" apart from a slight
initial retardation that may be due to adaptation to extrauterine
life and to delayed feeding in some infants. From term to 6 years,
the growth in head circumference of the preterm infants is identical
with that of the full-term control infants (p > 0.1). Contrary to
the findings for weight and supine length, growth in head circumference is not diminished (Brandt, 1978, 1979b).

     The necessary period for age adjustment is from birth to 17
months, because there are significant differences in head circumference between corrected and uncorrected age, decreasing from 6.3
to 0.5 cm (Fig. 5). With further decreasing growth velocity, this
difference diminishes and becomes nonsignificant at 18 months,

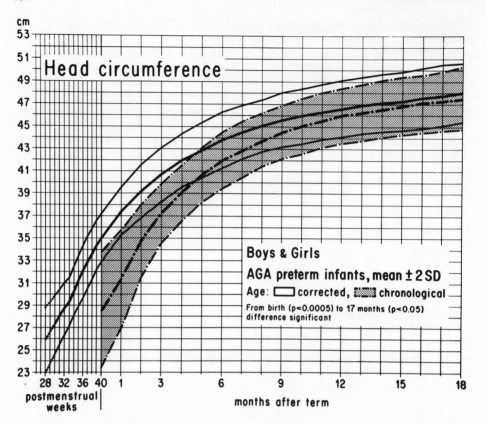

Fig. 5.   Head circumference of AGA preterm infants, mean and two
          standard deviations; corrected age (clear area, continu-
          ous lines) versus uncorrected age (shaded area, broken
          lines).

being then 0.4 cm. At 6 years it is only 0.04 cm. This "assimi-
lation" of the non-age-corrected curve to the corrected curve,
which is due to the rapid decrease in growth velocity, has led to
erroneous assumptions of catch-up growth in normal AGA preterm
infants. In other studies of preterm infants, where postmenstrual
age has been considered and the infants have been grouped into AGA
and SGA, growth in head circumference of the AGA infants agrees
with national standards (Babson, 1970; Davies, 1975; Fitzhardinge,
1975).

     Comparisons among studies from different countries show the
Bonn preterm and full-term infants' head circumferences are smaller
than those of full-term infants of the Berkeley Growth Study
(Eichorn and Bayley, 1962) and similar or bigger than those of
full-term infants of other European studies (Tanner et al., 1966;

Karlberg et al., 1976; Prader and Budliger, 1977) and of the U.S.A.
(Hamill et al., 1977). For example, at 12 months the preterm boys'
mean head circumference of 47.1 cm is similar to those from the
U.S.A. and Zurich (47.0 cm; Hamill et al., 1977; Prader and
Budliger, 1977). At 36 months, the preterm girls' mean head circumference of 49.5 cm agrees well with data from Hamburg (Spranger
et al., 1968), London (Falkner, 1958), Oxford (Westropp and Barber,
1956), and Zurich (Prader and Budliger, 1977). The head circumference of the Bonn infants agrees also with the "composite international and interracial graphs" of Nellhaus (1968) with a tendency
for the Bonn values to be larger.

The extrauterine mean growth velocity of head circumference
for the preterm infants, calculated in centimeters per month, from
30 to 40 postmenstrual weeks is significantly more rapid than after
term with a peak of 4.3 cm at 33.5 weeks (Fig. 6, upper part).

Soon after term, the velocity slows markedly. In the first
month it is 2.5 cm in the preterm infants and is similar to that
of the full-term control infants who grow 2.4 cm per month (Fig. 6,
lower part). At 6 months, the velocity has slowed in both groups
to 0.8 cm per month. Thus a period of rapid head growth extends
from the 31st postmenstrual week to the sixth month after term,
corresponding to a phase of rapid brain development. Subsequently
the velocity of growth in head circumference in the preterm infants
agrees with that of the full-term control infants. At 4.5 years of
age, the velocity decreases to 0.04 cm/month which is only one-
hundredth of the peak rate during the 34th postmenstrual week.
During the subsequent months to 6 years of age, the velocity remains
at about this level.

If age is not corrected for prematurity, the peak of the
velocity curve becomes flat and does not demonstrate the individual
growth rate. A similar observation can be made for stature velocity
at puberty where the peak broadens and flattens if the different
maturity stages of children of the same chronological age are not
considered in calculating the mean growth spurt (Tanner et al.,
1966).

Relationship Between Head Circumference Growth and Brain Size

Recently Dobbing and Sands (1978) published an approximate
formula linking head circumference and brain weight:

$$g = \frac{x^3}{100} - \frac{3000}{2x} \qquad \text{where } g = \text{brain weight in g} \quad \text{and} \\ x = \text{head circumference in cm}$$

This formula makes it possible to convert longitudinal head

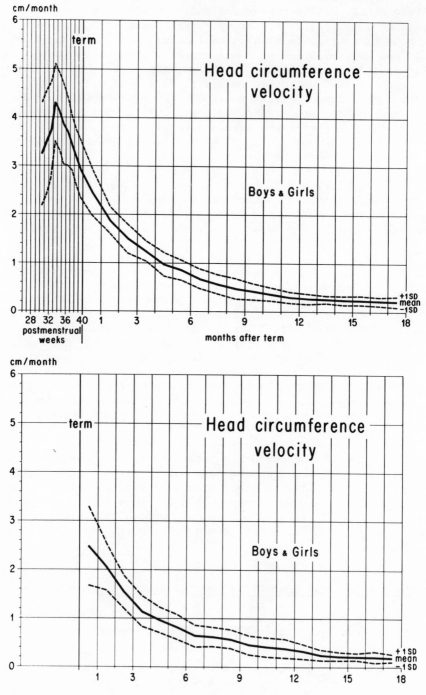

Fig. 6.   Head circumference velocity, calculated in cm per month,
          AGA preterm infants above and full-term infants below.

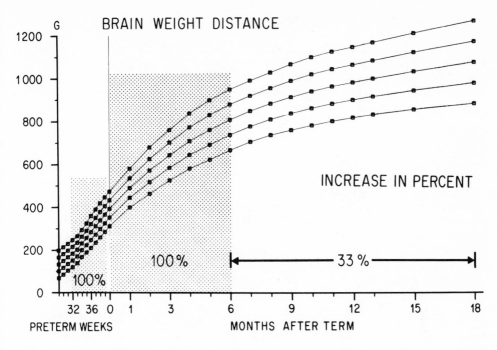

Fig. 7.   Calculated brain weight (g) of AGA preterm infants (mean
± 1 and 2 s.d.).

circumference data of AGA preterm infants to estimated brain
weights. Fig. 7 demonstrates unsmoothed estimated brain weights
from 29 postmenstrual weeks to 18 months after term. The high
growth rate during the perinatal period, defined as the time between
28 postmenstrual weeks and the seventh day after term, is evident.
Between 32 and 39 weeks the brain doubles in weight from 183 g to
365 g. During the first six months after term, brain weight is
doubled again, i.e., from 391 g at term to 807 g at 6 months.
Thereafter growth slows considerably; at 18 months brain weight
amounts to 1072 g, an increase of only 32% over the value at 6
months.

A comparison of the calculated brain weight of preterm infants
from 30 to 40 postmenstrual weeks shows a close correspondence with
brain weight data from autopsies of normal infants published by
Larroche and Maunoury (1973) and by Gruenwald and Minh (1960). For
example, brain weight at 38 weeks amounts to 339 g in all three
groups.

GROWTH PATTERNS OF SGA PRETERM INFANTS: CATCH-UP

Since the classic publication of Prader et al. (1963) on catch-up growth following illness or starvation, this concept has been accepted in pediatrics and has attained increasing relevance. Catch-up has occurred when the measurements of SGA preterm infants, being significantly below the mean at birth, reach the values for the full-term control infants; this is achieved by a period of significantly more rapid growth velocity than in the control infants.

Head circumference catch-up growth has been chosen here as a criterion for separation of the heterogeneous SGA preterm infants into two groups, after excluding infants with malformations and prenatal infections. In Group A (N = 22) there was catch-up growth in head circumference. In Group B (N = 22) there was no catch-up growth in head circumference. Due to the rapidly decreasing growth velocity of head circumference after 6 months of age, it could be suggested that the chance for catch-up occurs only during the first 6 to 9 months of life.

Until recently, catch-up growth of head circumference, and thus presumably of the brain, after intrauterine growth retardation has not been reported except by Falkner (1966) and Babson and Henderson (1974), and information has not been reported about the timing of the catch-up. Also Commey and Fitzhardinge (1979), in their recent study of 71 SGA preterm infants, did not observe catch-up growth. Catch-up growth in supine length and/or weight has been observed at later ages independently of whether catch-up has or has not occurred in head circumference (Stoch and Smythe, 1976; Varloteaux et al., 1976).

The postnatal head circumference measurements of a group of 22 SGA preterm infants of the Bonn study with a mean birthweight of 1380 g and a mean postmenstrual age of 34.5 weeks were significantly below the norms for AGA preterm infants from 34 to 40 postmenstrual weeks, and remained so until one month after term (Table 1). By 2 months after term, the means approach the values of the AGA control infants; the difference of 0.5 cm between the groups is not significant ($p > 0.05$). At the age of 6 months, the difference is 0.3 cm (nonsignificant), and by 12 months the mean for the SGA infants is within 0.2 cm of the mean for the AGA control infants and remains this close until the age of 5 years. This signifies these SGA infants have exhibited complete catch-up after their prenatal retardation (Brandt, 1978). This catch-up is brought about by significantly more rapid growth velocity than normal at 35.5 postmenstrual weeks ($p < 0.01$) and also at 1.5 months after term ($p < 0.05$).

Table 1. Head Circumference of AGA Preterm Infants Compared to SGA Preterm Infants with Catch-up Growth (Mean, Boys and Girls)

Corrected age	AGA preterm infants	SGA preterm infants	Difference between AGA and SGA
36 postmenstrual weeks	32.1 cm	30.4 cm	1.7 cm ($p < 0.0005$)
40 postmenstrual weeks	35.1 cm	33.9 cm	1.2 cm ($p < 0.0025$)
6 months	43.7 cm	43.4 cm	0.3 cm ($p > 0.1$)

Two major groups of factors favor catch-up growth. First, early diagnosis of intrauterine growth retardation by ultrasound, follow-up and prenatal care; and secondly, nutrition and postnatal care. The amount of calories given seems to play an important role in the further development of very small SGA infants. The capacity for "catch-up" depends on the duration, the timing and the severity of restriction. Further, the different growth patterns of weight, supine length and head circumference suggest that the capacity for catch-up depends also on the specific velocity (Brandt, 1976). When growth has slowed significantly, as for head circumference by the tenth month of life, one may assume that beyond this age there is little chance for catch-up after an intrauterine or early post-natal retardation. Supine length and weight velocity, however, decrease in the tenth month only to one-third of their mean peak velocity during the perinatal period and in the fifth year to about one-sixth of this velocity. These data suggest a continuing capacity for catch-up in these measurements if nutrition is adequate. The extent to which intrauterine deprivation can be tolerated without resultant damage, and of the conditions under which prenatal growth retardation of head circumference can be overcome by catch-up after birth, needs further research. Even if several factors are involved in intrauterine growth retardation, there exists, at least in children with malnutrition, the chance to overcome resultant deficits by early and adequate postnatal nutrition.

ACKNOWLEDGMENTS

This research was carried out with grants from the Bundes-minister für Jugend, Familie und Gesundheit, from the Minister für Wissenschaft und Forschung des Landes Nordrhein-Westfalen, and from the Fritz Thyssen Stiftung which are gratefully acknowledged. My thanks are due to my colleagues and assistants for support of this study at the University Children's Hospital Bonn (Director:

Professor Dr. Heinz Hungerland until 1974, and Professor Dr. Walther
Burmeister from 1975).

I particularly wish to thank all the mothers and fathers in the
study for their faithful cooperation, without which the frequent
examinations at regular intervals would not have been possible.

REFERENCES

Babson, S. G., 1970, Growth of low-birth-weight infants, J. Pediatr.,
    77:11.
Babson, S. G., and Henderson, N. B., 1974, Fetal undergrowth:
    Relation of head growth to later intellectual performance,
    Pediatrics, 53:890.
Bäckström, L., and Kantero, R.-L., 1971, Cross-sectional studies of
    height and weight in Finnish children aged from birth to 20
    years, Acta paediatr. Scand., Suppl. 220:9.
Bjerkedal, T., Bakketeig, L., and Lehmann, E. H., 1973, Percentiles
    of birth weights of single, live births at different gesta-
    tion periods, Acta paediatr. Scand., 62:449.
Brandt, I., 1976, Growth dynamics before and after term, including
    catch-up growth in weight, length and head circumference of
    preterm infants, in: "Perinatal Medicine," G. Rooth and
    L.-E. Bratteby, eds., Almqvist & Wiksell International,
    Stockholm.
Brandt, I., 1978, Growth dynamics of low-birth-weight infants with
    emphasis on the perinatal period, in: "Human Growth," Vol. 2,
    F. Falkner and J. M. Tanner, eds., Plenum Publishing Cor-
    poration, New York.
Brandt, I., 1979a, Patterns of early neurological development, in:
    "Human Growth," Vol. 3, F. Falkner and J. M. Tanner, eds.,
    Plenum Publishing Corporation, New York.
Brandt, I., 1979b, Perzentilkurven für das Kopfumfangswachstum bei
    Früh- und Reifgeborenen in den ersten sechs Jahren, der
    kinderarzt, 10:185.
Brandt, I., 1979c, Perzentilkurven für die Gewichtsentwicklung bei
    Früh- und Reifgeborenen in den ersten fünf Jahren, der
    kinderarzt, 10:713.
Brandt, I., in press, Hirnwachstum bei fetaler Mangelversorgung und
    die Hypoglykämiegefahr - Klinische Konsequenzen, Klin.
    Pädiat.
Buda, F. B., Reed, J. C., and Rabe, E. F., 1975, Skull volume in
    infants - methodology, normal values, and application,
    Am. J. Dis. Child., 129:1171.
Commey, J. O. O., and Fitzhardinge, P. M., 1979, Handicap in the
    preterm small-for-gestational-age infant, J. Pediatr., 94:
    779.

Davies, P. A., 1975, Perinatal nutrition of infants of very low
     birth weight and their later progress, Mod. Probl. Paediatr.,
     14:119.
Dobbing, J., and Sands, J., 1978, Head circumference, biparietal
     diameter and brain growth in fetal and postnatal life, Early
     Hum. Dev., 2:81.
Eichorn, D. H., and Bayley, N., 1962, Growth in head circumference
     from birth through young adulthood, Child Dev., 33:257.
Falkner, F., 1958, Some physical measurements in the first three
     years of life, Arch. Dis. Childh., 33:1.
Falkner, F., 1966, General considerations in human development, in:
     "Human Development," F. Falkner, ed., W. B. Saunders
     Company, Philadelphia.
Fitzhardinge, P. M., 1975, Early growth and development in low-
     birthweight infants following treatment in an intensive
     care nursery, Pediatrics, 56:162.
Gruenwald, P., and Minh, H., 1960, Evaluation of body and organ
     weights in perinatal pathology. I. Normal standards derived
     from autopsies, Am. J. Clin. Path., 34:247.
Hackeloer, B.-J., and Hansmann, M., 1976, Ultraschalldiagnostik in
     der Frühschwangerschaft, Gynäkologe, 9:108.
Hamill, P. V. V., Drizd, T. A., Johnson, C. L., Reed, R. B., and
     Roche, A. F., 1977, "NCHS Growth Curves for Children.
     Birth-18 years, United States," Vital and Health Statistics
     Series 11, No. 165, DHEW Publ. No. (PHS) 78-1650, U.S.
     Government Printing Office, Washington, D.C.
Hansmann, M., Schuhmacher, H., Foebus, J., and Voigt, U., in
     press, Ultraschallbiometrie der fetalen Scheitelsteisslänge
     in der ersten Schwangerschaftshälfte, Geburtsh. u.
     Frauenheilk.
His, W., 1874, "Unsere Körperform und das physiologische Problem
     ihrer Entstehung," Verlag von F. C. W. Vogel, Leipzig.
Hohenauer, L., 1973, Intrauterines Längen- und Gewichtswachstum,
     Pädiat. Pädol., 8:195.
Hosemann, H., 1949, Schwangerschaftsdauer und Neugeborenengewicht,
     Arch. Gynäk., 176:109.
Karlberg, P., Taranger, J., Engström, I., Lichtenstein, H., and
     Svennberg-Redegren, I., 1976, The somatic development of
     children in a Swedish urban community. A prospective
     longitudinal study, Acta paediat. Scand., Suppl. 258:1.
Kunze, D., 1974, Percentilkurven von Körpergrösse und Körpergewicht
     6-14jähriger Kinder, Klin. Pädiat., 186:505.
Larroche, J.-C., and Maunoury, M.-T., 1973, Analyse statistique de
     la croissance pondérale du foetus et des viscères pendant
     la vie intra-uterine, Arch. Franç. Pédiat., 30:927.
Lenz, W., 1954, 2. Aufl., Wachstum: Körpergewicht und Körperlänge.
     Proportionen. Habitus, in: "Biologische Daten für den
     Kinderarzt," Bd. 1, J. Brock, ed., Springer Verlag, Berlin,
     Göttingen, Heidelberg.

Lubchenco, L. O., Hansman, C., Dressler, M., and Boyd, E., 1963, Intrauterine growth as estimated from live born birth-weight data at 24 to 42 weeks of gestation, Pediatrics, 32:793.

Lubchenco, L. O., Hansman, C., and Boyd, E., 1966, Intrauterine growth in length and head circumference as estimated from live births at gestational ages from 26 to 42 weeks, Pediatrics, 37:403.

Maaser, R., 1974, Eine Untersuchung gebräuchlicher Längen-Gewichtstabellen. Zugleich ein Vorschlag für ein Somatogramm O - 14jähriger Kinder, Mschr. Kinderheilk., 122:146.

Miller, H. C., and Hassanein, K., 1971, Diagnosis of impaired fetal growth in newborn infants, Pediatrics, 48:511.

Nellhaus, G., 1968, Head circumference from birth to eighteen years: Practical composite international and interracial graphs, Pediatrics, 41:106.

Nellhaus, G., 1975, Practical composite international and interracial head circumference graphs: A reappraisal, Abstracts 1st International Congress of Child Neurology, Toronto.

Neumann, C. G., and Alpaugh, M., 1976, Birthweight doubling time: A fresh look, Pediatrics, 57:469.

Prader, A., Tanner, J. M., and von Harnack, G. A., 1963, Catch-up growth following illness or starvation. An example of developmental canalization in man, J. Pediatr., 62:646.

Prader, A., and Budliger, H., 1977, Körpermasse, Wachstumsgeschwindigkeit und Knochenalter gesunder Kinder in den ersten zwölf Jahren (Longitudinale Wachstumsstudie Zürich), Helv. Paediat. Acta, Suppl. 37:1.

Robinson, H. P., 1973, Sonar measurement of fetal crown-rump-length as means of assessing maturity in first trimester of pregnancy, Brit. Med. J., iv:28.

Robinson, H. P., and Fleming, J. E. E., 1975, A critical evaluation of sonar "crown-rump-length" measurements, Brit. J. Obstet. Gynaec., 82:702.

Rohrer, F., 1921, Der Index der Körperfülle als Mass des Ernährungszustandes, Münch. Med. Wschr., 68:580.

Sempé, M., Tutin, C., and Masse, N. P., 1964, La croissance de l'enfant de 0 à 7 ans, Arch. Franç. Pédiat., 21:111.

Spranger, J., Ochsenfarth, A., Kock, H. P., and Henke, J., 1968, Anthropometrische Normdaten im Kindesalter, Z. Kinderheilk., 103:1.

Stoch, M. B., and Smythe, P. M., 1976, 15-year developmental study on effects of severe undernutrition during infancy on subsequent physical growth and intellectual functioning, Arch. Dis. Childh., 51:327.

Tanner, J. M., Whitehouse, R. H., and Takaishi, M., 1966, Standards from birth to maturity for height, weight, height velocity, and weight velocity: British children, 1965, Arch. Dis. Childh., 41:454 and 613.

Thompson, D. W., 1942, "On Growth and Form," Cambridge University Press, Cambridge.

Varloteaux, C.-H., Gilbert, Y., Beaudoing, A., Roget, J., and
Rambaud, P., 1976, Avenir lointain de 128 enfants agés de
13 à 14 ans de poids de naissance inferieur à 2500 grammes,
Arch. Franç. Pédiat., 33:233.

Weber, H. P., Kowalewski, S., Gilje, A., Möllering, M., Schnaufer,
I., and Fink, H., 1976, Unterschiedliche Calorienzufuhr
bei 75 "low birth weights": Einfluss auf Gewichtszunahme,
Serumeiweiss, Blutzucker und Serumbilirubin, Eur. J.
Pediatr., 122:207.

Westropp, C. K., and Barber, C. R., 1956, Growth of the skull in
young children. Part I: Standards of head circumference,
J. Neurol. Neurosurg. Psychiat., 19:52.

Wieringen van, J. C., Wafelbakker, F., Verbrugge, H. P., and Haas
de, J. H., 1971, "Growth Diagrams 1965 Netherlands Second
National Survey on 0-24-Years-Olds," Wolters-Noordhoff
Publishing, Groningen.

9. ADOLESCENT GROWTH

Roland Hauspie

Belgian National Science Foundation
Free University Brussels
Pleinlaan 2, 1050 Brussels, Belgium

A major characteristic of the normal pattern of growth is the presence of an adolescent growth spurt during the second decade of life. This spurt is a marked acceleration in growth of most body dimensions during a period of about two years, leading towards a peak in growth velocity. After reaching this maximum rate, growth slows down and finally reaches a more or less stable level, mature size. Although universally present in all normal boys and girls, there is a great variability in the timing and the intensity of the spurt among different individuals, among sexes and among different body dimensions.

The adolescent growth spurt is important because about 20% of adult size is completed during this period and most of the sex differences in adult phenotype are brought about by differential patterns of adolescent growth among boys and girls. Considerable shape changes within an individual also occur during the adolescent cycle as a result of differential growth rates in various body dimensions.

The present paper attempts to summarize and discuss some major findings related to adolescent growth, its variation in timing, and sex differences and interrelationships of different aspects of the pattern of growth.

DIFFERENTIAL TIMING OF THE ADOLESCENT SPURT IN DIFFERENT BODY MEASURES WITHIN THE SAME INDIVIDUAL

The mean ages at which the adolescent growth spurts are observed in various body dimensions are quite similar but neverthe-

Table 1. Differences (in years) Between Mean Age at Peak Velocity
          in Various Body Dimensions and Mean Age at Peak Height
          Velocity

	Sitting Height		Leg Length		Biacromial Diameter		Biiliac Diameter		Weight	
	BOYS	GIRLS	BOYS	GIRLS	BOYS	GIRLS	BOYS	GIRLS	BOYS	GIRLS
(1)	.34	.32	-.33	-.30	.30	.35	.07	.37		
(2)		.40		-.60		-.20		-.40		.60
(3)		.32		-.53				-.23		.63
(4)	.24	.32	-.27	-.25	.26	.51				
(5)									.3	.6
Aver.	.3	.3	-.3	-.4	.3	.2	.1	-.1	.3	.6

(1) Tanner et al., 1976
(2) Bielicki and Welon, 1973
(3) Bielicki, 1975
(4) Marubini et al., 1972
(5) Lindgren, 1978

less tend to occur in a more or less constant sequence. The differences in timing of the take-off of the adolescent spurt in different measurements, being of the order of one month in both sexes,
is less pronounced than the timing of peak velocity. Some comparable figures on the differences between mean age at peak velocity
in various body dimensions and mean age at peak height velocity,
as seen in different samples, are shown in Table 1. From this
table it seems that only for leg length, sitting height and weight
are the data somewhat homogenous among the different samples. Mean
age at peak length velocity in the legs precedes peak height velocity on the average by 0.3 years in boys and by 0.4 years in girls,
while the mean age of peak growth in trunk length is on the average
0.3 years later than age at peak height velocity. Weight reaches
a peak about 0.6 years after height in girls and the only figure
available for boys indicates a delay of 0.3 years. The scatter in
the values of the differences is much greater for the two transverse diameters (biacromial diameter, biiliac diameter). This may
be partly due to the greater difficulty in determining the peak of
the growth spurt for these body dimensions. If, however, we consider this variation to be due to errors in sampling and technique
and we use the average value as an indication, it seems that the
peak for growth in hip width coincides almost with peak height velocity, while the peak in biacromial diameter lags behind the peak
in height growth, but is close to the peak for sitting height.
This order is in agreement with Tanner (1962); also, he reported

that chest breadth coincides in timing with hip width, while the spurt in chest depth occurs at the same mean age as the spurt in trunk length. Furthermore, he stated that the peripheral parts of the limbs tend to have their spurts earlier than the more proximal parts. Lindgren (1978) found that the mean time difference between the peak in height and that in weight decreased with the time of occurrence in a highly significant manner. In boys with late age of peak velocities, the mean age at peak weight velocity was slightly younger than the mean age at peak height velocity.

Singh (1976) measured longitudinally the growth in trunk surface area in boys and found that the thoracic and abdominal surface had a peak in growth, very close to the age at peak height velocity of the same children. The maximum rate of muscle growth occurs at the same mean age as the minimal increase in subcutaneous fat thickness; both are very close in timing to peak height velocity (Marshall, 1970). Finally, the maximum rate of growth of head width and of the mandibular length coincides with peak height velocity (Singh et al., 1967; Thompson et al., 1976).

In fact, the differences between mean ages at peak velocity in different parts of the body are rather small and it was not surprising that the variability of timing of maximum growth rate is reflected in individual sequence variability (Roche, 1974). Roche observed that among nine girls selected from the Fels sample, none followed the mean order. He suggested a true biological variation in the order, but it seems likely that some error, introduced by estimating the peak, has contributed at least in part to the observed variability.

SEX DIMORPHISM IN ADULT STATURE

Although sex difference in stature before adolescence is only slightly pronounced, boys being on the average slightly taller than girls, mature height differs significantly between the sexes. Deming (1957) found a significant mean difference of 14.5 cm between the statures of men and women when fitting the Gompertz function to longitudinal growth data of 24 boys and 24 girls. She concluded that the pattern of growth in length during adolescence is characterized by a larger total gain in boys than in girls. The sex difference in adult height was brought about by a 5.3 cm greater adolescent gain in boys (K-parameter) and by a 9 cm greater lower asymptote in boys. Somewhat different conclusions were reached by Tanner et al. (1976). These workers analyzed longitudinally the growth in height of Harpenden boys and girls by means of the logistic function. They reported that the sex difference in adult height is mainly due to the later onset of the pubertal growth spurt in boys than in girls, rather than to a difference in adolescent gain. Table 2 shows comparable data on

Table 2. Components of Sex Difference in Adult Height

	Sex difference at girls' age of take-off (cm)	Amount due to boys' delay in spurt (cm)	Amount due to boys' greater adolescent spurt (cm)	Adult sex difference for stature (cm)
(1)	1.0	7.0	2.5	10.5
(2)	1.6	6.4	4.6	12.5
(3)	1.3	9.0	4.2	14.5
(4)	3.3	4.7	6.0	14.0

(1) Harpenden Growth Study (Tanner et al., 1976)
(2) Zurich Longitudinal Study (Largo et al., 1978)
(3) Health Examination Survey (Hamill et al., 1973)
(4) Sarsuna-Barisha Growth Study (Hauspie et al., unpublished data)

the components of sex difference in adult stature observed in four different samples. From Tanner's data it can be seen that the means for height in boys exceed those for girls by about 1.0 cm at the girls' age of take-off. A gain of 7 cm is experienced by the boys between age at take-off in the girls and age at take-off in the boys; this is the amount due to the boys' delay in onset of the adolescent spurt. The greater adolescent gain in height in boys amounts to only 2.5 cm. Some of the discrepancies between the observations of Deming and those of Tanner may be due to a difference in defining adolescent gain. Deming's adolescent gain is defined as the difference between the upper and lower asymptote of the fitted Gompertz function. Tanner's value is the adult height less height at take-off, which is closer to the real adolescent gain.

Similar figures were derived from Swiss data (Largo et al., 1978). Although less pronounced than in the British sample, the sex difference in adult height in this group is due more to the delay of the spurt in boys than to a greater adolescent gain in boys. The data in this sample were analyzed by smoothing spline functions and take-off was defined as the point of minimal pre-spurt velocity in height. An American cross-sectional sample (Hamill et al., 1973), again, shows an important contribution of the delay in the adolescent spurt in boys to the sex difference in adult height. The sex difference in adult height observed in Indian (Bengali) boys and girls (Hauspie et al., unpublished data) seems to be brought about in a different way. The sample consisted of 63 boys and 42 girls, analyzed longitudinally by fitting Preece Model I (Preece and Baines, 1978). The point at take-off was determined as the age of minimal prepubertal height velocity

and the adolescent gain as the difference between adult size and
size at take-off. The striking dissimilarity with the previous
studies is in the greater prepubertal sex difference in height of
3.3 cm and in the relatively smaller adult stature difference due
to the delay in the spurts of boys.

Some differences observed among different samples may be explained in different ways. Perhaps the various techniques for
estimating the growth parameters are partly responsible for the
observed differences. Population differences in the patterns of
growth may also be responsible for some of the variation observed
among the four studies. Valenzuela et al. (1978) stated that
there is a strong genetic component of sex dimorphism in adult
stature; this is confirmed by Eveleth (1975). In the case of the
Indian data, the relatively greater prepubertal growth of boys
compared to girls may, to some extent, be due to better treatment
of boys in this society. This mechanism was sugggested by Eveleth
(1975) to explain the relatively greater sex dimorphism of adult
height in Amerindians, compared to other populations. Pingle
(personal communication) suggests the same mechanism, when analyzing sex dimorphism in adult height in various rural groups in
Andra Pradesh (India). Bock et al. (1973) stated that the differences in adult height, not only between but also within sex, are
determined more by the differential timing of the adolescent cycle
than by variations in the amount of growth during this period.
Finally, the generally slightly greater adolescent gain in height
growth in boys is due to a slightly longer period of growth, rather
than to the minor difference in peak velocity (Deming, 1957;
Malina, 1974).

SEX DIFFERENCES IN MEASURES OTHER THAN STATURE

Sex differences may appear at all parts of the growth cycle,
as early as during foetal life, or gradually during the course of
the growth period, or at adolescence (Tanner, 1962; Miklashevskaya,
1969). They occur in most body measurements and are usually slight
during childhood; it is particularly during adolescence that most
of the anthropometric differences between males and females
become obvious (Malina, 1974). The mean patterns of growth of
most skeletal body dimensions in boys exceed very slightly those
observed in girls during childhood. Then comes a period during
which girls overtake the boys, due to the earlier onset of the
adolescent spurt in girls. This period during which the means for
girls are larger than those for boys lasts for about 2.5 years,
after which the boys grow to a greater mean size than girls for
almost all body dimensions.

Sex dimorphism in adult stature has already been discussed,
but it is interesting to note that the two main components of

height, trunk length (or sitting height) and leg length, behave
somewhat differently in their expression of sex difference. The
relative length of the legs is greater in men than in women.
Tanner (1962) explains this as being the result of the combined
effect of the delay in the boys' adolescent spurt and the relatively more rapid growth rate of the legs during the period just before
this spurt, giving a greater gain in leg length, in proportion to
stature, before the spurt. The effect of this is reflected in the
sitting height/height index which is almost identical in boys and
girls up to the age of 11 years, but becomes slightly higher in
girls after that age (Malina, 1974). The relatively longer arm
length in boys is partly due to the same mechanism as the one
acting on leg length but in the arm the sex difference is also in
part due to a more rapid growth rate in boys than girls, starting
at an early age (Tanner, 1962).

        The sex differences in transverse diameters is quite obvious
in adults with men having wider shoulders and women having relatively wider hips. The absolute amount of growth in hip width is
about the same in boys and girls, but the adolescent spurt in
biacromial diameter is much larger in boys (Bayley, 1943;
Marshall, 1970; Malina, 1974).

        The sex differences in head and face dimensions differ from
those for most other body measurements in that the mean values for
boys are larger than those for girls at all ages; consequently,
there is no crossing of the mean growth curves of boys and girls.
Within a particular racial or regional group, boys tend to have
larger head circumferences than girls (Meredith, 1971; Kantero and
Tiisala, 1971). Similar findings for bigonial diameter were reported by Newman and Meredith (1956). However, in the sample
studied by Hautvast (1971), morphological face height and also
bizygomatic diameter in boys exceed temporarily the mean values
for girls.

GROWTH OF THE HEAD AND FACE

        The head and the face have a pattern of growth that is quite
different from that of the rest of the body. At young ages, the
growth of the head is well advanced in its development compared to
height. About 70% of adult height is achieved by the age of 6
years, but the head has already completed 90% of its adult size
by that age (Baughan et al., 1979). Tanner (1962) reports that
head length, breadth and circumference are about 96% of adult size
at the age of 10 years. This pattern of growth has been defined
by Scammon (1930) as the neural type. Growth of the brain case is
related to the growth of the brain, but growth of the face,
although in contact with cranial structures, develops relatively
independently (Graber, 1966). This was shown by Newman and

Meredith (1956) who reported independence between the patterns of growth of biparietal diameter and bigonial diameter, but a great similarity between the growth of the upper and lower jaws. The growth of morphological face height and partly also of bizygomatic breadth is visceral in type, as is the case for most skeletal structures (Hautvast, 1971). Studying craniofacial growth in French-Canadian girls, Baughan et al. (1979) discerned a differential pattern for the cranial base (sella-nasion), the height of the face and the length of the mandible. The head had achieved 92% of its 15-year-old size by the age of 6 years; the face had achieved about 83%. Miklashevskaya (1969) showed that the growth of the upper part of the face is more advanced than that for the lower part. Some, if not all, of these observations may be interpreted in the light of the general cephalocaudad gradient discussed by Tanner (1962).

Goldstein (1939) and Shuttleworth (1939) showed that some parts of the head respond to the "general stimulus" at adolescence. The use of lateral radiographs of the head and the face in more recent studies has greatly enhanced the accuracy of the studies of individual patterns of growth. An adolescent spurt in the growth of facial dimensions has been shown clearly. However, it has been a matter of discussion for a long time whether the brain case has a growth spurt as well (Tanner, 1962). Meredith (1971), however, studied longitudinally the growth of the frontal bone as the rectilinear distance from nasion to bregma in girls during childhood and adolescence and discovered in 60% of the individuals an adolescent spurt coinciding with or occurring near the time of peak height velocity. The other 40% of girls showed a steady increase with decreasing velocity. A recent study by Lestrel and Brown (1976) has provided some more evidence for a spurt in head dimensions. They analyzed growth of the cranial vault longitudinally, applying Fourier analysis, and demonstrated an adolescent growth spurt in the cranial vault coinciding with peak height velocity. They could not find a substantial thickening of the cranial vault related to the spurt of the ectocranium but, at least for boys, there was a spurt for the endocranial size, suggesting a possible involvement of neural tissue in the adolescent spurt.

Peak growth velocity for facial measurements is reached on average a few months after peak height velocity according to Nanda (1955) but Baughan et al. (1979) reported that the maximum increment for most facial measures occurs between 6 months and 1 year after peak height velocity. A differential adolescent pattern of growth between and within bones of the face is observed, also, entailing considerable shape changes in the face at adolescence (Graber, 1966). Of the three dimensions of the face--height, width and depth--the vertical and anteroposterior growth are more pronounced than changes in width (Graber, 1966). This was

particularly shown for the growth of the maxillae in girls aged 3
to 16 years (Singh and Savara, 1966). Of all facial measurements,
the spurt in mandibular length seems to be largest, changing the
profile of the face towards a more projected lower part (Tanner,
1962).

INTERRELATION OF SEVERAL ASPECTS OF THE PATTERN OF GROWTH

A study of the interrelationships of different aspects of the
pattern of growth implies the analysis of longterm serial data
for individuals. Among one of the first studies on such relationships is that of Boas (1932). He showed that, in boys and girls,
the velocity of adolescent growth is the less, the later adolescence occurs. He also found that the period of maximum growth
was unrelated to adult height. Palmer and Reed (1935) and Palmer
et al. (1937) studied growth in height and weight during a large
longitudinal survey of elementary school children (boys and girls).
They studied the correlations between increments for height and
weight attained during the prepubertal and pubertal periods.
They found almost no correlation between height status and height
velocity in the prepubertal period but a marked positive correlation during adolescence. For weight, there was a moderate to
strong correlation between status and velocity during both periods.
Probably their observations merely reflect the differential pattern
of mean increments of height and weight. In the above-mentioned
age periods, height and weight increase with age. For height,
preadolescent mean increments show a rather constant pattern yielding no correlation with height attained during that period. In
early adolescence the correlation is strongly positive because the
height attained and the rate of growth in height both tend to increase. For weight, the mean increments also increase with age,
slowly in the preadolescent period and more pronounced during the
first half of the adolescent spurt (Tanner et al., 1966a,b). This
may have produced the moderate to strong correlations between increments for weight and weight attained.

Often interrelationships between different characteristics of
the pattern of growth have been studied in terms of coefficients
of correlation, for example, between age at take-off, size at take-
off, velocity at take-off, age at peak velocity, size at peak
velocity, intensity of peak velocity, adult size. Some correlations obtained for height in different studies are summarized in
Table 3. The values above the diagonal are for boys; those below
the diagonal, for girls.

Perhaps one of the most interesting relationships is that
between adult stature and the different aspects of the pattern of
growth. In none of the reported studies is there a relationship
between adult stature and age at peak velocity. However, Bock

et al. (1973), fitting the double logistic function to their growth data, found a moderate, but non-significant, positive correlation between adult value and the age at maximum rate of growth in the second component. Also, the lack of a relationship between adult height and age at peak velocity was reported by Anguélov (1970) and Thompson et al. (1976). Adult height is rather unrelated to the rate of growth at peak velocity itself, except for the significant and high positive correlation in a Belgian sample (Wachholder, personal communication). Age at take-off is in all but one sample (Swiss girls; Largo et al., 1978) unrelated to adult height. Highly significant positive correlations are present for all samples (boys and girls) between adult height and height at take-off and height at peak velocity. Largo et al. (1978) showed that adult height is independent of the duration of prepubertal growth and the duration of the adolescent growth spurt.

Tanner et al. (1976) analyzed the relationship between the adult sizes of measures other than stature and some characteristics of their patterns of growth. They found mature size was independent of age at take-off and age at peak velocity for sitting height, subischial leg length, biacromial diameter and biiliac diameter. The size at take-off, i.e., the amount of prepubertal growth, was correlated significantly with adult size, but this relationship was less close for biacromial diameter than for the other variables. They conclude adult shoulder width is less predictable than the other measures from size before the adolescent spurt. It is interesting that Pařízková (1968) found adult shoulder breadth but not adult height could be influenced by regular physical training. Similar findings were reported by Buckler and Brodie (1977).

Peak height velocity is in general, although not always, significantly negatively correlated with age at peak height velocity. The value for Bengali girls (Hauspie et al., unpublished data) is exceptionally low in this respect. Many have reported that peak height velocity is greater in early maturers and smaller in late maturers (e.g., Shuttleworth, 1939; Simmons, 1944; Bayley, 1956; Deming, 1957; Tanner et al., 1966a,b), but that adult height is not noticeably different between these groups (Richey, 1937; Deming, 1957; Tanner, 1962). Frisch and Revelle (1969) and Hamill et al. (1973) consider the positive correlation between height and age at peak height velocity reduces the differences in adult height between late and early maturers because the slower peak velocity in late maturers is compensated by a greater height at the peak and vice versa. A lack of correlation between weight at peak velocity and peak weight velocity may explain why early and late maturers differ in adult weight. The above-mentioned findings with regard to the compensating mechanism for growth in height of early and late maturers are indirectly reflected in the negative correlations found between prepubertal growth and adolescent gain as seen in Bock's data ($r = -.46$ for boys and $r = -.58$

Table 3. Correlation Coefficients for Height between Different Aspects of the Growth Curve

	Age at Take-off	Height at Take-off	Velocity at Take-off	Age at Peak Velocity	Height at Peak Velocity	Peak Velocity	Adult Height
Age at Take-off		.50°° (1) .64°°° (2) .61°°° (3)	-.34°°° (2) .36°° (3)	.65°°° (2) .79°°° (3)	.20° (2) .39°° (3)	-.11 (2) -.11 (3)	.11 (1) .09 (2) .09 (3)
Height at Take-off	.37° (1) .67°°° (2) .58°°° (3) .49°° (8)		.17 (2) .20 (3)	.24° (2) .49°°° (3)	.81°°° (2) .87°°° (3)	-.04 (2) -.15 (3)	.84°° (1) .74°°° (2) .62°°° (3)
Velocity at Take-off	-.54°°° (2) -.41° (3) -.88°°° (8)	.04 (2) -.05 (3) -.14 (8)		-.48°°° (2) -.17 (3)	.35°°° (2) .22 (3)	-.01 (2) -.14 (3)	.40°°° (2) .23 (3)
Age at Peak Velocity	.88°°° (3) .94°°° (8)	.28°° (2) .34° (3) .32 (8)	-.72°°° (2) -.67°°° (3) -.91°°° (8)		.27° (1) .22° (2) .37°° (3)	-.50°° (1) -.36°°° (2) -.20 (3) -.30°°° (4) -.75°°° (6) -.06 (7)	.02 (1) .04 (2) .15 (3) .11 (6) .25 (7)
Height at Peak Velocity	.48°°° (2) .33° (3) .18 (8)	.87°°° (2) .88°°° (3) .79°°° (8)	.12 (2) -.07 (3) .08 (8)	.21 (1) .33 (2) .25 (3) .41°°° (5) .18 (8) .21 (10)		-.04 (2) -.08 (3)	.95°°° (2) .91°°° (3)

Table 3 - Continued

	Age at Take-off	Height at Take-off	Velocity at Take-off	Age at Peak Velocity	Height at Peak Velocity	Peak Velocity	Adult Height
Peak Velocity	-.30°°° (2)	-.13 (2)	.39°°° (2)	-.29 (1)	.04 (2)		.11 (2)
	-.09 (3)	-.11 (3)	-.16 (3)	-.36°°° (2)	.11 (3)		-.07 (3)
	-.31 (8)	-.04 (8)	.19 (8)	-.05 (3)	.42°° (8)		
				-.24°°° (4)			
				-.16 (5)			
				-.60°° (6)			
				-.30 (7)			
				-.21 (8)			
				-.29°° (9)			
				-.21° (10)			
Adult Height	-.01 (1)	.81°° (1)	.32°°° (2)	-.03 (1)	.88°°° (2)	.18 (2)	
	.22° (2)	.73°°° (2)	.12 (3)	.05 (2)	.90°°° (3)	-.10 (3)	
	-.02 (3)	.65°°° (3)	.50°° (8)	-.00 (3)	-.86°°° (8)	.36° (8)	
	-.23 (8)	.55°° (8)		-.16 (6)	.84°°° (10)		
				.21 (7)			
				-.19 (8)			
				.03 (10)			

Significance: °p < .05 °°p < .01 °°°p < .001

(1) Tanner et al., 1976 (55 boys; 35 girls) GREAT BRITAIN
(2) Largo et al., 1978 (112 boys; 110 girls) SWITZERLAND
(3) Hauspie et al., unpublished data (63 boys; 42 girls) INDIA
(4) Lindgren, 1978 (354 boys; 330 girls) SWEDEN
(5) Onat and Ertem, 1974 (65 girls) TURKEY
(6) Deming, 1957 (24 boys; 24 girls) U.S.A.
(7) Bock et al., 1973 (56 boys; 51 girls; double logistic model) U.S.A.
(8) Wachholder, personal communication (35 girls; Preece Model 1) BELGIUM
(9) Marubini et al., 1971 (121 girls; Gompertz fit) ITALY
(10) Marubini et al., 1971 (121 girls; Logistic fit) ITALY

Note: Above diagonal, boys; below diagonal, girls.

for girls). Tanner et al. (1976), however, found a lower degree
of dependency (r = -.2) between prepubertal growth and adolescent
gain.

Beneath the relationships found between different aspects of
the pattern of growth of the same measurements, there are also
high correlations for some aspects between different measures, such
as age at take-off and at peak velocity for height, sitting height,
leg length and biacromial diameter (Tanner et al., 1976). Singh
(1976) found that the correlation between thoracic and abdominal
surface area increased with age, suggesting that growth of the
thorax and abdomen become more closely related as growth proceeds.
There are low associations between growth of the head and face
(Newman and Meredith, 1956) and between adolescent gains in longitudinal and transverse diameters of the body, suggesting shape
changes during adolescence (Tanner et al., 1976).

REFERENCES

Anguélov, G. A., 1970, Dynamique de la croissance corporelle et de
      l'évolution de la puberté chez les enfants de 10 à 17 ans,
      Biométrie Humaine, 5:85.
Baughan, B., Demirjian, A., Levesque, G. Y., and Lapalme-Chaput, L.,
      1979, The pattern of facial growth before and during puberty,
      as shown by French-Canadian girls, Ann. Hum. Biol., 6:59.
Bayley, N., 1956, Growth curves of height and weight by age for
      boys and girls, scaled according to physical maturity, J.
      Pediatr., 48:187.
Bayley, N., 1943, Size and body build of adolescents in relation
      to rate of skeletal maturation, Child Dev., 14:47.
Bielicki, T., 1975, Interrelationships between various measures of
      maturation rate in girls during adolescence, Stud. Phys.
      Anthropol., 1:51.
Bielicki, T., and Welon, Z., 1973, The sequence of growth velocity
      peaks of principal body dimensions in girls, Mater. Prac.
      Antropol., 86:3.
Boas, F., 1932, Studies in growth, Hum. Biol., 4:307.
Bock, R. D., Wainer, H., Petersen, A., Thissen, D., Murray, J.,
      and Roche, A., 1973, A parameterization for individual
      human growth curves, Hum. Biol., 45:63.
Buckler, J. M. H., and Brodie, D. A., 1977, Growth and maturity
      characteristics of schoolboy gymnasts, Ann. Hum. Biol.,
      4:455.
Deming, J., 1957, Application of the Gompertz curve to the observed
      pattern of growth in length of 48 individual boys and girls
      during the adolescent cycle of growth, Hum. Biol., 29:83.
Eveleth, P. B., 1975, Differences between ethnic groups in sex
      dimorphism of adult height, Ann. Hum. Biol., 2:35.

Frisch, R. E., and Revelle, R., 1969, The height and weight of adolescent boys and girls at the time of peak velocity of growth in height and weight: longitudinal data, Hum. Biol., 41:536.

Goldstein, M. S., 1939, Development of the head in the same individuals, Hum. Biol., 11:197.

Graber, T. M., 1966, Craniofacial and dentitional development, in: "Human Development," F. Falkner, ed., W. B. Saunders Company, Philadelphia.

Hamill, P. V. V., Johnston, F. E., and Lemeshow, S., 1973, "Height and Weight of Youths 12-17 Years," Vital and Health Statistics, Series 11, No. 124 (PHS), U.S. Government Printing Office, Washington, D.C.

Hautvast, J., 1971. Growth in stature and head and face measurements in Dutch children aged 7 to 14, Hum. Biol., 43:340.

Kantero, R. L., and Tiisala, R., 1971, Growth of head circumference from birth to 10 years, Acta Paed. Scand., Suppl. 220:27.

Largo, R. H., Gasser, T., Prader, A., Stuetzle, W., and Huber, P. J., 1978, Analysis of the adolescent growth spurt using smoothing spline functions, Ann. Hum. Biol., 5:421.

Lestrel, P. E., and Brown, H. D., 1976, Fourier analysis of adolescent growth of the cranial vault: a longitudinal study, Hum. Biol., 48:517.

Lindgren, G., 1978, Growth of schoolchildren with early, average and late ages of peak height velocity, Ann. Hum. Biol., 5:253.

Malina, R. M., 1974, Adolescent changes in size, build, composition and performance, Hum. Biol., 46:117.

Marshall, W. A., 1970, Sex differences at puberty, J. Biosoc. Sci., Suppl. 2:31.

Marubini, E., Resele, L. F., and Barghini, G., 1971, A comparative fitting of the Gompertz and logistic functions to longitudinal height data during adolescence in girls, Hum. Biol., 43:237.

Marubini, E., Resele, L. F., Tanner, J. M., and Whitehouse, R. H., 1972, The fit of Gompertz and logistic curves to longitudinal data during adolescence on height, sitting height and biacromial diameter in boys and girls of the Harpenden Growth Study, Hum. Biol., 44:511.

Meredith, H. V., 1971, Human head circumference from birth to early adulthood: racial, regional, and sex comparisons, Growth, 35:233.

Miklashevskaya, N., 1969, Sex differences in growth of the head and face in children and adolescents, Hum. Biol., 41:250.

Nanda, R. S., 1955, The rates of growth of several facial components measured from serial cephalometric roentgenograms, Am. J. Orthod., 41:658.

Newman, K. J., and Meredith, H. V., 1956, Individual growth in skeletal bigonial diameter during the childhood period from 5 to 11 years of age., Am. J. Anat., 99:157.

Onat, T., and Ertem, B., 1974, Adolescent female height velocity: relationships to body measurements, sexual and skeletal maturity, Hum. Biol., 46:199.

Palmer, C. E., Kawakami, R., and Reed, L. J., 1937, Anthropometric study of individual growth. II. Age, weight, and rate of growth in weight, elementary school children, Child Dev., 8:47.

Palmer, C. E., and Reed, L. J., 1935, Anthropometric studies of individual growth. I. Age, height and growth in height, elementary school children, Hum. Biol., 7:319.

Pařízková, J., 1968, Longitudinal study of the development of body composition and body build in boys of various physical activity, Hum. Biol., 40:212.

Preece, M. A., and Baines, M. J., 1978, A new family of mathematical models describing the human growth curve, Ann. Hum. Biol., 5:1.

Richey, H., 1937, The relation of acceleration, normal and retarded puberty to the height and weight of school children, Monogr. Soc. Res. Child Dev., Vol. 2, No. 1, Series 8.

Roche, A. F., 1974, Differential timing of maximum length increments among bones within individuals, Hum. Biol., 46:145.

Scammon, R. E., 1930, The measurement of the body in childhood, in: "The Measurement of Man," J. A. Harris, C. M. Jackson, D. G. Paterson, and R. E. Scammon, eds., University of Minnesota Press, Minneapolis.

Shuttleworth, F., 1939, The physical and mental growth in girls and boys age 6 to 19 in relation to age at maximum growth, Monogr. Soc. Res. Child Dev., 4, No. 3.

Simmons, K., 1944, The Brush Foundation study of child growth and development. II. Physical growth and development, Monogr. Soc. Res. Child Dev., 9, No. 1.

Singh, I. J., and Savara, B. S., 1966, Norms of size and annual increments of seven anatomical measures of maxillae in girls from three to sixteen years of age., Angle Orthod., 36:312.

Singh, I. J., Savara, B. S., and Newman, M. T., 1967, Growth in the skeletal and non-skeletal components of head width from 9 to 14 years of age, Hum. Biol., 39:182.

Singh, R., 1976, A longitudinal study of the growth of trunk surface area measured by planimeter on standard somatotype photographs, Ann. Hum. Biol., 3:181.

Tanner, J. M., 1962, "Growth at Adolescence," Blackwell Scientific Publications, Oxford.

Tanner, J. M., Whitehouse, R. H., Marubini, E., and Resele, L. F., 1976, The adolescent growth spurt of boys and girls of the Harpenden study, Ann. Hum. Biol., 3:109.

Tanner, J. M., Whitehouse, R. H., and Takaishi, M., 1966a, Standards from birth to maturity for height, weight, height velocity, and weight velocity: British children, 1965, Part I, Arch. Dis. Childh., 41:454.

Tanner, J. M., Whitehouse, R. H., and Takaishi, M., 1966b,
        Standards from birth to maturity for height, weight, height
        velocity and weight velocity: British children, 1965.
        Part II, Arch. Dis. Childh., 41:613.
Thompson, G. W., Popovich, F., and Anderson, D. L., 1976, Maximum
        growth changes in mandibular length, stature and weight,
        Hum. Biol., 48:285.
Valenzuela, C. Y., Rothhammer, F., and Chakraborty, R., 1978, Sex
        dimorphism in adult stature in four Chilean populations,
        Ann. Hum. Biol., 5:533.

10. PREDICTION

Alex F. Roche

Fels Research Institute and
Department of Pediatrics
Wright State University School of Medicine
Yellow Springs, Ohio 45387

In the present context, "prediction" refers to the use of one
or more variables noted at one age to predict a value at an older
age. To develop any prediction method one must have serial data.
When a prediction method is developed, replication studies are
necessary; the method may be less accurate in children of other
groups, particularly if they differ from the original group in eth-
nicity or socioeconomic circumstances.

ADULT STATURE

There are more methods for the prediction of adult stature
than for any other variable partly because the correlations between
childhood and adulthood statures are rather high and because there
is widespread interest in adult stature.

The methods to which major attention will be given predict from
data recorded at a single examination; this is essential if the
method is to be useful clinically. It is appropriate to begin this
survey with the 1952 method of Bayley and Pinneau (BP). Using
serial data from 90 boys and 103 girls (mean number at each 6 months
of age about 46 boys and 63 girls), Bayley and Pinneau noted a close
relationship between skeletal age, within chronological age groups,
and the percentage of adult stature achieved. In addition, they
showed that, at the same skeletal age, accelerated children had
achieved a smaller percentage of adult stature than children who
were retarded in skeletal maturation. This led them to publish
tables giving the percent adult stature achieved at particular
skeletal ages within groups of accelerated, average and retarded
children. The criterion for classification as "average" was a

skeletal age within one year of the chronological age. This is
approximately the range ± 1 s.d. Consequently their prediction
tables for accelerated and retarded children are based on very
small groups.

To use the BP tables, one must have available a Greulich-Pyle
(1959) skeletal age for the child; the details of this skeletal age
were not specified. The tables give the estimated percentage of
adult stature achieved for the skeletal maturity level. In combination with present stature, this percentage provides an estimate
of adult stature. Parental stature is not used in this prediction
method. However, Bayley (1962) showed the use of mid-parent stature
increases the accuracy of predictions made during infancy. Bayley
and Pinneau validated their tables using data from about 20 boys
and 20 girls. The standard deviations of the errors decrease from
3.6 cm at 8 years to 3.1 cm at 14 years in boys; the corresponding
values for girls are 4.3 and 1.0 cm. The accuracy of predictions
for accelerated or retarded children was not tested separately.

In the BP method the continuum of differences between skeletal
age and chronological age is divided to three groups. This has led
others to develop regression models. Roche, Wainer and Thissen
(1975) had available about 100 sets of serial data at each 6 months
of age in each sex from one to 18 years when they developed the RWT
method. They examined 78 possible predictors most of which were
bone-specific skeletal ages for the hand-wrist, knee and foot-ankle
or combinations of these ages. In addition, recumbent length,
weight and the adult statures of both parents were measured.

A selection was made between the many skeletal ages that was
based primarily on their interrelationships. After principal component and cluster analyses, 18 variables were chosen for further
testing. In this phase, all possible combinations between these
variables were considered using two, three and four predictor
models. Finally, a set of four predictors was chosen that was
applicable to both sexes throughout the age ranges considered. At
some ages, not all these predictors were useful but it was considered desirable to retain a consistent model for both sexes at all
ages. The final predictors chosen are recumbent length, weight and
skeletal age (median of Greulich-Pyle bone-specific skeletal ages
for the hand-wrist) of the child and mid-parent stature. Recumbent
length was preferred to stature because it can be obtained at all
ages and its serial changes are more regular than those for stature.

Regression techniques were used to estimate weightings for
each predictor variable. Multivariate smoothing was applied because these weightings were somewhat irregular across age. In the
process, some information was lost because the unsmoothed values
were the best estimates for the separate ages but the decreases in
R^2 values were trivial. Two advantages were gained. Continuous

functions of age were derived from the weightings for each predictor variable; consequently, predictions can be made at any age. Also, the method for deriving these functions utilized some serial properties of the data; in particular, estimates at ages with large samples improved the estimates at ages with small samples, thus yielding more robust estimates of predictor weightings (Wainer and Thissen, 1975).

One-month and three-month tables of these weightings are provided for boys from 1 to 16 years and for girls from 1 to 14 years (Roche et al., 1975, 1975a). Slightly more precise estimates for other ages within these age ranges can be obtained by using the polynomial functions that generated these tables (Wainer and Thissen, 1976).

The regression weightings contain much of interest but the pattern of change is difficult to interpret because of the interrelationships between the weightings for the four predictors. The weightings for recumbent length are positive and are similar in magnitude in each sex. The weightings decrease until about the age of the pubescent spurt in stature. When the β weightings are multiplied by median values for recumbent length, the products increase during childhood and decrease during adolescence.

The β weightings for body weight are much smaller and generally negative. The trends are similar across age in each sex with particularly large negative weightings at about 5 years in boys and 4 years in girls. When considered in combination with median values, the contribution of weight to the prediction decreases with age. Presumably this reflects the increase in the usefulness of the other predictors as age increases. Caution is necessary before any interpretation that the negative coefficients for weight reflect an effect of childhood obesity on adult stature. The findings are confounded by the differences in stature and skeletal maturity between obese and normal children (Bruch, 1939; Garn and Haskell, 1960; Maresh, 1961).

The β weightings for mid-parent stature are positive at all ages and are higher in boys than girls. Mid-parent stature does not differ systematically between the sexes; consequently, this variable made a larger contribution to the predicted adult statures of boys than of girls. This would be expected because men systematically exceed women in stature. The patterns of change with age in the weightings are similar in each sex but the inflections occur about two years earlier in the girls. The weightings become almost zero near the end of growth when other predictors, especially recumbent length, are more important.

The β weightings for skeletal age are negative at most ages and are larger in girls than boys. These negative values become

larger until about 14 years in boys and 13 years in girls. The
products of skeletal age and its β weighting make comparatively
small contributions to the predicted values because there are
comparatively few units (years) for skeletal age.

     The RWT method predicts stature at 18 years although recumbent
length, not stature, is used as a predictor. The amount of growth
in stature after 18 years is small (median values: 8 mm, boys; 6
mm, girls; Roche and Davila, 1972). This method is applicable over
longer age ranges than others. The standard deviations of the
residuals (errors) for the RWT method are less than 2 cm at all ages.
They show only a slight age trend until they decrease markedly near
the end of growth. The 90% error bounds for the RWT method, when
applied to the Fels children, are about 6 cm at all ages in each sex.

     The prediction errors were not associated significantly with
illnesses in parents during their growth, birth order, birthweight,
illness or growth pattern of the child, prediction errors in siblings, Tanner-Whitehouse skeletal age, or differences between bones
or groups of bones in skeletal age. Furthermore, the errors were
not associated with the present recumbent length of the child,

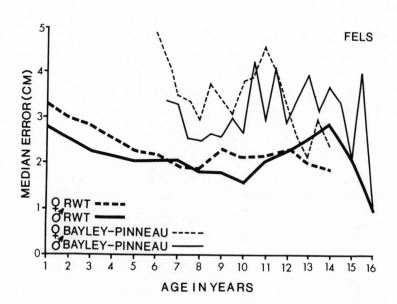

Fig. 1.   Mean errors (cm) for predictions of adult stature in chil-
          dren of the Fels sample using the Roche-Wainer-Thissen
          (RWT) or the Bayley-Pinneau method.

parental stature or the differences in stature between the two parents.

The RWT method is more accurate than the BP method when applied to the children in either the Fels, Denver or Harvard Growth studies with one qualification (Figures 1-3). RWT predictions for older Denver or Harvard children are less accurate than those made using the BP method. When the RWT method was being developed it was considered predictions were not needed for children who had almost completed their growth. Furthermore, satisfactory Greulich-Pyle skeletal ages cannot be obtained when maturation is almost complete. The upper limit of maturity for application of the RWT method is when half the bones of the hand-wrist are adult but the BP method is applicable until maturation is complete. Only area Greulich-Pyle skeletal ages are available

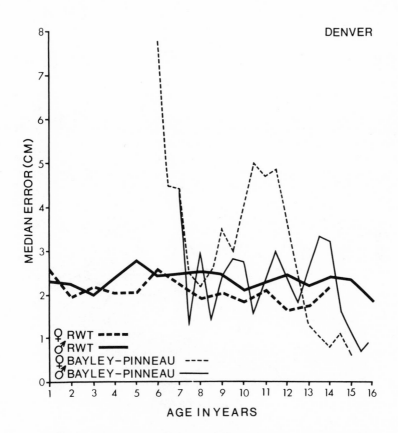

Fig. 2. Mean errors (cm) for predictions of adult stature in children of the Denver sample using the Roche-Wainer-Thissen (RWT) or the Bayley-Pinneau method.

for the Denver and Harvard children and, therefore, the older age
groups in these studies include children to whom the RWT method is
inapplicable.

The RWT prediction errors are much more regular across age
than the BP errors for the children in the Denver and Harvard
studies. Both RWT and BP methods tend to overpredict slightly for
the Denver boys and underpredict in the girls; these underpredic-
tions are considerably larger with the BP method. Similarly, both
methods tend to overpredict slightly for the boys in the Harvard
study; the BP method underpredicted in the girls. The RWT method
can be applied when skeletal age or the father's stature (or both)
are unavailable by substituting population means for these values.
There is a slight loss of accuracy that is larger at young ages.

Serial RWT predictions have been examined in the Fels and
Harvard samples. The mean changes during annual intervals are near
zero except in boys from 15 to 16 years in the Fels sample. The
larger differences for this interval may reflect sampling errors.
The standard deviations of these changes are about 1.0 cm at most
ages (Table 1). These findings are important in evaluating the

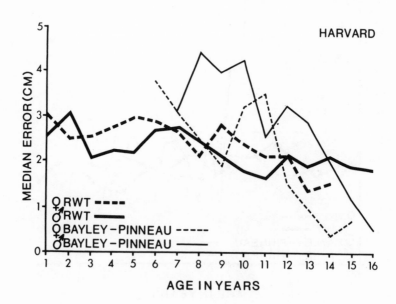

Fig. 3. Mean errors (cm) for predictions of adult stature in
         children of the Harvard sample using the Roche-Wainer-
         Thissen (RWT) or the Bayley-Pinneau method.

Table 1. Changes (cm) in Estimated Adult Stature Using
          the RWT Method   (Early Less Later)

Age Interval (Years)	Boys		Girls	
	Mean	S.D.	Mean	S.D.
1–2	-0.4	1.80	-0.7	1.81
2–3	-0.2	1.65	0.2	1.15
3–4	-0.2	1.07	0.0	1.09
4–5	0.0	1.31	-0.1	1.08
5–6	0.2	0.09	0.0	0.83
6–7	0.0	0.92	0.1	0.97
7–8	-0.3	0.98	0.0	0.85
8–9	-0.1	0.90	-0.1	0.95
9–10	0.0	0.84	-0.4	1.06
10–11	0.2	0.87	-0.4	1.29
11–12	0.3	1.17	-0.0	1.53
12–13	-0.1	1.44	0.0	1.79
13–14	-0.0	1.76	-0.6	1.73
14–15	-0.2	2.01	----	----
15–16	-0.5	2.07	----	----

effects of treatment and in determining the sample sizes necessary
to demonstrate significant effects on predicted adult stature.
The sample sizes needed are relatively small if analyses are based
on changes in predicted adult statures.

It is appropriate to consider how the accuracy of this method
might be increased. The instructions of the authors indicate 1.25
cm should be added to stature to make it approximately equivalent
to recumbent length. The median differences between recumbent
length and stature in the Fels sample are age-dependent but differ
little between the sexes although they differ among individuals
(Roche and Davila, 1974); Hamill et al., 1977). Slightly greater
as well as slightly smaller differences between these variables
have been observed in other growth studies. A small increase in

accuracy would be expected if age-specific adjustments were made
when stature is adjusted to "recumbent length" for use as a predictor.   Body build could be helpful as may the separation of girls to
premenarcheal and postmenarcheal groups.   Slightly greater accuracy
would be achieved by using the mean of two independent assessments
of skeletal maturity and perhaps by substituting RWT measures of
skeletal maturity (Roche et al., 1975b) for the Greulich-Pyle skeletal age.   Finally, hormonal values may be useful predictors.

The TW prediction method of Tanner and his colleagues (1975)
was developed using mixed longitudinal data from 116 boys and 95
girls; the number available at each age was not stated.   Regression
equations were developed for chronological age groups using stature,
chronological age and skeletal age as predictors.   The skeletal age
employed is the RUS (radius, ulna, short bones) subset of the TW
skeletal age method (Tanner et al., 1975).   The model is "consistent" across age but the RUS skeletal age does not add information
from 4 to 7 years in boys and from 4 to 5 years in girls; consequently, it has a zero β weighting at these ages.

The weightings obtained for the regression equations were
smoothed subjectively across age for one variable at a time.   Separate regression equations are used for girls aged 11 years or more
depending on whether they have reached menarche.   Mid-parent
stature is included by adjusting the predicted value by one-third
the amount by which the mid-parent stature deviates from the mean
for the population.   The standard deviations of the residuals for
TW predictions are about 3.0 to 3.5 cm at younger ages but decrease
with age to about 2.0 cm at 16 years in boys and 13 years in girls.
The authors replicated the method using data from 57 ballet girls
aged 9 to 12 years.   The mean error was 2.2 cm (s.d., 1.6 cm).

Comparisons Between Methods

As noted earlier, Roche and others (1975) compared the BP and
RWT methods using data for normal children from the Denver and
Harvard studies.   Zachmann and others (1978) reported comparisons
between the BP, RWT and TW methods using, primarily, serial data
from 56 normal children aged 9 to 16 years.   The mean errors for
the other methods are less than 2 cm except at older ages when the
TW method tends to underestimate.   The s.d. of the errors tend to
be smaller for the RWT method except at 16 years in boys and 13 and
14 years in girls when they are smaller for the TW method.

Zachmann and his associates reported a tendency for each
method to overestimate in early maturing children and to underestimate in those who were late maturing; this tendency was least
marked for the RWT method.   All three methods are reasonably
accurate in children with familial tall stature.   The RWT and TW

Table 2. Age Ranges (Years) During Which Selected
          Methods are Applicable

Method	Boys	Girls
Bayley-Pinneau	6.0-18.5*	6.0-18.0*
Roche-Wainer-Thissen	1.0-16.0	1.0-14.0
Tanner-Whitehouse	4.0-17.5	4.5-15.5

*Slightly different for accelerated and retarded
 children.

methods are satisfactory in endocrinopathies in which appropriate
treatment restores normal growth but they are grossly inaccurate
in conditions such as Turner's syndrome and precocious puberty.
This is to be expected, as stated by those who developed the
methods. These regression models assume the child will reach the
population mean for stature with adjustments for present size and
maturity and for parental size. This assumption is false for such
children. Finally, Zachmann and others concluded that, while all
three methods tend to overpredict, the BP method is the most accurate when applied to 10 children with primordial short stature.
This is not in agreement with the earlier findings of Roche and
Wettenhall (1977) who reported the RWT method was more accurate
than the BP method when applied to 28 short boys. In comparing
various methods, notice should be taken of the age ranges during
which they can be applied (Table 2).

Schreiber and others (1976) compared the errors of prediction
of the BP, RWT and TW methods. They had data from 70 children
studied until they had grown less than 1 cm during a year. For
predictions made at 8 years, BP tended to overpredict in boys and
underpredict in girls. The RWT and TW methods underpredicted in
both sexes by about 1.5 cm. However, these authors used stature,
not recumbent length, as a predictor when applying the RWT method.
When predictions were made at 12 years each method was reasonably
accurate except that TW underpredicted markedly in the boys. The
means and standard deviations of the errors were smaller for the
RWT method than for the others.

A comparison of methods has been reported by Lenko and others
(Kantero and Lenko, 1976; Lenko, 1979). They had available data
from 60 children but due to missed visits the number of sets of
data at each age varied from 16 to 28. These workers used area
Greulich-Pyle skeletal ages obtained omitting the carpals. Since
carpal bones are among the earliest hand-wrist bones to reach adult

levels of maturity, it is probable that some of the older children
did not qualify for inclusion in the group to which the RWT method
is applicable. Also they applied the RWT method to children who
were older than the upper limits of age for which the prediction
equations apply. Moreover, in applying the TW method they did not
adjust for mid-parent stature. Finally, they used chronological
age rounded to whole years. Such comparisons are only acceptable
if the instructions of the authors are followed.

The mean errors reported by Lenko and his associates for
girls are similar for predictions made with the BP, RWT and TW
methods. In the boys, the mean errors are largest for BP and
smallest for RWT except after 14 years when the order is reversed.
The TW method markedly underpredicted for boys from 13 to 16 years
of age. Otherwise the errors tend to be small for all methods.
The mean differences between successive predictions of adult stature were considerably smaller when the RWT method was used than
when the BP or TW methods were used except near the end of the age
range when, almost certainly, predictions were made for children
to whom the RWT method should not be applied.

Some other methods of stature prediction depend on the availability of serial data. These methods are unlikely to be used
widely by clinicians but they are of biological interest. Walker
(1974) reported a method in which the predictors are present stature, the increment in stature during the previous 9 to 18 months
and a judgment as to whether the child has passed peak height velocity. Consequently, this method is applicable only near the end
of growth. When Walker replicated his findings using reported
data the errors were large. However, when the method was tested
by Schreiber and others (1976) the accuracy was quite good.

Welch (1970) fitted orthogonal polynomials to stature data
recorded at serial examinations from 21 to 126 months of age. The
parameters of these curves, together with mid-parent stature, led
to predicted adult statures that had s.d. of errors of 3.16 cm in
boys and 3.62 cm in girls. Onat (1975) reported predictions of
adult stature for girls using the percentage of adult stature
achieved at the onset of particular pubertal events. Serial data
are needed to judge the age at onset and, even then, it is not
easily determined. The s.d. of the estimates range from 4.1 to 4.7
cm. Any method developed from such data would be applicable only
during a restricted age range.

Filippson and Hall (1975) published a method based on dental
eruption and present stature. The standard deviation of the residuals, using stature when 12 teeth were erupted as a predictor, was
4.2 cm. When growth rate in a chronological age year was added as
a predictor, the standard deviation of the residual was 2.3 cm at
ages 6 to 10 years. The variability of adult stature was low in

the group studied and the findings have not been replicated.

PREDICTING OTHER VARIABLES

Age at Menarche

    Frisch (1974) estimated total body water as a percentage of
body weight using the formula of Mellits and Cheek (1970). Re-
gressions within quartiles of percent total body water were used
to predict age at menarche. The errors of the estimates exceed
6 months in 41 to 53% at ages from 9 to 12 years. The clinical or
biological usefulness of this approach is unclear.

Craniofacial Variables

    Without doubt, accurate predictions of craniofacial growth
would be very important for orthodontists. However, despite considerable interest in these predictions, little has been achieved.
The aims of prediction include: size, relationships between parts,
timing of events, directions and rates of growth.

    The problem is difficult because, with the exception of the
shape of the pituitary fossa (Kier, 1968), the form of the spheno-
occipital synchondrosis (Powell and Brodie, 1963; Konie, 1964),
the presence of the sphenoid sinus (Terracol and Ardouin, 1965;
Vidic, 1968), and the profile of the mandibular symphysis (Meredith,
1957), little is known of the maturation of the skull and mandible
in regard to radiographically visible features. In the absence of
measures of craniofacial maturity, those for other areas of the
skeleton should be used as predictors.

    Ricketts (1957, 1961, 1972, 1973) has written extensively on
the prediction of craniofacial growth. His method is based on the
directions and amounts by which radiographic points move during
growth. These changes are made on a tracing of a radiograph in a
stepwise fashion moving inferiorly from the cranial base. In
recent versions of this method, age changes in growth rates and
variations in directions of growth have been included (Schulhof
and Bagha, 1975). A firm statistical basis has not been reported
for the amounts and directions of growth that are incorporated.

    Johnston (1968) used data from 90 children each of whom had
cephalometric radiographs separated by a 5-year interval. He used
a regression approach and obtained a wide range of R^2 values (.02
to .81) when predicting various dimensions. In general, the mandibular, palatal and occlusal plane angles and the sizes of dis-
crete anatomical structures were not effective predictors. This

is in agreement with the findings of Ødegaard (1970) who showed the
direction of condylar growth was dependent on the morphology of the
mandible, particularly the gonial angle, but not upon the relationship of the mandible to the skull. Later, Johnston (1975) developed a grid for "easy" prediction that extends each point to be
predicted by average amounts and directions assuming all children
grow similarly irrespective of their facial patterns. Johnston
tested this method using data at 7.5 years to predict status at
12.5 years. The RMS of the errors were about 3 cm.

The accuracy of the Ricketts (Ricketts et al., 1972) and
Johnston (1968) methods was compared by Schulhof and Bagha (1975)
using radiographs at about 6 years to predict status at 16 years.
They defined the objectives of prediction in relation to the positions of points in the facial profile, the lower first molar tooth
and a point representing the "center" of the ramus. The method of
Ricketts was more accurate than that of Johnston. Hirschfeld and
Moyers (1971), using time series, attempted to predict several
craniofacial distances. The mean percentage error for prediction
across a 5-year interval was 7.5% for Ar - Gn (a measure of mandibular length) and 3.2% for A-B (a measure of the relative positions of the maxilla and mandible).

As stated earlier, there is no adequate method for the prediction of craniofacial growth. The development of such a system
is dependent on the availability of serial data, the definition
of growth patterns, the measurement of craniofacial maturity, and
it will involve complex mathematical procedures.

CONCLUSION

Realistically, a prediction method should be based on data
that can be obtained at a single examination. Consequently, regression methods are appropriate although other alternatives are
discussed by Bock and Thissen elsewhere in this volume. The
methods presently available are applicable only to normal children
and selected groups of unusual children. Methods could be developed for abnormal children if sufficient data were available from
homogeneous groups. Finally, it must be emphasized that whenever
a prediction method is applied, the instructions of the authors
should be followed closely and the confidence limits of each prediction should be given.

REFERENCES

Bayley, N., 1962, The accurate prediction of growth and adult
       height, Mod. Probl. Paediatr., 7:234.

Bayley, N., and Pinneau, S. R., 1952, Tables for predicting adult height from skeletal age: revised for use with Greulich-Pyle hand standards, J. Pediatr., 40:423.

Bruch, H., 1939, Obesity in childhood. Physical growth and development of obese children, Am. J. Dis. Child., 58:457.

Filippson, R., and Hall, K., 1975, Prediction of adult height of girls from height and dental maturity at ages 6-10 years, Ann. Hum. Biol., 2:355.

Frisch, R. E., 1974, A method of prediction of age of menarche from height and weight at ages 9 through 13 years, Pediatrics, 53:384.

Garn, S. M., and Haskell, J. A., 1960, Fat thickness and developmental status in childhood and adolescence, Am. J. Dis. Child., 99:746.

Greulich, W. W., and Pyle, S. I., 1959, "Radiographic Atlas of Skeletal Development of the Hand and Wrist," 2nd ed., Stanford University Press, Stanford.

Hamill, P. V. V., Drizd, T. A., Johnson, C. L., Reed, R. B., and Roche, A. F., 1977, "NCHS Growth Curves for Children Birth-18 Years, United States," (Vital and Health Statistics, Series 11, No. 165, DHEW Publ. No. (PHS) 78-1650), U.S. Government Printing Office, Washington, D.C.

Hirschfeld, W. J., and Moyers, R. E., 1971, Prediction of craniofacial growth: the state of the art, Am. J. Orthod., 60:435.

Johnston, L. E., 1968, A statistical evaluation of cephalometric prediction, Angle Orthod., 38:284.

Johnston, L. E., 1975, A simplified approach to prediction, Am. J. Orthod., 67:253.

Kantero, R.-L., and Lenko, H. L., 1976, Prediction of adult height, Compte-Rendu de la XIIIe Réunion, des Equipes Chargées des Etudes sur la Croissance et le Développement de l'Enfant Normal, Rennes.

Kier, E. L., 1968, The infantile sella turcica; new roentgenologic and anatomic concepts based on a developmental study of the sphenoid bone, Am. J. Roentgenol., 102:747.

Konie, J. C., 1964, Comparative value of x-rays of the spheno-occipital synchondrosis and of the wrist for skeletal age assessment, Angle Orthod., 34:303.

Lenko, H. L., 1979, Prediction of adult height with various methods in Finnish children, Acta Paediatr. Scand., 68:85.

Maresh, M. M., 1961, Bone, muscle and fat measurements. Longitudinal measurements of the bone, muscle and fat widths from roentgenograms of the extremities during the first six years of life, Pediatrics, 28:971.

Mellits, E. D., and Cheek, D. B., 1970, The assessment of body water and fatness from infancy to adulthood, Monogr. Soc. Res. Child Dev., 35:12.

Meredith, H. V., 1957, Change in the profile of the osseous chin during childhood, Am. J. Phys. Anthropol., 15:247.

Ødegaard, J., 1970, Growth of the mandible studied with the aid of
    metal implants, Am. J. Orthod., 57:145.
Onat, T., 1975, Prediction of adult height of girls based on the
    percentage of adult height at onset of secondary sexual
    characteristics, at chronological age, and skeletal age,
    Hum. Biol., 47:117.
Powell, T. V., and Brodie, A. G., 1963, Closure of the spheno-
    occipital synchondrosis, Anat. Rec., 147:15.
Ricketts, R. M., 1957, Planning treatment on the basis of the
    facial pattern and an estimate of its growth, Angle Orthod.,
    27:14.
Ricketts, R. M., 1961, Cephalometric analysis and synthesis, Angle
    Orthod., 31:141.
Ricketts, R. M., 1972, The value of cephalometrics and computerized
    technology, Angle Orthod., 42:179.
Ricketts, R. M., 1973, New findings and concepts emerging from the
    clinical use of the computer, in: "Proceedings, Interna-
    tional Orthodontic Conference," London.
Ricketts, R. M., Bench, R. W., Hilgers, J. J., and Schulhof, R.,
    1972, An overview of computerized cephalometrics, Am. J.
    Orthod., 61:1.
Roche, A. F., and Davila, G. H., 1972, Late adolescent growth in
    stature, Pediatrics, 50:874.
Roche, A. F., and Davila, G. H., 1974, Differences between recum-
    bent length and stature within individuals, Growth, 38:313.
Roche, A. F., and Wettenhall, H. N. B., 1977, Stature prediction
    in short boys, Aust. Paediatr. J., 13:261.
Roche, A. F., Wainer, H., and Thissen, D., 1975, Predicting adult
    stature for individuals, Monogr. Paediatr., 3, Karger,
    Basel.
Roche, A. F., Wainer, H., and Thissen, D., 1975a, The RWT method
    for the prediction of adult stature, Pediatrics, 56:957.
Roche, A. F., Wainer, H., and Thissen, D., 1975b, "Skeletal
    Maturity. The Knee Joint as a Biological Indicator," Plenum
    Publishing Corporation, New York.
Schreiber, A., Patois, E., and Roy, M. P., 1976, Etude comparative
    de quatre methodes de prédiction de la taille adulte, Compte-
    Rendu de la XIIIe Réunion des Equipes Chargées des Etudes
    sur la Croissance et le Développement de l'Enfant Normal,
    Rennes.
Schulhof, R. J., and Bagha, L., 1975, A statistical evaluation of
    the Ricketts and Johnston growth-forecasting methods, Am. J.
    Orthod., 67:258.
Tanner, J. M., Whitehouse, R. H., Marshall, W. A., Healy, M. J. R.,
    and Goldstein, H., 1975, "Assessment of Skeletal Maturity
    and Prediction of Adult Height (TW 2 Method)," Academic
    Press, London.
Terracol, J., and Ardouin, P., 1965, "Anatomie des Fosses Nasales
    et des Cavités Annexes," Libraire Moloine, S. A., Paris.
Vidic, B., 1968, The postnatal development of the sphenoidal sinus

and its spread into the dorsum sellae and posterior clinoid processes, Am. J. Roentgenol, Radium Ther. & Nucl. Med., 104:177.

Wainer, H., and Thissen, D., 1975, Multivariate semi-metric smoothing in multiple prediction, J. Am. Statis. Assoc., 70:568.

Wainer, H., and Thissen, D., 1976, Two programs for predicting adult stature for individuals, Pediatrics, 58:368.

Walker, R. N., 1974, Standards for somatotyping children: I. The prediction of young adult height from children's growth data, Ann. Hum. Biol., 1:149.

Welch, Q. B., 1970, Fitting growth and research data, Growth, 34:293.

Zachmann, M., Sobradillo, B., Frank, M., Frisch, H., and Prader, A., 1978, Bayley-Pinneau, Roche-Wainer-Thissen, and Tanner height predictions in normal children and in patients with various pathologic conditions, J. Pediatr., 93:749.

11. ABNORMAL GROWTH

Roland Hauspie

Belgian National Science Foundation
Free University Brussels
Pleinlaan 2, 1050 Brussels, Belgium

To say a child's growth is "abnormal" implies one knows what is "normal" growth. The definition of normal growth is a matter of convention, originating from the need for some practical scale by which an individual's growth can be evaluated as aberrant or not. In one way or another, such scales express the most usual situation of some aspect of growth. Indeed, in the field of growth and development, the term "normal" is mostly used in the sense of "commonly occurring" or "ordinary" rather than in the sense of an ideal target to be achieved (Healy, 1978). Hence, the assessment of the normality of growth is, as a matter of fact, related to a certain standardizing group and all conclusions made about such an assessment are valuable only with respect to this group (Defrise-Gussenhoven, 1954). The standardizing group, norm or reference group should be representative of the population to which the child who is to be evaluated belongs, and should be homogenous in its geographic, ethnic, racial, social and other characteristics. Standards should also be quite recent to avoid effects of secular trends.

In this way, the normality of a child's growth can be evaluated in terms of frequencies of occurrence of a certain event of growth in the reference population. It is generally accepted to consider some event or measure of growth abnormal if it has a chance of less than 5% of being observed in the reference population. Of course, this level is chosen arbitrarily and, depending on the decisions to be made in relation to the assessment of the normality of the child's growth, one can choose any probability of occurrence as discriminatory between normal and abnormal.

It is quite important also to bear in mind that the assessment

of the normality of a particular event or measure of growth is
valuable only for that particular observation at that occasion or
over that period of time. Growth is a process in which quantitative and qualitative changes in body structures occur during a
period of almost two decades. It is totally different to assess,
for example, a child's height at age 10 years, than to check whether
the child's growth in height has been normal between the ages of 10
and 11 years, or even to see whether a series of measurements of
height between the ages of 10 and 20 years, for example, show an
acceptable pattern of growth. The first observation has mainly to
do with a very static approach to the dynamic process of growth,
and only allows one to say whether the height attained at that particular age is normal. Therefore, it can hardly be considered a
measure of the normality of growth as such. The second and third
ways of assessing growth data provide more information about the
dynamic aspects of growth and can show whether the change in growth
during a given period, or velocity, is within normal limits and if
the pattern of growth is acceptable. Specific reference material
are available for comparing the first two kinds of data.

Another approach to assessing the normality of growth is to
consider simultaneously the growth and development of several
aspects of the body (Tanner, 1958). One can be interested, for
example, in evaluating whether the weight of a child is appropriate
for the height, or if the height of a child aged 10 years is normal,
given the height of the parents, or if the time interval between
age at menarche and peak height velocity is within normal limits,
etc. Such an approach yields a measure of the degree of harmony of
growth and is certainly an equally important indication of normality
as the knowledge of the general degree of advancement or retardation
of growth (Royer and Rappaport, 1969). Falkner (1966) states that
the assessment of normality of a child's physical development should
be in relation to a background of several parameters necessitating
a multidisciplinary approach. Examples occur in the medical or
clinical assessment of growth, which may differ from a purely biometric assessment (Defrise-Gussenhoven, 1954). A child beyond the
5% limits of the normal distribution is biometrically abnormal by
convention, but will not necessarily be pathological or medically
abnormal, although a close clinical examination is probably
justified (Rappaport and Cachin, 1971).

Finally, it is quite different to state that the growth of an
individual child is abnormal than it is to state that the growth of
a group of children is abnormal. Indeed, the average growth of a
group may well deviate significantly in a statistical sense from
the population mean, while the growth of each child in this group
is within limits of normal variation. Even when the deviation of
the mean is not statistically significant, abnormality of mean
growth is not necessarily excluded in about the same way as normal
height for a single child at a particular age does not necessarily

reflect a normal pattern of growth. Suppose we have a series of
mean values for height in a cross-sectional sample at all annual
age classes between birth and 20 years, with none of the means
differing significantly from the reference data. If the number of
alternations in sequences of equally signed deviations is not randomly distributed, as shown by the runs-test (Siegel, 1956), one
can suspect that some common effect has been acting on the sample
at different age periods, producing some abnormal patterns of the
means. This is true if the means are independent from each other,
as is the case in a cross-sectional survey. Also, one has to assume
that the pattern of the sample means should follow the pattern of
the population means. Of course, such usually small and systematic
deviations of the means can be due to slightly inappropriate reference values.

SETS OF REFERENCE DATA

     Reference data for continuous measures of body growth are
usually constructed so that we can easily compare an individual's
measurement to them. They are composed of centile lines or some
measure of central tendency and dispersion of the values at each
age. The former type gives the point at a certain age or the level
during some age range below which a certain percentage of the individuals in the reference population lie, irrespective of the nature
of the distribution of the values in this population. The 50th
percentile divides the population into equally numerous halves and
is a measure of central tendency. Whenever the distribution of the
values in the reference group is symmetrical around the central
value, which is the case for most anthropometric measurements, this
distribution can be described fairly well by a mathematical model,
known as the Gaussian distribution. One can then take advantage of
the mathematical properties of the two parameters of this model (the
mean and the standard deviation); for example, about 95% of the
population values are included in the limits set by the mean plus
and minus two standard deviations.

     Assessing the normality of a single measurement of growth in
height, for instance, can be done in relation to any appropriate
reference data (cross-sectional or longitudinal), provided they
give limits of normal variation (95% limits, for example), corresponding to the child's age. Hence, accurate location of this
range of variation in the population is of great importance. It
should be noted that most published norms present means and standard
deviations based on age classes, most of which are for one year
intervals. Provided the observations are distributed homogenously
within the age class and assuming that growth progresses linearly
during the interval, the mean of all observations in the age class
is an unbiased estimate of the actual mean at the midpoint of the
interval. Assessment of the normality of an individual's growth in

height can be improved by allowing for the height of the parents, using charts of Tanner et al. (1970) for British children aged 2 to 9 years.

It is more difficult to assess the normality of multiple measurements of the same child at a single occasion. In the case of two measurements, such as height and weight, it is possible to evaluate both measurements together on a bivariate distribution (Defrise-Gussenhoven and Deshommes, 1970). A set of several measurements on the same subject can be compared and analyzed by expressing each measure in terms of standard scores, as was done by Johnston and Krogman (1964), for example, in a study on the growth of children with thalassemia major. Also standard scores are included in the computer program designed for the assessment of child growth in a clinical context (Carter, 1973). Standard scores can be used to construct biometric profiles, such as the ones used by Twiesselmann (1975) in a study of children with Down's syndrome and by Van der Linden et al. (1970) for growth changes. From these profiles, one can get an impression of the harmony in the development of various parts of the body, but it is very difficult to discern normal from abnormal.

Assessing the normality of growth during yearly intervals, for example, can be done in relation to population norms for growth velocity, such as those published by Tanner et al. (1966) for height and weight of British children. During adolescence, if there is no measure of maturity available, such assessments can be very inefficient because of the great variation of growth velocity during that period.

Whenever a series of anthropometric measurements are available over an extended age range, it is possible, although quite difficult, to assess the normality of the growth pattern. It has been stated by several authors that the pattern of growth is normal if a child follows a certain centile line. However, norms for physical development usually present means at each age, eventually connected by a smoothed curve that absorbs all small variations in the individual pattern of growth. The mean growth curve or the 50th centile line gives an approximate indication of the midpoint of the range (Falkner, 1966). During adolescence, it is normal for a child's growth in height, for example, to deviate temporarily from his prepubertal centile line, because the adolescent growth spurt of an individual is much more marked and sharper than the pattern of the mean increments at adolescence as shown in cross-sectional reference data. The latter spurt is flattened by the effect of averaging pubertal growth spurts of children who differ greatly in the timing of this event (Tanner et al., 1966). Tanner and White-house (1976), however, have partly overcome these problems by constructing clinical longitudinal reference data that allow for variation in the timing of the adolescent growth spurt between

early, average and late maturing children. On these charts, the
individual pattern of velocity in growth (height and weight) can
be evaluated against centile limits for age, corresponding to the
timing of the individual's adolescent spurt. Unfortunately, such
reference data exist only for British children and the norms for
growth available in other countries are far less powerful with
respect to the evaluation of the individual pattern of growth.

   Another approach is to derive biologically meaningful parameters from the observed pattern of growth; the variable is usually
stature. These parameters include age at peak growth velocity,
rate at peak growth velocity, gain during adolescence, age at minimum pre-pubertal velocity, size at take-off or size at peak velocity.
These parameters can be estimated objectively from the fit of an
appropriate mathematical model to the data (Preece and Baines,
1978), and compared with the ranges of variation of these parameters
in the population. A major problem, however, is that adequate
reference data for such parameters are still very scarce. This
method has another important shortcoming. Mathematical models are
only capable of describing those characteristics of the growth curve
for which they were designed, for example, the increase in height
at a decelerating rate during pre-pubertal ages or the adolescent
growth spurt. They express the variation in a number of features
of the pattern of growth and can, therefore, show abnormalities in
these features. They can be used to describe unforeseen changes in
the growth pattern, such as temporary decelerations or accelerations
in velocity other than the adolescent growth spurt. Such unusual
alterations in the growth pattern could be detected as an abnormal
peak or dip in the curve. Theoretically, one could design models
that describe such irregularities in the pattern of growth. These
would require many more parameters in the function, making the
fitting procedure much more complex and reducing the statistical
validity of the fit. In the field of assessing the normality of
the pattern of growth of an individual child, there are still many
methodological problems to be solved.

CATCH-UP GROWTH

   A very interesting phenomenon related to abnormal growth is
that of catch-up growth. An individual with a retarded pattern of
growth tends to restore his growth deficit (or excess) as soon as
the growth-disturbing conditions are partly or completely eliminated.
Forbes (1974) has described the process in mathematical terms and
states catch-up growth is complete only when the integrated velocity
excess during recovery matches the previous deficit. Prader et al.
(1963) illustrated the phenomenon of catch-up growth for height,
weight and skeletal maturity during and after treatment of illness
and in children with restored food intake after starvation. They
concluded the amount of catch-up growth depends on the magnitude of the

growth deficit and the duration of the growth disturbance. In another series of examples, Prader (1978) illustrated that the process of catch-up growth showed some rather constant characteristics, such as a sharp increase of the growth velocity followed by a progressive deceleration until the original "growth channel" is reached.

Tanner (1978) states there are two different ways in which catch-up growth can be achieved and that a mixture of the two is common. The first he calls "true catch-up growth." This matches the description by Prader in that it consists of a considerable increase in growth velocity until the original curve or pattern is reached. Thereafter, growth proceeds normally. The other way is a delayed maturation and prolonged period of growth, without an abnormal increase in velocity.

SOME OBSERVATIONS ON ABNORMAL GROWTH IN ASTHMATIC CHILDREN

Several authors have shown height and weight are commonly retarded in children with chronic respiratory diseases (Cohen et al., 1940; Falliers et al., 1961, 1963; Smith, 1963; Spock, 1965; Snyder et al., 1967).

We analyzed data from a mixed longitudinal sample of 568 asthmatic boys aged 2.5 to 20 years, living in a Residential Institute for asthmatic children (Zeepreventorium), in De Haan, Belgium. The sample had a distribution of socioeconomic levels that did not differ significantly from the reference population. The mean patterns of growth were determined for height, weight, a series of longitudinal and transverse body dimensions, and head and face measurements. The way in which the mixed longitudinal data were treated to obtain mean values at each age is described elsewhere (Hauspie et al., 1976).

The main conclusions of this study can be summarized as follows. The mean pattern of growth for most of the anthropometric measurements appears to differ from the reference growth curves. Except the dimensions of the head, all longitudinal and transverse measures as well as weight show a delay during adolescence. Also longitudinal dimensions appear to be constantly below the average norms during the prepubertal period, though the deviation is always less pronounced than during adolescence. Towards adulthood, a catch-up growth is seen for the mean pattern of growth in height and biacromial diameter; a corresponding catch-up for weight is not observed. The pattern of the mean annual increments shows a delay of the pubertal growth spurts for height and weight; the other measurements cannot be analyzed in this way because the patterns of the means are irregular.

A retardation of growth due to a delay in the adolescent growth spurt is typical of delayed maturers. Hauspie et al. (1977) showed that a slow rate of growth during adolescence is associated with delayed development of pubic hair and slow skeletal maturation. The catch-up observed in the patterns of change in the mean values across age may well reflect a true individual catch-up growth because the mean yearly increments for height in asthmatic boys after the age of 15 years are consistently larger than the average velocity in the reference data. The average growth period is prolonged by about one year, compared to the reference population, and the final height of the asthmatic boys is equal to the average adult height in the reference group. Growth in weight of asthmatic boys remains significantly below average but weight is normal at adulthood.

The adolescent delay of growth in height and weight of asthmatic children found in this study is in agreement with the recent findings of Wittig et al. (1978) and Hauspie et al. (1979) in a study of a cross-sectional sample of 500 asthmatic boys from Hungary. This latter study is another example of abnormal growth that is hardly detectable for an individual child but is significant in terms of means and patterns of change in the means across age.

REFERENCES

Carter, B. S., 1973, A program for assessing the effect of treatment on growth and development in children with growth disorders, Comput. Biol. Med., 3:443.
Cohen, M. B., Weller, R. R., and Cohen, S., 1940, Anthropometry in children, Am. J. Dis. Child., 60:1058.
Defrise-Gussenhoven, E., 1954, Croissance et débilité, Institut Royal des Sciences Naturelles de Belgique, Mémoire No. 128.
Defrise-Gussenhoven, E., and Deshommes, M., 1970, Graphiques de croissance corrélée du poids, de la taille et de la somme des périmètres des membres, Publication du Centre National de Radiobiologie et de Génétique, Brussels.
Falkner, F., 1966, General considerations in human development, in: "Human Development," F. Falkner, ed., W. B. Saunders, Philadelphia.
Falliers, C. J., Szentivanyi, J., McBride, M., and Bukantz, S. C., 1961, Growth rate of children with intractable asthma, J. Allergy, 32:420.
Falliers, C. J., Tan, S., Szentivanyi, J., Jorgensen, J. R., and Bukantz, S. C., 1963, Childhood asthma and steroid therapy as influences on growth, Am. J. Dis. Child., 105:127.
Forbes, G. B., 1974, A note on the mathematics of "catch-up" growth, Pediatr. Res., 8:929.

Hauspie, R., Susanne, C., and Alexander, F., 1976, A mixed longi-
    tudinal study of the growth in height and weight in asth-
    matic children, Hum. Biol., 48:271.

Hauspie, R., Susanne, C., and Alexander, F., 1977, Maturational
    delay and temporal growth retardation in asthmatic boys,
    J. Allerg. Clin. Immunol., 89:200.

Hauspie, R., Gyenis, G., Alexander, F., Simon, G., Susanne, C., and
    Madách, A., 1979, Heights and weights of Hungarian and
    Belgian asthmatic boys, Hum. Biol., in press.

Healy, M. J. R., 1978, Statistics of growth standards, in: "Human
    Growth," Vol. 1., F. Falkner and J. M. Tanner, eds.,
    Baillière Tindall, London.

Johnston, F. E., and Krogman, W. M., 1964, Patterns of growth in
    children with thalassemia major, Ann. N. Y. Acad. Sci.,
    119:667.

Prader, A., 1978, Catch-up growth, in: "Paediatrics and Growth,"
    D. Barltrop, ed., Fellowship of Postgraduate Medicine,
    London.

Prader, A., Tanner, J. M., and von Harnack, G. A., 1963, Catch-up
    growth following illness or starvation: an example of
    developmental canalization in man, J. Pediatr., 62:646.

Preece, M. A., and Baines, M. J., 1978, Analysis of the human
    growth curve, Brit. Postgrad. Med. J., 54:77.

Rappaport, R., and Cachin, D., 1971, Abord pratique des retards de
    croissance avant la puberté, Rev. Pédiatr., 7:629.

Royer, P., and Rappaport, R., 1969, Les ressources thérapeutiques
    dans les défauts de développement statural, Rev. Prac., 19:
    2279.

Siegel, S., 1956, "Nonparametric Statistics for the Behavioral
    Sciences," McGraw-Hill, London.

Smith, J. M., 1963, Prolonged treatment with prednisolone in
    children with asthma, Tubercle, 44:281.

Snyder, R. D., Collip, P. J., and Greene, J. S., 1967, Growth and
    ultimate height of children with asthma, Clin. Pediatr.,
    5:389.

Spock, A., 1965, Growth patterns in 200 children with bronchial
    asthma, Ann. Allergy, 23:608.

Tanner, J. M., 1958, Growth and the prediction of abnormality,
    Dent. Pract., 8:220.

Tanner, J. M., 1978, "Education and Physical Growth," Hodder and
    Stoughton, London.

Tanner, J. M., and Whitehouse, R. H., 1976, Clinical longitudinal
    standards for height, weight, height velocity, weight veloc-
    ity and stages of puberty, Arch. Dis. Childh., 51:170.

Tanner, J. M., Whitehouse, R. H., and Takaishi, M., 1966, Standards
    from birth to maturity for height, weight, height velocity,
    and weight velocity: British children 1965, Part I,
    Arch. Dis. Childh., 41:454.

Tanner, J. M., Goldstein, H., and Whitehouse, R. H., 1970, Stan-
    dards for children's height at ages 2 - 9 years allowing
    for height of parents, Arch. Dis. Childh., 45:755.
Twiesselmann, F., 1975, Biométrie comparée de trisomique G et de
    crétins endémiques, Population et familles, 34:81.
Van der Linden, F. P., Hirschfield, W. J., and Miller, R. L., 1970,
    On the analysis and presentation of longitudinally collected
    growth data, Growth, 34:385.
Wittig, H. J., McLaughlin, E. T., and Belloit, J. D., 1978, Growth
    retardation in children with chronic asthma in the absence
    of prolonged steroid therapy, Allergol. et Immunopathol.,
    6:203.

12. AGEING, CONTINUOUS CHANGES OF ADULTHOOD

Charles Susanne

Free University Brussels
Pleinlaan 2, 1050 Brussels, Belgium

Developmental processes or changes in morphology continue
after puberty. Ageing is difficult to define, since it is a continuous process and it is impossible to distinguish between effects
related only to time and the effects of degenerative diseases.
These diseases are the cause or the result of senescence. The
theories of ageing are very numerous but it is quite clear that the
processes of formation or destruction are present in all stages
from conception to death, the ratio between the processes being,
however, different. There is no clear starting point of senescence.

It is probable that the onset and the rate of senescence are
genetically determined. Studies of twins have shown a very high
concordance between monozygotic twins for characters of the aged,
such as grey hair, baldness, and wrinkled skin (Vogt et al., 1939;
Von Verschuer, 1954; Nishimura and Shimizu, 1963). A genetic component has been postulated also for the timing of menopause
(Moretti, 1953). These different genetic factors, but also the
influence or interaction with environmental factors, determine
longevity. That some genetic factors could have an influence on
this very complex character is demonstrated by the fact that the
maximum observed lifespan of a species can be predicted for mam-
malia and especially for primates with an accuracy of about 25%
from a multiple regression of lifespan on brain and body weight
(Sacher, 1975). A heritable component but of very low level has
been suggested for human longevity by twin studies and by familial
studies (Kallmann, 1957; Jarvik et al., 1960, see also Table 1).
An environmental component is present also; Philippe (1978) showed
the coefficients of longevity between spouses were of the same
level as the coefficients between relatives, suggesting that the
familial likeness in age at death could be due to a common way of
life.

Table 1. Coefficient of Correlation of Age at Death

	FS	FD	MS	MD	B-B	Si-Si	Spouses
Beeton and							
Pearson, 1901	0.14	0.13	0.13	0.15	0.29	0.33	
Pearl, 1931	0.06	0.05					
Nöllenburg, 1932	0.14	(0.07)	0.10	0.10	0.11	0.12	
Stoessiger, 1932	0.11		0.16		0.23	0.20	
	0.11				0.26		
	0.14						
Pearl and							
Dewitt, 1934	(0.09)	(0.02)	0.16	(0.07)			
Jalavisto, 1951[a]	(0.12)	(0.04)	(0.16)	(0.20)			
Philippe, 1978	(0.10)	(0.07)	(0.05)	0.16	(0.09)	0.21	0.12

a = coefficient of regression; F:father, M:mother, S:son, D:daughter, B:brother, Si:sister. Values in parentheses are not significant.

PHYSIOLOGICAL CHANGES

     With ageing, mitosis begins to fail to compensate for the
loss of dead cells resulting in a phase of negative growth which is
first observed in the central nervous system, because cell replacement does not occur here. Time of reaction increases, special
senses and movement accuracy gradually deteriorate, and a diffuse
atrophy of the brain begins shortly after puberty. Other modifications are noticeable after 20 or 30 years of age (Sinclair, 1973).
The lymphoid component of the spleen decreases, as well as the
number of hair follicles; there is atrophy of the ovaries, breast
tissue, and the intertubular areas of the testes; the pancreas,
liver, heart, and kidney tend to become smaller; there is diminution of the extensibility of the elastic fibers, and calcification
of cartilages is observed. All these processes are very gradual;
consequently, a physiological age is undefinable.

     The definition of a period of complete maturation is impossible
for vital capacity also. This reaches a maximum at 20 years and
decreases afterwards (Norris et al., 1963). In maximum breathing
capacity (volume breathed during a 15-second period of deep and
rapid breathing) corrected for surface area, the reported mean
values are 80 l/square meter/min at age of 20 years but 36.5
l/square meter/min at age 80 years. The diminution of the elastic-
ity of the lungs and calcification of rib cartilages are implicated.
The increase with age in mean serum cholesterol level is also well-
known (Abraham et al., 1978).

An increase of blood pressure, especially of systolic blood pressure, is observed during the entire lifespan (Wolański and Pyžuk, 1973; Roberts, 1975; Roberts and Maurer, 1978). A gradual loss of metabolizing tissue with advancing age is translated into a diminution of oxygen consumption per unit of lean body mass (Pařízková, 1963; Astrand et al., 1973), of the basal heat production expressed in cal per square meter per hour and of total body water (Shock et al., 1963). A diminution of metabolism per unit body weight is observed between 20 and 40 years (Keys et al., 1973).

An increase in cell volume of lymphocytes is observed in vivo (Simons and Van Den Broek, 1970). This supports the hypothesis that ageing is due to an increase of inactive protein or of ir-removable substances (Walford, 1967). Age changes in differential leucocyte count have been studied longitudinally by Polednak (1978): a decrease in leucocyte count may be related to "ageing" of lymphoid organs, and an increase of eosinophils and monocytes to responses to mild infections. These results confirm those from cross-sectional studies (Alexopoulos and Babitis, 1976; Augener et al., 1974) on T lymphocytes. Even in muscles, effects of ageing are evident; diminution of muscle width (Meema et al., 1973), increase in capsule thickness (Swash and Fox, 1972), decrease in cytoplasm and in total number of muscle fibers, increase in connective tissue, and fat cells (Inokuchi et al., 1975).

Adulthood is not a stable physiological and biochemical period; also, changes are numerous and constantly observed at osteological and anthropometric levels.

OSTEOLOGICAL CHANGES

Skeletal changes are very numerous during the senescent period. Remodelling of bones has been observed together with increases in bone diameters due to continued periosteal apposition but simultaneous decrease in cortical thickness of the tubular bones and increases of diameters of ribs (Epker and Frost, 1966; Semine and Damon, 1975), femur (Smith and Walker, 1964; Trotter et al., 1968), second metacarpal (Garn et al., 1967; Dequeker, 1972) and other tubular bones (Virtama and Helela, 1969). This imbalanced bone remodelling, with reduced new bone formation and less marked reduction in bone resorption, results in skeletal rarefaction (Meema et al., 1973). Trotter and Hixon (1974) observed a decrease in the weight of the dry, fat-free osseous skeletons of 15.6 gm/y starting from 40 years of age.

The bodies of the lumbar vertebrae become significantly shorter and broader, accompanied by the development of vertical columns of periosteal bone between large osteophytes (Ericksen, 1978) and increasing trabecular atrophy, particularly of horizontal

trabeculae (Tanaka, 1975). The entire skeletal volume decreases
due to the loss of cancellous bone, particularly horizontal trabeculae; irregular thickening of vertical trabeculae is observed also.
The percentage of vertebral trabecular surfaces covered with
osteoid is highest in infancy and decreases until the age of 40
years when growth remodelling is in equilibrium (Jung Kuei Wei and
Arnold, 1972). After 40 years of age, there is progressive loss
of bone mass with ageing and the level of osteoid increases progressively. In young adults, this osteoid is present only on
transverse trabeculae; in old age it is present on vertical trabeculae also. An enlargement of marrow cavities has been observed
at the frontozygomatic suture (Kokich, 1976), in the mandible
(Manson and Lucas, 1962) and in the ribs (Epker et al., 1965).

ANTHROPOMETRIC CHANGES (FACE AND HEAD)

     The patterns of change are related to the osteological
changes; apposition ectocranially and resorption endocranially
throughout adulthood and senescence alter the skull dimensions
(Table 2). Israel (1973) reported cranial thickening at the
frontal region and increases in skull size from adulthood to
senescence; the outer skull diameters tend to increase also.
Overall mandibular size increases consistently. These findings of
Israel are, however, contested on the basis of methodological
aspects by Tallgren (1974).

     Enlargement of the head in breadth and length is observed
commonly. Most transverse studies show an increase of head length
with age (Pfitzner, 1899; Saller, 1930, 1931; Jarcho, 1935; Hooton
and Dupertuis, 1951; Lasker, 1953) but a few non-significant decreases have been reported (Dahlberg and Wahlund, 1941; Coon, 1950;
Marquer and Chamla, 1961). In a longitudinal study, Büchi (1950)
and Susanne (1977) found increases in head length; in the latter
study, a mean increase of 2.86 mm was observed between about 32
and 54 years of age. This change with age in individuals is compensated by secular changes; as a result, transverse studies show
only small changes. In the longitudinal study of Susanne, individual alterations with age are more evident for head breadth
(5.27 mm increase during the same period) than for head length.
This increase is observed also in transverse studies (significant
for Saller, 1930, 1931; Coon, 1950; Goldstein, 1943; Lasker, 1953;
non-significant for Pfitzner, 1899; Hrdlička, 1935; Dahlberg and
Wahlund, 1941; Hooton and Dupertuis, 1951; Marquer and Chamla,
1961). The face also continues to grow during old age; some facial
features grow slowly to the fourth decade, others to the fifth
decade or later. These changes involve face heights and diameters,
and the morphology of mouth, nose and ears.

     In transverse studies, a net increase in bizygomatic width,

Table 2. Changes with Age of Cephalic Characters

	Sample	No. Years Longitud.	Observation
Transverse studies			
Israel (1971)		---	no changes, excepted increase in thickness of bregma region
Boersma (1974) lateral radiographs	58-91y ♂ and ♀	---	no increase, excepted length of nasal floor in ♀
Fenart et al. (1975) vestibular orientation	♂ and ♀ ?	---	depression and retirement of pre-vestibular region
Longitudinal studies			
Thompson & Kendrick (1964) cephalometry	n=71 ♂ 22-34y	1 y	significant increase in skull height, and upper, lower and total facial height
Tallgren (1967) lateral radiographs		7 y	no changes in cranial base, upper face and mandibular base
Carlsson & Persson (1967)		5 y	no changes in cranial base, upper face
Kendrick & Risinger (1967) cephalometry	n=71 ♂ 22-34y	1 y	significant increase of anterior and posterior cranial length, of upper, middle and lower facial depth
Israel (1968) lateral radiographs	24-56y n=43 ♂ n=53 ♀	13-28 y	increase external, internal skull diameters, intersutural distances, thickness frontal and parietal bones, length of cranial base, height of upper face
Israel (1973) lateral radiographs	n=26 24-64y	13-28 y	increase in the size of the sella turcica
Israel (1970) lateral radiographs			continual growth of craniofacial complex
Tallgren (1974) lateral radiographs	20-73y n=32 ♀	15 y	no changes, excepted increase of the distances sella-glabella, slight apposition thickening in glabellar and frontal areas

probably until at least 60 years of age, suggests continuing periosteal apposition. An increase in the length of the nose due to a
growth of cartilage and deposition of fat has been observed constantly, with a variable age-limit situated between 30 and 60 years.
On the contrary, the increase in nose breadth is constant during
adulthood and could be due to an increase of adipose tissue with
bulbous enlargement of the wings of the nose. Other changes during
adulthood include, for example, increase in the size of the ears,
decrease in the height of the lips. An extensive bibliography is
to be found in Susanne (1974). Longitudinal studies show these
changes are related to senescence per se (Büchi, 1950; Susanne,
1977). Individual increases with age in bizygomatic breadth are
very evident (4.86 mm between 32 and 54 years of age; Susanne,
1977) and result in the observation of increases in many transverse
samples (Pfitzner, 1899; Saller, 1930, 1931; Jarcho, 1935;
Hrdlička, 1935; Dahlberg and Wahlund, 1941; Goldstein, 1943; Coon,
1950; Hooton and Dupertuis, 1951; Lasker, 1953; Marquer and
Chamla, 1961). Periosteal apposition could be responsible for
these individual changes that are perhaps also due to changes in
fat tissue. Indeed, when a diminution of fat is observed at a
later age, a decrease in bizygomatic breadth is observed (Dahlberg
and Wahlund, 1941; Büchi, 1950; Marquer and Chamla, 1961). Other
changes of senescence have been demonstrated by Büchi (1950) and
Susanne (1974, 1977), such as increases in bigonial breadth,
morphological height of the face, nasion-stomion height, and ear
height and a decrease in lip height.

ANTHROPOMETRIC CHANGES (BODY)

The study of weight typifies the difficulties of interpreting
data relative to adulthood. In transverse studies of Western populations, mean weights increase during the first decades of adulthood but after 60 years a clear and very significant decrease is
observed (Master et al., 1959; Parot, 1959; Bourlière, 1963;
Norris et al., 1963; Bourlière et al., 1966). These variations,
however, are not entirely due to individual changes with age but
also to differential mortality (Susanne, 1977).

The changes in weight depend moreover on the nutritional
status of the populations studied; a decrease in body mass is sometimes marked in populations with unsatisfactory nutritional status
(Sinnett et al., 1973; Harvey, 1974). The percent contribution of
fat and water to body mass changes very regularly with age. A
decrease of the water component and increase of the fat component
is observed from 20 to 90 years of age (Young et al., 1963;
Brožek, 1965). In an attempt to reflect the general development
of subcutaneous fat by the sum of ten skinfolds, Pařizkova (1963)
reported a constant increase in both sexes between 20 and 60 years
of age. These results are in agreement with those of Parot (1959,

1961), and Wessel et al. (1963). However, in subjects studied
longitudinally from 70 to 90 years of age, Pařizková and Eisett
(1971) did not find significant changes in relative or absolute
amounts of depot fat. Increases in skinfold thicknesses with age
are not observed in poorly nourished populations; this is in agreement with the findings for weight (Slome, 1960; Abbie, 1967;
Crognier, 1969). Changes are observed in transverse studies of
other body measurements. Only slight changes occur in biacromial
diameter till 55 years of age, but a large decrease is observed
after this age (Saller, 1930, 1931; Hooton and Dupertuis, 1951;
Lasker, 1953; Parot, 1961; Marquer and Chamla, 1961; Wessel et al.,
1963; Susanne, 1971). A marked increase with age has been observed
in biiliac diameter by Marquer and Chamla (1961), Parot (1961),
Wessel et al. (1963), and Susanne (1971). Significant decreases
in sitting-height between 45 and 65 years of age were observed by
Hooton and Dupertuis (1951), Lasker (1953), Parot (1961), and
Marquer and Chamla (1961). An increase in upper arm circumference
has been observed by Wessel et al. (1963) and Susanne (1971).

A decrease in stature is observed in many transverse studies
(Quetelet, 1870; Weissenberg, 1895; Pfitzner, 1899; Bartucz, 1917;
Saller, 1930; Boas, 1935; Jarcho, 1935; Hrdlička, 1935; Dahlberg
and Wahlund, 1941; Goldstein, 1943; Coon, 1950; Hooton and Dupertuis, 1951; Lasker, 1953; Takahashi and Atsumi, 1955; Kaufman et
al., 1958; Lee and Lasker, 1958; Parot, 1961; Marquer and Chamla,
1961; Bourlière et al., 1966; Susanne, 1967). The ageing process
per se involving stature is, presumably, the result of shrinkage
or compression of the intervertebral discs, osteoporosis, increasing curvature of the spine (Milne and Lauder, 1974) and inability
to stand erect. However, factors such as arthritic lipping of
articular margins and appositional bone growth (Lasker, 1953) may
contribute also to age changes. Moreover, in the transverse method
of study, differences cannot be directly identified with age
changes in individuals. Indeed, secular changes interfere with
clear expression of individual age changes.

SENESCENCE OR SECULAR CHANGES

Because data for studies of adults are often cross-sectional,
it is necessary to separate the changes due to secular changes
from those resulting from senescence or continuing growth, especially in the face. Moreover, selective survival, for instance of
more robust individuals, must also be taken into account in the
interpretation of cross-sectional data.

Some authors have studied long bones because their lengths are
highly correlated with stature and are influenced by secular changes
but not by age-associated factors. Trotter and Gleser (1951)
estimated the decrease of stature at 0.06 cm/y between 20 and 90

years of age. Hertzog et al. (1969) found a good agreement between
longitudinally derived statural loss and estimates calculated from
regression equations using age-specific tibial lengths. By multiple regression of stature and age, controlling for subischial
length, the ageing changes per se of stature were estimated in a
sample from rural Colombia at 0.12 cm/y for men of 28 to 81 years
of age and at 0.03 cm/y for females from 22 to 62 years of age
(Himes and Mueller, 1977a). However, there may be a small ageing
phenomenon in subischial length also due to increasing frequency
of bowed legs, flat feet or thinning of articular cartilages. With
this same method, Himes and Mueller (1977b) showed that groups at
low socioeconomic levels tended to lose stature at a faster rate
than did higher socioeconomic groups; the differences were significant for women.

Longitudinal studies are more successful in distinguishing
age changes from secular trends, but their numbers are limited. A
decrease in stature is always observed (Table 3), but there are
considerable population differences in the timing of this ageing
process. In a longitudinal study of a Belgian population, and in
comparison with a transverse sample, Susanne (1967) observed a
secular change of 1.24 cm per decade for stature; individual
changes in stature were not observed in adulthood before 45 years
of age but changes at older ages were estimated at 0.83 cm per
decade. These results were observed in a longitudinal study with
measurements at an interval of 22 years and with individuals ranging in age to a maximum of 65 years. These results cannot be
extrapolated after 65 years of age; the senescent changes within
individuals are not necessarily a linear function of age.

Longitudinal studies for other measurements are still more
limited (Table 4): significant decreases in sitting height, arm
span, and forearm circumference are observed, together with significant increases in bicristal diameter, and chest and abdominal
circumferences. These are attributed to ageing processes such as
relaxation of the muscles of the abdominal wall (abdominal circumference) and senile emphysema of the lungs (chest circumference).
Although a decline of lean body mass is not observed for all subjects in longitudinal studies, a mean decline of 6.3% of the initial
value per decade between 22 and 57 years has been reported (Forbes,
1976). This indicates that an increase of body fat is associated
with a constant body weight during ageing. Ageing leads to thinner
extremities and a thicker trunk partly because of fat redistribution and a decrease in some lean tissues (Borkan and Norris, 1977).

CONCLUSION

Morphological, physiological and psychological traits change
during adulthood: an important factor in the sampling of a

Table 3. Longitudinal Studies of Stature in Aged

	Sample	Max. Age	Interval	Observation
Büchi, 1950	129 ♂	64 y	9 y	increase 0.75 cm between 20-37 y; decrease 1.75 cm (0.064 cm/y)
	67 ♀	64 y	9 y	increase 0.54 cm between 20-28 y; decrease 2.64 cm (0.073 cm/y)
Lipscomb and Parnell, 1954	44 ♂	72 y		no decrease
Damon, 1965	187 ♂	56 y		no decrease
Gsell, 1966	♂			declining from 30 y
Miall et al., 1967	♂			increase to age 35-40
	326	70 y	6-8 y	decrease 1.7 cm (0.056 cm/y)
	428	70 y	6-8 y	decrease 3.5 cm (0.12 cm/y)
	♀			increase to age 25
	405	70 y	6-8 y	decrease 3.5 cm (0.077 cm/y)
	430	70 y	6-8 y	decrease 4.3 cm (0.095 cm/y)
Hertzog et al., 1969	52 ♀	63 y	10-40 y	decrease of 0.134 cm/y from 45 y 30-45 y: -.14 cm; 30-55 y: -1.02 cm; 30-65 y: -2.82 cm
Parizková and Eisett, 1971	14 ♂	70 y	8-10 y	1 cm decrease between 60-70 y (0.1 cm/y)
	21 ♂	70 y	8-10 y	1.3 cm decrease between 60-70 y (0.13 cm/y)
	10 ♂	80 y	8-10 y	1.49 cm decrease between 70-80 y (0.149 cm/y)
	10 ♂	80 y	8-10 y	1.55 cm decrease between 70-80 y (0.155 cm/y)
Susanne, 1974 1977	44 ♂		22 y	decrease from 45 y of 0.083 cm/y
Borkan and Norris, 1977	50 ♂	84 y	6,8 y	decrease from 25 y

Table 4. Longitudinal Studies of Other Body Measurements by Age

Weight

Pařízková and Eisett (1971)	between 60 and 80 y	+0.239 kg/y to -0.284 kg/y
Borkan and Norris (1977)	between 25 and 85 y	increase till 55 years (0.311 kg/y)
		decrease between 55 and 75 years
		(0.149 kg/y) corresponds with a de-
		crease of fat-free weight from 25 y
		but an increase of body fat weight
		till 65 years
Susanne (1977)	between 30 and 55 y	individual increase (0.398 kg/y)

Sitting height

Büchi (1950)	between 20 and 70 y	decrease from 55 y
Pařízková and Eisett (1971)	between 60 and 80 y	decrease: 0.282 cm/y to 0.623 cm/y
Susanne (1977)	between 30 and 55 y	decrease: 0.023 cm/y

Biacromial diameter

| Pařízková and Eisett (1971) | between 60 and 80 y | decrease: 0.025 cm/y to 0.115 cm/y |
| Susanne (1977) | between 30 and 55 y | NS; +0.003 cm/y |

Bicristal diameter

| Pařízková and Eisett (1971) | between 60 and 80 y | increase: 0.286 cm/y to 0.306 cm/y |
| Susanne (1977) | between 30 and 55 y | increase: 0.09 cm/y |

Arm circumference (relaxed)

| Pařízková and Eisett (1971) | between 60 and 80 y | +0.033 cm/y to -0.093 cm/y |
| Susanne (1977) | between 30 and 55 y | increase: 0.05 cm/y |

population is the age of the individuals. The growth of a child occurs between limits defined by its genotype; it is very likely that changes in individuals during senescence also occur within limits defined by genetic factors, although environmental factors are very important also.

The longitudinal method is the most suitable for the study of changes in individuals during old age. In transverse studies, these individual changes are associated with differences due to secular changes, and perhaps with changes due to selective survival. Longitudinal studies of twins or sibs may help understand the interactions between genetic and different environmental factors that determine the complex changes of ageing.

REFERENCES

Abbie, A., 1967, Skinfold thickness in Australian aborigines, Arch. Phys. Anthr. in Oceania, 2:207.
Abraham, S., Johnson, C. L., and Carroll, M. D., 1978, "Total Serum Cholesterol Levels of Adults 18-74 Years," Vital and Health Statistics, Series 11, No. 205, U.S. Government Printing Office, Washington, D.C.
Alexopoulos, C., and Babitis, P., 1976, Age dependence of T lympho-cytes, Lancet, 1:426.
Astrand, I., Astrand, P. O., Hallback, I., and Kilborn, A., 1973, Reduction in maximal oxygen uptake with age, J. Appl. Physiol., 35:649.
Augener, W., Cohen, G., Reuter, A., and Bittinger, G., 1974, Decrease of T lymphocytes during ageing, Lancet, 1:1164.
Bartucz, L., 1917, Die Körpergrösse der heutigen Magyaren, Arch. Anthrop., 15:44.
Beeton, M., and Pearson, K., 1901, On the inheritance of the dura-tion of life, and on the intensity of natural selection of man, Biometrika, 1:50.
Boas, F., 1935, Studies in growth, Hum. Biol., 7:303.
Boersma, H., 1974, Alteration of skull dimensions in aged persons, J. Dent. Res., 53:678.
Borkan, G. A., and Norris, A. H., 1977, Fat redistribution and the changing body dimensions of the adult male, Hum. Biol., 49: 495.
Bourlière, F., 1963, Principes et méthodes de mesure de l'âge bio-logique chez l'homme, Bull. et Mém. Soc. d'Anthropologie de Paris, 4:561.
Bourlière, F., Clement, F., and Parot, S., 1966, Normes de vieilli-sement morphologique et physiologique d'une population de niveau socio-économique élevé de la région parisienne, Bull. et Mém. Soc. d'Anthrop. Paris, 10:11.
Brožek, J., 1965, Age trends and adult sex differences in body com-position, Homenaje a Juan Comas, Mexico, Editorial, Libros

de Mexico, Mexico.

Büchi, E. C., 1950, Aenderung der Körperform beim erwachsenen Menschen, Anthrop. Forsch. (Anthrop. Gesellsch. in Wien), 1:1.

Carlsson, G. E., and Persson, G., 1967, Morphologic changes of the
mandible after extraction and wearing of dentures. A longitudinal clinical and X-ray cephalometric study covering 5
years, Odont. Rev., 18:27.

Coon, C. S., 1950, The mountain of giants: a racial and cultural
study of the North Albanian mountain Ghegs, Pap. Peabody
Mus., 23:106.

Crognier, E., 1969, Données biométriques sur l'état de nutrition
d'une population Africaine tropicale: Les Sara du Tchad,
Biometrie humaine, 4:37.

Dahlberg, G., and Wahlund, S., 1941, "The Race Biology of the
Swedish Lapps," II, Anthropometrical survey, Uppsala.

Damon, A., 1965, Discrepancies between findings of longitudinal
and cross-sectional studies in adult life: physique and
physiology, Hum. Dev., 8:16.

Dequeker, J., 1972, Bone loss in normal and pathological conditions,
Diss. Univ. Leuven, Belgium.

Epker, B. N., and Frost, H. M., 1966, Periosteal appositional bone
growth from age two to age seventy in man, A tetracycline
evaluation, Anat. Rec., 154:573.

Epker, B., Kelvin, M., and Frost, H., 1965, Magnitude and location
of cortical bone loss in human rib with ageing, Clin.
Orthop., 41:198.

Ericksen, M. F., 1978, Aging in the lumbar spine III: L5, Am. J.
Phys. Anthropol., 48:247.

Fenart, R., Deblock, R., and Dufresnoy, P., 1975, Modifications
apportées par la sénescence, au profil cranien, en orienta-
tion vestibulaire, Bull. Soc. Anthr. Paris, 13 II:231.

Forbes, G. B., 1976, The adult decline in lean body mass, Hum.
Biol., 48:161.

Garn, S. M., Rohmann, C. G., Wagner, B., and Ascoli, W., 1967,
Continuing bone growth throughout life: a general phenomenon, Am. J. Phys. Anthropol., 26:313.

Goldstein, M. S., 1943, Demographic and bodily changes in descendants of Mexican immigrants with comparable data on parents
and children in Mexico, Publ. Inst. Latin American Studies,
Univ. Texas (cited by Lasker, 1953).

Gsell, 1966, Longitudinale Alterforschung, Med. Wochenschrift,
96:1541.

Harvey, R. G., 1974, An anthropometric survey of growth and
physique of the populations of Karkar Island and Lufa sub-
district, New Guinea, Phil. Trans. R. Soc. Lond. B., 268:
279.

Hertzog, K., Garn, S. M., and Hempy, H., 1969, Partitioning the
effects of secular trend and ageing on adult stature, Am.
J. Phys. Anthropol., 31:111.

Himes, J. H., and Mueller, W. H., 1977a, Ageing and secular change in adult stature in rural Colombia, Am. J. Phys. Anthropol., 46:275.

Himes, J. H., and Mueller, W. H., 1977b, Age associated statural loss and socio-economic status, J. Am. Geriatr. Soc., 25:171.

Hooton, E. A., and Dupertuis, C. W., 1951, Age changes and selective survival in Irish males, Stud. Phys. Anthropol., 2:1.

Hrdlička, A., 1935, The Pueblos, with comparative data on the bulk of the tribes of southwest and northern Mexico, Am. J. Phys. Anthropol., 20:235.

Inokuchi, S., Ishikawa, H., Iwamoto, S., and Kimura, T., 1975, Age-related changes in the histological composition of the rectus abdominis muscle of the adult human, Hum. Biol., 47:231.

Israel, H., 1968, Continuing growth in the human cranial skeleton, Arch. Oral Biol., 13:133.

Israel, H., 1970, Continuing growth in sella turcica with age, Am. J. Roent. Rad. Ther. and Nucl. Med., 108:516.

Israel, H., 1971, "The impact of aging upon the adult cranio-facial skeleton," Ph.D. Thesis, Univ. Alabama.

Israel, H., 1973, Age factor and the pattern of change in craniofacial structures, Am. J. Phys. Anthropol., 39:111.

Jalavisto, E., 1951, Inheritance of longevity according to Finnish and Swedish geneologies, Ann. Med. Int. Fenn., 40:263.

Jarcho, A., 1935, Die Aeltersveränderungen der Rassenmerkmale bei Erwachsenen, Anthrop. Anz., 12:173.

Jarvik, L. F., Falek, A., Kallmann, F. J., and Lorge, I., 1960, Survival trends in a senescent twin population, Am. J. Hum. Genet., 12:170.

Jung, K. W., and Arnold, J. S., 1972, Variation in osteoid pattern with age in human vertebrae, Okajimas Folia Anat. Jap., 49:157.

Kallmann, F. J., 1957, Twin data on the genetics of ageing, in: "Colloquia on Ageing," (Ciba Foundation, No. 3), Churchill, London.

Kaufmann, H., Hägler, K., and Lang, R., 1958, Analyse anthropologique et statistique de Walsers orientaux et de Romanches de l'Oberhallstein, Arch. Suisses Anthrop. Gén., 23:1.

Kendrick, G. S., and Risinger, H. L., 1967, Changes in the antero-posterior dimensions of the human male skull during the third and fourth decade of life, Anat. Rec., 159:77.

Keys, A., Taylor, H. L., and Grande, F., 1973, Basal metabolism and age of adult man, Metabolism, 22:579.

Kokich, V. G., 1976, Age changes in the human frontozygomatic suture from 20 to 95 years, Am. J. Orthod., 69:411.

Lasker, G. W., 1953, The age factor in bodily measurements of adult male and female Mexicans, Hum. Biol., 25:50.

Lee, M. C., and Lasker, G. W., 1958, The thickness of subcutaneous fat in elderly men, Am. J. Phys. Anthropol., 16:125.

Lipscomb, F. M., and Parnell, R. W., 1954, The physique of Chelsea pensioners, J. Royal Army Med. Corps, 100:247.

Manson, J. D., and Lucas, R. B., 1962, A microradiographic study
    of the age changes in the human mandible, Arch. Oral Biol.,
    7:761.
Marquer, P., and Chamla, M. C., 1961, L'évolution des caractères
    morphologiques en fonction de l'âge chez 2,089 Français de
    20 à 91 ans., Bull. et Mém. Soc. d'Anthrop. Paris, 2:1.
Master, A. M., Lasser, R. P., and Bechman, G., 1959, Analysis of
    weight and height of apparently healthy population, ages
    65 to 94 years, Proc. Soc. Expt. Biol. Med., 102:367.
Meema, S., Reid, D. B. W., and Meema, H. E., 1975, Age trends of
    bone mineral mass, muscle width and subcutaneous fat in
    normals and osteoporotics, Calcif. Tissue Res., 12:101.
Miall, W., Ashcroft, M., Lovell, H., and Moore, F., 1967, A
    longitudinal study of the decline of adult height with age
    in two Welsh communities, Hum. Biol., 39:445.
Milne, J. S., and Lauder, I. J., 1974, Age effects in kyphosis and
    lordosis in adults, Ann. Hum. Biol., 1:327.
Moretti, I., 1953, Comportamento della menopausa in gemelle mono-e
    biovulari, Fol. Hered. Path. (Pavia), 2:1.
Nishimura, H., and Shimizu, S., 1963, Studies on various ageing
    phenomena in Japanese twins and siblings, Acta Genet. Med.,
    12:22.
Nöllenburg, W. auf der, 1932, Statistische Untersuchungen über die
    Erblichkeit der Lebenslänge, Z. Konstit.-Lehre, 16:707.
Norris, A. H., Lundy, T., and Shock, N. W., 1963, Trends in selected
    indices of body composition in men between the ages of 30
    and 80 years, Ann. N.Y. Acad. Sci., 110:623.
Paŕízková, J., 1963, Impact of age, diet and exercise on man's
    body composition, Ann. N.Y. Acad. Sci., 110:661.
Paŕízková, J., and Eisett, E., 1971, A further study on changes in
    somatic characteristics and body composition of old men
    followed longitudinally for 8-10 years, Hum. Biol., 43:318.
Parot, S., 1959, Les variations de poids liées à l'âge: étude
    transversale à taille constante, Rev. Soc. Biom. Humaine,
    1:78.
Parot, S., 1961, Recherches sur la biométrie du vieillissement
    humain, Bull. et Mém. Soc. d'Anthrop. Paris, 2:299.
Pearl, R., 1931, Studies on human longevity, IV: The inheritance
    of longevity (preliminary report), Hum. Biol., 3:245.
Pearl, R., and Dewitt, R., 1934, Studies on human longevity, IV:
    The distribution and correlation of variation in the total
    immediate ancestral longevity of nonagenarians and centen-
    arians, in relation to the inheritance factor in duration
    of life, Hum. Biol., 6:98.
Pfitzner, W., 1899, Social-anthropologische Studien, I. Der Ein-
    fluss des Lebens alters auf die anthropologischen Charak-
    tere, Z. Morph. Anthrop., 1:325.
Philippe, P., 1978, Familial correlations of longevity: an isolate-
    based study, Am. J. Med. Genet., 2:121.

Polednak, A. P., 1978, Age changes in differential leukocyte count among female adults, Hum. Biol., 50:301.

Quetelet, A., 1870, Anthropométrie ou mesure des différentes facultés de l'Homme, Bachelier, Bruxelles.

Roberts, J., 1975, "Blood Pressure of Persons 18-74 Years," Vital and Health Statistics, National Center for Health Statistics, DHEW Pub. No. (HRA) 75-1632, Series 11, No. 150, U.S. Government Printing Office, Washington, D.C.

Roberts, J., and Maurer, K., 1978, "Blood Pressure Levels of Persons 6-74 Years," Vital and Health Statistics, Series 11, No. 203, National Center for Health Statistics, DHEW Pub. No. (HRA) 78-1648, U.S. Government Printing Office, Washington, D.C.

Sacher, G. A., 1975, Maturation and longevity in relation to cranial capacity in hominid evolution, in: "Primates: Functional Morphology and Evolution," R. Tuttle, ed., Mouton, The Hague.

Saller, K., 1930, Die Fehmaraner, Deutsche Rassenkunde, 4:1.

Saller, K., 1931, Süderdithmarsische Geestbevölkerung, Deutsche Rassenkunde, 7:1.

Semine, A. A., and Damon, A., 1975, Costochondral ossification and ageing in five populations, Hum. Biol., 47:101.

Shock, N. W., Watkin, D. M., Yiengst, M. J., Norris, A. H., Gaffney, G. W., Gregerman, R. I., and Falzone, J. A., 1963, Age differences in water content of the body as related to basal oxygen consumption in males, J. Geront., 18:1.

Simons, J. W., and Van den Broek, C., 1970, Comparison of ageing in vitro and in vivo by means of cell size analysis using a Coulter counter, Gerontologia, 16:340.

Sinclair, D., 1973, "Human Growth After Birth," Oxford Univ. Press, London.

Sinnett, P. F., Keig, G., and Craig, W., 1973, Nutrition and age-related changes in body build of adults: Studies in a New Guinea Highland community, Hum. Biol. in Oceania, 2:50.

Slome, C., Campel, B., Abramson, J. H., and Scotch, N., 1960, Weight, height and skinfold thickness of Zulu adults in Durban, South Afr. Med. J., 34:505.

Smith, R. W., and Walker, R. R., 1964, Femoral expansion in aging women: Implications for osteoporosis and fractures, Science, 145:156.

Stoessiger, B., 1932, On the inheritance of duration of life and cause of death, Ann. Eugen. (Lond.), 5:105.

Susanne, C., 1967, Les changements de la taille liés à l'âge (Phénomènes normaux de sénescence), L'Anthropologie, 72:297.

Susanne, C., 1971, Hérédité des caractères anthropologiques mesurables, Bull. et Mém. Soc. d'Anthrop. Paris, 7:169.

Susanne, C., 1974, Les changements morphologiques liés à l'âge, L'Anthropologie, 78:693.

Susanne, C., 1977, Individual age changes of the morphological characteristics, J. Hum. Evol., 6:181.

Swash, M., and Fox, K. P., 1972, The effect of age on human skeletal muscle. Studies of the morphology and innervation of muscle spindles, J. Neurol. Sci., 16:417.

Takahashi, E., and Atsumi, H., 1955, Age differences in the thoracic form as indicated by thoracic index, Hum. Biol., 27:65.

Tallgren, A., 1967, The effect of denture wearing on facial morphology. A 7-year longitudinal study, Acta Odont. Scand., 25:563.

Tallgren, A., 1974, Neurocranial morphology and ageing: a longitudinal roentgen cephalometric study of adult Finnish women, Am. J. Phys. Anthropol., 41:285.

Tanaka, J., 1975, A radiographic analysis on human lumbar vertebrae in the aged, Virchows Arch. A. Path. Anat. and Hist., 366:187.

Thompson, J. L., and Kendrick, G. S., 1964, Changes in the vertical dimensions of the human male skull during the third and fourth decades of life, Anat. Rec., 150:209.

Trotter, M., and Gleser, G., 1951, The effect of ageing on stature, Am. J. Phys. Anthropol., 9:311.

Trotter, M., Peterson, R. R., and Wette, R., 1968, The secular trend in the diameter of the femur of American whites and Negroes, Am. J. Phys. Anthropol., 28:65.

Trotter, M., and Hixon, B. H., 1974, Sequential changes in weight, density and percentage ash weight of human skeletons from an early fetal period through old age, Anat. Rec., 179:1.

Von Verschuer, O., 1954, "Wirksame Faktoren im Leben des Menschen, Beobachtungen an ein- und zweieiigen Zwillingen durch 25 Jahre," Steiner, Wiesbaden.

Virtama, P., and Helela, T., 1969, Radiographic measurements of cortical bone, Acta Radiol., Suppl. 293:1.

Vogt, A., Wagner, H., Richner, H., and Meyer, G., 1939, Das Senium bei eineiigen und zweieiigen Zwillingen, Arch. Klaus-Stift. Vererb.-Forsch., 14:475.

Walford, R. L., 1967, The role of auto-immune phenomena in the ageing process, Symp. Soc. Ex. Biol., XXI, "Aspects of the Biology of Ageing."

Weissenberg, S., 1895, Die Südrussischen Juden, Arch. Anthrop., 23:347.

Wessel, J. A., Ufer, A., Van Huss, W. D., and Cederquist, D., 1963, Age trends of various components of body composition and functional characteristics in women aged 20-69 years, Ann. N.Y. Acad. Sci., 110:608.

Wolański, N., and Pyzuk, M., 1973, Psychomotor properties in 1.5-99 year old inhabitants of Polish rural areas, Studies in Hum. Ecology, 1:134.

Young, C. M., Blondin, J., Tensuan, R., and Fryer, J. H., 1963, Body composition studies of older women, thirty to seventy years of age, Ann. N.Y. Acad. Sci., 110:589.

III.   FACTORS

13. DEVELOPMENTAL GENETICS OF MAN

Charles Susanne

Free University Brussels
Pleinlaan 2, 1050 Brussels, Belgium

This paper deals with an analysis of present knowledge about
the genetic influences on growth and development in normal human
beings. Human genetics includes study of the continuum from mole-
cules to populations. Some single genes can be clearly detected,
such as the dominant gene for achondroplasia. But more often, particularly in normal individuals, single genes that determine morphological characteristics cannot be detected. These characteristics are determined not only by factors of genetic origin but
also by factors of environmental origin. The regulation of continuously distributed characters cannot be understood without an
analysis of environmental and genetic factors. What is the relative
importance of genetic and environmental factors on human development? It must be stressed that these two kinds of factors are very
rarely separable and they almost invariably interact. In particular, the environment common to individuals of the same family has
to be taken into account, adding to the ambiguity of the evidence.
Also environmental influences may be more important in some individuals than in others.

HERITABILITY

The term heritability refers to the proportion of the phenotypic variance (V_p) due to additive genetic variance
(V_A, genic variance) ($h^2 = V_A/V_p$).
Also it could be defined as the regression of the additive genetic
value on the phenotypic value

$$(b_{AP} = cov/AP, /V_p).$$

Heritability in the narrow sense determines a selective breeding
program but this is illusory in human population where environmental correlations cannot be eliminated. A reliable estimate of
heritability cannot be obtained when the environment is non-random.
Moreover, different factors can influence heritability coefficients
such as dominant factors (V_D), epistatic factors (V_i) or
environmental factors

$$(V_E) (V_p = V_A + V_D + V_i + V_E).$$

In human populations, heritability is commonly used in a broad
sense as the proportion of the total variance that is partitioned
into the genetic variance

$$(h^2 = \frac{V_A + V_D + V_i}{V_p}).$$

Different measures of heritability have been proposed (Table 1).

Estimations of heritability can be calculated from studies of
twins: the correlation between monozygotic twins is a measure of
heritability if no significant common family environmental effect
exists. The presence of such an effect inflates the estimate of
heritability. Traditional estimates of heritability using MZ and
DZ twins are:

$$h^2 = \frac{\sigma^2_{DZ} - \sigma^2_{MZ}}{\sigma^2_{DZ}} \qquad \text{and} \qquad h^2 = \frac{r_{MZ} - r_{DZ}}{1 - r_{DZ}}.$$

With these formulae the common familial effect is less marked but
is not totally eliminated if we do not admit that the environment
is equivalent for MZ and DZ twins. These estimates are affected
also by assortative mating, which will influence the concordance
of DZ but not of MZ twins.

Measurements of heritability can be calculated from the comparison of parents and children. A good estimate is the child on
mid-parent regression which is not affected by selection of parents,
assortative mating, dominance or epistasis, but it is considerably
affected by common family environmental effects. Twice the regression of child on one parent is also an estimate of heritability,
but is inflated by environmental effects common to both parents and
child and by assortative mating. This heritability coefficient can
be calculated by the method of Fisher (1918) from the correlation
coefficients between parents and children, between sibs and between
spouses (Susanne, 1976, 1977).

A third kind of measure can be obtained from an analysis of
data for sibs. Twice the correlation between sibs is an estimate
of heritability. However, a quarter of any dominance effects are

Table 1. Coefficients of Heritability and Other Estimates from Correlations Between Relatives

Formulae	Comments
Twin $h^2 = r_{MZ}$	if complete genetic control $r_{MZ} = 1.0 \qquad r_{DZ} = 0.5$
$h^2 = \dfrac{\sigma^2_{DZ} - \sigma^2_{MZ}}{\sigma^2_{DZ}}$	
$h^2 = \dfrac{r_{MZ} - r_{DZ}}{1 - r_{DZ}}$	less inflated by familial environment; affected by assortative mating
Parent-child $r_{p.c}$	correlation parent-child $r_{p.c} = 0.50$ - inflated by familial environment and by assortative mating; decreased by dominance - for X-linkage $r_{MS} = 0.71;\ r_{FD} = r_{MS} = 0.5;$ $r_{FS} = 0.0$
$h^2 = b_{mp,c}$	regression midparent-child, inflated by familial environment
$h^2 = 2b_{p,c}$	twice regression parent-child, inflated by familial environment and assortative mating
$h^2 = \dfrac{2r_{pc}}{1 + m_p}$	m_p = correlation between spouses (Fisher, 1918); an estimation (h^2_o) in the panmictic condition can be calculated
Sibling r_{sibs}	r = 0.50 - inflated by familial environment and by assortative mating
$h^2 = 2r\ sibs$	
$r_{sibs} = \dfrac{1}{2} h^2 + \dfrac{1}{4} \dfrac{V_D}{V_p}$	for X-linkage (Mather and Jinks, 1971) $r_{SS} = 0.75;\ r_{BB} = 0.50;\ r_{BS} = 0.35$
rth degree $b_r = (\dfrac{1}{2})^r h^2$	from Falconer, 1960

included, together with effects of assortative mating, as well as
common environmental effects that are probably greater for sibs
than for parent-child pairs.

Lastly, data from other degree relatives could be used.
Measures of heritability will be four times the correlation between
second-degree, and eight times the correlation between third-degree
relatives. These estimates may be less affected by dominance and
common environmental factors but data are not easily collected.

Many methods can be used but, in each case, the estimates of
the coefficients of heritability are relative to the studied population, in its specific environment and time (Feldman and Lewontin,
1975). The coefficients of heritability are specific for a particular gene pool and environment, as well as for a particular interaction between genotypes and environments. Indeed, not only socioeconomic factors, individual age factors and other environmental
factors but also factors of genetic origin may influence pheno-
typical variations. We have to take into account factors that
influence the frequency of genes such as mutation, selection, and
mixing as well as factors that influence the distribution of genes
such as inbreeding and assortative mating.

This implies that the interpretation of heritability estimates
is very difficult. The environments of relatives are often positively correlated, resulting in inflated heritability estimates.
The method of sampling has primary importance: the population has
to be as homogeneous as possible. Positive assortative mating and
consanguinity lead to overestimates of heritability measurements.
On the contrary, dominant factors will lead to underestimates of
heritabilities. Other possible complications of the method are
the influence of X-linked loci, where the following relation is
expected:

$$r_{father-daughter} = r_{mother-son} > r_{mother-daughter} > r_{father-son}$$
$$\text{and } r_{sisters} > r_{brothers} > r_{brother-sister}.$$

The environmental covariance is expected to have less influence
on parent-child comparisons than on comparisons between sibs or
twins. In a familial study, the different covariances have to be
taken into account:

$$cov._{(genotypes\ parents\ and\ children)} + cov._{(genotypes\ parents}$$

$$_{and\ environments\ children)} + cov._{(genotypes\ children\ and}$$

$$_{and\ environments\ parents)} + cov._{(environments\ parents\ and}$$

$$_{children)}.$$

The second and fourth covariances are positive in most cases.

Despite these numerous difficulties, it is possible to define in a specific population a decreasing order of heritability for different anthropological characters. Some quantitative traits are more subject to genetic factors than other traits; these traits are less influenced by environmental factors (Susanne, 1971). For this last kind of approach, definition of a decreasing order of heritability, not real coefficients of heritability, could be used, such as correlation coefficients midparent-child, parent-child, sibs, analysis of variance. On a Belgian sample, for which 36 anthropometric measurements were recorded (Susanne, 1975), we calculated coefficients of correlation between different estimates, real or unreal, of heritability (Table 2). These correlations are, of course, highly significant but are clearly lower with the correlation coefficients between sibs; the coefficients of correlation between sibs are much more affected by the common familial environment and are therefore less accurate than regression coefficients of child on midparent or coefficients of heritability (Fisher, 1918). But these results in Table 2 show that the coefficient of correlation between parent and child, although not really a coefficient of heritability, is a good first approximation for the quantitative traits considered.

MORPHOLOGY AT BIRTH

The interactions of genetic and environmental factors are already complex by the time of birth (Roberts, 1978; Robson, 1978). Many genes are responsible for cellular and sexual differentiation during the embryonic period; at the same time, the influence of the environment increases progressively.

The results of Penrose (1961) demonstrate the small influence of fetal hereditary constitution in determining the body size of the newborn child: the fetal genetic factors are responsible for 16% of the variability of birthweight and the maternal hereditary

Table 2.   Correlation Coefficients between Different Approaches of
           Heritabilities (36 anthropometric variables; Belgian
           sample; Susanne, 1975)

	1	2	3	4
1. Regr. coeff. child-midparent	1	0.88	0.59	0.95
2. Coeff. correl. parent-child		1	0.64	0.92
3. Coeff. correl. between sibs			1	0.56
4. Coeff. heritability (Fisher, 1918)				1

constitution for 20% of this variability. This small genetic influence is observed in some domesticated animals, too, and thus
may be characteristic of the physiology of gestation as shown by
some crosses of horses, of cattle, of swine and of rabbits (Morton,
1955). Table 3 emphasizes the role of the maternal environment in
the determination of birthweight. Like-sex twins, with a high
degree of genetic relationship, are no more alike than full sibs or
even than half sibs from the same mother. Even factors related to
timing, expressed by the number of births between the members of
a sibship, influence the level of the correlation (Table 3). In
twins, the varying degrees of vascular anastomoses between the
placentas result in lower within-pair correlations for monozygotic
twins than for dizygotic twins at birth (Wilson, 1976). In linear
models of familial correlation derived from a Wright path analysis,
Rao and Morton (1974) showed a good fit of a model with no heritability (h^2 = 0) and with effects of common environment estimated
at 55% of the phenotypic variance. In joint estimates, these
effects of common environment are estimated at 49%, only 8% of the
phenotypic variance being the result of genetic control. This
limited genetic influence allowed, however, the calculation of
expected birthweights, taking into account maternal height and
weight (Tanner and Thomson, 1970) or the mean birthweight of the
previous sibs (Tanner et al., 1972).

AUTOCORRELATIONS

Later the genetic potential of the child is increasingly
asserted. This developmental increase in the hereditary component
of control can be expressed by autocorrelations, where the measurements of a child during growth are correlated with his or her
measurements in adulthood. In the first year, the autocorrelations for stature increase very rapidly. Later they increase more slowly and decrease somewhat during the pubescent
growth spurt. This general increase from birth to maturity reflects the increasing contribution of the child's own genes to the
determination of stature (Tanner, 1960; Furusho, 1968; Ashizawa
et al., 1977).

The evolution of autocorrelation of other measurements is
somewhat different as shown by Tanner et al. (1956). In their
data, the increase in the autocorrelations for weight from birth
to 5 years is rather regular but less rapid than for stature.
Also, in these data, the autocorrelations for biacromial and bitro-
chanteric diameters increase to 3 years but decrease afterwards,
but the autocorrelations for head length and breadth have patterns
of change similar to those for stature.

PARENT-OFFSPRING CORRELATIONS

From inspection of the resemblance between the height of adult parents and the height of growing children (Bayley, 1954; Hewitt, 1957; Tanner and Israelsohn, 1963; Bielicki and Welon, 1966; Tanner et al., 1970; Necrasov and Critescu, 1971; Tiisala and Kantero, 1971; Welon and Bielicki, 1971, Gerylovova and Bouchalova, 1974), it is clear that the similarity increases dramatically during the first years after birth and then more slowly until a transitory diminution occurs during pubescence. This corresponds in timing to the decrease in autocorrelations and could be explained by assuming that the timing of the pubescent spurt and adult height are independently influenced by genetic factors. Similar results are obtained in domestic animals: the autocorrelations are smaller during the suckling period and higher after weaning (Dickerson, 1954).

The literature is less abundant for measurements other than stature. Chrzastek-Spruch (1977) observed a continuous increase in parent-child correlations for weight although the coefficients were low and sometimes not significant. The correlations for skinfolds and subcutaneous fat thicknesses between parents and offspring are near zero (Bayley, 1954; Tanner and Israelsohn, 1963). Hewitt (1958) showed that, between 6 months and 5 years of age, the coefficients of correlation between sisters change independently for muscle, bone and fat thicknesses measured in the calf: the correlation for muscle breadth increases to 5 years; on the contrary, the fat decreases and the correlation relative to bone does not change significantly. It is unlikely that different body characters are determined by the same genetic factors during development.

Many authors have sought evidence of sex-linked genes in relation to growth in stature but there is no present evidence of one major sex-linked gene (Susanne, 1971). Schull and Neel (1963), analysing different measurements of daughters of first cousin spouses, did not find a relation with a sex-linked genetic coefficient of inbreeding. The possibility of an X chromosome participation in a polygenic system cannot, however, be excluded, but the resultant effect on quantitative traits would be limited. Similarly, in the development of mammals and birds, Beilharz (1963) did not find conclusive evidence of sex linkage on reviewing 36 reports, except perhaps for the body weight of rabbits, mice and sheep. Moreover, the finding that adult males with Klinefelter's syndrome and adult girls with Turner's syndrome show correlation coefficients with their parents of the same level to those found with normal children suggests the genetic mechanisms are, for the most part, located on autosomes (Lemli and Smith, 1963; Brook et al., 1974, 1977).

Table 3. Birth Weight: Correlation Between Relatives or Heritability

	half sibs (same mother)	half sibs (same father)	twins	sibs
Donald, 1939				.53(454)[4]
				.62(191)[4]
				.44(135)[5]
				.41(891)[4]
Karn and Penrose, 1951				.47(314)[4]
				.44(228)[5]
				.72(201)[1]
Karn, 1952				.67(103)[3]
				.71(163)[1]
Karn, 1953				.64(92)[3]
Karn, 1954				.80(1232)[1]
				.76(355)[3]
				.58(146)[1]
Penrose, 1954				.66(133)[1]
				.59(157)[3]
				.50[9]
Robson, 1955	.581(30)		.557(220)[1]	.543(365)[4]
Morton, 1955		.102(168)	.655(40)[3]	.425(652)[5]
				.363(151)[6]
				.54
Karn, 1956			.77(159)[1]	
Fraccaro, 1957			.79(78)[3]	
Namboodiri and Balakrishnan, 1959			.70(85)[1]	
			.78(78)[1]	
Penrose, 1961			.66(58)[3]	
			.58[3]	
Vandenberg and Falkner, 1965			no diff. DZ - MZ	

Record et al., 1969
Tanner et al., 1972

.50 (5042)
.54 (198) [8]
.56 (198) [8]
.58 (49) [8]
.53 (49) [8]
.46 (6702) [7]
.53 (6702) [7]

Billewicz and Thomson, 1973

Nikityuk, 1973

.655 (158) [1]
.574 (194) [1]
.520 (140) [3]

Wilson, 1976

.61 (159) [2]
.70 (107) [3]

Robson, 1978

.69 (152) [1]
.66 (134) [1]
.63 (202) [3]

The figures in parentheses are the numbers of pairs

1. like-sex twins; 2. monozygotic; 3. dizygotic; 4. adjoining births; 5. one intermediate birth; 6. two intermediate births; 7. after adjustment for parity; 8. after adjustment for maternal height; 9. after adjustment for sex, maternal age and parity.

CORRELATION COEFFICIENTS BETWEEN SIBS

Correlations of a measurement between growing siblings of the same age continuously increase during the developmental period (Garn and Rohmann, 1966; Furusho, 1974). In twins, also, the genotype regularly exerts a larger differential effect, compensating for prenatal inequalities between monozygotic twins and producing a differentiation in the growth of dizygotic twins. Using data from twins studied longitudinally from birth to 4 years, Wilson (1976) and Ljung et al. (1977) show a high concordance for dizygotic twins at birth due to common factors of maternal origin but the within-pair concordance correlation progressively decreases afterwards. On the contrary, the concordance increases in monozygotic twins. It is suggested the differences at birth are largely due to placental anastomosis; after birth there is an increasing genetic influence. Von Verschuer (1934) and Fukuoka (1937) studied, as a function of age, the mean intrapair differences (expressed in percentages), and reported they are higher for dizygotes than for monozygotes. It is interesting that in these studies the intrapair differences for dizygotic twins become larger with age, especially for characters with a high environmental component such as weight. The authors consider these increased differences reflect increasing environmental differences, especially after puberty. Similar results have been reported by Palmer (1934) for same-sex siblings followed longitudinally. On the average, the correlations between sibs are higher than those for parent-child pairs. Indeed, for purely genetic reasons, the correlation between parents and children may be lower than between sibs if dominant factors influence the character. However, it is unlikely the differences observed by Susanne (1975) and by Mueller (1977) are due only to dominance. These differences could be attributable to environmental factors, too. Sibs growing up together may have a higher environmental similarity than parents have with their children. Differences of environmental covariance for somewhat labile measurements, more similar gene-environment interactions, and similar genetic influences at critical periods during growth explain also the fact that correlations between school-aged sibs are larger than correlations between adult sibs (Mueller, 1977). Similarly, correlation coefficients between sibs of different ages are diminished when the age differences between members of a sibling pair increase; this is marked for weight, muscle and fat measurements but not for bone measurements (Furusho, 1968; Mueller, 1978). Here, too, differences of environmental covariance for rather labile measurements are probably responsible.

Due to the interaction with environmental factors, the correlations between growing sibs are approximately at the same level for different measurements. There is a trend, however, in adult sibs: heritabilities are highest for longitudinal measurements,

less for breadths and circumferences and least for skinfolds
(Susanne, 1971, 1975).

INFLUENCE OF ENVIRONMENTAL FACTORS ON THE LEVEL OF COEFFICIENTS OF
CORRELATION

Generally, higher correlation coefficients are observed in
populations of European origin than in non-European ones (Malina et
al., 1976; Mueller, 1976; Russell, 1976): the existence of positive
assortative mating in the first group of populations is one explanation of these higher values. Another may be that the phenotype is
better expressed when there is a good standard of living. The
heritability level depends, indeed, not only on the geographical
origin of the populations studied, but also on standard of living.
However, in opposition to these findings, some studies (Charzewski
and Wolański, 1964; Bielicki and Welon, 1966; Welon and Bielicki,
1971; Mueller and Titcomb, 1977) have shown higher coefficients of
correlation in populations with low standards of living and nutrition (village versus town, poorly-nourished versus well-nourished).
The lower correlation coefficients could be due to different environmental experiences in parents and offspring, or to a decrease
of similarity of living standards of children in relation to that
of their parents during childhood. The same kinds of arguments
could explain the higher correlation coefficients observed by sibs
close together in age, and the higher correlation coefficients for
parent-child pairs when those including younger parents are compared with those including older parents (Furusho, 1964; Rao et al.,
1975; Mueller, 1978). Also, genotype-environment interaction may
influence the level of heritability. In well-nourished samples,
appetite may be important in the determination of body size, while
with malnutrition the ability to utilize available food may be
reduced. All these results show the need to stress that the correlation between the environments of relatives can vary greatly.

It has been suggested that women are more resistant to the
effects of malnutrition and disease than men (Waddington, 1957;
Tanner, 1962); i.e., men are more ecosensitive (Wolański, 1975).
A decrease in height in response to moderate undernutrition is
observed in men, while women react in this way only to more severe
disturbances of living conditions. Some samples, indeed, show a
marked secular trend in stature for males but not females (Acheson
and Fowler, 1964; Bielicki and Charzewski, 1977).

GENETIC DETERMINATION OF OSSIFICATION

Different statistical analyses are summarized in Table 4.
Garn et al. (1963) reported there was no variation in the correlation coefficient for ossification rate and ossification timing

Table 4.   Correlation Coefficients Between Times of Onset of Ossification Centres and Between Ossification Rate

Ossification timing	Age	Monozygotic twins	Dizygotic twins	Sibs	Parent child	First cousin
Reynolds, 1943	0-6.5y	.71(178)		.28(666)		.12(256)
Sontag and Lipford, 1943	0.5-5y	.82(228)		.32(912)		
Hewitt, 1957				.35(83)[1] .56(23)[2] .40(27)[3]		
Garn and Rohmann, 1962	1 - 5y	.96(108)	.33(62)	.47(2171)[1] .40(1260)[2] .54(854)[3]	.13(2016)	
Garn et al., 1963	1 - 7y				.25(834)	
Hertzog et al., 1969				.32[1] .23[2] .48[3]		
Garn et al., 1969 round bones	1m-15y			.48[1] .37[2] .44[3]		
ep. metacarpals						
Ossification rate						
Garn and Rohmann, 1962	1 - 5y	.88(68)	.20(62)	.40(1223)[1] .39(688)[2] .62(494)[3]	.32(2016)	
Garn et al., 1963	1 - 7y				.32(377)	
Hertzog et al., 1969						

The figures in parentheses are the numbers of pairs.
1 = unlike sex; 2 = brothers; and 3 = sisters.
ep = epiphyses.

during the age range 1 to 7 years. The same authors observed
higher correlations for sisters than for brothers and propose an
x linkage mechanism. However, Hewitt (1957) observed a higher
correlation between brothers than sisters. Ossification timing
appears to be largely gene-determined while ossification sequence
appears to be almost entirely gene-determined (Garn and Rohmann,
1962; Garn and Bailey, 1978). Hertzog et al. (1969) reported the
discordance in ossification sequence is 3.5 times more common
between like-sexed dizygotic twins 1 to 5 years of age than between
monozygotic twins. Heritability of tooth formation timing and of
tooth emergence has been demonstrated also (Garn and Bailey, 1978).

GENETIC DETERMINATION OF PUBERTAL MATURATION

Menarche is the most noteworthy event during pubertal maturation; it is a qualitative event that is easily recorded. Moreover,
age at menarche is highly and positively correlated with other
measures of biological maturation, e.g., age at peak height velocity, breast development (Marshall and Tanner, 1969). Evidence of
hormonal, nutritional, and socioeconomic determinants of age of
menarche have been published from many studies.

It has been suggested genetic factors play a significant role
in determination of age at menarche. Roberts (1969) detected an
apparent genetic component in racial differences. Results from
twin and familial studies are shown in Table 5. These correlations
are generally low and prove little of the possible genetic inheritance. In interpreting these results, one must, however, take
into account the environmental correlation between twins or sisters
and between mother and daughters. The disappearance of socioeconomic differences for age of menarche in contemporary industrial
societies shows the importance of environmental influences (Susanne,
Chapter 21). Other maturational phenomena, such as the magnitude
and timing of the pubescent spurt and the first signs of sexual
maturation, occur at very similar ages in twins (Sklad, 1972).

GENETIC DETERMINATION OF PATTERNS OF GROWTH

Isolated studies of longitudinal curves on twins or even
triplets (Sontag and Nelson, 1933; Brander, 1938; Stenborg, 1938;
Zeller, 1940; Dearborn and Rothney, 1941; Reynolds and Schoen,
1947; Von Sydow and Rinne, 1958; Garn, 1961; Tanner, 1962) are
difficult to interpret although monozygotic twins show growth
curves generally more alike than those of dizygotic twins.
Similarity of growth curves and of growth rate have been reported
also from longitudinal studies of sibs (King, 1910; Guttmann, 1916;
Baldwin, 1926; Palmer, 1934; Simmons and Greulich, 1943; Meredith,
1947; Mansfeld, 1956; Ford, 1958).

Table 5. Mean Differences of Age at Menarche Between Relatives (in months), or Coefficients of Correlations (r) of the Age at Menarche

	Monozygotic twins	Dizygotic twins	Sisters	Mother-daughter	Random
Bolk (1926)					
Popenoe (1928)			r=.39(351)	14.6m(71)	
Petri (1935)			12.9m(145)	r=.40(351)	
Feigel (1935)	2.8m(51)	12.0m(47)	14.4m(120)	18.4m(120)	18.6m(120)
Tietze and Grutzner (1937)	3.9m(10)	14.6m(9)			
Reymert and Jost (1947)	3.3m(23)				
Tisserand-Perrier (1953)			10.6m(72)		13.9m(100)
Damon et al. (1969)	2.2m(46)	8.2m(39)		r=.54(from Bolk)	
Kantero and Widholm (1971)				r=.24(78)	
Necrasov and Critescu (1971)				r=.283(1946)	
Widholm and Kantero (1971)				r=.51(55)	
Orley (1977)				.72y(8000)	
Garn and Bailey (1978)				13.5m(1916)	
				r=.25(550)	
				r=.23(546)[1]	
Bakshi (1979)			r=.83(53)	13.22m(300)	
				r=.35(300)	

The figures in parentheses are the numbers of pairs. 1 = correction for fatness.

Still more difficult to interpret are studies of twins of different ages grouped to broad age classes (Dahlberg, 1926; Newman et al., 1937; Lamy et al., 1954; Kimura, 1956). Quantitative estimation of heritability in patterns of growth are infrequent; they have been hindered by the difficulties of characterising the human growth curve. Bock and Thissen (1978) used triple logistic curve fitting by unweighted nonlinear least squares in the study of two sets of triplets, where two sibs were identical and one fraternal. The curves of the identical sibs were clearly more similar to each other than to that of the fraternal sib; the heritable component was primarily evident in the appearance of the pubescent growth spurt. Vandenberg and Falkner (1965), in a sample of 29 monozygotic and 31 dizygotic twins, did not find a significant difference in intrapair variance of length at 1 month, but the intradizygotic variance was significantly greater than the intra-monozygotic variance for the linear component of growth rate between 1 month and 4 years ($p < .05$) and for the deceleration in growth rate during the same period ($p < .01$). Karn (1956) observed a gradual decrease in the influence of maternal factors on the weights of siblings from birth to 3 years; thereafter the correlations between siblings increased. In a longitudinal study of twins (Fischbein and Nordqvist, 1978), growth curves were more similar in monozygotic twins than in dizygotic like-sex twins. Analysing data for height and weight, these authors plotted the square root of the sum of squared differences between corresponding points against an intraclass correlation for profiles estimated from an interaction term of an analysis of variance.

Welch (1970a,b) fitted third degree orthogonal polynomials
$$(y = b_o + b_1 x + b_2 x^2 + b_3 x^3)$$
for height, leg length, stem length, head length, lip width and weight to analyse data from 36 male and 42 female Berkeley Growth Study subjects and 90 of their children studied up to 10.5 years. Interpretation of the results is difficult because the overall size of the parent-child correlation is not given. Also, some half-sibs were included, some parents were represented more than once, and the variations between the four different parent-child correlations are very large. The only reasonable conclusion is that a tendency to genetic influences is observed for b_o and b_1 but not for b_2 and b_3. A slight trend for full-sib correlations to be larger than parent-offspring correlations is observed. The additional effects of dominance and of environmental variation tending to bias upwards the correlations between siblings may be responsible.

CONCLUSION

Many studies give indirect or direct evidence of the effects

of genetic factors on the patterns of growth and development. Most
of these studies are based on coefficients of correlation rather
than analyses of covariance or coefficients of heritability. These
coefficients of heritability, in the broad sense, are relative to
a particular array of genotypes and environments in a specific
population at a specific time. In these conditions, it is illusory
to separate a genetic variance that depends on the environment from
an environmental variance that depends on the genotype. Fluctuations in the coefficient of heritability are observed as a function
of differences in gene frequencies and differences in environmental
components. Furthermore, positive assortative mating or consanguinity will lead to overestimation of heritabilities; positive
correlations between the environments of the relatives may have
the same result. The interpretation of these coefficients is
difficult. Also, it is difficult to collect suitable longitudinal
data to characterise the human growth curve. Consequently, there
are few studies of the inheritance of growth patterns.

REFERENCES

Acheson, R. M., and Fowler, G. B., 1964, Sex, socio-economic status,
        and secular increase in stature: a family study, Brit. J.
        Prev. Soc. Med., 18:25.
Ashizawa, K., Takahashi, C., and Yanagisawa, S., 1977, Stature and
        body weight growth patterns from longitudinal data of Japan-
        ese children born during World War II, J. Human Ergol.,
        6:29.
Bakshi, R., 1979, "Anthropometric measurements and age at menarche
        of Punjabi mothers and daughters," Thesis, University of
        Delhi.
Baldwin, B. T., 1926, Anthropometric measurements, in: "Genetic
        Studies of Genius. 1. Mental and Physical Traits of a
        Thousand Gifted Chindren," V. Terman, ed., Stanford Univ.
        Press, Stanford.
Bayley, N., 1954, Some increasing parent-child similarities during
        the growth of children, J. Educ. Psychol., 55:1.
Beilharz, R. G., 1963, On the possibility that sex-chromosomes
        have a greater effect than autosomes on inheritance, J.
        Genet., 58:441.
Bielicki, T., and Charzewski, J., 1977, Sex differences in the
        magnitude of statural gains of offspring over parents,
        Hum. Biol., 49:265.
Bielicki, T., and Welon, Z., 1966, Parent height correlation at
        ages 8 to 12 years in children from Wrocław, Poland,
        Hum. Biol., 38:167.
Billewicz, W. Z., and Thomson, A. M., 1973, Birthweights in con-
        secutive pregnancies, J. Obstet. Gynaec. Brit. Commonwealth,
        80:491.

Bock, R. D., and Thissen, D., 1978, Familial resemblance in patterns of growth in stature, in: "Twin Research, Part A, Psychology and Methodology," W. E. Nance, ed., Alan R. Liss Inc., New York.

Bolk, L., 1926, Untersuchungen über die Menarche bei der Niederlandischen Bevölkerung, Z. Geburtsch. Gynäk., 89:364.

Brander, T., 1938, Uber die Bedeutung des unternormalen Geburtsgewichts für die weitere körperliche und geistige Entwicklung der Zwillingen, Z. Konstit.-Lehre, 21:306.

Brook, C. G., Gasser, T., Werder, E., Prader, A., and Vanderschueren-Lodewijkx, M. A., 1977, Height correlations between parents and mature offspring in normal subjects and in subjects with Turner's and Klinefelter's and other syndromes, Ann. Hum. Biol., 4:17.

Brook, C. G., Mürset, G., Zachmann, M., and Prader, A., 1974, Growth in children with 45 XO, Turner's syndrome, Arch. Dis. Child., 49:789.

Charzewski, J., and Wolański, N., 1964, Influences of parental age and body weight on the physical development of their offspring, Prace i Materialy, Naukove IMD, 3:9.

Chrzastek-Spruch, H., 1977, Some genetic and environmental problems of physical growth and development of children aged 0-7 years, in: "Growth and Development," O. Eiben, ed., Akadémiai Kiadó, Budapest.

Dahlberg, G., 1926, "Twin births and twins from a hereditary point of view," Dissertation, Stockholm.

Damon, A., Damon, S. T., Reed, R. B., and Valadian, I., 1969, Age at the menarche of mothers and daughters, with a note on accuracy of recall, Hum. Biol., 41:161.

Dearborn, W. F., and Rothney, J. W. M., 1941, "Predicting the Child's Development," Science Art Publishers, Cambridge, Mass.

Dickerson, G. E., 1954, Hereditary mechanisms in animal growth, in: "Dynamics of Growth Processes," J. Boell, ed., Princeton Univ. Press, Princeton, N.J.

Donald, H. P., 1939, Sources of variance in human birth weight, Proc. Royal Soc. Edinb., 59:91.

Falconer, D. S., 1960, "Introduction to Quantitative Genetics," Wiley, New York.

Feigel, S., 1935, Ginek., 5:1 (cited by Knussmann, 1968).

Feldman, M. W., and Lewontin, R. C., 1975, The heritability hangup, Science, 190:1163.

Fischbein, S., and Nordqvist, T., 1978, Profile comparisons of physical growth for monozygotic and dizygotic twin pairs, Ann. Hum. Biol., 5:321.

Fisher, R. A., 1918, The correlation between relatives on the supposition of Mendelian inheritance, Trans. Royal Soc. Edinb., 52:399.

Ford, E. H., 1958, Growth in height of ten siblings, Hum. Biol., 30:107.

Fraccaro, M., 1957, A contribution to the study of birth weight based on an Italian sample twin data, Ann. Hum. Genet., 21:224.

Fukuoka, G., 1937, Anthropometric and psychometric studies on Japanese twins, in: "Studies on Japanese Twins," T. Komai and T. Fukuoka, eds., Kyoto.

Furusho, T., 1964, Factors affecting parent-offspring correlation of stature, Jpn. J. Hum. Genet., 9:35.

Furusho, T., 1968, On the manifestation of genotypes responsible for stature, Hum. Biol., 40:437.

Furusho, T., 1974, Genetic study on stature, Jpn. J. Hum. Genet., 19:1.

Garn, S. M., 1961, The genetics of normal human growth, in: "De Genetica Medica, II (1)," L. Gedda, ed., Mendel Institute, Rome.

Garn, S. M., and Bailey, S. M., 1978, Genetics of maturational processes, in: "Human Growth, 1. Principles and prenatal growth," F. Falkner and J. M. Tanner, eds., Plenum Publishing Corp., New York.

Garn, S. M., and Rohmann, C. G., 1962, Parent-child similarities in hand-wrist ossification, Am. J. Dis. Child., 103:603.

Garn, S. M., and Rohmann, C. G., 1966, Interaction of nutrition and genetics in the timing of growth and development, Pediatr. Clin. North Am., 13:353.

Garn, S. M., Rohmann, C. G., and Davis, A. A., 1963, Genetics of hand-wrist ossification, Am. J. Phys. Anthropol., 21:33.

Garn, S. M., Rohmann, C. G., and Hertzog, K. P., 1969, Apparent influence of the X chromosome on timing of 72 ossification centers, Am. J. Phys. Anthropol., 30:123.

Gerylovova, A., and Bouchalova, M., 1974, The relationship between children's and parents' heights in the age range 0-6 years, Ann. Hum. Biol., 1:229.

Guttmann, M., 1916, Einige Beispiele individueller körperlicher Entwicklung, Z. Kinderheilk., 13:248.

Hertzog, K. P., Falkner, F., and Garn, S. M., 1969, The genetic determination of ossification sequence polymorphism, Am. J. Phys. Anthropol., 30:141.

Hewitt, D., 1957, Some familial correlations in height, weight and skeletal maturity, Ann. Hum. Genet., 22:26.

Hewitt, D., 1958, Sib resemblance in bone, muscle and fat measurements of the human calf, Ann. Hum. Genet., 22:213.

Kantero, R. L., and Widholm, O., 1971, Correlation of menstrual traits between adolescent girls and their mothers, Acta Obstet. Gynecol. Scand., Suppl. 14:30.

Karn, M. N., 1952, Birth weight and length of gestation of twins, together with maternal age, parity and survival rate, Ann. Eugen., 16:365.

Karn, M. N., 1953, Twin data. A further study of birth weight, gestation time, maternal age, order of birth and survival, Ann. Eugen., 17:233.

Karn, M. N., 1954, Data of twins in Italy 1936-1951, Acta Genet. Med. Gemell., 3:42.

Karn, M. N., 1956, Sibling correlations of weight and rate of growth and relation between weight and growth rate over the first five years, Ann. Hum. Genet., 21:177.

Karn, M. N., and Penrose, L. S., 1951, Birth weight and gestation time in relation to maternal age, parity and infant survival, Ann. Eugen., 16:147.

Kimura, K., 1956, The study on physical ability of children and youths. On twins in Osaka City, J. Anthropol. Soc. Nippon, 64:172.

King, J., 1910, Measurements of the physical growth of two children, J. Educ. Psychol., 1:279.

Knussmann, R., 1968, Entwicklung, Konstitution, Geslecht, in: "Humangenetic," P. E. Becker, ed., George Thieme Verlag, Stuttgart.

Lamy, M. C., Pognan, C., and Maroteaux, P., 1954, Etude de quelques caractères normaux et pathologiques chez les jumeaux. Confrontation de mille paires, Atti. 9 Congr. Inst. Genetica, Bellagio.

Lemli, L., and Smith, D. W., 1963, The XO syndrome: A study of the differentiated phenotype in 25 patients, J. Pediatr., 63:577.

Ljung, B. O., Fischbein, S., and Lindgren, G., 1977, A comparison of growth in twins and singleton controls of matched age followed longitudinally from 10 to 18 years, Ann. Hum. Biol., 4:405.

Malina, R. M., Mueller, W. H., and Holman, J. D., 1976, Parent-child correlations and heritability of stature in Philadelphia black and white children 6 to 12 years of age, Hum. Biol., 48:475.

Mansfeld, E., 1956, Uber den Wachstumsverlauf einer Geschwisterreihe im Schulkindalter, Off. Gesundh. Dienst, 18:119.

Marshall, W. A., and Tanner, J. M., 1969, Variations in pattern of pubertal changes in girls, Arch. Dis. Childh., 44:291.

Mather, K., and Jinks, J. L., 1971, "Biometrical Genetics," Chapman and Hall, London.

Meredith, H. V., 1947, Length of upper extremities in homo sapiens from birth to adolescence, Growth, 11:1.

Morton, N. D., 1955, The inheritance of human birth weight, Ann. Hum. Genet., 20:125.

Mueller, W. H., 1976, Parent-child correlations for stature and weight among school aged children: A review of 24 studies, Hum. Biol., 48:379.

Mueller, W. H., 1977, Sibling correlations in growth and adult morphology in a rural Colombian population, Ann. Hum. Biol., 4:133.

Mueller, W. H., 1978, Transient environmental changes and age limited genes as causes of variation in sib-sib and parent-offspring correlations, Ann. Hum. Biol., 5:395.

Mueller, W. H., and Titcomb, N., 1977, Genetic and environmental determinants of growth of school-aged children in a rural Colombian population, Ann. Hum. Biol., 4:1.

Namboodiri, N. K., and Balakrishnan, V., 1959, A contribution to the study of birth weight and survival of twins based on an Indian sample, Ann. Hum. Genet., 23:334.

Necrasov, O., and Critescu, M., 1971, Sur l'hérédité de la croissance et du développement des enfants, Bull. Soc. Anthr. Paris, 7:317.

Newman, H. H., Freeman, F. N., and Holzinger, K. H., 1937, "Twins. A Study of Heredity and Environment," University of Chicago Press, Chicago.

Nikityuk, B. A., 1973, An anthropogenetic analysis of familial similarity, IXth Internat. Congr. Anthr. Ethnol. Sci., paper No. 158.

Orley, J., 1977, Analysis of menarche and gynaecological welfare of Budapest school girls, in: "Growth and Development. Physique," O. Eiben, ed., Adadémiai Kiadó, Budapest.

Palmer, C. E., 1934, Age changes in the physical resemblance of siblings, Child Dev., 5:351.

Penrose, L. S., 1954, Some recent trends in human genetics, Caryologia, 6(Suppl.).

Penrose, L. S., 1961, "Recent Advances in Human Genetics," Churchill, London.

Petri, E., 1935, Untersuchungen zur Erbbedingtheit der Menarche, Z. Morph. Anthrop., 33:43.

Popenoe, P., 1928, Inheritance of age of onset of menstruation, Eugen. News, 13:101.

Rao, D. C., Macklan, C. J., Morton, N. E., and Yee, S., 1975, Analysis of family resemblance. V. Height and weight in Northeastern Brazil, Hum. Genet., 27:509.

Rao, D. C., and Morton, N. E., 1974, Path analysis of family resemblance in the presence of gene environment interaction, Am. J. Hum. Genet., 26:767.

Record, R. G., McKeown, T., and Edwards, J. H., 1969, The relation of measured intelligence to birth weight and duration of gestation, Ann. Hum. Genet., 33:71.

Reymert, M. L., and Jost, H., 1947, Further data concerning the normal variability of the menstrual cycle during adolescence and factors associated with age of menarche, Child Dev., 18:169.

Reynolds, E. L., 1943, Degree of kinship and pattern of ossification, Am. J. Phys. Anthropol., 1:405.

Reynolds, E. L., and Schoen, G., 1947, Growth patterns of identical triplets from 8 through 18 years, Child Dev., 18:130.

Roberts, D. F., 1969, Race, genetics and growth, J. Biosoc. Sci., Suppl. 1:43.

Roberts, D. F., 1978, The genetics of human fetal growth, in:
    "Human Growth. 1. Principles and Prenatal Growth," F.
    Falkner and J. M. Tanner, eds., Plenum Publishing Corp.,
    New York.
Robson, E. B., 1955, Birth weight in cousins, Ann. Hum. Genet.,
    19:262.
Robson, E. B., 1978, The genetics of birth weight, in: "Human
    Growth. 1. Principles and Prenatal Growth," F. Falkner
    and J. M. Tanner, eds., Plenum Publishing Corp., New York.
Russell, M., 1976, Parent-child and sibling-sibling correlations of
    height and weight in a rural Guatemalan population of pre-
    school children, Hum. Biol., 48:501.
Schull, W. J., and Neel, J. V., 1963, Sex linkage, inbreeding and
    growth in childhood, Am. J. Hum. Genet., 15:106.
Simmons, K., and Greulich, W. W., 1943, Menarcheal age and the
    height, weight and skeletal age of girls aged 7 to 17 years,
    J. Pediatr., 22:518.
Skład, M., 1972, Certain growth and maturation phenomena in twins,
    Mat. Prac. Anthrop., 83:121.
Sontag, L. W., and Lipford, J., 1943, The effects of illness and
    other factors on the appearance pattern of skeletal epi-
    physes, J. Pediatr., 23:391.
Sontag, L. W., and Nelson, V. L., 1933, A study of identical trip-
    lets. I. Comparison of the physical and mental traits of a
    set of monozygotic dichorionic triplets, J. Hered., 24:473.
Stenborg, G., 1938, Wachstum schwedischer Mädchen und ein neuer
    Konstitutionsindex, Lunds Univ. Arsskrift N.F. adv. II,
    Bd. 34, Leipzig.
Susanne, C., 1971, Hérédité des caractères anthropologiques mesur-
    ables, Bull. Mém. Soc. Anthr. Paris, 7:169.
Susanne, C., 1975, Genetic and environmental influences on morpho-
    logical characteristics, Ann. Hum. Biol., 2:279.
Susanne, C., 1976, Heredity of anthropometric measurements:
    analysis with the method of Fisher (1918), Glasnik Antr.
    Drustva Yugoslavye, 13:11.
Susanne, C., 1977, Heritability of anthropological characters,
    Hum. Biol., 49:573.
Tanner, J. M., 1960, Genetics of human growth, in: "Human Growth.
    Symposia of the Society for the Study of Human Biology,"
    Pergamon Press, Elmsford, New York.
Tanner, J. M., 1962, "Growth at Adolescence," Blackwell, Oxford.
Tanner, J. M., Healy, M. J. R., Lockhart, R. D., MacKenzie, J. D.,
    and Whitehouse, R. H., 1956, Aberdeen growth study. I. The
    prediction of adult body measurements from measurements
    taken each year from birth to 5 years, Arch. Dis. Childh.,
    31:372.
Tanner, J. M., and Israelsohn, W. J., 1963, Parent-child correla-
    tions for body measurements of children between the ages of
    one month and seven years, Ann. Hum. Genet., 26:245.

Tanner, J. M., and Thomson, A. M., 1970, Standards for birthweight
    at gestation periods from 32 to 42 weeks, allowing for
    maternal height and weight, Arch. Dis. Childh., 45:566.

Tanner, J. M., Goldstein, H., and Whitehouse, R. H., 1970, Stan-
    dards for children's height at ages 2-9 years allowing for
    height of parents, Arch. Dis. Childh., 45:755.

Tanner, J. M., Lejanaga, H., and Turner, G., 1972, Within family
    standards for birth-weight, Lancet, 2:193.

Tietze, K., and Grutzner, R., 1937, Studien zur Ovarialfunction
    und ihren Störungen an eineiigen Zwillingen, Zbl. Gynäk.,
    61:1467.

Tiisala, R., and Kantero, R. L., 1971, Some parent-child correla-
    tions for height, weight and skeletal age up to ten years,
    Acta Paed. Scand., Suppl. 220:42.

Tisserand-Perrier, M., 1953, Etude comparative de certains pro-
    cessus de croissance chez les jumeaux, J. Génét. Hum., 2:87.

Vandenberg, S. G., and Falkner, F., 1965, Hereditary factors in
    growth, Hum. Biol., 37:357.

Von Sydow, G., and Rinne, A., 1958, Very unequal identical twins,
    Acta Paediatr., 47:163.

Von Verschuer, O., 1934, Die Erbbedingtheit des Körperwachstums,
    Z. Morph. Anthrop., 34:398.

Waddington, C. H., 1957, "The Strategy of Genes," Allen and Unwin,
    London.

Welch, Q. B., 1970a, Fitting growth and research data, Growth,
    34:293.

Welch, Q. B., 1970b, A genetic interpretation of variation in
    human growth patterns, Behav. Genet., 1:157.

Welon, Z., and Bielicki, T., 1971, Further investigations of parent-
    child similarity in stature, as assessed from longitudinal
    data, Hum. Biol., 43:517.

Widholm, O., and Kantero, R. L., 1971, A statistical analysis of
    the menstrual pattern of 8,000 Finnish girls and their
    mothers, Acta Obstet. Gynaecol. Scand., 30:Suppl. 14.

Wilson, R. S., 1976, Concordance in physical growth for monozygotic
    and dizygotic twins, Ann. Hum. Biol., 3:1.

Wolański, N., 1975, "Human Ecology and Contemporary Environment of
    Man," Skola Bioloska Antropologie, Zagreb.

Zeller, W., 1940, Wachstum und Reifung in Hinsicht auf Konstitution
    und Erbanlage, in: "Handbuch der Erbbiologie des Menschen,"
    G. von Just, K. H. Bauer, E. Hanhart, J. Lange, eds.,
    J. Springer, Berlin.

14. METHODOLOGY OF TWIN STUDIES: A General Introduction

Paolo Parisi

Department of Medical Genetics, University of Rome;
and The Mendel Institute, Rome

The birthdate of twin research is usually considered to be
the year 1875, when Francis Galton, in his paper, "The History of
Twins as a Criterion of the Relative Powers of Nature and Nurture,"
first suggested the respective influences of heredity (nature) and
environment (nurture) on any given trait or condition in man be
assessed through the comparison of twin partners. Systematic
scientific investigations using twins were initially confined to
psychology, but the interest soon spread and the "twin method" was
enthusiastically applied in most areas of human biology. Inevitably, perhaps, there also were indiscriminate applications, ill-
designed studies and uncritical conclusions. This gave momentum
to criticism of the method, with doubt being cast on some of its
basic assumptions. Thus, in the fifties and sixties, the method
became much less popular than it used to be. This called for a
serious revision of the classic design and of its assumptions, as
a result of which possible limitations and pitfalls have been identified, corrections suggested, and new approaches and methodologies
developed.

In fact, recent years have witnessed a renewed interest in
twin research, the potentialities of which are now clearer and may
perhaps be better exploited. Although there still are problems to
be solved and criticisms to be met, the classic twin method, with
its more modern refinements, has again come to represent to many a
powerful device for research into human variability. Moreover,
different designs have grown out of the classical one, and different
applications have been and can be suggested, so that the study of
twins may also offer new, still largely unexploited, possibilities.

BIOLOGY OF TWINNING

Twinning is rather frequent in nature and represents the rule in a number of mammalian orders, such as mice, cats, dogs, sheep, and swine. However, most likely in relation with the general evolution of reproductive strategies, whereby large litter size is gradually substituted by higher parental care, twinning is not as common in all the higher vertebrates and represents an exception in primates (cf. Gedda, 1951). In the human species, twin births average 1:100 total maternities; triplets 1:10,000; quadruplets 1:1 million; and quintuplets 1:100 million (or, respectively, $1:100$, $1:100^2$, $1:100^3$, $1:100^4$, etc., according to an empirical principle known as Hellin's rule).

Twinning is generally considered to originate through one of two possible mechanisms. Monozygotic (MZ) twinning originates when the single zygote, resulting from the union of one sperm and one ovum, splits in two, at some early stage during its embryological development, thus eventually producing two siblings who are genetically identical, i.e., have identical genes. Dizygotic (DZ) twinning originates when, as a result of more or less simultaneous double ovulation and double fertilization, two different zygotes develop at the same time, eventually producing two twins who, like ordinary full siblings, have only a 0.5 probability of identical genes at any one locus. Higher multiple births can originate through either mechanism or a combination of the two, so that triplets, for example, can be monozygotic, dizygotic, or trizygotic. A monochorial placenta is found in only about two-thirds of MZ twins, while the remaining one-third, and all DZ twins, have a dichorial placenta (that may be fused and erroneously considered monochorial) or even two placentae.

Whereas MZ twinning is essentially constant across time and in different populations, except for a slight increase with maternal age (Figure 1), DZ twinning is influenced by a variety of factors. Its rate increases considerably with parity and maternal age, possibly in response to higher gonadotropin levels. Social factors, especially nutritional ones, also appear to play a role; a decrease in DZ twinning rates occurs under conditions of starvation (Bulmer, 1970). Variations have been noted also at the individual, family, and population levels, and must at least partly reflect the influence of genetic factors. There is a considerable variability from one mother to the other in the propensity to have DZ twins, the rate being ∿4 times higher in women who have already had one set of DZ twins, and ∿9 times in mothers of trizygotic triplets (Bulmer, 1970). The DZ rate is also higher than usual in the families of twins; at least, as one would expect, in the maternal line. Finally, DZ rates vary from one population to another, being up to 20 times as high among Negroid than among Mongoloid populations. In Caucasoid populations they used to be in the range of 6-9 per

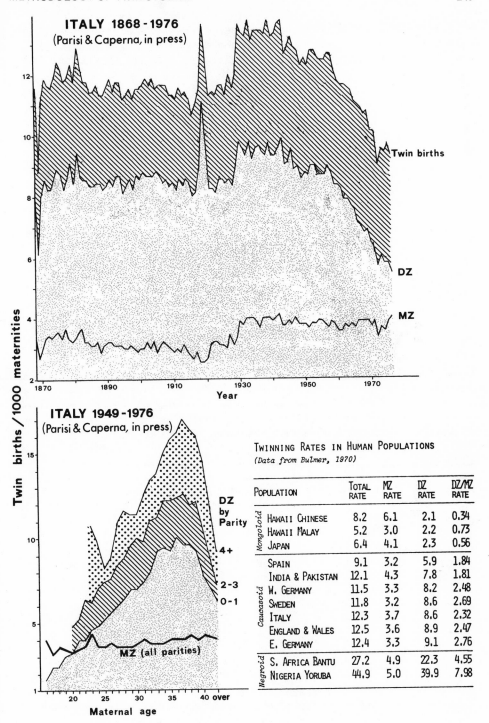

ITALY 1868 - 1976
(Parisi & Caperna, in press)

Twin births

DZ

MZ

Year

ITALY 1949 -1976
(Parisi & Caperna, in press)

DZ
by
Parity

4+

2-3

0-1

MZ (all parities)

Maternal age

Twin births / 1000 maternities

TWINNING RATES IN HUMAN POPULATIONS
(Data from Bulmer, 1970)

POPULATION		TOTAL RATE	MZ RATE	DZ RATE	DZ/MZ RATE
Mongoloid	HAWAII CHINESE	8.2	6.1	2.1	0.34
	HAWAII MALAY	5.2	3.0	2.2	0.73
	JAPAN	6.4	4.1	2.3	0.56
Caucasoid	SPAIN	9.1	3.2	5.9	1.84
	INDIA & PAKISTAN	12.1	4.3	7.8	1.81
	W. GERMANY	11.5	3.3	8.2	2.48
	SWEDEN	11.8	3.2	8.6	2.69
	ITALY	12.3	3.7	8.6	2.32
	ENGLAND & WALES	12.5	3.6	8.9	2.47
	E. GERMANY	12.4	3.3	9.1	2.76
Negroid	S. AFRICA BANTU	27.2	4.9	22.3	4.55
	NIGERIA YORUBA	44.9	5.0	39.9	7.98

Fig. 1. Twinning rates in relation to calendar year and maternal age

million until, in recent decades, partly because of the reduction
in maternal age and parity and of the truncation of sibships resulting from increased birth control, DZ rates started to decline in
most industrialized countries (Figure 1).

THE CLASSIC TWIN METHOD:
AN EXAMINATION OF FUNDAMENTAL ASSUMPTIONS

Because MZ cotwins originate from one and the same fertilized
egg, they will have identical genes: any phenotypic difference
between them must therefore be the result of nongenetic, "environmental" factors. This is the basic assumption of the classic twin
method, directly stemming from Galton's formulation in which
heredity and environment are somewhat simplistically seen as clear-
cut, opposing forces. DZ twins, in turn, provide an ideal control
sample. In fact, because they originate from two zygotes, they
share only an average of 50% of their genes and may therefore
differ on account of both genetic and environmental factors. In
this perspective, they are just as similar as two ordinary siblings. However, they are much more comparable than the latter to
MZ twins: in fact, whether MZ or DZ, any two cotwins obviously
are of the same age, have simultaneously developed in the same
prenatal environment, and simultaneously develop, initially at
least, in very similar postnatal environments.

Consequently, the method assumes that the extent to which the
average within-pair similarity with respect to any given trait or
condition is higher in MZ than DZ twins reflects the extent to
which that particular variable is under genetic control. For this
to hold general value, the method must further assume that, at
least for the variable under study, genotypic and environmental
variances in twins are the same as those of the singleton population, i.e., that twins are representative of the general population.

Because one of the main objections to the twin method has
been that it is liable to biases of various natures because the
assumptions on which it is based are questionable, these will now
be examined in some detail. The issue of whether the twins are
representative of the general population will be examined later
in relation to sample ascertainment.

Possible Genetic Bias

According to the method's first fundamental assumption, twins
are of two types: MZ, sharing 100% of their genes, and DZ, sharing
an average of 50% of their genes. However, it has been claimed,
non-MZ twins might not necessarily derive from an independent
release and fertilization of two ova, which is the usually accepted

mechanism of DZ twinning. Other mechanisms could be possible, con-
sisting in the double fertilization of ova that have not been released independently but have both developed (1) from the same
primary oocyte, or (2) from the same secondary oocyte as a result
of an equal, rather than the usual unequal, first or second meiotic
division, or even (3) from a subdivision of the ovum immediately
before fertilization. The resulting twins, collectively indicated
as dispermatic or third-type twins, would be genetically more
similar than the usual DZ twins.

Elston and Bocklage (1978) have recently reexamined this issue
and proposed a test to genetically detect dispermatic monovular
twins, suggesting that it be applied to a large battery of genetic
markers. If this can be done, it will certainly prove a valuable
contribution. From a practical viewpoint, however, it should be
noted that, although some biological evidence suggests dispermatic
twins might in fact occasionally occur in some animal groups, the
possiblity that they exist in man is, as yet, only a speculation.
In fact, for example, the concordance values observed in numerous
samples of nonidentical twins with respect to many blood group
systems are very close to the values expected for DZ twins, whereas
they should have been higher had dispermatic twins been present to
any appreciable extent. According to Bulmer (1970), who has extensively reviewed the subject, ". . . several lines of investigation
have failed to reveal any evidence of the existence of a third type
of twinning in man. It can be concluded that such twins must be
very rare if they occur at all." Should any appreciable number of
dispermatic twins exist in man, however, it can be speculated that,
because identity of maternal recombination would hold only for the
monovular twins, but not the oocytary ones, their average probability of identical genes will not much exceed 0.5 and will be lower
than 0.75. Moreover, it is likely that some of them would be
excluded from the sample (unless very extensive blood-typing is
done, which is frequently not the case) because of difficult zygosity
determination. Of the remaining pairs, some might be classified as
MZ and most as DZ, thus respectively decreasing and increasing the
average degree of within-pair similarity in the two groups. Should
that eventually result in any considerable bias, which seems
questionable, at best, it is likely that heritability would be
underestimated.

For the sake of completeness, it is desirable to consider the
two related phenomena of superfecundation, i.e., the fertilization
of simultaneously released ova by sperms released in different
coital acts, and superfetation, i.e., the fertilization of ova
released in different menstrual cycles. Conclusive evidence that
these occur is lacking (e.g., Nance et al., 1978). The resulting
twins may differ in gestational age, but will be genetically as
similar as any other pair of DZ twins. However, if the mother had
intercourse with two men in a short period of time this could

produce a pair of twins who are actually half sibs, i.e., share
only an average of 25% of their genes. Despite the relaxation of
sexual morality in our present society, it seems doubtful that
twins of different fathers are likely to seriously bias the twin
method. The effect of such theoretical twins would be to reduce
the average within-pair similarity of the DZ sample, in which they
would obviously be introduced, and thus somewhat balance the equally
theoretical effect of dispermatic twins.

Possible Environmental Bias

The second fundamental assumption of the twin method, i.e.,
that the conditions in which cotwins develop have the same degree
of similarity for MZ and for DZ twins, has been questioned repeatedly and possible antenatal and postnatal differences have been
noted.

Antenatal Bias. Following Bronson Price's widely known paper
in 1950, "Primary Biases in Twin Studies," it has become increasingly clear that the twin condition presents peculiarities that
make twins not always directly comparable to singletons; these
conditions can differ between MZ and DZ pairs. The implications of
this for twin sample ascertainment and study design will be examined
later. Such a prenatal environmental bias, to the extent that it
exists, will usually increase the MZ within-pair variance and thus
reduce heritability estimates, as suggested by Price. However,
often the increased variance will be present for only a relatively
short time and then tend to disappear. Height and weight can be
considered as examples. As a result of intrauterine restrictions,
competition, and differences in antenatal nourishment, MZ cotwins
frequently have very different birthweights and sizes. After birth,
however, as shown clearly by a recent study of 900 twin pairs
followed longitudinally from birth to 9 years, they soon tend to
converge on a common growth curve, while the opposite is true of
DZ cotwins whose differences become increasingly clear with time
(Wilson, in press).

Postnatal Bias. The existence and effects of a possible postnatal environmental bias in twin studies has been a much debated
issue in the field of psychology. Such a bias would essentially
concern psychological traits and be originated by parental behavior
and/or the twin situation itself.

Parental behavior has been claimed to encourage similarity
between MZ cotwins, but dissimilarity between DZ cotwins. Should
that be true, heritability would be overestimated. However, the
claim has not been substantiated, and the effect may be less
important than commonly believed. First of all, similarity will
usually take some time to be evident (few weeks to a few years)

and the appearance of the twins at birth may be misleading, within-pair correlations for weight and size being higher for DZ than for MZ cotwins (Wilson, in press). Furthermore, birth trauma and other complications can mask genetic effects. For example, the choice of names is influenced by zygosity, but not in the way critics would expect; similarity of names being higher in DZ than in MZ and opposite-sex cotwins (Vandenberg, 1976). Early infant care and child-rearing practices are unlikely to be more similar for MZ than for DZ cotwins. The few reports supporting differential treatment may be biased because they have been obtained by interviewing parents long after the birth of the twins when their reports might be influenced by the similarities or differences that have become apparent. Adult MZ cotwins are indeed more similar than DZ cotwins in terms of having the same friends, studying together, etc., but it is questionable whether this is due to parental behavior rather than genetic factors.

Secondly, one would imagine parental behavior to be determined much more by the birth of a twin pair rather than a singleton and by related and purely practical considerations, than by the extent of the similarity between the two twins. In other words, it is likely that similarity will be stressed, but this may be largely independent of zygosity. Even siblings may occasionally be dressed alike and sent to the same school, but this is essentially deter-mined by practical considerations. In a recent study in which the issue of parental behavior has been reexamined and, adopting a method proposed by Scarr (1968), within-pair IQ differences have been compared for pairs correctly and incorrectly classified by their parents. Matheny (in press) concludes: "The results from the present study, in combination with those from previous studies, indicate that parents most often correctly ascribe zygosity to same-sex twin pairs, but when errors occur, the pairs erroneously classified provide data similar to data from twin pairs correctly classified. . . . Until strong evidence shows that parental bias results in an exaggeration of differences between identical and fraternal pairs, the rejection of data accruing from the study of twins does not seem warranted on empirical grounds."

A second mechanism whereby environmental bias could be intro-duced into twin studies has been claimed to derive from the twin situation as such. MZ cotwins might be influenced by their own similarity so as to stress this similarity, whereas DZ cotwins could conversely tend to stress their dissimilarities. The combined effect would be an overestimation of genetic factors. Zazzo (1960) in France and Koch (1966) in the United States have studied the twin situation quite extensively and found it induces some division of labor and roles, making one twin more dominant and one more submissive. These and similar effects could increase the within-pair variance. Because similar situations apply to MZ twin pairs, but much more rarely to DZ ones, they might produce an underestimation

of genetic factors, thus somewhat contrasting the above possible
overestimation.   However, according to Vandenberg, who has extensively reviewed the subject, "The overall conclusion that may be
drawn . . . is that twins are not importantly different from
single-born children, nor identical twins from fraternal. . . .
It seems possible that the fashionable tendency to question the
twin method gives too much weight to dramatic instances of a twin
pair with a large difference in dominance or a very shy pair."
(Vandenberg, 1976).

THE CLASSIC TWIN METHOD

Twin Sample Ascertainment

     The twin method assumes twins to be representative of the
general population with respect to the variable under study.   This
may not always be true, so that the peculiarities of the twin condition and their possible effects should be carefully considered
when designing a twin study and ascertaining the twin sample.

     The twin pregnancy is usually considered a high-risk pregnancy
on account of the increased frequency of complications, of abnormal
presentations (breeches and transverse presentations are about 10
times more frequent than in single deliveries), and of the difficulties of dealing with a double delivery within optimal intervals.
This results, among other things, in an increased frequency of
birth trauma, especially brain injury.   However, on account of
possible intrauterine restrictions and competition between the twin
fetuses, as well as a generally shorter period of gestation (by an
average of ∿20 days), the twin newborn is frequently premature.
Over 50% of twins, vs. less than 10% of singletons, have a birthweight less than 2.5 kg (Bulmer, 1970; Nylander and MacGillivray,
1974; MacGillivray, 1974).   Even when these and other complications
do not result in fetal or early infant death, they can considerably
affect postnatal development.   Twins, in fact, generally experience
a delay in both mental and physical development, although they show
a remarkable tendency to recovery immediately after birth and
eventually catch up (Wilson, in press).

     Most monochorial twins (all of whom are MZ) experience some
fusion of their placental circulations.   In extreme cases this may
result in the twin-transfusion syndrome, with one anemic and one
polycythemic twin, the former having bled into the latter.   Because
the syndrome has been found to affect ∿15% of monochorial twin
births, with an infant mortality rate that may exceed 60%, only ∿6%
of the surviving MZ twins (over one-third of the MZs are dichorial)
may be involved (Farr, 1974).   However, a higher frequency of the
syndrome is presumably masked by prenatal loss.   Moreover, less

serious degrees of fusion between the placental circulations may
also have undesirable effects, so that, at least for research on
variables likely to be influenced by this situation, the MZ sample
should be grouped into monochorial and dichorial pairs (Corey et
al., 1979).

If these problems, including possible psychological concomi-
tants of twinning, have been accounted for, and the desirable characteristics relating to size and type of sample have been defined,
ascertainment problems have to be solved and biases avoided.
Samples collected through announcements and similar procedures are
usually non-random because of the presumably higher motivation of
respondents that may be in turn related to specific problems. Also
samples from hospital populations are subject to bias because of
the specific risks of the twin condition. Obviously, however, for
many research purposes, some selection may be necessary. However,
whenever possible, the sample should be obtained from a school
population, or from large twin registers. The latter are now being
developed in several countries: Detailed information can be
obtained through the International Society for Twin Studies or The
Mendel Institute in Rome.

Twin Zygosity Determination

Once the twin sample has been ascertained, it usually has to
be classified by zygosity. Opposite-sex pairs are obviously DZ
and it is in most cases a very desirable practice to consider them
as a separate class (MF). Monochorial pairs may be safely considered as MZ and should, whenever possible, be considered separately (MC). In many cases, however, the information on placentation
may not be available or reliable. If so, not only the dichorial
(DC), but all the same-sex pairs (MM and FF) need to be classified.
This can be done through objective or subjective criteria and the
degree of accuracy of this assessment should vary according to the
kind of research and the sample size.

Objective Method. This requires the analysis of blood groups
and/or other genetic polymorphisms: The more systems tested, the
higher the probability that DZ pairs be detected because of the
discordance(s) they show. Cost-efficiency should be considered in
selecting the systems. The serologically concordant pairs are not
necessarily all MZ. Improbable as it is, two DZ cotwins (or, for
that matter, unrelated individuals) can be concordant for even all
of genetic polymorphisms. Thus, the determination of monozygosity
must be probabilistic in nature and its probability of error, i.e.,
the probability that any given pair classified as MZ is actually a
DZ pair, will be lower the more concordant genetic polymorphisms
are observed. A method originally developed by Smith and Penrose
(1955) is usually followed.

When parental phenotypes are known (those of other relatives may also be helpful), the likelihoods of obtaining the phenotypes observed in the twins can be calculated, on the hypothesis that they are MZ (L_M) or DZ (L_D). The likelihoods of obtaining the observed sex combination in the twin pair can be calculated similarly: two sex combinations (MM, FF) being equally probable for MZ pairs and four combinations (MM, FF, MF, FM) for DZ ones, for any given same-sex twin pair it will then be: $L_M = 0.5$ and $L_D = 0.25$. Given the relative frequencies of MZ and DZ twins in the general population, taking into account, whenever possible, modifying factors, such as ethnic group, maternal age and parity, year of birth, the prior probabilities of monozygosity (m) and dizygosity (d) are then calculated.

Using Bayes' theorem, the posterior probabilities of the twins' being MZ (P_M) or DZ (P_D) can be calculated as follows:

$$P_M = m L_M / (m L_M + d L_D)$$

$$P_D = d L_D / (m L_M + d L_D)$$

so that the relative odds in favor of the twins being DZ will be:

$$P_D/P_M = d L_D / m L_M = d/m \times L_D/L_M$$

The following example may be considered. Two twin girls, born in Italy in the seventies ($d/m \simeq 1.5$) are found to have blood types O,MN, their father being A,M and their mother O,MN. The likelihoods can be calculated as follows:

	Both twins female	Both O	Both MN	Total
$L_M =$	1/2	1/2	1/2	1/8
$L_D =$	1/4	1/4	1/4	1/64

The relative odds in favor of the twins being DZ will be:

$$P_D/P_M = d L_D / m L_M = d/m \times L_D/L_M = 1.5 \times 1/8 = 0.19.$$

That is obviously a much too high probability of error, and at least one or two more markers must be examined.

Of course, parental phenotypes may not be known, in which case a similar procedure is used, based on the calculation of the likelihood that the two twins are of the same phenotype, on the hypothesis that they are DZ, given the gene frequencies in the specific population. Thus, given the prior probability, d, in favor of DZ pairs, and the individual likelihoods that a DZ pair in that population be of the same sex, and of the same phenotype for genetic markers 1,2,3,...,n, a final combined probability is obtained, which is lower the more genetic polymorphisms examined. For example, data on a pair of twins born in England in the late forties (d/m = 2.33), both male, B,MsNs,CDe/cDE, gave a combined probability of the pair being DZ of 2.33 x 0.25 x 0.47 x 0.47 x 0.42 = 0.05 (see Smith and Penrose, 1955, for details). Today, because of the decline in DZ twinning rates and the lower d value ($d/m \simeq 1.5$), the same probability would have been $\sim$ 0.03.

The study of dermatoglyphics has been advocated to provide useful clues to zygosity assessment. In particular, the total finger ridge count is almost completely genetically determined and is easy and economic to measure, and shows a high population variability. Although its mode of inheritance is not clearly established, and thus it cannot be properly considered a genetic marker, it has been used frequently in probabilistic determinations of zygosity. For instance, based on a complex discrimination function developed by Parisi and Di Bacco (1968), any given same-sex pair can be classified as MZ or DZ according to whether the within-pair difference in the total finger ridge count is respectively $\leq$ 11 or > 11. The error of classification of this method was estimated as 0.14, which is possibly the lowest from any single trait. When combined with a few genetic markers the method will allow an accuracy of $\sim$ 95%.

Subjective Methods. Extensive analyses may not always be practical nor economic, and for many research purposes and sufficiently large samples they are not needed. An experienced observer can classify twins as MZ or DZ with considerable accuracy by simply looking at them. Race and Sanger (1968) found that bloodgrouping practically never contradicted Shields' (1962) opinion on the twins' zygosity. A less subjective approach may involve the detailed assessment of the twins' physical similarity with respect to anthropological markers, such as eye color, hair color and form, ear form and attachment, form of the nose. Extensions of this method, originally developed by Siemens (1927) and von Verschuer (1928) have appeared in recent years and been found to be highly accurate (Fairpo, 1979). Because the genetic determination of these traits is still rather obscure and environmental influences are always possible, this approach should be considered with caution. Moreover, because it is essentially subjective, it should be employed only after validation and reliability estimates have been obtained.

For some research studies, usually of an epidemiologic nature, zygosity can be assessed through suitable questionnaires (Cederlöf et al., 1961; Nichols and Bilbro, 1966) simply asking the parents to answer such questions as: "When growing up, were the two twins as alike as two peas in a pod?" or "Were the twins ever mixed up by their parents?" When validated against objective evaluations, these methods usually prove accurate in 95-97% of cases. However,

before any questionnaire method is applied, it may be desirable to
validate it on the specific population to which it is to be directed.
Finally, for population-based data (vital statistics, twin registers,
large hospital records, etc.), Weinberg's differential method, based
on sex combinations, can be used. Because, in the general population, the departure from equality of the two sexes at birth is not
large (the sex ratio being $\sim$106M:100F for most Caucasian populations), the four sex combinations possible for DZ pairs (MM, FF,
MF, FM) may safely be assumed as equally probable at 0.25. Let then
d and m be the estimates of DZ and MZ twin pairs, respectively, and
U = MF + FM be the number of unlike-sex pairs. Then:

$$d = 2U \quad \text{and} \quad m = 1 - d$$

Twin Data Analysis

When the twin data have been collected, the analysis is
usually based on a comparison of the MZ and the DZ samples (1) in
terms of percentages of concordant vs. discordant pairs, if the
study is concerned with a categorical, all-or-none variable, or (2)
in terms of pair differences or correlation coefficients, if the
research is concerned with a quantitative, continuous variable.
The extent of the increase in similarity in the MZ with respect to
the DZ pairs is taken as an indication of the amount of genetic
control over the trait or condition under examination. The efforts
to isolate and quantify this amount through heritability estimates
have produced a few formulae some of which are very widely used
although they probably lack theoretical value. The attempts to
estimate heritability have also led to more complex approaches and
continuing controversies.

Concordance Studies are mostly concerned with diseases.
Problems of ascertainment have to be carefully considered. Two
stages may be needed to correctly estimate the twin concordance
rate for the given disease. The first stage involves the ascertainment of the condition in the general population or population
sample: Twins found to be affected become probands. However, it
is necessary to take into account the possibility of incomplete
ascertainment. The members of a twin pair may live in different
cities, attend different hospitals, etc. Consequently, further
investigation of those pairs with only one proband is needed:
This will usually lead to the discovery of more concordant pairs.
The methodology to be followed in concordance studies has been
discussed extensively by Allen and Hrubec (1979) who developed a
mathematical model allowing for continuous variation in completeness of ascertainment in both stages, and for within-pair correlations in the primary ascertainment and in the occurrence of the
disease.

   When reliable concordance estimates   (or an analogous parameter, related to correlation in primary ascertainment) have been
obtained, the data can usually be summarized conveniently into an
heritability coefficient. The following formula (attributed to
Holzinger, perhaps because it resembles his H index used for quantitative traits, cf below) has been used commonly:

$$H_C = (C_{MZ} - C_{DZ})/1 - C_{DZ} \tag{1}$$

where C_{MZ}, C_{DZ} are the proportions of concordant twin pairs in
the two zygosity classes. A transformation table of proband concordance rate into an index of genetic determination, G, has been
provided by Smith (1974). The latter, however, frequently yields
unrealistic values, even > 1. Both approaches have been reviewed
recently by Allen (in press) who has suggested the following
revised formula:

$$H'_C = (C_{MZ} - C_{DZ})/C_{MZ} = 1 - C_{DZ}/C_{MZ} \tag{2}$$

except when $C_{MZ} + C_{DZ} > 1$, in which case formula (1) may still
be preferable. Also Allen has stressed that, rather than estimating heritability or the degree of genetic determination, "These
indexes . . . should be regarded as crude statements of the relative
degree of familial determination."

   Quantitative Studies. The classic approach to the analysis of
twin data for continuous variables consisted in the calculation of
within-pair correlations or variances and the subsequent estimation
of some coefficient describing the relative importance of genetic
vs. environmental factors in the determination of the character
under study. Such are the heritability estimates introduced by
Holzinger in 1929 and respectively based on correlations and on
variances:

$$H_1 = (\text{var}DZ - \text{var } MZ)/\text{var}DZ \tag{3}$$

Holzinger, 1929

$$H_2 = (r_{MZ} - r_{DZ})/1 - r_{DZ} \tag{4}$$

Though very widely applied until recently, these two formulae are
considered imprecise and unjustifiable on theoretical grounds.
Improvements have been suggested and the following formulae have
been used:

$$h^2 = 2(r_{MZ} - r_{DZ}) \qquad \text{Falconer, 1960} \tag{5}$$

$$H_R = 2(r_{MZ} - r_{DZ})/r_{MZ} = h^2/r_{MZ} \qquad \text{Nichols, 1965} \tag{6}$$

$$F = \text{var}DZ/\text{var}MZ = 1/1 - H^1 \qquad \text{Vandenberg, 1965} \tag{7}$$

Further improvements have been suggested by Jensen (1967) and by Elston and Gottesman (1968) among others. When different formulae are applied to the same set of data, considerably different results can be obtained. However, this may be done to obtain a range of values as a better approximation to heritability.

In general, heritability estimates have met with considerable criticism and the possibility of applying them to the study of human variability has been questioned, essentially on account of the difficulties in the partitioning of variance. The geneticists who introduced the concept of heritability as a guide in the selection of economically important traits in animal breeding differentiated between a broad heritability, meaning the total portion of variance due to genetic differences, and a narrow heritability, restricted to the measure of the additive portion of genetic variance, other portions such as the effects of dominance, genic interaction, assortative mating, being difficult to estimate. The controversies that have until recently characterized the genetic analysis of quantitative variables in man, and specifically the application of heritability estimates as derived from twin studies, essentially refer to the actual importance of the nonadditive portions of genetic variance, to the extent of genotype-environment interactions, and to the techniques whereby these components are estimated.

A more comprehensive approach than heritability estimates has been developed in the sixties by Cattel (1960, 1965) and further examined by Loehlin (1965): the Multiple Abstracts Variance Analysis (MAVA). This is based on the comparison of within- and between-family variances of full and half-sib families as well as MZ and DZ twins and allows an assessment of the importance of genetic vs. environmental factors, including the correlation between the two. The usefulness of including data on siblings and parents of twins for a simultaneous analysis of quantitative inheritance was stressed by Elston and Gottesman (1968).

A general approach to the quantitative analysis of twin data was provided by the extension of Fisher's biometric genetic analysis proposed by Jinks and Fulker (1970) in which the classic estimates and the MAVA approach are included as special cases. The techniques of the biometric genetic analysis, as described and illustrated by these authors and further extended by their colleagues of the Birmingham group (Eaves et al., 1977, 1978; Martin et al., 1978; Fulker, 1978; Eaves, 1978), allow a more critical assessment of the different components of variance and have greatly contributed to the new, widespread interest in twin studies and the extension of their potentialities.

In general, modern methods of analysis are based on the following variance analysis set of data:

Source of	MZ pairs		DZ pairs	
variation	df	Mean squares	df	Mean squares
Among pairs	nMZ-1	M_{AMZ}	nDZ-1	M_{ADZ}
Within pairs	nMZ	M_{WMZ}	nDZ	M_{WDZ}

df = degrees of freedom; nMZ, nDZ = number of MZ, DZ pairs

When the mean squares for MZ and DZ pairs have been calculated,
their values are interpreted in terms of a model describing the
different contributions to the total variation. The theoretical
model is fitted and estimates of the various parameters are obtained. Detailed descriptions and applications of the various,
frequently complex, procedures are to be found in the articles
cited above. Simpler procedures in the quantitative analysis of
twin data, with special respect to tests for heterogeneity of twin
means and variances along with estimates of genetic variance, have
been reviewed by Christian (1979).

OTHER TWIN DESIGNS

Over the years, a number of different approaches have grown
out of the classic twin method and new applications and perspec-
tives found for the study of twins, the potentialities of which
have thus been greatly expanded. Some of these approaches will be
mentioned briefly, with reference to sources where systematic
treatment and applications may be found.

MZ Twins Reared Apart (MZA)

A theoretically simple and extremely powerful variation of the
classic twin method consists in the study of MZ cotwins who were
separated soon after birth and raised in different environments.
The advantages are obvious, since the covariance between such
cotwins can provide us with a direct estimate of the genetic variance in the population with respect to the variable under study.
However, the point has been made that some selection in placement,
through adoptions, etc., being likely, the two environments might
be related to some extent. Moreover, the peculiarities of such
situations would make it even more difficult to derive findings of
general value from such studies.

Such twins are extremely difficult to identify because they
are quite rare, and because adoption agencies and similar bodies
are usually eager to protect the privacy of their records. In
fact, though isolated pairs have been described, there have been

only four studies of MZA series (Newman et al., 1937: 19 pairs; Shields, 1962: 38 pairs; Juel-Nielsen, 1965: 12 pairs; and Burt, 1966: 53 pairs. There is some dispute about this latter study). These studies, totalling 122 pairs (or just 69, if Burt's series is disregarded), have been of particular interest to psychologists; they essentially concerned behavioral variables, and specifically IQ measures. Useful reviews can be found in Jensen (1970) and Shields (1978).

Cotwin Control Studies

The method of cotwin control is essentially experimental in nature. It allows the testing of hypotheses about cause and effect through the comparison of two perfectly matched sets of subjects, one twin of each pair being placed in the experimental group and the cotwin in the control group. It essentially involves MZ cotwins, although DZ cotwins may be used also.

Possibly introduced by Gesell and Thompson (1929), at first the method was used only in the fields of psychology and education to determine the importance of training and teaching systems. In more recent years, the method has been applied increasingly to the testing of drugs and differential treatments, as well as in epidem- iology to evaluate the effects of differential exposure to factors such as smoking, alcohol, etc. (e.g., Cederlöf et al., 1977). The potential of this powerful approach is still far from fully exploited.

The Half-Sib Method

Half-sib analysis is a useful technique for quantitative genetic studies in organisms other than man, allowing, in conjunc- tion with other family data, estimates of genetic and environmental variance, as well as the partitioning of the former into its addi- tive, dominance, and epistatic components. In man, however, half- sib analysis is subject to practical difficulties and potential biases, and is usually not as powerful as in other species because human half-sibs are frequently reared in the same environment, so that genetic and environmental effects remain confounded.

These and similar problems may be circumvented by the analysis of the offspring of MZ cotwins, who are genetically related to each other in the same way as are conventional half-sibs, but usually live in different households and belong to sibships of the same expected size and mean age. The structure of the data is illus- trated in Figure 2. A model for the application of the half-sib method to the genetic analysis of quantitative variables in man, based on the data structure illustrated by the scheme in Figure 2,

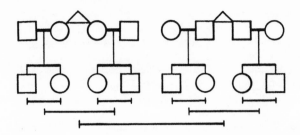

Fig. 2.   Structure of MZ twin half-sibship data, illustrating how
           total variation may be partitioned into within sibship,
           between sibship-within half-sibship and among half-
           sibship components.

has been developed by Nance (1974) who has applied it successfully
and has stressed its flexibility. More recently, the extension of
the model to include data on the grandchildren of MZ twins has
been advocated as a useful tool in the study of maternal effects
and for the resolution of the single-major-locus vs. multifactorial-
inheritance controversy in the analysis of birth defects (Corey et
al., 1978).

     Besides the above variations of the classic design, other
approaches have been developed and different applications and prospective uses advocated for twin research. A model for the qualitative analysis of population-based twin data independent of
zygosity has been developed by Gedda et al. (1979). The study of
sex differences between MF cotwins compared to those in the general
population has been proposed by Vandenberg (1976) to assess the
influence of the presence of an opposite-sex sibling of the same
age on personality development and on sex differentiation. The
striking synchronies that are frequently observed in MZ cotwins
have led to inferences and general models related to the timing
of the genetic program (Gedda and Brenci, 1978; Wilson, 1978).
The peculiarities of the twin situation have been used in an effort
to better understand the psychological dynamics of couples in
general (Zazzo, 1978). Similarly, as critics of conventional
approaches have recently noted (Elston and Bocklage, 1978), the
biologic, and specifically the embryologic, peculiarities of
twins can be of great use in helping to elucidate fundamental
developmental processes.

     Far from being obsolete, as its critics have sometimes con-
tended, twin research is still an active field with promising
achievements and avenues for further development.

REFERENCES

Allen, G., in press, Holzinger's Hc revised, Acta Genet. Med.
     Gemellol., 28.
Allen, G., and Hrubec, Z., 1979, Twin concordance. A more general
     model, Acta Genet. Med. Gemellol., 28:3.
Bulmer, M. G., 1970, "The Biology of Twinning in Man," Clarendon
     Press, Oxford.
Burt, C., 1966, The genetic determination of differences in intel-
     ligence: A study of monozygotic twins reared together and
     apart, Br. J. Psychol., 57:137.
Cattell, R. B., 1960, The multiple abstracts variance analysis.
     Equations and solutions for nature-nurture research on con-
     tinuous variables, Psychol. Rev., 67:353.
Cattell, R. B., 1965, Methodological and conceptual advances in
     evaluating hereditary and environmental influences and their
     interaction, in: "Methods and Goals in Human Behavior
     Genetics," S. G. Vandenberg, ed., Academic Press, New York.
Cederlöf, R., Friberg, L., Jonson, E., and Kaaij, L., 1961, Studies
     on similarity diagnosis in twins with the aid of mailed
     questionnaires, Acta Genet., 11:338.
Cederlöf, R., Friberg, L., and Lundman, T., 1977, "The Interactions
     of Smoking, Environment and Heredity and Their Implications
     for Disease Etiology," Acta Med. Scand., Suppl. no. 612.
Christian, J. C., 1979, Testing twin means and estimating genetic
     variance. Basic methodology for the analysis of quantitative
     twin data, Acta Genet. Med. Gemellol., 28:35.
Corey, L. A., Nance, W. E., and Berg, K., 1978, A new tool in birth
     defects research: The MZ half-sib model and its extension
     to grandchildren of identical twins, in: "Annual Review of
     Birth Defects, 1977. Part A: Cell Surface Factors, Immune
     Deficiencies, Twin Studies," R. L. Summitt and D. Bergsma,
     eds., A. R. Liss, New York.
Corey, L. A., Nance, W. E., Kang, K. W., and Christian, J. C.,
     1979, Effects of type of placentation on birthweight and
     its variability in monozygotic and dizygotic twins, Acta
     Genet. Med. Gemellol., 28:41.
Eaves, L. J., Last, K., Martin, N. G., and Jinks, J. L., 1977, A
     progressive approach to non-additivity and genotype-
     environmental covariance in the analysis of human differ-
     ences, Br. J. Math. Stat. Psychol., 30:1.
Eaves, L. J., Last, K. A., Young, P. A., and Martin, N. G., 1978,
     Model-fitting approaches to the analysis of human behaviour,
     Heredity, 41:249.
Eaves, L. J., 1978, Twins as a basis for the causal analysis of
     human personality, in: "Twin Research. Part A: Psychology
     and Methodology," W. E. Nance, G. Allen, and P. Parisi, eds.,
     A. R. Liss, New York.

Elston, R. C., and Gottesman, I. I., 1968, The analysis of quantitative inheritance simultaneously from twin and family data, Am. J. Hum. Genet., 20:512.

Elston, R. C., and Bocklage, C. E., 1978, An examination of fundamental assumptions of the twin method, in: "Twin Research. Part A: Psychology and Methodology," W. E. Nance, G. Allen, and P. Parisi, eds., A. R. Liss, New York.

Fairpo, C. G., 1979, The problem of determining twin zygosity for epidemiological studies, Acta Genet. Med. Gemellol., 28:21.

Falconer, D. S., 1960, "Introduction to Quantitative Genetics," Oliver & Boyd, Edinburgh.

Farr, V., 1974, Prognosis for the babies, early and late, in: "Human Multiple Reproduction," I. MacGillivray, P. P. S. Nylander, and G. Corney, eds., W. B. Saunders, London.

Fulker, D. W., 1978, Multivariate extensions of a biometrical model of twin data, in: "Twin Research. Part A: Psychology and Methodology," W. E. Nance, G. Allen, and P. Parisi, eds., A. R. Liss, New York.

Galton, F., 1875, The history of twins as a criterion of the relative powers of nature and nurture, Fraser's Magazine, 12:566.

Gedda, L., 1951, "Studio dei Gemelli," Orizzonte Medico, Rome. (English translation of first part: "Twins in History and Science," Charles C Thomas, Springfield, 1961.)

Gedda, L., and G. Brenci, 1978, "Chronogenetics. The Inheritance of Biological Time," Charles C Thomas, Springfield.

Gedda, L., Rossi, C., Brenci, G., 1979, Twin azygotic test for the study of hereditary qualitative traits in twin populations, Acta Genet. Med. Gemellol., 28:15.

Gesell, A., and Thompson, H., 1929, Learning and growth in identical twins: An experimental study by the method of co-twin control, Genet. Psychol. Monogr., 6:1.

Holzinger, K. J., 1929, The relative effect of nature and nurture on twin differences, J. Educ. Psychol., 20:241.

Jensen, A. R., 1967, Estimation of the limits of heritability of traits by comparison of monozygotic and dizygotic twins, Proc. Nat. Acad. Sci., 58:149.

Jensen, A. R., 1970, IQ's of identical twins reared apart, Behav. Genet., 1:133.

Jinks, J. L., and Fulker, D. W., 1970, Comparison of the biometrical, genetical, MAVA, and classical approaches to the analysis of human behavior, Psychol. Bull., 73:311.

Juel-Nielsen, N., 1965, "Individual and Environment. A Psychiatric-Psychological Investigation of Monozygotic Twins Reared Apart," Acta Psychiatrica Scandinavica, Suppl. no. 183.

Koch, H., 1966, "Twins and Twin Relations," University of Chicago Press, Chicago.

Loehlin, J. C., 1965, Some methodological problems in Cattell's Multiple Abstracts Variance Analysis, Psychol. Rev., 72:156.

MacGillivray, I., 1974, Labour in multiple pregnancies, in: "Human
    Multiple Reproduction," I. MacGillivray, P. P. S. Nylander,
    and G. Corney, eds., W. B. Saunders, London.

Martin, N. G., Eaves, L. J., Kearsey, M. J., and Davies, P., 1978,
    The power of the classical twin method, Heredity, 40:97.

Matheny, A. P., Appraisal of parental bias in twin studies:
    Ascribed zygosity and IQ differences in twins, Acta Genet.
    Med. Gemellol., in press.

Nance, W. E., 1974, Genetic studies of the offspring of identical
    twins. A model for the analysis of quantitative inherit-
    ance in man. First International Congress on Twin Studies,
    Rome, 1974, Acta Genet. Med. Gemellol., 25:103.

Nance, W. E., Winter, P. M., Segreti, W. O., Corey, L. A., Parisi-
    Prinzi, G., Parisi, P., 1978, A search for evidence of
    hereditary superfetation in man, in: "Twin Research.
    Part B: Biology and Epidemiology," W. E. Nance, G. Allen,
    and P. Parisi, eds., A. R. Liss, New York.

Newman, H. H., Freeman, F. N., Holzinger, K. J., 1937, "Twins: A
    Study of Heredity and Environment," University of Chicago
    Press, Chicago.

Nichols, R. C., 1965, The National Merit twin study, in: "Methods
    and Goals in Human Behavior Genetics," S. G. Vandenberg,
    ed., Academic Press, New York.

Nichols, R. C., and Bilbro, W. C., 1966, The diagnosis of twin
    zygosity, Acta Genet., 16:265.

Nylander, P. P. S., and MacGillivray, I., 1974, Complications of
    twin pregnancy, in: "Human Multiple Reproduction,"
    I. MacGillivray, P. P. S. Nylander, and G. Corney, eds.,
    W. B. Saunders, London.

Parisi, P., and Di Bacco, M., 1968, Fingerprints and the diagnosis
    of zygosity in twins, Acta Genet. Med. Gemellol., 17:333.

Price, B., 1950, Primary biases in twin studies, Am. J. Hum.
    Genet., 2:293.

Race, R. R., and Sanger, R., 1968, "Blood Groups in Man," F. A.
    Davis, Philadelphia.

Scarr, S., 1968, Environmental bias in twin studies, Eugen. Q.,
    15:34.

Shields, J., 1962, "Monozygotic Twins Brought up Apart and Brought
    up Together," Oxford University Press, London.

Shields, J., 1978, MZA twins: Their use and abuse, in: "Twin
    Research. Part A: Psychology and Methodology," W. E.
    Nance, G. Allen, and P. Parisi, eds., A. R. Liss, New York.

Smith, C., 1974, Concordance in twins: methods and interpretation,
    Am. J. Hum. Genet., 26:454.

Smith, S. M., and Penrose, L. S., 1955, Monozygotic and dizygotic
    twin diagnosis, Ann. Hum. Genet., 19:273.

Vandenberg, S. G., 1965, Multivariate analysis of twin differences,
    in: "Methods and Goals in Human Behavior Genetics," S. G.
    Vandenberg, ed., Academic Press, New York.

Vandenberg, S. G., 1976, Twin studies, in: "Human Behavior
       Genetics," A. R. Kaplan, ed., Charles C Thomas, Springfield.
Von Verschuer, O., 1928, Die Aenlichkeitsdiagnose der Eineiigkeit
       von Zwillingen, Anthropol. Anz., 5:244.
Wilson, R. S., 1978, Synchronies in mental development: An epi-
       genetic perspective, Science, 202:939.
Wilson, R. S., Twin growth: Initial deficit, recovery, and trends
       in concordance from birth to nine years, Ann. Hum. Biol.
       in press.
Zazzo, R., 1960, "Les Jumeaux: Le Couple et la Personne," Presses
       Universitaires de France, Paris.
Zazzo, R., 1978, Genesis and peculiarities of the personality of
       twins, in: "Twin Research. Part A: Psychology and
       Methodology," W. E. Nance, G. Allen, and P. Parisi, eds.,
       A. R. Liss, New York.

15. STATISTICAL PROBLEMS OF FITTING INDIVIDUAL GROWTH CURVES[1]

R. Darrell Bock

University of Chicago

Chicago, IL   60637

David Thissen

University of Kansas

Lawrence, KS   66045

A thorough-going longitudinal study of a child's growth can produce upward of forty observations spaced over the years from birth to maturity. Such a data record is too long and inevitably too noisy (because of measurement error and short-run growth variation) to be interpreted without some sort of condensation and smoothing. The length of the record forces attention to certain critical regions or features of the curve, but the noisiness of the data makes it risky to characterize these regions or features by a few isolated measurements. The only safe approach to interpretation of individual growth data is via a statistical method capable of revealing the essential trend and concisely describing its main features.

In broad terms there are two, sometimes opposed, sometimes complementary, philosophies of how data reduction of this type should be undertaken. They can be contrasted as "nonstructural" vs. "structural." In the nonstructural approach, the data are smoothed locally to suppress measurement error and short-term variation. The surface features of the smooth curve then serve to describe and summarize the pattern of variation. A good example in the growth literature is the use by Largo, et al. (1978) of cubic spline functions to smooth the growth velocity curve and to estimate the preadolescent minimum and adolescent maximum of velocity.

In the structural approach, the objective is to find a mathematical model, usually expressed as a family of functions relating

---
[1]Supported in part by NSF Grant BNS 76-02849 to the University of Chicago and NSF Grant BNS 76-22943 A02 to the Center for Advanced Study in the Behavioral Sciences, Stanford, California.

observable quantities in terms of unobservable parameters. The
parameters are then estimated by those values that best fit the
function to the particular data record. If the model is found to
fit sufficiently well and the number of parameters is small relative
to the number of observations, the statistical estimation of the
parameters is tantamount both to summarizing and to smoothing the
record. The critical features of the record can be accurately
inferred from the fitted curve, and the parameter estimates convey
all of the information needed to reproduce the essential trend in
the data. Moreover, the parameter estimates can stand in place of
the data in multivariate analyses of group differences or relations
to background variables and thus reduce the dimensionality of these
analyses to a manageable number. Finally, if the mathematical
function reflects actual processes responsible for the phenomenon,
the parameters may have an interpretation in terms of the physical
or biological processes responsible for the observed relationships.

As will be apparent in the sequel, the present authors are of
the persuasion that, in the long run, the structural model-fitting
approach to data analysis is more productive of applications and
articulates better with physical or biological theory than does the
nonstructural. Accordingly, we devote the present paper almost
entirely to model fitting methods of analyzing longitudinal data.
We discuss procedures for this purpose based on increasingly refined
statistical techniques--namely, least-squares, maximum likelihood
(or generalized least squares), Bayes estimation, and linearly constrained Bayes estimation. We illustrate these techniques by fitting
the triple-logistic model of Bock and Thissen (1976) to data from
the Berkeley Guidance Study. The techniques are entirely general,
however, and could be applied to the same data using other proposed
growth functions, such as those of Jenss and Bayley (1937), Preece
and Baines (1978), or Stützle (1977). The problems of fitting the
triple-logistic function are typical of those encountered with any
relatively good-fitting, nonlinear, heavily parameterized growth
model.

1.   Statistical Properties of Longitudinal Data

In the fitting of growth models, longitudinal data present
quite different problems from those of cross-sectional data. Because each subject in a cross-sectional study contributes a measurement at only one time point, the measures and means of measures at
the various time points are logically unrelated to one another and
are stochastically independent. As a result, conventional methods
of linear and curvilinear regression may be used to fit curvilinear
polynomial growth models (see Bock, 1975, Cpt. 4 or Bock, 1979).
Straightforward generalizations, described in the following
section, make these methods available for nonlinear models such as
logistic growth curves.

When the data are longitudinal, on the other hand, the observations made on the same subject at different times are logically associated and are in general statistically correlated. Much, but not all, of this correlation is suppressed when individual growth models are fitted and variation due to systematic trend is removed. The correlation that remains in the residual variation (i.e., in the differences between the observed measures and the predicted values calculated from the individually fitted models) is due to short-run fluctuations in growth appearing at more or less random times in different individuals, possibly as a result of environmental influences. Not being part of systematic growth that can be captured by the model, this short-run variation produces correlation among residuals, and its effects must be accounted for in any efficient method of curve fitting. A suitable method is discussed in Section 3. This method exploits the fact that deviations from trend in time-dependent data typically have a simple correlation structure that can be modeled and incorporated into the curve-fitting procedure.

To provide for modeling of the residual correlation structure, it is essential that the data be collected at fixed, regularly spaced time points. Data with this property have been termed "time structured" (Bock, 1979). Longitudinal data that are not time structured are not suitable for the investigation of residual correlation structures. Once the structure has been characterized, however, the results can be used in curve fitting procedures for longitudinal data that do not require time-structured data (see Section 5). This has obvious advantages in anthropological and pediatric applications where strict time structuring is difficult to achieve.

In the remaining sections of this paper, we describe a series of curve-fitting procedures based on successively less restrictive assumptions. First, a method appropriate for fitting a non-linear growth model to complete data with underlined residuals is discussed. Then, the correlation of residuals is admitted in time-structured data; next, the requirement of time structuring is relaxed; finally a method suitable for incomplete data records is presented and illustrated.

2.   Nonlinear Least Squares

The least-squares method of Gauss and Legendre, when applied to models that are linear in the parameters to be estimated and in the error component, yields estimators that are explicit linear functions of the observations. (The formulas for simple and multiple regression coefficients and for class-effects in analysis of variance are familiar examples.) But when applied to nonlinear models (i.e., to models in which the parameters appear not as separate coefficients of additive terms, but as products or quotients, or in exponents), the estimators are nonlinear in the observations and in many cases

expressable only as infinite recursion. With a good choice of the
numerical method, however, the estimates of the parameters often can
be determined with sufficient accuracy for practical work in a small
number of recursions. In such favorable cases, nonlinear estimation
is not inordinately more difficult than linear estimation of the same
number of parameters. (See Jennerich and Ralston, 1978.)

There is now fairly general agreement that the best method of
minimizing a multiparameter nonlinear function is the so-called
"conditioned Newton-Raphson" solution (Gill and Murray, 1974;
Chambers, 1977). In the context of the present application, it may
be described as follows:

Let the statistical model for the stature of subject i at age
x_j be

$$y_{ij} = f(x_j, \underline{\theta}_i) + \varepsilon_{ij}, \quad j = 1, 2, \ldots, n, \tag{2-1}$$

where f represents a twice-differentiable function of age and

the individual growth parameters $\underline{\theta}_i = (\theta_{i_1}, \theta_{i_2}, \ldots, \theta_{i_m})$, and

ε_{ij} is an independent residual.

To obtain the estimator of $\underline{\theta}_i$, we minimize the (weighted) sum
of squared residuals,

$$q_i = \sum_{j}^{n} w_j [y_{ij} - f(x_j, \underline{\theta}_i)]^2, \tag{2-2}$$

where the w_j are positive-valued weights. (In growth data it is
advisable to weight the data points inversely as their density in
time. That is, annual measures might be given the weight 1 and semi-
annual measures, the weight 1/2.)

A necessary condition on the minimum may be obtained by differentiating (2-2) and equating to zero to obtain the so-called
"extremal" equations,

$$\frac{\partial q_i}{\partial \theta_{ig}} = -2 \sum_{j=1}^{n} w_j [y_{ij} - f(x_j, \underline{\hat{\theta}}_i)] \left[\frac{\partial f(x_j, \underline{\theta}_i)}{\partial \theta_{ig}} \right]_{\underline{\theta} = \underline{\hat{\theta}}_i} \tag{2-3}$$

$$= 0, \quad g = 1, 2, \ldots, m.$$

For "reasonable" functions f and, with n "large" relative to m, this
system of implicit nonlinear equations in the m unknowns,

$\hat{\underline{\theta}} = [\hat{\theta}_{i1}, \hat{\theta}_{i2}, \ldots, \hat{\theta}_{im}]$, usually can be solved by a conditioned Newton-Raphson process based on the iterative corrections

$$\hat{\theta}_{ig}^{(\ell+1)} = \hat{\theta}_{ig}^{(\ell)} + \gamma_{ig}^{(\ell)} \tag{2-4}$$

where $\gamma_{ig}^{(\ell)}$ is obtained at iteration ℓ by solving the linear system,

$$\sum_{h=1}^{m} \gamma_{ih}^{(\ell)} \left[\frac{\partial^2 q_i}{\partial \theta_{ig} \partial \theta_{ih}} + c_\ell \delta_{gh} \right]_{\underline{\theta}_i = \hat{\underline{\theta}}_i^{(\ell)}} = \left[\frac{\partial q_i}{\partial \theta_{ig}} \right]_{\underline{\theta}_i = \hat{\underline{\theta}}_i^{(\ell)}} . \tag{2-5}$$

In (2-5), $\delta_{gh} = 1$ for $g = h$ and 0 otherwise (Kronecker's delta), and c_ℓ is a constant chosen to accelerate convergence of the iterations (see Chambers, 1977). To start the process, the elements of $\underline{\theta}_i^{(\ell)}$ are assigned initial estimates, $\underline{\theta}_i^{(0)}$. A good choice for $\underline{\theta}_i^{(0)}$ in the present instance is the set of mean values of the growth parameters in the population from which the subject was drawn (if these measures are unknown, some amount of trial and error may be required to find satisfactory initial values for the first few subjects, after which accumulated means can be used). Provided the initial values are not too far removed from the solution point, the corrections will quickly become small, c_ℓ will approach zero, and stable estimates of the parameters, if they exist, will be obtained. When the curvature of the criterion function is positive at this point, i.e., if

$$\sum_{g=1}^{m} \sum_{h=1}^{m} \left[\frac{\partial^2 q_i}{\partial \theta_{ig} \partial \theta_{ih}} \right]_{\underline{\theta} = \hat{\underline{\theta}}_i} z_g z_h > 0 , \tag{2-6}$$

for all z_g such that $\Sigma z_g^2 = 1$, a minimum of the **squared residuals** has been found. Provided the parameter values at this point are plausible, the solution is then usually assumed to be the proper minimum and the least square estimates therefore obtained.

For residuals that can be assumed to have zero mean, have finite, homogeneous variance and be normally independently distributed, the least-squared solution can be justified statistically as a best asymptotic normal or BAN estimator. As n increases without limit, the sampling variation of the BAN estimator is multivariate normal and has the minimum possible variance, i.e., the limiting standard error or the estimator is minimal. But we can take very little comfort in the fact, not so much because n can never be really large in longitudinal growth studies, but because the residuals in longitudinal data are not in general independent. In fact, they can be fairly highly correlated if the interval between observations is small. This type of dependency in residual variation about trend lines in serial data is so universally encountered that it has, in recent years, become the subject of a vast literature (see Cochran and Orcutt, 1949; Jenkins and Watts, 1968; Fuller, 1976; Box and Jenkins, 1976; Brillinger, 1975 and Glass, et al., 1975). This work has established that conventional least-squares for minimizing independent errors cannot be relied on for analysis of longitudinal data, but must be replaced by the method of maximum likelihood, or the computationally equivalent method of generalized least squares, on the assumption of correlated errors.

3.   <u>Maximum Likelihood Estimation in the Presence of Correlated</u>
     <u>Residuals</u>

We now assume that n residuals in (2-1) have the multivariate normal distribution, $N(\underline{0}, \Sigma_\varepsilon)$, i.e., all components of the vector mean are zero, and each of the $n(n + 1)/2$ distinct elements in the n×n covariance matrix, Σ_ε, is arbitrary. (Later we will assume a structure for Σ_ε that restricts its elements). The j-th diagonal element of Σ_ε is σ_j^2, the variance of the residual at age x_j; the j, k off-diagonal element, $j \neq k$, is the covariance $\sigma_{jk} = \sigma_{kj} = \rho_{jk}\sigma_j\sigma_k$, where ρ_{jk} is correlation between residuals at ages x_j and x_k.

In this notation, the logarithm of the likelihood of the parameters, given the data, which when maximized with respect to variation in the parameters yields the maximum likelihood estimates, has the form

$$\lambda_i = C - \tfrac{1}{2}\sum_{jk}^{nn}\sum_i \sigma^{jk}[y_{ij} - f(x_j,\underline{\theta}_i)][y_{ik} - f(x_k, \underline{\theta}_i)] \qquad (3\text{-}1)$$

where C is a term not involving $\underline{\theta}_i$, and σ^{jk} is an element of Σ_ε^{-1}, the inverse of the covariance matrix of the residuals, given by the solution of the linear system,

$$\sum_k^n \sigma^{jk}\sigma_{jk} = \delta_{jk} \quad ,$$

in which $\sigma_{jj} = \sigma_j^2$ and δ_{jk} is the previously defined Kronecker delta.

The log likelihood criterion differs from the least-squares criterion in that cross-products as well as squares of the residuals appear in the sum, and each term in the sum if weighted by the element σ_i^{jk} from the inverse covariance matrix of the residuals for subject i. These weights provide a rigorous treatment of the problem of irregular spacing of observations that was handled by the heuristic weights assigned in the least-squares criterion.

Given numerical values for the σ^{jk}, the maximum likelihood estimates are obtained in a manner analogous to nonlinear least squares: The first derivatives of the likelihood function are set equal to zero to obtain the so-called likelihood equations,

$$\frac{\partial \lambda_i}{\partial \theta_{ig}} = \sum_{jk}^{nn} \sigma_i^{jk} [y_{ij} - f(x_j, \hat{\theta}_i)] \left[\frac{\partial f(x_k, \theta_i)}{\partial \theta_{ig}}\right]_{\theta_i = \hat{\theta}_i} = 0 \quad . \quad (3-2)$$

Like the extremal equations in nonlinear least squares, the system (3-2) can usually be solved in cases of interest by a conditional Newton-Raphson process. The second derivatives of the log likelihood function, $\partial^2 \lambda_i / \partial \theta_{ig} \partial \theta_{ih}$, which are required in this process, are more lengthy than in (2-5) because of the possibly large number of terms in (3-2).

The practical difficulty in the maximum likelihood method is, however, not so much in the calculation of the derivatives, which in the case of the triple logistic model is tedious but otherwise straightforward (see Thissen and Bock, 1979), as in the specification of values for σ^{jk}. They are assumed known in (3-2), but in fact are unknown.

Fortunately, these quantities merely play the role of weights and, as such, do not need to be known with great accuracy. Except in unusual cases that are not likely to occur in the present application (in which the determinant of Σ_ε approaches zero), the σ_{jk} and consequently the σ^{jk} can vary appreciably without altering much the solution of (3-2). This fact encourages us to study empirically the structure of Σ_ε in the hope of finding an approximation for it that will serve the purposes of maximum likelihood estimation. If we are successful, we have the advantage not only of avoiding the biases in the fitted curve due to irregular spacing of the observations, but also of favorable statistical properties of the estimator--namely, that the estimator is BAN under much more realistic assumptions than the least-squares estimator and that the large sample standard error of the estimator of θ_{ig} is given simply by the square root of

$$\left[\frac{\partial^2 \lambda_i}{\partial \theta_{ig} \partial \theta_{ih}}\right] gg,$$

$$\underline{\theta}_i = \hat{\underline{\theta}}_i$$

(3-3)

that is, of the g-th diagonal element of the inverse matrix of second derivatives of the log likelihood at the solution point of (3-2).

4.   The Structure of the Covariance Matrix of Residuals from Triple-Logistic Growth Curves[1]

In considering how to determine Σ_ε, we realize immediately that the data for any one subject is far too limited to estimate a personal error covariance matrix for each subject. The best we can do is to assume that the covariance matrices are homogeneous within certain subclasses of subjects (e.g., within sexes) and to estimate a common within-group matrix. This estimate may not be optimal for any given subject, but on average it should provide a more accurate evaluation of the likelihood than some more arbitrary choice.

The following strategy for estimating an expected Σ_ε has been proposed by Fearn (1975): First calculate least-squares estimates of the growth parameters for a number of subjects, call these values $\hat{\underline{\theta}}_i^*$, i = 1,2,..., N, and calculate the provisional residuals,

$$\hat{e}_{ij}^* = y_{ij} - f(x_j, \hat{\underline{\theta}}_i^*), \quad j = 1,2,\ldots, n.$$

(4-1)

From the latter, calculate provisional covariance estimates

$$\hat{\sigma}_{jk}^* = \frac{1}{N}\sum_i^N [y_{ij} - f(x_j, \underline{\theta}_i^*)][y_{ik} - f(x_k, \underline{\theta}_i^*)],$$

(4-2)

then go back to the data and obtain provisional maximum likelihood estimates using (3-2) and substituting $(\sigma^*)^{jk}$ for σ^{jk}. Once again compute residuals and re-estimate covariances by appropriate substitutions in (4-1) and (4-2). Since only a rough approximation of Σ_ε is required, the latter estimates should be sufficiently accurate to be used in calculating the final maximum likelihood estimates of the growth parameters.

---

[1] We are indebted to John Tukey and David Brillinger for suggestions in this section.

This strategy, while workable in high quality data, is unfortunately limited by the requirement that the numbers and values of time points, x_j, be identical for all subjects. It can be applied only in longitudinal growth studies in which the times of observation have been kept rigorously regular in all subjects, and results obtained from one study would not be useful for data with a different choice of time points (and thus not for data from a typical field study). For a suitably general procedure, we need a method of computing the expected covariance matrix of residuals for observations taken in an arbitrary pattern of age points.

From our work with the Berkeley data, a practical method appears to be available. Using Faern's approach, we find that the covariance structure of residuals from the triple-logistic model in these data seems to be consistent with the assumption that the residuals are generated by a stationary, normal, stochastic process in continuous time. That is, the residuals at any age x_j are normally distributed with constant mean, μ, and constant variance, σ, and the correlation between residuals at ages x_j and x_k depends only upon the absolute value of the "lag," $x_j - x_k$, between age points. With these assumptions, the covariance structure simplifies from $n(n+1)/2$ arbitrary elements to $n-1+2 = n+1$ elements. Moreover, the correlations between residuals tend to "die out," or at least become negligible, as the lag becomes large, and the number of arbitrary elements is reduced still further. Assuming the distribution of the residuals to be stationary, we can calculate the expected covariances, σ_{jk}, and hence, the weights, σ^{jk}, for maximum likelihood fitting, merely from the common mean (which is zero), the common standard deviation, and an autocorrelation function expressing the correlation between residuals in terms of $|x_j - x_k|$.

Evidence of the validity of these assumptions is presented in Figure 4-1, which shows the means and standard deviations of the residuals from a provisional least-squares fitting of the triple-logistic curve for a sample of 67 boys and 62 girls in the Berkeley Guidance Study. The measures of stature were obtained quarterly between one and two years of age, annually between two and eight, and semi-annually thereafter. In the mean residuals for girls there is some "end effect" beyond age 15 that should disappear when the observations are correctly weighted. In both sexes there is some indication of runs in the mean residuals during adolescence. The shape of the adolescent component possibly could be altered slightly to correct this, but the means of the residuals in this region are too small to have much effect on the correlations, and we will ignore them for the present.

The standard deviations are quite uniform in the range 8 to 18 years, but are somewhat elevated in the range two to 8 years. This may be an artifact of the fitting due to less dense measures in the years two through 8, or it may represent a real tendency of children to experience more short-run variability of growth at younger ages. Although it will be possible to correct for this effect if it is real, we have not yet attempted to do so and have computed the estimated autocorrelations in Figure 4-1 on the assumption of a common standard deviation equal to 1/3 cm at all time points.

To make use of the standard maximum likelihood estimator of autocovariances (see Fuller, 1976), it is necessary that the observations be equally spaced. If the fixed interval is then chosen as the unit of time, the m.l. estimator for the autocovariance at lag k can be expressed for the residuals of subject i as

$$\hat{\gamma}_i(k) = \frac{1}{n-k} \sum_{j=1}^{n-k} (\hat{\varepsilon}_{ij} - \mu)(\hat{\varepsilon}_{i,j+k} - \mu) \qquad (4-3)$$

(see Fuller, 1976, p.236). But we are assuming N realizations of this series and are taking $\mu = 0$; hence,

$$\hat{\gamma}_i(k) = \frac{1}{N(n-k)} \sum_{j}^{n-k} \sum_{i}^{N} \hat{\varepsilon}_{ij} \hat{\varepsilon}_{i,j+k} \qquad (4-4)$$

Then $\hat{\sigma}^2 = \gamma(0)$, and the estimated <u>autocorrelation</u> is

$$\hat{\rho}(k) = \hat{\gamma}(k)/\gamma(0) \quad . \qquad (4-5)$$

The Berkeley data required some preconditioning to put them in a form suitable for estimating the autocorrelations by (4-4) and (4-5). For this purpose, we first minimized end-effects by limiting the boys' data to the range two through 17 years and the girls', two through 15. We then interpolated linearly to obtain estimates of stature for the half years between 2 and 8. Finally, for the variances of these interpolated points, we used $(1/3)^2 \mathrm{cm}^2$.

The resulting autocorrelations are shown in Figure 4-2 for lags 0 through 16 (in half-year units). The autocorrelations follow the typical pattern of an autoregressive process of order greater than one (see Box and Jenkins, 1976, pp.53-66).

Other evidence of the autoregressive nature of the process can be seen in the spectral density functions estimated from the auto-correlations and plotted in Figure 4-3 as a function of the frequency 0 to 1/2. These functions give the probability density for a cosine function of frequency f in the Fourier transform of population auto-correlation function. They have been computed in this instance by

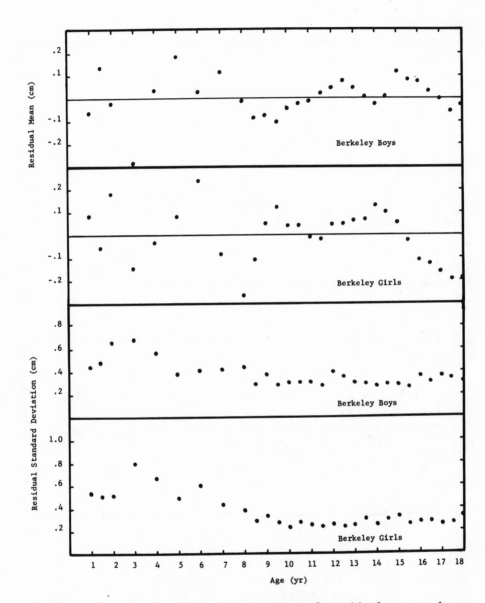

Fig. 4-1. Means and standard deviations of residuals at each age point from least squares fits of the data for Berkeley boys and girls.

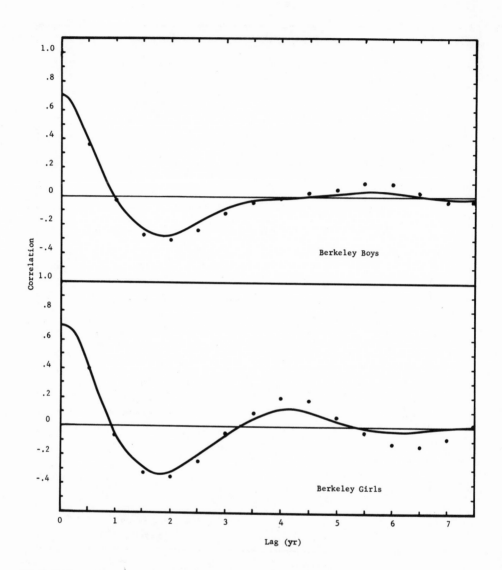

Fig. 4-2.   Autocorrelations of residuals from least-squares fits of
the data for Berkeley boys and girls. The solid line is
the autocorrelation function obtained by inverting the
spectral density functions in Figure 4-3.

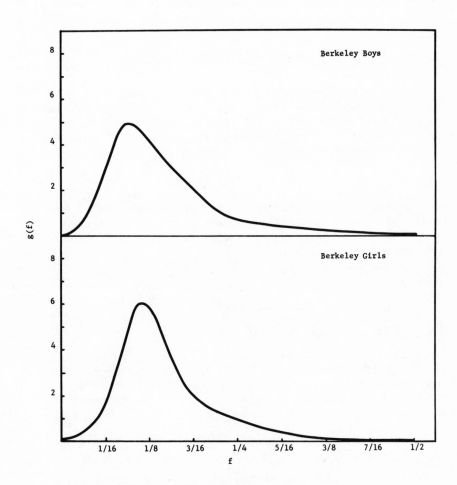

Fig. 4-3.   The spectral density functions computed from the auto-
            correlations for the first 16 half-year lags.·

the formula

$$g(I) = 2[0.7 + 2 \sum_{K=1}^{M-1} \hat{\rho}(K)W(K)\cos\frac{\pi KI}{N_F}] \quad , \qquad (4-6)$$

For $M = 16$, $N_F = 40$ and $I = 1,2,\ldots, N_F$. The weight function,

$$W(K) = \tfrac{1}{2}[1 + \cos\frac{\pi K}{M}] \quad , \qquad (4-7)$$

called a "Tukey Window," serves to smooth the estimated spectrum.[1]

Because the observations are affected by independent measurement error, the autocorrelations cannot approach 1 as the time points approach lag zero. Some fraction of the variance of the residuals must be attributed to measurement error. We have set this fraction at 0.3, which accounts for the 0.7 in (4-6).

The main interest in the spectral density in the present context is that it can be inverted to obtain an approximation of the estimated autocorrelation function that satisfies the assumption of a stationary stochastic process in which the autocorrelations go to zero at large lags. In the present example, the autocorrelations for monthly lags up to 8 years are approximated by

$$\rho(K) = 2[0.7 + 2 \sum_{I=1}^{N_F} g(I)\cos\frac{\pi KI}{N_F}] \quad , \qquad (4-8)$$

for $K = 1$ to $M - 1$ steps of $1/12$.

In Figure 4-3, the smooth curve connects the values given by (4-8). The expected autocorrelations for low lags agree closely with the observed, but as a result of lags greater than 8 years being truncated in approximating the spectra, the expected autocorrelations go to zero faster than the observed. The approximation to Σ_ε^{-1} that will be used in the maximum likelihood solution will therefore take the form $\frac{1}{\hat{\sigma}}\hat{R}_8^{-1}$, i.e., the inverse of a band correlation matrix in which correlations corresponding to $|x_j - x_k| > 8$ years are set to zero. Where the x_j are uniformly spaced, the inverse matrix has a simple recursive form that need not be computed in full. With non-uniform spacing, however, the easier course is to perform the

---

[1]Faster methods of performing these calculations are available (Fast Fourier transforms; see Brillinger, 1975, Sec. 3.5) but are hardly necessary in this application.

complete calculation.[1]

We suggest that the autocorrelation functions in Figure 4-2 could be used provisionally in the maximum likelihood fitting of the triple logistic model to data from other growth studies on the assumption that the covariance structure of the residuals is roughly similar from one study to another. If this is not the case, improved estimates of the autocorrelation functions could be computed from the residuals obtained in the provisional analysis. Indeed, better estimates of the functions for the Berkeley data will be available after we obtain final weighted best estimates of the growth parameters of the Berkeley subjects.

5.   Bayes Estimation when Data are Incomplete

Although least squares or maximum likelihood estimation may adequately fit a nonlinear growth model when complete annual or semi-annual measures of the subjects' stature are available, these methods may fail or may produce implausible results when the record is truncated at either end or contains gaps. They have the weakness of noticing only the incomplete information in the observations and ignoring the subject's origin in a population about which, in favorable instances, we have some knowledge. In particular, if the population has been the object of a longitudinal growth study, we may have information about the distribution of individual growth parameters in it. Inasmuch as knowledge of these distributions conditions our expectations about those aspects of the subject's growth curve that are not well determined by the data, we would like to have a method of estimation that takes these expectations into account.

For a specified growth model, this empirically derived information takes the form of a multivariate distribution of the model parameters in that population. Given knowledge of this so-called "prior" distribution, we are in a position to employ a form of Bayes estimation to obtain, in combination with the available data, the so-called "posterior" distribution of the particular subject's growth parameters.

The mean of the posterior distribution is called the "Bayes estimate" of the growth parameter. It combines optionally the information that we have observed in this subject with what we expect from our knowledge that the subject is drawn from a population specified by sex, ethnic background, stature of parents, etc., assuming the relevant normative data are available. Fearn (1975) has discussed results for the Bayes estimate that are already known

---

[1]In the actual calculation it is the inverse of the Cholesky decomposition of Σ_ε that is obtained (see Bock, 1975, pp.85-89).

for the case where the distribution of the residuals for the given
subject, as well as the distribution of growth parameters in the
population, is multivariate normal and the statistical model is linear
in its parameters and in the errors (see Smith, 1973). In the present
application, the normal distribution assumptions seem reasonable, but
as we have seen the triple logistic model is nonlinear in its paramete
and so the known results do not apply.

For nonlinear models, the simplest approach appears to be to
follow the example of Lindley and Smith (1972) and estimate the _mode_
of the posterior distribution rather than the mean. As the number of
data points increase, the posterior distribution can be expected to
approach a multivariate normal distribution, the mode will approach
the mean, and the negative reciprocal of the curvature at the mode
will approach the sampling variance.

On these presumptions, the limiting vector mean and covariance
matrix of the posterior distribution of the growth parameters may be
obtained as follows: Let the distribution of the residuals be
$N(\underline{0}, \Sigma_\varepsilon)$ and the prior distribution of growth parameters be
$N(\mu_\theta, \Sigma_\theta)$. Then the logarithm of the posterior density is

$$\phi_i = D - \frac{1}{2}\sum_{jk}^{nn}\sigma^{jk}[y_{ij} - f(x_j,\underline{\theta}_i)][y_{ik} - f(x_k,\underline{\theta}_i)] - \frac{1}{2}\sum_{gh}^{mm}\sigma_\theta^{gh}(\theta_{ig} - \mu_{\theta g})(\theta_{ih} - \mu_{\theta h}),$$

$$(5-1)$$

where D is a constant not involving $\underline{\theta}$, and σ_θ^{gh} is the g,h element of
Σ_θ^{-1}. A necessary condition on the maximum of the posterior density
(mode) with respect to variation in θ_{ig} is, therefore,

$$\frac{\partial\phi_i}{\partial\theta_{ig}} = \sum_{jk}^{nn}\sigma^{jk}[y_{ij} - f(x_j,\underline{\hat{\theta}}_i)]\left[\frac{\partial f(x_k,\underline{\theta}_i)}{\partial\theta_{ig}}\right]_{\theta = \underline{\hat{\theta}}} - \sum_h^m\sigma_\theta^{gh}(\hat{\theta}_{ig} - \mu_{\theta g}) = 0$$

$$(5-2)$$

Note that (5-2) differs from the likelihood equation (3-2) only
in the assumption that σ^{jk} is common for all subjects and the appearance of an additional term on the right derived from the prior density
of $\underline{\theta}$. This term acts as a "penalty" function to prevent the estimated
$\underline{\hat{\theta}}$ from straying too far from its population mean $\mu_{\theta g}$.

The curvature of ϕ_i in the vicinity of the maximum, described by

$$\frac{\partial^2\phi_i}{\partial\theta_{ig}\theta_{ih}} = \frac{\partial^2\lambda_i}{\partial\theta_{ig}\partial\theta_{ih}} - \sigma_\theta^{gh},$$

$$(5-3)$$

is always increased in magnitude relative to that in maximum likelihood estimation. As a result, special conditioning of the Newton-
Raphson iterations is seldom needed, and the limiting standard error
of the Bayes model estimator is less than that of the corresponding
maximum likelihood estimator.

The most attractive property of the Bayes estimator is that for
any amount or quality of data, it will always give a plausible estimate of the growth parameters. If there are few data (i.e., n is
small) or the independent error is large (i.e., the σ_j^2 are relatively
large and the σ^{jj} correspondingly small), the right hand term in
(5-2) will dominate and the estimate of θ_{ig} will be very near its
population value, $\mu_{\theta g}$. If there are extensive data (n, large) and
precision is high (σ^{jj}, large), the left-hand term in (5-2) will
dominate and the Bayes and maximum likelihood estimates will be
almost identical.

Because of this property, the Bayes estimator can serve as a
computer-based prediction system in clinical settings. On the basis
of all relevant independent information, including chronological age,
bone age if available, sex, markers of puberty, stature of parents
or siblings, ethnic background, etc., an appropriate prior mean and
covariance matrix would be selected for the particular subject. Each
time the subject visits the clinic his current measured stature would
be combined with the prior to obtain the posterior model estimates
of his or her personal growth parameters. These estimates would
determine the **expected** growth curve, including the predicted mature
stature.

6.   Linearly Constrained Bayes Modal Estimation

For the method of curve fitting in Section 5 to work properly,
it is essential that the parameters $\underline{\theta}$, be sufficiently independent
in the population that Σ_θ is "well conditioned" for matrix inversion;
that is, Σ_θ^{-1} must not have elements that are excessively large
relative to the reciprocals of the diagonal elements of Σ_θ. Otherwise, the calculation of the penalty function becomes inaccurate and
the stability of the entire procedure deteriorates.

The problem is likely to arise when a non-linear model has two
or more parameters that control very similar features of the curve.
These parameters may then tend to "trade off" their values from one
subject to another in such a way that they are highly dependent with
respect to variation in the population. Such appears to be the case
for the triple logistic model. The estimated parameter p in (7-1)

below and the estimated linear function

$$0.851 + 0.041b_1 - 0.018c_1 - 0.517b_2 - 0.042c_2 \qquad (6\text{-}1)$$

are correlated above .95 in the Berkeley samples. This correlation is not so high as to preclude empirical Bayes estimation, but it suggests that the standard errors of the parameters could be decreased without noticeable loss of goodness of fit by restricting these estimates so that p exactly equals (6-1).

Estimation under this restriction can be accomplished in a number of different ways. For greatest economy of computation, the best method is to substitute (6-1) for p in the model and express the first and second derivatives in one fewer parameters. For ease and flexibility of programming the method due to Gill and Murray (1974) is perhaps most convenient. In the latter method, the vector of first derivatives and matrix of second derivatives of the posterior density is projected into the 8 dimensional subspace orthogonal to the restriction (6-1). From these, the projected correction is computed for the current iteration of the Newton-Raphson process and the improved estimates of the parameters obtained. The procedure will then in general converge to stable values of the estimates that satisfy the restriction.

7. Applications

Thissen and Bock (1979) report an application of the method of Section 6 to the longitudinal data for 66 boys and 70 girls published by Tuddenham and Snyder (1954). In this application, the following form of the triple logistic model, describing the height of subject i at age x_j as a sum of a prepubertal component with contributions from early and middle childhood growth and an adolescent component, was used:

$$y_{ij} = a_1 \left\{ \frac{1 - p}{1 + \exp[-b_1(x_j - c_1)]} + \frac{p}{1 + \exp[-b_2(x_j - c_2)]} \right\}$$

$$+ \frac{a_2}{1 + \exp[-b_3(x_j - c_3)]} \qquad (7\text{-}1)$$

where

a_1 = contribution of prepubertal growth to mature stature

b_1 = slope of the early-childhood component at maximum velocity

c_1 = age of maximum velocity of the early-childhood component

b_2 = slope of the middle-childhood component at maximum velocity

c_2 = age at maximum velocity of the middle-childhood component

p = proportion of prepubertal growth attributable to the middle-childhood component

a_2 = contribution of the adolescent component to mature stature

b_2 = slope of adolescent component at maximum velocity

c_3 = age at maximum velocity of the adolescent component

The conception behind this model, which was proposed at earlier times by Robertson (1908) and by Burt (1937), is that mature stature is a summation of three processes, each of which responds logistically with a characteristic maximum velocity, age at maximum velocity, and final contribution to mature stature. Growth from each of these sources may be occurring simultaneously, i.e., may overlap, but in fact only two are effectively active at the same time.

In the range one year to maturity, this model is remarkably successful in reproducing with nine parameters both the amount of growth and the velocity of growth (El Lozy, 1978).

The role played by each component is illustrated in Figure 7-1, which shows curves for an "average" boy and girl in the Berkeley Guidance Study. The curves are constructed from the average estimated growth parameters reported by Thissen and Bock (1979) and reproduced here in Table 7-1. Figure 7-2 shows the velocity curves for overall growth and for each component. Note that the model conveys the small local maximum of velocity in middle childhood that is seen in some, but not all, growth records (El Lozy, 1978) as well as the more obvious preadolescent velocity minimum and adolescent velocity maximum. It is not yet clear whether the separate components have any physiological interpretation, but it is perhaps of interest that the first corresponds to the period in infancy of declining fetal adrenal functioning, the second to the onset of mature adrenal functioning in middle childhood, and the third, to the onset of mature gonadal functioning in adolescence.

As an example of the stability of Bayes estimation when the growth record is incomplete, Figure 7-3 shows the linearly restricted Bayes fits of the triple-logistic model to measures of standing height for two girls in the Berkeley study. The upper panel represents Case 301, a relatively short girl (5' 2" at maturity); the lower panel represents Case 310, a very tall girl (6' at maturity).

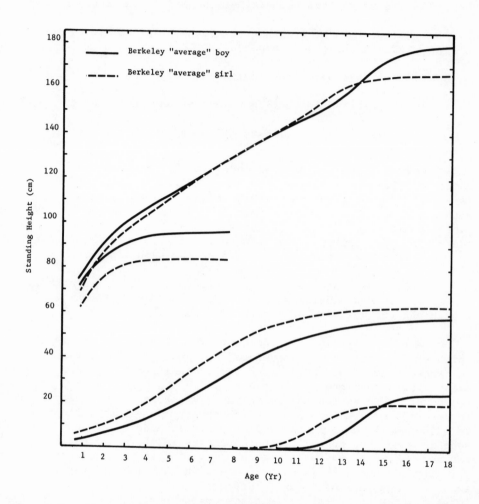

Fig. 7-1. The triple-logistic growth curves computed from average
           parameters of restricted Bayes fits in the samples of
           Berkeley boys and girls. The upper two curves are the
           triple logistics, and the lower six curves are the com-
           ponents of which they are the sums.

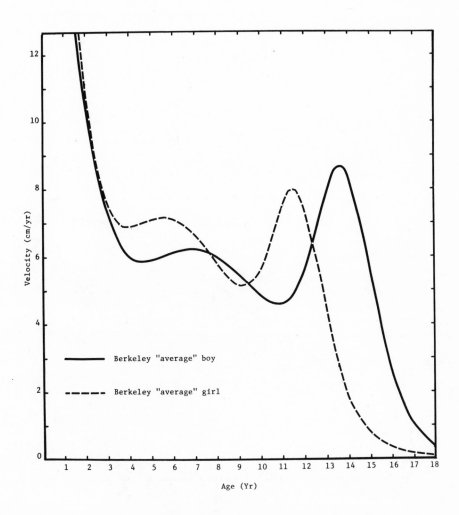

Fig. 7-2. Velocity curves computed from the derivatives of the
triple logistic curves in Figure 7-1.

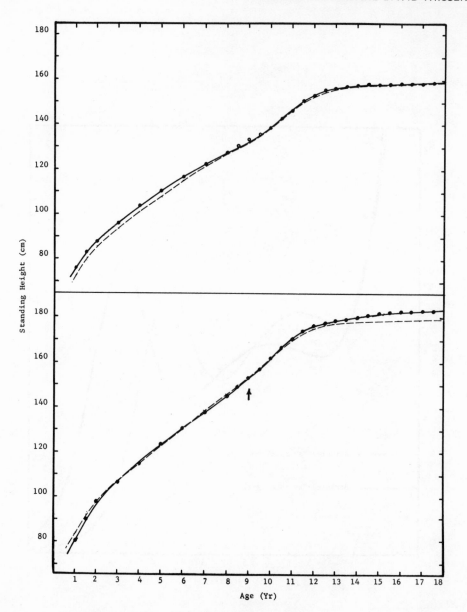

Fig. 7-3. Triple logistic growth curves for a short (top panel)
           girl and a tall (bottom panel) girl from the Berkeley
           study fitted by linearly restricted empirical Bayes esti-
           mation. The solid line is the fit to all data points;
           the broken curve in the upper panel is the fit to data
           from 11 to 18 years; the broken curve in the lower panel
           is the fit to the single data point at nine years (arrow).

Table 7-1.   Means and Standard Deviations of Restricted
             Individual Triple-logistic Growth Parameters
             Estimated for Boys and Girls in the Berkeley
             Guidance Study (from Thissen and Bock, 1979)

Parameters	Boys (N=66)		Girls (N=70)	
	Mean	S.D.	Mean	S.D.
a_1 (cm)	155.32	5.45	147.82	7.53
b_1 (logit/yr)	0.82	0.52	1.23	0.76
c_1 (yr)	− 0.47	0.46	− 0.24	0.44
b_2	0.41	0.06	0.44	0.12
c_2	7.15	1.41	5.69	1.67
a_3	25.28	4.31	19.39	5.17
b_3	1.14	0.22	1.27	0.24
c_3	13.75	1.07	11.64	0.87

The solid lines are constructed from the parameter estimates in Table
7-2.   These estimates were obtained by fitting triple logistic models
to all data at the points shown.   The diameter of the data points are
scaled at about 1 cm, which is roughly ± 1 standard error of measurement.   The curves obviously fit well, except perhaps at the ages 8.5
and 9 in Case 301, where curvature of the adolescent logistic component seems somewhat too high.

The broken line in the top panel is the model fitted only to
points from 11 years onward (solid dots).   Note that the curve dupli-
cates the result of the full fit in this region and is not far
removed from it in the region from 1 to 10.5 years where no data was
assumed.   This illustrates the power of the empirical Bayes method
to produce a plausible model when the data are incomplete.

In the lower panel of Figure 7-1, the broken line represents
the model fitted to a single data point at age 9 (arrow).   This
illustrates the predictive possibilities of the empirical Bayes
method.   The information contained in this one data point, when combined with the information in mean and covariance matrix of parameter
estimates in the sample of Berkeley girls, is sufficient to predict
mature stature to within 3.5 cm.

Table 7-2. Estimated Parameters and Descriptive Features
           for Growth Curves of Two Girls from the
           Berkeley Study

		Estimates (S.E.)	
		Case 301	Case 310
1.	Parameters		
	a_1 (cm)	140.81 (1.59)	169.48 (1.16)
	b_1 (logit/yr)	2.11 (.43)	.82 (.08)
	c_1 (yr)	−.02 (.16)	−.35 (.06)
	b_2	.34 (.01)	.37 (.03)
	c_2	2.98 (.38)	6.20 (.62)
	a_2	18.96 (1.44)	14.58 (1.30)
	b_3	1.30 (.11)	1.62 (.07)
	c_3	10.59 (.05)	10.16 (.07)

2. <u>Descriptive Features</u>

One Year			
	Stature (cm)	76.12	80.90
	Velocity (cm/yr)	16.84	17.57
Preadolescent Velocity			
Minimum			
	Stature	127.49	143.33
	Velocity	4.76	6.93
	Age	8.0	7.8
Adolescent Velocity			
Maximum			
	Velocity	8.21	10.18
	Age	10.5	10.0
Adolescent Increment		31.72	39.83
Mature Stature		159.21	183.16

   Table 7-2 shows in addition to the parameter estimates some
analytic features of the curve that might be of interest. Case 310
grew at a remarkable rate in middle childhood and adolescence. Her
preadolescent velocity minimum occurred early (7.8 years), and she
was already relatively tall at that time. Unlike more typical girls,
she was still growing appreciably in the range 16 to 18 years.

   Neither of these cases showed the post-infancy velocity minimum
or a middle childhood velocity maximum that are apparent in some

children.   In both girls the velocity of growth declined monoton-
ically from one year to the preadolescent minimum.

REFERENCES

Bock, R.D., 1975, "Multivariate Statistical Methods in Behavioral
    Research," McGraw Hill, New York.
Bock, R.D., 1979, Univariate and multivariate analysis of variance
    of time-structured data, in: "Longitudinal Research in Human
    Development: Design and Analysis," J.R. Nesselroade and
    P.B. Baltes, eds., Academic Press, New York (in press).
Bock, R.D., and Thissen, D., 1976, Fitting multi-component models
    for growth in stature, Proceedings of the 9th International
    Biometric Conference, 1:431-442.
Box, G.E.P., and Jenkins, G.M., 1976, "Time Series Analysis: Fore-
    casting and Control," (2nd Ed.), Holden-Day, San Francisco.
Brillinger, D.K., 1975, "Time Series: Data Analysis and Theory,"
    Holt, Rinehart and Winston, New York.
Burt, C., 1937, "The Backward Child," Appleton-Century, New York.
Chambers, J.M., 1977, "Computational Methods for Data Analysis,"
    Wiley, New York.
Cochrane, D., and Orcutt, G.H., 1949, Applications of least-squares
    regression to relationships containing auto-correlated error
    terms, J. Am. Stat. Assoc., 44:32-61.
El Lozy, M., 1978, A critical analysis of the double and triple
    logistic growth curves, Ann. Human Biol., 5:389-394.
Fearn, T., 1975, A Bayesian approach to growth curves, Biometrika,
    62:89-100.
Fuller, W.A., 1976, "Introduction to Statistical Time Series," Wiley,
    New York.
Gill, P.E., and Murray, W. (Eds.), 1974, "Numerical Methods for
    Constrained Optimization," Academic Press, London.
Glass, G.V., Willson, V.L., and Gottman, J.M., 1975, "Design and
    Analysis of Time-series Experiments," Colorado Associated
    University Press, Boulder (Colorado).
Jenkins, G.M., and Watts, D.G., 1968, "Spectral Analysis and its
    Applications," Holden-Day, San Francisco.
Jennerich, R.I., and Ralston, M.L., 1978, "Fitting Nonlinear Models
    to Data," Technical Report #6, Health Sciences Computing
    Facility, University of California at Los Angeles.
Jenss, R.M., and Bayley, N., 1937, A mathematical model for studying
    the growth of a child, Human Biol., 9:556-563.
Largo, R.H., Gasser, Th., Prader, A., Stuetzle, W., and Huber, P.J.,
    1978, Analysis of the adolescent growth spurt using smoothing
    spline functions, Ann. Human Biol., 5:421-434.
Lindley, D.V., and Smith, A.F.M., 1972, Bayes estimates for the
    linear model, J. Royal Stat. Soc., Series B, 34:1-41.

Preece, M.A., and Baines, M.J., 1978, A new family of mathematical models describing the human growth curve, Ann. Human Biol., 5:1-24.

Robertson, T.B., 1908, On the normal rate of growth of an individual, and its biochemical significance. Archiv für Entwicklungs Mechanik den Organismen, 25:581-614.

Smith, A.F.M., 1973, A general Bayesian linear model. J. Royal Stat. Soc., Series B, 35:67-75.

Stützle, W., 1977, "Estimation and Parameterization of Growth Curves," Juris, Zurich.

Thissen, D., and Bock, R.D., 1979, Bayes estimation of individual growth parameters (in preparation).

Tuddenham, R.D., and Snyder, M.M., 1954, Physical growth of California boys and girls from birth to eighteen years. University of California Publications in Child Development, 1:183-364.

16. NUTRITION AND GROWTH

Francis E. Johnston

Department of Anthropology
University of Pennsylvania
Philadelphia, Pa.   19104

One of the major criteria utilized in establishing a nutrient as essential is the failure of an animal to grow normally when that nutrient is removed from an otherwise well-balanced diet, followed by a resumption of normal growth upon its restoration. It is no wonder then that the relationship between nutrition and growth is an intimate one, directed by millions of years of evolutionary adaptation reflecting interrelationships among habitat, morphology, physiology, and behavior. The growth pattern which leads the individual to the mature state is provided by the genotype, while the processes of metabolism and regulation which actualize that pattern utilize, as raw material, the nutrients provided by the diet. A wide variety of nutrients have been shown to be essential for human growth, maintenance, and function, as seen in Table 1. While this list reflects the current state of nutritional knowledge, it may very well be incomplete. Nevertheless, it indicates the broad range of substances that is necessary for normal human existence which must be supplied by the diet.

The study of human nutrition is rendered difficult because human subjects cannot be manipulated in a laboratory as can other animals. While the use of animal models is basic to the determination of nutritional requirements, studies on humans are also necessary in order to elicit information from peoples living in a variety of environments and eating a broad range of foods obtained in many different ways.

The study of human nutrition is further difficult because we do not consume nutrients; rather we eat foods. While the nutrients we require are defined on biological criteria, the food we select is defined as food on criteria rooted deeply in our cultural experience, obtained from an extraordinary range of natural settings, each with its own ecological characteristics, and prepared in a variety of ways

which can alter the composition of the raw foodstuff, or the bioavai-
lability of the nutrients it contains (Robson, 1976). To partition
a human diet into individual nutrients and to quantify them so as to
obtain an estimate of actual intake can seldom be accomplished by direct analysis but must rely upon the methods of proximate composition
which, in the case of indigenous diets, introduces a disquieting uncertainty and a potentially significant error.

Table 1. Nutrients Established As Essential For Humans[a]

Carbohydrate	Minerals	Vitamins
Glucose	Calcium	Fat-soluble
Lipid	Phosphorus	A
Linoleic acid	Sodium	D
Protein	Potassium	E
Amino acids	Sulfur	K
Leucine	Chlorine	Water-soluble
Isoleucine	Magnesium	Thiamin
Lysine	Iron	Riboflavin
Methionine	Selenium	Niacin
Phenylalanine	Zinc	Biotin
Threonine	Manganese	Folacin
Tryptophan	Copper	Pyridoxine
Valine	Cobalt	B_{12}
Histodine	Molybdenum	Pantothenic acid
Nonessential N_2	Iodine	Ascorbic acid
	Chromium	Water
	Fluorine	
	Vanadium	
	Tin	
	Nickel	
	Silicon	

[a]From Guthrie (1979)

Another problem confronting those who study human nutrition away
from laboratory settings is in the range of interactions which characterize any human ecosystem. Sanitation, affluence, poverty, education, demographics, and the natural environment are factors which can
act on the human organism, either independently or jointly with nutritional factors, and which affect growth, morbidity, and mortality
in ways which may mimic the effects of nutritional variables and
which may be inseparable from nutritional effects.

Given the above problems, knowledge about the role of nutrition
in human growth, and of variation in nutrient intake as a determinant
of variation in growth, must be obtained through a number of research
designs. The four major types of designs are: 1) the study of normal
subjects; 2) the study of the effects of malnutrition upon humans; 3)
the analysis of the response to nutritional supplementation and

rehabilitation; and 4) experimental studies of animals.

NUTRIENT REQUIREMENTS DURING GROWTH

In considering nutrient requirements during the growing years, it is useful to separate conceptually the requirements for tissue maintenance from the requirements for growth. Maintenance requirements are determined largely by size, body somposition, and the degree of biochemical maturation. Requirements for growth are a function largely of the rate of synthesis of new tissue. Table 3 presents estimated energy requirements during the growing years. While maintenance is seen to account for the greater proportion of ingested energy, the requirements for growth are significant, especially during the first few months of postnatal life. Even a requirement for

Table 2. Energy Intake and Requirements Per Day
During the Growing Years[a]

Age (yr)	Weight (kg)	Energy Cost (Cal)		Pct. for Growth
		Maintenance	Growth	
B-0.25	4.6	365	128	23
0.75-1.0	9.6	800	60	6
2-3	13.6	1020	30	2
9-10	31.1	1750	30	1
16-17	60.3	2500	60	2

[a]From Payne and Waterlow (1977)

growth that is but 6% of intake is important. Consider, for example, the typical intake of a 1-year old in a developing country of 75 Cal/kg/day, with a weight of 8 kg; the energy intake per day will be 600 Cal. This value is below even the maintenance requirement for that body size, leaving nothing for growth or activity. It is obvious that the organism must undergo a marked alteration in order to survive under such conditions, involving a delay in growth as well as disturbances of normal activity patterns.

Because of difficulties in making estimates of levels of nutrients required for growth of children of different age and body size, our knowledge of nutrient requirements is far from perfect and subject to changes as new information is collected. Consider the recommended intakes of protein and energy, as reflected in the Recommended Daily Allowances (RDA's) which have been published periodically. Table 3 indicates how the allowances for protein and energy have changed since 1948, based upon estimates for a 1-year old. The allowance for energy has remained generally constant at 100 Cal/kg.

Table 3. Estimates of Protein and Energy Requirements at 1-Year of Age, 1948 to 1974[a]

Year	Protein[b] (g)	Energy[b] (Cal)	Source
1948	3.3	100	NRC(USA)
1957	2.0	100	FAO
1964	2.5	100	NRC(USA)
1965	1.1	100	FAO/WHO
1968	1.8	100	NRC(USA)
1969	1.3	110	DHSS(UK)
1973	1.27	105	FAO/WHO
1974	1.35	100	NRC(USA)

[a] Taken from Waterlow and Payne, 1975
[b] Per kg body weight

However, the allowance for protein has declined steadily from a high,
in 1948, of 3.3g/kg/day to the lows of the 1970's. This decline in
the RDA for protein is 700mg per decade for a 1-year old. It has not
resulted from changes in requirement, but from the results of research
which has demonstrated a protein need in 1-year olds which was below
that which was accepted in earlier decades.

In addition to infancy, the growth rate of the individual is
markedly elevated during the adolescent years and nutrient requirements show a concomitant increase, when compared to those of childhood. Table 4 presents the RDA's for selected nutrients, as set for
the U.S. population, for adolescence, expressed as a multiple of the
allowances for young adults. While these allowances are estimates,
they show the increased requirement associated with the adolescent
growth spurt, sometimes as much as 80% of the young adult RDA.

GROWTH AND THE REGULATION OF NUTRIENT INTAKE

Species have adapted their dietaries and their feeding behaviors
to their environments as part of their evolutionary histories. As a
consequence, each species exhibits mechanisms which regulate food intake so as to provide nutrients in amounts and balance which are adequate for survival. No less than in other species, human food intake is governed by factors which are intrinsic to the individual and
which regulate food intake, even though, at the same time, we must
recognize that these factors may be modified and even distorted by
the forces of socialization and conditioning.

In their recent review of nutrition and growth, Bergmann and
Bergmann (1979) concluded that energy needs determine the food intake
of infants. Even though excess intakes may predispose the individual

to a lifetime of overfatness, infants, in the absence of externally-imposed dietary excesses, seem able to vary their energy intake so as to integrate it with their needs for growth and maintenance.

Table 4. RDA's (USA, 1974) For Selected Nutrients During
Adolescence Relative to Young Adult (23-50) RDA's.

Nutrient	Males		Females	
	11-14	15-18	11-14	15-18
Energy	1.04	1.11	1.20	1.05
Protein	0.79	0.96	0.96	1.04
Vitamin A	1.00	1.00	1.00	1.00
Thiamin	1.00	1.07	1.20	1.10
Calcium	1.50	1.50	1.50	1.50
Iron	1.80	1.80	1.80	1.80
Magnesium	1.00	1.14	1.00	1.00
Zinc	1.00	1.00	1.00	1.00

Various lines of evidence support the concept of self-regulation of nutrient intake by infants. Ashworth (1969) analyzed the progress of 8 children hospitalized for severe protein-energy malnutrition; all were between 10 and 18 months of age, except for a 36 month old boy. During the period of rehabilitation, their energy intakes averaged 160 Cal/kg/day. There were virtually no refusals of food and their rates of growth were, on the average, 15 times those of normal children of the same age. After recovery from the acute malnutrition energy intakes fell to an average of 116 Cal/kg/day, growth rates paralleled those expected for their body weights, and food refusal became common.

The ability of children to alter food intake and rate of growth so as to catch-up to an expected body size, following a period of malnutrition, is also a function of the duration of the period of malnutrition. Scholl et al. (n.d.) analyzed the response of the growth rate of Mexican children who had developed severe protein-energy malnutrition, according to whether they had previously displayed evidence of chronic nutritional deprivation. During the period in which the children displayed the symptoms of severe malnutrition, when they were receiving appropriate medical treatment, they showed significant reductions in growth in weight and in arm muscle circumference. However, three months after the onset of the severe malnutrition, the children had caught up, in these variables, to their position prior to displaying the symptoms of malnutrition. On the other hand, if these children also displayed evidence of chronic protein-energy malnutrition, they caught up in growth only to the level displayed by the other children in the sample who were chronically, but not acutely malnourished. In other words, children seem able to catch-up in growth following a period of severe protein-energy malnutrition, providing that they receive adequate care and appropriate food intakes. However, their ability to catch-up so as to compensate for a longer period of chronic malnutrition is less clear and depends heavily upon the quality of the environment which they experience.

There are two other qualifications which must be made with regard to the ability of infants and young children to alter their food intakes following a period of malnutrition. First, it may be impossible for an undernourished child to consume a sufficient amount of food for normal growth. In developing countries, diets are high in starch and of low caloric density. The amount of food necessary to supply an adequate amount of energy may exceed the capacity of a child. Béhar (1977) has noted that even when Guatemalan children from poor, rural communities had access to sufficient amounts of their traditional diet, based upon corn and beans, the amount they consumed was below requirement. The addition of fat to the diet raised the caloric density and made possible the consumption of adequate levels of calories.

The second qualification to the concept of self-regulation of energy intake is with regard to the development of obesity. Overfeeding during the first year of life increases the risk of obesity during adolescence and into the adult years as well. The increased risk may be expressed as a risk ratio, which indicates the increased occurrence of obesity in infants who at the extreme of weight-for-height at 1-year of age, relative to those below this extreme. Johnston and Mack (1978) calculated this risk ratio at approximately 1.5, indicating a 50% greater likelihood of adolescent obesity associated with infant overgrowth in weight. This suggests that excess calories during the first year may have a conditioning effect upon subsequent food intake which, in some individuals, will predispose them to later obesity.

Just as nutrient intake seems to be regulated by the caloric content of the diet, the problem of malnutrition, on a worldwide basis, is one of energy. While protein deprivation may be the case in some areas and deficiencies of specific nutrients may be the cause in others, in general, energy is implicated as the limiting nutrient and the major cause of malnutrition. Table 5 presents data from several studies, in which food intakes were weighed and analyzed, and where the contribution of breast milk was not a factor. Though the sample sizes are small, the pattern is clear. Protein intake does not seem to be deficient and, for the combined data, was 108% of the RDA of the United Nations FAO/WHO. Only in the case of the sample from Thailand was protein intake markedly below the RDA.

On the other hand, energy intakes of all samples were below the RDA, ranging from 52% of the recommended allowance for the Thailand sample to 86% for the children from Ghana. Overall, energy intake was but 75% of the recommended. Despite innate regulatory abilities, chronic insufficiencies of energy in the diet are significant causes of growth deviation in children of lesser-developed nations.

Table 5。 Weighed Intakes of Protein and Energy
of Weaned 1-2 Year Old Children[a].

| Country | Child-Days | Intake/kg Body Weight | | | |
| | | Protein (g) | | Energy (Cal) | |
		$\overline{X}$	Pct[b]	$\overline{X}$	Pct[b]
Ghana	30	1.19	99	86	86
Guatemala	28	1.16	96	77	77
Jamaica	266	1.47	123	83	83
Polynesia	72	1.32	110	70	70
Thailand	54	0.61	51	52	52
Uganda	124	1.28	107	68	68
Total	574	1.30	108	75	75

[a]Taken from Waterlow and Payne (1975)
[b]Percentage of FAO/WHO recommended intakes

The role of nutrients other than protein and energy is also crucial to normal growth, although deficiencies are not nearly so ubiquitous. The striking retardation of growth and development associated with regional deficits in iodine, zinc, and vitamin A are well
known. However since, in many instances of malnutrition due to specific nutrients such as these, there are also associated shortages
of energy as well, it is difficult to isolate the relationship between a particular nutrient and growth.

The importance of specific nutrients to the growth process is,
more often, determined through clinical studies of individual infants
and children, rather than epidemiological studies of at-risk communities. For example, studies of low birth weight and preterm infants
have revealed them to be at risk for tocopherol (vitamin E) deficiency
which can contribute indirectly to poor growth through the role of
vitamin E deficiency in hemolytic anemia (Goldbloom, 1979). Other
fat-soluble vitamins, as well as the water-soluble ones, are also
important to normal growth, though deficiency states are uncommon
apart from such well-known conditions as beriberi and pellagra.

PRENATAL GROWTH

Nutritional factors are important determinants of prenatal
growth, as indicated by birth weights. Nutritional deficiencies of
the maternal diet may act directly upon the fetus, or they may act
upon the maternal environment. For example, Arroyo et al.(1978)
found that half of the pregnant women from a malnourished Mexican
community failed to add subcutaneous fat during pregnancy, many of
them losing fat as indicated by skinfold thicknesses.

Where maternal nutritional status is poor, low birth weights are common. In such communities, dietary supplementation of pregnant women can decrease the incidence of low birth weight by 50% (Klein et al, 1976). Where the supply of energy to the mother is more than ample, the opposite is the case. Udall et al (1978) have shown that maternal weight gain is a significant factor in the large for gestational age infant.

CHILDHOOD AND ADOLESCENCE

The years of childhood and adolescence comprise a period in which the sensitivity to nutritional factors is as important, though less well studied, as in the years of infancy. The straightforward relationship between national affluence, increased body size, and rate of maturation seems to imply a system in which nutrient intake is a significant component. While genetic factors at the population level may contribute to group differences, the role of the environment in regulating the growth rate and the rate of biological maturation is indisputable (Eveleth and Tanner, 1976; Johnston et al., 1976; Malina, 1978).

The response of children and youth to nutrient intake may be seen in the increased increments of the undernourished to nutritional supplementation. Table 6 presents the mean increments over an 8-month

Table 6. Mean Growth Increments of Bundi Children Receiving 10g and 20g Daily Protein Supplementation[a]

Variable	Controls	Supplemented Children		F
		10g	20g	
Height (cm)	1.75	3.23	3.45	37.46[b]
Weight (kg)	1.33	1.98	2.94	24.62[c]
Periosteal Breadth (mm)	0.14	0.26	0.36	6.63[b]
Endosteal Breadth (mm)	-0.19	-0.16	-0.11	0.28
Compact Bone Breadth (mm)	0.33	0.43	0.47	0.81
Skeletal Age (yr)	0.41	0.62	0.64	4.41[b]
Triceps (mm)	0.71	0.14	0.01	9.23[b]
Subscapular (mm)	1.07	-0.26	-0.04	5.04[b]

[a] From Lampl et al. (1978)
[b] Supplemented children different from controls
[c] Supplemented children different from controls and each other

period of supplementation of Papuan children, and a group of controls, ranging in age from 7.7 to 13.0 years (Lampl et al, 1978). The increments of each group are adjusted for differences in chronological age. Supplemented children received daily either 10g or 20g of protein in the form of skim milk powder. Whether the supplements were utilized as energy, or provided amino acids and nitrogen, is not known. What is significant is that supplemented children showed a response in the expected direction for each variable measured, with significant differences indicated. Supplementation was associated with increased increments of height, weight, the periosteal breadth of the second metacarpal, and skeletal age, as well as an increased increment (though not a significant one) in the compact bone breadth of the metacarpal. Significantly smaller increments were seen for skinfold thicknesses, as well as a smaller increment, though one that was not significant, in the endosteal breadth of the second metacarpal.

Children receiving a 20g supplement showed differences in the expected direction from those receiving 10g. However, the difference was significant only in the case of body weight.

While undernutrition delays maturation and reduces growth during childhood and adolescence, it is not clear just how much overnutrition can stimulate growth in dimensions other than those associated with fatness. Some researchers (e.g., Garn et al., 1975) have found increased stature among obese children and youths, suggesting that overnutrition stimulates skeletal growth. However, other studies indicate that fatness does not contribute to increased stature (e.g., Mack and Johnston, 1979).

SOME CONCLUDING STATEMENTS

Normal growth and development require adequate amounts of essential nutrients in proper balance. As expected, deficiencies of nutrient intake will, if severe or prolonged, produce abnormal growth patterns. Nutrient excesses may also adversely affect the normal course of human development. While the results of deviations from optimal intakes may be demonstrated in experimental conditions, especially if animal models are used, it is much more difficult, and often impossible, to relate deviations to growth as an outcome in an ecological setting. In part this results from the wide range of variation in energy intakes and the ubiquitous nature of the effect of that variation upon human growth. But the difficulty is also related to the tendency, in a human ecosystem, for nutritional deficiencies, or excesses, to be correlated. The diets of children in a developing country deficient in, for example, zinc are likely to be deficient in energy, protein, and other nutrients as well.

The role of the genotype in determining differential response to nutrient intake has been established in experimental animals and, in humans, for certain enzymatic defects such as lactase deficiency, phenylketonuria, and galactosemia. However, despite these examples, there is presently no solid evidence of differential responses to the same level of nutrient as a factor contributing to inter-population variability in growth. Where the existence of such suggestions has been postulated, the research design has not effectively ruled out confounding variables, or has not established the existence of clear nutritional differences. The detection of genetic differences among populations in nutrient utilization remains to be demonstrated.

It is likely that the majority of studies of the growth and development of children and youth conducted away from the laboratory will be forced to deal with composite measures of the environment, in which individual variation in nutrient intake is unknown or, if estimated, contains a high degree of error. Given this situation, we will be forced to focus upon estimates of mean intakes for groups. Nonetheless, the role of nutrition in growth may still be demonstrated clearly, even at the population level, and serves as a highly significant determinant of variability in the processes of human growth and development.

REFERENCES

Arroyo, P., Garcia, D., Llerena, C., and Quiroz, S.E., 1978, Subcutaneous fat accumulation during pregnancy in a malnourished population, Brit. J. Nutr., 40:485.
Ashworth, A., 1969, Growth rates in children recovering from protein-calorie malnutrition, Brit. J. Nutr., 23:835.
Béhar, M., 1977, Protein-calorie deficits in developing countries, Ann. N. Y. Acad. Sci., 300:176.
Bergmann, R. L. and Bergmann, K. E., 1979, Nutrition and growth in infancy, in: "Human Growth, 3, Neurobiology and Nutrition," F. Falkner and J. M. Tanner, ed., Plenum, New York.
Eveleth, P. B. and Tanner, J. M., 1976, "Worldwide Variation in Human Growth," Cambridge, London.
Garn, S. M., Clark, D. C., and Guire, K. E., 1975, Growth, body composition, and development of obese and lean children, in: "Childhood Obesity," M. Winick, ed., John Wiley, New York.
Goldbloom, R. B., 1979, Fat-soluble vitamins, in: "Developmental Nutrition," K. Oliver, B.G. Cox, T. R. Johnson, and W. M. Moore, ed., Ross Laboratories, Columbus, Ohio.
Guthrie, H. A., 1979, "Introductory Nutrition," Fourth edition, Mosby, St. Louis.
Johnston, F. E., Wainer, H., Thissen, D., and MacVean, R. B., 1976, Hereditary and environmental determinants of growth in height in a longitudinal sample of children and youth of Guatemalan and European ancestry. Amer. J. Phys. Anthrop., 44:469.
Johnston, F. E. and Mack, R. W., 1978, Obesity in urban, black adolescents of high and low relative weight at 1-year of age. Amer. J. Dis. Child., 132:862.
Klein, R. E., Arenales, P., Delgado, H., Engle, P. L., Guzman, M. Irwin, M., Lasky, R., Lechtig, A., Martorell, R., Mejia, V. P.,

Russell, P., and Yarbrough, C., 1976, Effects of maternal nutrition on fetal growth and infant development. PAHO Bull., 10: 301.

Lampl, M., Johnston, F. E., and Malcolm, L. A., 1978, The effects of protein supplementation on the growth and skeletal maturation of New Guinean school children, Ann. Human Biol., 5:219.

Mack, R. W. and Johnston, F. E., 1979, Height, skeletal maturation, and adiposity in adolescents with high relative weight at 1-year of age. Ann. Human Biol., 6:77.

Malina, R. M., 1978, Adolescent growth and maturation: selected aspects of current research, Yearbook of Phys. Anthrop., 21:63.

Payne, P. R. and Waterlow, J. C., 1977, Relative energy requirements for maintenance, growth, and physical activity, Lancet, 2(1):210.

Robson, J. R. K., 1976, Problems in assessing nutritional status in the field, Yearbook of Phys. Anthrop., 19:158.

Scholl, T. O., Johnston, F. E., Cravioto, J., and DeLicardi, E. R., in press, A prospective study of the effects of clinically severe protein-energy malnutrition on growth, Acta Paediat. Scand.

Udall, J. N., Harrison, G. G., Vaucher, Y., Walson, P. D., and Morrow, G., 1978, Interaction of maternal and neonatal obesity, Pediatrics, 62:17.

Waterlow, J. C. and Payne, P. R., 1975, The protein gap, Nature, 258: 113.

17. PHYSICAL ACTIVITY, GROWTH, AND FUNCTIONAL CAPACITY

Robert M. Malina

Department of Anthropology
University of Texas
Austin, Texas 78712

INTRODUCTION

Physical activity subjects the organism to a variety of stresses which give rise to measurable physiological and biomechanical responses. The magnitude and degree of response varies with the duration, intensity, and perhaps timing of the activity stimulus. The responses generated via regular physical activity initiated during childhood are believed by many to result in favorable influences on the organism during growth and into adulthood (Espenschade, 1960; Malina, 1969a, 1975a; Bailey, 1973; Rarick, 1974; Bailey et al., 1978). Some of the effects of regularly repeated physical activity on the growing organism are considered subsequently. Nevertheless, the precise role of properly graded activity, training or exercise programs in influencing growth and development is not completely understood, and the results of studies are equivocal. The terms activity, exercise and training are used as being synonymous, although they are variably used in the literature.

Growth depends on the integration of many factors, and it must be emphasized that physical activity is only one of many factors that may affect the growth of a child. The broad range of developmental plasticity characteristic of the human species must also be considered in evaluating the effects of physical training. Growth and development can be inhibited or perhaps facilitated by environmental circumstances, of course within the limits established by the genotype. It is within this framework that the effects of physical activity on the growing organism must be understood, as such exercise-induced responses may become permanent features.

Before proceeding to an examination of the effects of physical activity on specific tissues, dimensions and functions, it should be noted that a significant amount of data is derived by extrapolation from experimental animals. The concept of species specificity must be recognized. Training programs of varying intensity and duration are used, and are commonly described as being mild, moderate and severe activity stress without more specific definition. Training is a continuum, ranging from mild work to severly stressing activity. It is not a single entity and varies considerably in type, e.g., strength, endurance, or skill training. Specific training programs tend to have specific effects (Edgerton, 1976; McCafferty and Horvath, 1977; Scheuer and Tipton, 1977). Regarding growth and development, the timing or age at initiation of the training program may be a significant factor.

Among humans, variable and composite age groups are used in training studies, as are small samples. Attrition rates tend to be high. There is also a lack of studies in which the exercise factor has been regularly applied and changes monitored over a sufficiently long period during growth. Difficulties inherent in conducting longitudinal programs with humans are obvious. Studies on children are further confounded by problems inherent in any attempt to partition training-induced effects from changes accompanying normal growth and development. Thus, it is essential to monitor the effects of regular activity over and above "normal" childhood activity, given, of course, adequate dietary and health conditions. Measures or estimates of "normal" childhood activity are presently inadequate. Comparisons are ordinarily made between individuals characterized by high and low levels of habitual activity, or by levels of extra activity, especially training for a specific sport.

STUDY DESIGNS

A variety of approaches have been used to evaluate the effects of physical activity on growth and development in humans. Several are considered.

Experimental studies involve the comparison of trained (treatment) and untrained (control) subjects. The training stimulus varies in type, intensity, duration and age at initiation. Problems are often encountered in defining and quantifying the training stimulus within and across studies. Selection of experimental subjects, motivation to train, and control of outside activity or practice are critical factors.

Comparisons of athletes and non-athletes during childhood and adolescence are commonly used to make inferences about the effects of physical activity on growth. It is assumed that the athletes had been training regularly, and differences relative to

non-athletes are attributed to the training stimulus. The problem
with this approach is subject selection. Youngsters proficient in
sports are undoubtedly selected for skill and in some sports for
size. Size, physique, strength and motor ability are related
(Malina, 1975b; Malina and Rarick, 1973). An individual's level
of strength and motor proficiency may also influence his level of
habitual activity. Maturity differences also characterize youngsters
who excel in sports (Malina, 1978a). Males who are successful in
athletic competition are generally advanced in biological maturity
status. This probably reflects the size, strength and performance
advantages associated with earlier maturation (Malina, 1975b, 1979).
In contrast, females who excel in sports, except for swimmers, more
often tend to be later maturers (Malina, 1978a). The data, however,
are not as extensive as for young male athletes. Late maturing girls
have more linear physiques, which may be more suitable for athletic
performance (Malina, 1975b, 1979). In addition, the role of social
factors, i.e., socialization into or away from sport or physical
activity must be considered, especially as interacting with growth
and maturation of the young athlete (Malina et al., 1978).

Comparisons of adult athletes with non-athletes or the general
population are also used to make inferences on the effects of regular
physical activity during growth. It is assumed that the adult athletes began training during their youth, and differences relative
to non-athletes reflect positive training effects on growth.
Problems associated with selection for athletic ability and motivation are the same as mentioned for young athletes.

Extreme unilateral activity involving specialized use of an
extremity, e.g., tennis, baseball pitching, and specific manual
occupations, is occasionally used to illustrate training effects.
The individual is his own control, as the dominant limb (trained)
is compared to the non-dominant limb (untrained).

The co-twin control method (see Parisi, this volume) has been
more recently used to assess growth and activity effects. Comparisons of monozygotic twins discordant for regular physical activity
provide an indication of the effect of activity on the organism.

ACTIVITY AND BONE LENGTH

Growth of bone comprises a unique series of events. Using long
bones, the development from an embryologic cartilaginous model into
an adult bone entails growth in length and width, plus the maintenance of shape. Growth in bone length, or in linear dimensions such
as extremity length or stature, are dependent upon epiphyseal
mechanisms, i.e., cartilage proliferation. Growth in width is a
function of periosteal bone deposition and endosteal resorption,

while maintenance of shape during growth is a function of remodelling at the metaphysis.

Evidence concerning the effects of exercise on linear bone growth is not clear, such that the conclusion of Steinhaus (1933), over 45 years ago, is still plausible: the pressure effects of physical activity (tensile, compressive) may stimulate epiphyseal growth to an optimal length, but excessive and prolonged pressure can retard linear growth.

With swimming as the exercise stimulus, experimental studies on prepubertal rats (Lamb et al., 1969; Van Huss et al., 1969) showed significantly longer tibiae and femora in sedentary rats compared to voluntarily and forced exercising animals. Lengths were especially reduced in the forced group. Thus, forced exercise during the prepubertal age in rats resulted in reduced bone lengths. Similar results were reported with moderate or intensive running programs in mice (Kiiskinen, 1977) and rats (Tipton et al., 1972).

Corresponding data in children are difficult to find. Limited observations by Kato and Ishiko (1966) are suggestive of detrimental effects of excess compressive forces on epiphyseal growth of the lower extremities of children. They reported 116 cases (out of 4,000 observations) of obstructed epiphyseal growth in the lower extremities of Japanese children exposed to strenuous physical labor. Distal femoral and proximal tibial epiphyses showed earlier closure by several years; hence, stature was reduced. The authors attributed the premature closure to excessive loads carried on the shoulders resulting in severe compressive stresses across the epiphyses of the knee. It should be noted, however, that the environment in which these children were reared and in which they worked was poor economically and substandard nutritionally. In contrast, some data suggest that persistent, unilateral physical activity may stimulate bone growth in length. Buskirk et al. (1956) found the dominant hands and forearms of seven nationally ranked tennis players to have longer bones than the non-dominant extremity. Since the tennis players participated extensively in this activity during their teen-age years, it was suggested that the length differences were due to the effects of vigorous exercise on bone growth during the adolescent years. Prives (1960) also reported similar results for individuals engaged in specialized sport and work occupations.

ACTIVITY AND STATURE

There is no consistent evidence that regular training leads to an increase in stature. Although some early data suggest an increase in stature with physical training (Beyer, 1896; Schwartz et al.,

1928; Adams, 1938), the observed changes are usually quite small, and are derived from studies that did not control for subject selection and for maturity status at the time of training or the comparison. Several specific examples from the recent literature are considered. Ekblom (1969a, 1969b) subjected 5 boys to endurance training for 32 months. The boys (11 years old at the start of the training) had heights and weights at the start of training that corresponded to Swedish reference data, but showed an accelerated growth during the training program. It is difficult to consider the accelerated growth relative to the training program as maturity status was not controlled, and the boys could have experienced all or part of their adolescent spurts. In another study Eriksson (1972) studied 12 boys, 11 to 13 years of age, over 16 weeks of endurance training. The boys increased, on the average, 3.5 cm in stature. Although the accelerated growth was attributed to the training program, the average gain over four months would correspond to an annual gain of about 10 cm, which is suggestive of the adolescent height spurt. Further, maturity status was not reported. Daniels and Oldridge (1971) studied 6 boys, 10 to 14 years of age, during 22 months of endurance running. At the start of training, the boys' stature equaled United States reference data. After 22 months of training, stature was slightly below the standard, in contrast to the preceding studies.

In a study of young boys, 11 to 13 years of age (n=28), selected for swimming training, Milicer and Denisiuk (1964) noted slightly greater average increments in stature over two years of training compared to a control population. The rate differences for stature probably reflect maturity differences. The young swimmers included a greater percentage of early maturers (25%) compared to the general population of young boys (17%), and did not include late maturers.

Astrand et al. (1963) studied the growth and functional capacities of 30 female swimmers of national caliber over several years. The girls were 11.9 to 16.4 years of age and were taller than Swedish reference data at the start of the study. Examination of school records indicated that the girls were taller than the average since 7 years of age. After age 12, their heights appeared to accelerate relative to the reference data. The mean height was +0.6 standard deviation units at the time of the study, while it was +0.4 at 7 years of age. The apparent acceleration was not related to the intensity of swimming training. It was probably related to the swimmers' somewhat earlier maturation: 8 girls attained menarche between 11.0 and 11.9 years, 7 girls in the 13th year, 10 girls in the 14th year, and 4 girls in the 15th year. The average age at menarche of the group (12.9 years) was slightly earlier than the Swedish data by about one-half of a year. Menarche generally follows peak height velocity, so that one might expect the young swimmers to be somewhat taller. Their tallness most likely represents earlier maturation and not the effects of intensive swimming training.

Observations on activity and stature in humans and experimental studies of specific bone lengths in rats are in contrast to data on the effects of unilateral activity, which suggest that physical activity may stimulate bone growth of the upper extremity in length. A major portion of stature is comprised of the long bones of the lower extremities which are constantly subjected to the compressive pressures of weight bearing in addition to those of many physical activities. Physical activity may, perhaps, stimulate growth of the upper extremity bones in length in the absence of the compressive pressures of weight bearing.

ACTIVITY AND BONE MINERALIZATION

In contrast to linear growth, physical activity is known to increase bone mineralization, while inactivity decreases mineralization. Experimental studies on animals (Saville and Smith, 1966; Saville and Whyte, 1969; King and Pengelly, 1973; Kiiskinen, 1977) and observations on adults (Buskirk et al., 1956; Prives, 1960; Mashkara, 1969; Dalen and Olsson, 1974; Jones et al., 1977) indicate greater skeletal mineralization and density, and wider, more robust bones with prolonged physical training. Buskirk et al.'s (1956) observations on 7 nationally ranked tennis players, whose dominant hand and forearm bones were wider and more robust than the non-dominant member, suggest a training-mediated effect on bone width during the growing years. Jones et al. (1977) more recently reported similar results of 84 active professional tennis players. There was a marked hypertrophy of cortical bone of the humerus in the playing arm compared to the non-playing arm. Cortical thickness of the dominant arm was about 35% greater than the non-dominant arm in males, while the difference among women tennis players was about 28%. The mean age of the males was 27 years and that of females was 24 years, and the average length of playing experience was 18 years in the men and 14 years in the women. These observations thus suggest a training-mediated response, probably begun during childhood. Similar hypertrophy of the humeral cortex has been reported in the throwing arms of adolescent (Tullos and King, 1972) and professional baseball pitchers (King et al., 1969). These clinical reports, however, do not offer quantitative data on the degree of cortical hypertrophy.

Nilsson and Westlin (1971), reported greater bone densities in young adult athletes compared to non-athletes. There was a clear gradient from highest densities in "top" athletes through "ordinary" athletes and "exercising" controls to "not exercising" subjects.

Within the athletes, those participating in sports including a
heavy load on the lower limbs had especially higher densities.
Since the mean ages of the four groups was approximately 22-23 years,
beneficial effects of physical activity on bone mineralization
during growth was speculated.

Activity-related bone mineralization data for children are
not as conclusive as those for adults. In a study of bone mineralization of the dominant and non-dominant arms of amateur baseball
players 8 to 19 years of age, Watson (1973) reported marked mineralization and width differences only for the dominant humerus compared to the non-dominant member. Inconsistent patterns of greater
mineralization and width were noted in the dominant radius and
ulna. Further, differences in the mineral content between the
dominant and non-dominant humeri increased with age, while those
for the dominant and non-dominant radii and ulnae did not. Although
these observations suggest possible activity-mediated effects,
mineral dominance was not related to indicators of physical activity
stress (limb girths and grip strength) after body weight was controlled in the analysis. These indicators of physical stress are
essentially estimates of muscularity, and radiographic studies of
bone and muscle show little relationship between widths of the two
tissues (Malina, 1969b).

The data thus suggest, though not equivocally, a training-
mediated effect on bone growth in width and mineralization. The
exact mechanism underlying these effects is not clear. Saville and
Smith (1966) suggest that they are the specific effects of muscular
contraction acting on bone. Other postulated mechanisms suggest
neural, circulatory, and in the case of limb bones, compression or
weight bearing stress (Lamb, 1968).

ACTIVITY AND SKELETAL MATURATION

Regular physical activity does not accelerate or retard skeletal maturity of the child. An obvious example is the minor right-
left differences in skeletal maturation of the hand and wrist
(Greulich and Pyle, 1959; Acheson, 1966). Since the right hand is
generally exercised more than the left, it may be inferred that
regular physical activity does not affect the rate of skeletal
maturation of the hand and wrist. Regarding physical training in
general as opposed to unilateral activity effects, Cerny (1969)
reported no significant differences in skeletal maturity among boys
undergoing different programs of physical activity from 11 through
15 years of age. Variation in skeletal maturity within different
activity groups was greater than between.

ACTIVITY AND MUSCLE GROWTH

Growth of muscle tissue after the first few months of postnatal
life is characterized by constancy in number of muscle fibers, an
increase in fiber size, and a considerable increase in number of
muscle nuclei (Montgomery, 1962; Malina, 1978b). Muscle fibers
grow in length by an increase in the number of sarcomeres in series
along myofibrils, and possibly by an increase in length of individual sarcomeres (Goldspink, 1972). Growth in length occurs primarily at the musculotendinous junction, and the differential growth
of limb segments requires similar length increases in individual
muscles. Growth of a muscle fiber in girth and length is associated
with an increase in the number of nuclei, so that the number of
nuclei observed in fiber cross-sections or along a fiber's length
increases with age. The additional nuclei are apparently derived
from satellite cells (Montgomery, 1962; Goldspink, 1972; Burleigh,
1974; Cheek et al., 1971). The incorporation of nuclei into the
muscle fiber seemingly assures sufficient nuclear control for the
new fiber components added through growth in length and girth.

Postnatal increase in muscle girth is due almost entirely to
hypertrophy of existing muscle fibers, and not to hyperplasia
(Goldspink, 1972). Muscle fibers increase in diameter with age and
body size postnatally. Increase in fiber diameter varies with the
muscle studied, and is apparently related to function or intensity
of workload(Malina, 1978b). Changes in muscle tissue with regular
physical activity are well documented. Physical training results
in muscular hypertrophy, and the intensity of muscular work is the
critical factor underlying the hypertrophy observed in normal muscle
subjected to training(Steinhaus, 1933, 1955; Rarick, 1974). Hypertrophy is accompanied by an increase in contractile substances
(Helander, 1961), myofibrils (Goldspink, 1964), and functional
capacity, e.g., strength, oxygen uptake, enzyme activity (Holloszy,
1967). Strength of a muscle is related to its cross-section, such
that larger muscles generate more strength. Strength is thus related
to muscle and body size (Malina, 1975b). Observations are limited
in many instances to adult humans and experimental animals, so that
it is difficult to partition training-induced changes from those
accompanying normal growth.

Age changes in the number of nuclei in skeletal muscle during
growth had recently received attention in experimental animals and
children (Cheek, 1968; Malina, 1978b). The number of nuclei is
estimated from measures of DNA, which is relatively constant per
nucleus. Studies of DNA content and thus nuclear number of muscle
in growing animals undergoing regular training indicate a significant rise in DNA content above that expected from normal growth
(Buchanan and Pritchard, 1970; Bailey et al., 1973; Hubbard et al.,
1974). The normal pattern of change in DNA content of muscle tissue

with growth is one of steady increase until puberty, with a constant
level thereafter. The increased DNA content of exercised muscles
would seem to indicate that training is a significant factor influencing nuclear number during growth and determining adult levels
of DNA in muscle tissue. Training-induced increases in DNA and
presumably nuclear number of skeletal muscle have also been reported in adult animals (Christensen and Crampton, 1965).

Functional implications of changes in muscle tissue with training merit consideration. As a result of the biochemical responses
to chronic exercise, there is improved functioning at the molecular
level in muscle tissue (Holloszy, 1967; Jeffress and Peter, 1970;
Edgerton, 1976). Changes with training include, for example, enhanced oxidative enzyme activity, which is a mechanism through
which muscle tissue adapts to the chronic overload of vigorous
physical activity. Most of the observations, however, are derived
from experimental animals, with limited information on humans,
especially children and youth.

In a small sample of 11-year-old boys (n=5) trained for 6
weeks, Eriksson (1972; Eriksson et al., 1974) observed no change
in the muscle fiber population of the tissue samples, but did note
a marked increase in the oxidative potential of both the slow-
and fast-twitch fibers. A 30% increase was noted in succinatedehydro-
genase (SDH) activity. In contrast, maximal oxygen uptake increased
by only 8%, suggesting that the oxidative capacity of muscle tissue
may not limit oxygen consumption. Phosphofructokinase (PFK) activity,
though low compared to adult values, increased markedly with the
short term training program (83%). PFK is regarded as the rate-
limiting enzyme for glycolysis, and increased activity with training
indicates enhanced glycolytic potential.

Gollnick et al. (1973) reported similar results for adult males
(n=6). After 5 months of endurance training, there was no change
in the percentages of slow- and fast-twitch muscle fibers. Maximal
oxygen uptake increased, on the average, by 13%, while SDH and
PFK activities increased by 95% and 11% respectively. Oxidative
potential increased in both slow- and fast-twitch fibers, while
glycolytic capacity apparently increased only in fast-twitch fibers.
In contrast, the relative area of muscle composed of slow-twitch
fibers increased with endurance training.

Using an 8 week progressive strength training program in adult
males (n=14), Thorstensson (1976) observed no change in the percentage distribution of fast-twitch and slow-twitch muscle fibers.
Changes in the ratio of fast- to slow-twitch fiber area suggested
a specific hypertrophy of fast-twitch fibers with the strength
training program. On the other hand, the strength training program

had an insignificant effect on selected "contractility" enzymes
(myokinase, creatine phosphokinase).

Results of the studies using human subjects suggest that the
distribution of fiber types is probably not altered by training;
either endurance or strength. This would suggest that genetic factors
are of primary significance in skeletal muscle fiber distribution.
Monozygous (MZ) twins are quite similar in skeletal muscle fiber
composition, while dizygous (DZ) twins are more variable (Sjodin,
1976; Komi et al., 1977). However, the relative area of muscle
composed of fast- or slow-twitch fibers may change in response to
training. The direction of change apparently depends on the type
of training stimulus.

In muscle enzyme activities, MZ and DZ twin pairs show similar
variation, i.e., the former show as much variation as the latter
(Howald, 1976; Sjodin, 1976; Komi et al., 1977). The observations
may reflect training differences. With one member of an MZ twin
pair (n=7 pairs) participating in a 23-week endurance training
program while the other maintained his usual activity, SDH and
hexokinase activities increased with training by 28% and 17% respectively in one member on the MZ twin pair compared to the other
(Howald, 1976). Although genetic factors are important in the
fiber composition of muscle tissue, the results emphasize the importance of physical training in the functional capacity of muscle
tissue.

ACTIVITY AND ADIPOSE TISSUE

There is much current emphasis on adipose tissue cellularity
during growth. Adipose cell growth may result from increases in
fat cell number or size. Estimates of fat cell (adipocyte) development in children, however, are not consistent across several
studies, probably reflecting methodological and site differences
in estimating adipose cell size and number (Brook, 1972; Knittle,
1972, 1978; Knittle et al., 1977; Hager, 1977; Hager et al., 1977).
Physical activity is associated with smaller fat cell size in experimental animals (Booth et al., 1974; Oscai et al., 1974; Askew and
Hecker, 1976), and in adult humans (Björntorp et al., 1972).

A question that merits consideration is the potential of regular physical activity programs, initiated during early childhood,
to influence the development of adipose cellularity. Experimental
evidence suggests that training initiated very early in life (pre-
weaning) effectively reduced the rate of fat cell accumulation in
growing rats, thus producing a significant reduction in fat cells
and body fat later in life (Oscai et al., 1972, 1974). On the other
hand, endurance running begun after seven weeks of age in rats had

no effect on cell number, but significantly reduced adipose cell
size (Booth et al., 1974; Askew and Hecker, 1976). These experimental
observations thus suggest a role for regular physical activity in
influencing fat cell number and size. For training to influence fat
cell number, it must be initiated very early in the life of rats.
By about 7 weeks of age in rats, the pattern of fat cell proliferation is apparently established so that adipocyte number is not
influenced by a later training stimulus. Thus, training
applied after 7 weeks in rats is not effective in limiting fat cell
numbers.

One can inquire as to possible implications of these findings
for fat cell development in humans, and to what age can cell numbers
be influenced by activity programs, if at all? Observations on human
infants (Hager et al., 1977) and on obese rats (Johnson et al.,
1976) suggest a coupling between fat cell size and multiplication.
Multiplication of adipocytes occurs when the cells are filled with
lipid to a size comparable to that of young adults (Hager et al.,
1977). This coupling may simply be a coincidence or may be biologically meaningful. It would be interesting to speculate a possibly
significant role for regular training. Since physical training can
reduce adipose cell size in experimental animals, and in light of
a suggested coupling of size and multiplication, a reduced cell
size may delay or inhibit adipocyte proliferation.

ACTIVITY, LEANNESS AND FATNESS

Physical activity is important in the maintenance and regulation of body weight (see Oscai, 1973). Weight is a heterogeneous
mass, quite frequently partitioned into lean body mass and fat
(Malina, 1969b, also this volume). Regular training produces an
increase in lean body mass and a corresponding decrease in body fat
in children and youth (Pařízková, 1963, 1973; v. Döbeln and Eriksson, 1972). Training produces similar effects on adults, quite
often without any appreciable change in body weight (Pařízková,
1963). Results, however, are not consistent across studies (Forbes,
1978).

The magnitude of change in body composition with regular activity varies with the intensity and duration of the training regime.
Greater changes in body composition are associated with more intense
training programs. Results may also vary with the method used for
estimating lean body mass or fatness. Prediction equations based
on skinfolds may not be sufficiently sensitive to detect lean body
mass changes with training (Wilmore et al., 1970).

Body composition changes during growth are considerable so that
it is difficult to separate the effects of growth and of training.
In one of the more comprehensive studies, Pařízková (1968, 1970,

1974) reported the results of longitudinal observations on teenage
boys exposed to different degrees of sports participation and physical training over a 7 year period (11 to 18 years). Three levels
of training were compared: regularly trained (intensive; 6 hours
per week); trained, but not on a regular basis (went to sport
schools; about 4 hours organized exercise per week); and untrained
(about 2 1/2 hours per week including school physical education).
Sample sizes for the three groups at the conclusion of the study
were 8, 18 and 13 respectively. The groups did not differ markedly
in selected anthropometric dimensions, though the group with the
highest physical activity level was on the average taller and heavier. The groups also did not differ in relative body composition at
the beginning of the study. At the end of 7 years the most active
boys had significantly more lean body mass and less fat than the
least and moderately active boys. Body composition differences
between moderately active and least active adolescent boys were
small.

V. Döbeln and Eriksson (1972) observed functional and morphological changes in 12 boys, 11 to 13 years of age, after 16 weeks of
endurance training (see Eriksson, 1972, cited earlier). Nine of the
12 boys had their total body potassium measured before and after
the endurance program. They gained, on the average, 0.5 kg in weight,
but about 12 grams in potassium. A 12 gram increase in potassium
corresponds to a gain of about 4 kg of muscle tissue, which would
indicate that the 0.5 kg gain in body weight was accompanied by a
loss of about 3 kg of fat during the endurance training program
(V. Döbeln and Eriksson, 1972). Relative to the growth of boys in
stature the increase in potassium was 6% more than expected, while
the gain in body weight was about 5% less than expected. Whether
these changes are the result of training or normal adolescent
growth is not clear. The boys gained, on the average, 3.5 cm in
stature, which would correspond to an annual gain of about 10 cm.
This may suggest the adolescent spurt occurred with its concomitant
increase in muscle mass (see Malina, 1978b).

ACTIVITY AND PHYSIQUE

Physique is a composite, referring to an individual's body
form, i.e., the conformation of the entire body as opposed to emphasis on specific features (Tanner, 1953). Studies of training and
physique, however, have generally considered height-weight relationships, specific dimensions, and proportions (Malina and Rarick,
1973). Several studies of teenagers indicate beneficial effects of
short-term training on body bulk, specifically muscular development
(Godin, 1920; Simon, 1923; Takahashi, 1966). Physique-related
changes with training are usually most apparent in those body parts
specifically exercised, e.g., thoracic and arm measurements with
gymnastic training (Godin, 1920).

In a longitudinal study of the effects of different training programs on the growth of boys from 11 to 15 years, Pařízková (1968) noted that the most active boys (see preceding section) developed, on the average, relatively narrower pelves in relation to stature and shoulder breadth. There was, however, much overlap among the different activity groups, such that the significance of the change is not clear. It could reflect differential timing of the adolescent spurt in stature, thus influencing the ratio of hip width to stature. Further, the more active boys were taller and this could alter the index without a change in the width of the pelvis.

Pařízková and Carter (1976) also considered the stability of anthropometric estimates of somatotype in this longitudinal sample (n=39) from 11 to 18 years. The distribution of somatotypes did not differ among the three activity groups, suggesting no marked effect of the training programs on somatotype. Individuals changed considerably in somatotype over the 7 year span. Changes occurred in a random fashion and were not attributable to physical activity. All boys changed in somatotype ratings at least once, and 67% changed in component dominance. Individual variation in somatotype stability over adolescence thus confounds the evaluation of possible training-related changes. In a follow-up analysis of a small sample of the original series at 24 years of age (n=14), the mesomorphy increased from 18 to 24 years, even though the boys had ceased regular training (Carter and Pařízková, 1978).

The relationship between age, physique, and response to training programs, and between physique and activity pursuits also needs consideration. In his early review Steinhaus (1933), for example, reported increased muscle girths in children and youth with training. However, during periods of rapid growth in body length (presumably the adolescent height spurt), exercise had less effect on muscle girths than in periods when the tendency to grow in width predominated. Peak adolescent gains in weight and muscle tissue generally occur after the peak height velocity in boys and girls (Tanner, 1962, 1965), while the apex of the male strength spurt occurs after both the height and weight spurts (Stolz and Stolz, 1951; Carron and Bailey, 1974). The pattern of maximum strength development in girls, on the other hand, is not so clear. The apex of strength development occurs more often after peak height velocity than before in girls, but there is wide variation in the timing of peak strength gains (Faust, 1977).

ACTIVITY AND AEROBIC POWER

Definitions of physical fitness vary considerably, but most agree that aerobic power (maximal oxygen uptake) is a sensitive index. During childhood, aerobic power (ℓ/min) increases with age in both sexes. However, when body size is accounted for, i.e.,

ml/min/kg body weight, observations on Canadian and United States
children indicate no increase with age from 8 to 14 years; rather,
there appears to be a slight decrease (Bailey, 1973). Similar data
for German boys show an almost constant level of aerobic power per
unit of body weight in boys from 5 to 17 years, while the data for
girls show a decrease (Mocellin, 1975). Data for Scandinavian girls
also show a decrease with age, but aerobic power per unit body weight
shows an increase with age in boys (Astrand and Rodahl, 1977; Hermansen and Oseid, 1971; Andersen and Ghesquirre, 1972). The different age trends perhaps reflect physical education program differences.

Children exposed to regular endurance-type training programs
show different age-associated trends in aerobic power (Malina, 1978a).
The degree of improvement in aerobic power per unit body weight,
however, is variable. Summarizing 6 studies of children in different
age groups, 6 through 15 years of age, Mocellin (1975) reported
relative changes ranging from -2% to +14%, with 6 of the 10 reported
changes with endurance training showing a small increase (+1 to +4%).

The age groups showing no increase or only small increases with
training ranged from 6 to 10 years. Motivation to train could also
be a factor at young ages. The data of Schmucker and Hollmann (1974)
on athletes (swimming, cycling, field hockey), from 6 to 7 years of
age on, suggest that changes in relative aerobic power as an effect
of endurance training could not be established before 11 years of
age. However, training-associated improvements after 11 years in
boys suggested an increased trainability of the heart and circulatory system circumpuberally. Data for young female athletes suggested similar age relationships, but with a smaller degree of improvement. Ekblom (1969a) and Sprynarova (1974) indicated similar enhanced
trainability in boys during adolescence, but Eriksson (1972) and
Berg and Bjure (1974) concluded that the adolescent period is not
critical for training, and that it is difficult to separate training-
associated increases in aerobic power from those associated with
growth.

The role of hereditary factors in maximal aerobic power during
childhood adds another dimension to the assessment of training and
growth effects. Evidence from twins suggests that the principal
determinant of variability in maximal aerobic power and aerobic
capacity among individuals who have lived under similar environmental conditions is genetic (Klissouras, 1971, 1972; Holmer and
Astrand, 1972; Klissouras et al., 1973; Komi et al., 1973; Howald,
1976; Leitch, 1976). Training, of course, is an environmental factor.

Using the co-twin control design, Weber et al. (1976) studied
the effects of physical training on one member of an MZ twin pair
while the other served as a control. Twelve pairs of identical
twin boys were studied, 4 pairs at each of 3 age levels, 10, 13,
and 16 years. The trained members of each twin pair experienced a

10-week endurance program, while the untrained member went through
normal daily routines and regularly scheduled physical education
classes. The twins did not differ in functional measures prior to
the training program. After 10 weeks, the trained 10 and 16-year-
old twins improved significantly in maximal oxygen uptake (ℓ/min)
compared to their untrained counterparts (23.5% and 20.5% respectively in the trained twins compared to 11.8% and 3.2% respectively
in the untrained twins). In contrast, both the trained and untrained
13-year-old twins improved commensurately (14.2% for the trained and
15.9% for the untrained twins). Based on these observations, Weber
et al. (1976) suggested that the "...old hypothesis that more might
be gained by introducing extra exercise at a time when the growth
impulse is the strongest is no longer tenable." Note, however, that
the untrained twins did in fact experience regular physical education
classes, and this may be a sufficient activity stimulus during peak
growth velocity. Also using the co-twin control design, Howald (1976)
studied the effects of a 23-week, low intensity endurance program
in 7 pairs of MZ twins (mean age, 18 years, range 15 to 25). Maximum ergometric performance and maximal oxygen uptake **increased 10.1%**
and 15.4% respectively in the trained compared to the untrained
twins.

Holmer and Astrand (1972) compared the maximal oxygen uptake
of a single pair of 19-year-old MZ twins on a variety of work tests.
One twin trained for competitive swimming from 14 through 19 years
of age, while the other trained similarly from 14 to 17 years, but
stopped training for three years prior to the study. Both girls
were almost identical in maximal oxygen uptake measured during running (3.61 and 3.56 ℓ/min), and only slightly different in maximal
oxygen uptake measured on a bicycle ergometer (3.44 and 3.13 ℓ/min).
However, the twins differed considerably in maximal oxygen uptake
measured during swimming. For example, the twin who was presently
training exceeded the non-training twin by 49% in maximal oxygen uptake measured during arm work (2.74 and 1.84 ℓ/min) while swimming.
A smaller difference (24%) between the trained and non-trained twins
was evident in maximal oxygen uptake measured during leg kick work
as in front crawl swimming (3.37 and 2.72 ℓ/min). Although these
observations are based on a single MZ twin pair, they emphasize both
the hereditary aspects of maximal oxygen uptake, and the specificity
of training effects and of aerobic power (see Bouchard et al., 1979).

PERSISTENCE OF ACTIVITY EFFECTS

The question of the persistence of training-associated changes
also needs consideration. Changes in response to short-term training are generally not permanent, and vary with the training stimulus.
This was especially clear in the fluctuating levels of fatness
associated with training and not training. Fatness varied inversely
with the quantity of training (Pařizková, 1973). The same was true

in experimental studies of adipocyte size in rats. With training
there was a reduction of fat cell size, while with detraining cell
size was similar to that of sedentary rats (Booth et al., 1974).
A study of weight training in adult males showed increased muscle
girths after four months; however, measurements taken on the subjects
four months after the prescribed training program had ceased showed
that almost all measurements had reverted to pre-training values
(Tanner, 1952). Similar questions can be asked on the persistence
of biochemical alterations in muscle with the cessation of training,
as well as of the persistence of training-related functional changes,
especially those changes occurring during growth.

      The fact that such positive changes depend on continued activity
was strikingly evident in a follow-up study of the young female
swimmers studied by Astrand et al. (1963). The girls trained intens-
ively for several years. Functional measures of the young swimmers
were consistently above those for normal girls of corresponding
body size: 11 to 15% for lung volumes except residual volume, 14%
for blood volume, 19% for total hemoglobin, 22% for heart volume,
and 10% for maximal oxygen uptake relative to body weight. Within
the sample of 30 girls, differences in the functional measures were
related to the individual girl's "training volume" (hours/week; meter/
week); i.e., the girls with greater training volumes generally had
greater lung volumes, heart volume and functional capacity, and vice
versa. The swimmers were re-studied 7 to 8 years (mean age 21.4)
and then 10 years (mean age 23.9) after the initial study (Eriksson
et al., 1971, 1978). Changes were marked in functional measures relative to age and body size. In the original study, the young swimmers
had maximal oxygen uptakes which were 20% higher than untrained girls
(51.5 ml/kg/min). At the follow-ups, this functional measure was 37.9
and 36.4 ml/kg/min respectively, the former swimmers' maximal oxygen
uptake decreasing, on the average, by almost 29%. The decrease reflects in part changes in body composition with the cessation of
training. Heart and lung volumes, on the other hand, did not change
appreciably after regular training ceased. This would imply that the
young women retained the capacity for higher functional levels even
though actual functional levels decreased considerably due to lesser
physical activity or persistent inactivity. Thus, continued training
is necessary to maintain the high level functional efficiency attained via training during adolescence.

      The foregoing has implications for the evaluation of effects of
exercise and training on children and adolescents. Are training-
associated changes produced during the growing years permanent? The
available data would seem to indicate that continued activity is
necessary to maintain the favorable functional and body composition
changes. Of relevance to functional changes associated with training is recent experimental evidence which suggests beneficial and
persistent effects of mild exercise during pregnancy on the microstructure of neonatal and adult heart muscle of rats (Pařížková,

1975, 1978; Bonner et al., 1978). Changes associated with activity during pregnancy persisted postnatally into adulthood.

ACTIVITY AND LONGEVITY

Physical activity may be one of a number of factors related to longevity (see Susanne, this volume), although the evidence indicating a beneficial effect of physical activity on longevity is not compelling (Skinner, 1968; Norris and Shock, 1974). More active individuals generally show greater functional capacity at all ages, and this may function to alleviate changes with aging. Further, changes in a general sense of well being (physical and perhaps psychological) associated with regular physical activity are probably significant. More active individuals also have less fat. Thus, the extent to which regular physical activity reduces fatness or prevents fat accumulation may be significant in that fat reduction in itself can lead to improved functional capacity and perhaps to increased longevity. However, whether physical activity during youth and adulthood substantially alters the rate of aging needs careful longitudinal study.

A significant role of continued training in slowing the age-associated reduction in aerobic power and perhaps a significant role for training during youth are further suggested by the data of Saltin and Grimby (1968). Among other variables, they reported maximal oxygen uptakes for middle-aged and older athletes compared to colleagues who were former athletes of the same ages now living a sedentary life. Most of the athletes started to train in adolescence. While competing the two groups were quite similar in their performance in "orientering" -- long distance cross-country running most commonly practiced in Scandinavian countries between April and October. Hence, the study was based on the assumption that the two groups were, at the time of competition, not significantly different in maximal oxygen uptake. At the time of testing, currently active older athletes had greater aerobic power than the nonactive athletes at all ages (maximal oxygen uptake, ml/min/kg). Both groups of athletes had aerobic power values higher than that found in the general population at the same ages. The greater aerobic power in the nonactive athletes compared to the general population perhaps reflects to some degree a positive effect of training during their youth. It could also reflect their genotype and the result of selective practices involved in competitive athletics. Differences between the active and nonactive athletes, on the other hand, are a function of continued training in the former.

SUMMARY

   Physical activity has no apparent effect on stature, although
prolonged unilateral activity may influence specific bone lengths.
Prolonged training favorably influences body weight regulation, the
ratio of leanness to fatness, skeletal mineralization, muscle size
and metabolism, and cardiorespiratory function. The changes associated with physical activity are a function of the intensity and
duration of training, and some changes are specific to the type of
training. The persistence of some observed changes is apparently
dependent upon continued regular physical activity. Regular activity
during childhood and adolescence may be significant in determining
the quantity and/or quality of fat and muscle tissues, bone mineral,
and aerobic function in adulthood. More active individuals generally
show less fatness and greater functional capacity at all ages, and
this may function to alleviate aging-associated changes.

   Just how much physical activity is necessary during the growing years is not known. Individual variation is great. A certain
level of physical exercise is apparently necessary to support normal
growth, maintain the integrity of osseous, muscle and adipose tissues, regulate fatness, and maintain aerobic fitness. Just what the
minimum level is or should be, and what effects more regular and
extended training programs may have on the growth and functional
development of the young child and adolescent, remain to be determined. More data are obviously necessary, especially longitudinal
observations in which the exercise variable is controlled or monitored. There is also a need to more carefully define, quantify and
control the training stimulus, and to develop sensitive methods of
monitoring and quantifying the amount and intensity of physical
activity in children and youth.

REFERENCES

Acheson, R.M. 1966, Maturation of the skeleton, in: "Human Develop-
      ment," F. Falkner, ed., Saunders, Philadelphia, p. 465.
Adams, E.H., 1938, A comparative anthropometric study of hard labor
      during youth as a stimulator of physical growth of young
      colored women. Res. Quart., 9;102.
Andersen, K.L., and Ghesquiere, J., 1972, Sex differences in maximal
      oxygen uptake, heart rate, and oxygen pulse at 10 and 14
      years in Norwegian children. Human Biol., 44:413.
Askew, E.W., and Hecker, A.L., 1976, Adipose tissue cell size and
      lipolysis in the rat: response to exercise intensity and food
      restriction. J. Nutr., 106: 1351.
Astrand, P.-O., Engstrom, L., Eriksson, B.O., Karlberg, P., Nylander,
      I., Saltin, B., and Thoren, C., 1963, Girl Swimmers. Acta
      Paediat., Suppl. 147.

Astrand, P.-O., and Rodahl, K., 1977, "Textbook of Work Physiology," (2nd. ed.), McGraw-Hill, New York.

Bailey, D.A., 1973, Exercise, fitness and physical education for the growing child -- a concern, Canad. J. Pub. Health, 64:421.

Bailey, D.A., Bell, R.D., and Howarth, R.E., 1973, The effect of exercise on DNA and protein synthesis in skeletal muscle of growing rats, Growth, 37:323.

Bailey, D.A., Malina, R.M., and Rasmussen, R.L., 1978, The influence of exercise, physical activity, and athletic performance on the dynamics of human growth, in: "Human Growth, 2, Postnatal Growth," F. Falkner and J.M. Tanner (eds.), Plenum Press, New York, p. 475.

Berg, K., and Bjure, J., 1974, Preliminary results of long-term physical training of adolescent boys with respect to body composition, maximal oxygen uptake, and lung volume, Acta Paediat. Belgica, 28:183.

Beyer, H.G., 1896, The influence of exercise on growth, J. Exper. Med., 1:546.

Björntorp, P., Grimby, G., Sanne, H., Sjöström, L., Tibblin, G., and Wilhelmsen, L., 1972, Adipose tissue fat cell size in relation to metabolism in weight-stabile, physically active men, Hormone Metab. Res., 4:178.

Bonner, H.W., Buffington, C.K., Newman, J.J., Farrar, R.P., and Acosta, D., 1978, Contractile activity of neonatal heart cells in culture derived from offspring of exercised pregnant rats, Eur. J. Appl. Physiol., 39:1.

Booth, M.A., Booth, M.J., and Taylor, A.W., 1974, Rat fat cell size and number with exercise training, detraining and weight loss, Fed. Proc., 33:1959.

Bouchard, C., Godbout, P., Mondor, J.-C., and Leblanc, C., 1979, Specificity of maximal aerobic power, Eur. J. Appl. Physiol., 40:85.

Brook, C.G.D., 1972, Evidence for a sensitive period in adipose-cell replication in man, Lancet, 2:624.

Buchanan, T.A.S., and Pritchard, J.J., 1970, DNA content of tibialis anterior of male and female white rats measured from birth to 50 weeks, J. Anat., 107:185.

Burleigh, I.G., 1974, On the cellular regulation of growth and development in skeletal muscle, Biol. Rev., 49:267.

Buskirk, E.R., Andersen, K.L., and Brožek, J., 1956, Unilateral activity and bone and muscle development in the forearm, Res. Quart., 27:127.

Carron, A.V., and Bailey, D.A., 1974, Strength development in boys from 10 through 16 years, Mon. Soc. Res. Child Dev., 39, no. 4.

Carter, J.E.L., and Pařížková, J., 1978, Changes in somatotypes of European males between 17 and 24 years, Amer. J. Phys. Anthrop., 48:251.

Cerný, L., 1969, The results of an evaluation of skeletal age of boys 11-15 years old with different regime of physical activity, in: "Physical Fitness Assessment," Charles University, Prague, p. 56.

Cheek, D.B., 1968, "Human Growth," Lea & Febiger, Philadelphia.

Cheek, D.B., Holt, A.B., Hill, D.E., and Talbert, J.L., 1971, Skeletal muscle cell mass and growth: the concept of the deoxyribonucleic acid unit, Pediatr. Res., 5:312.

Christensen, D.A., and Crampton, E.W., 1965, Effects of exercise and diet on nitrogenous constituents in several tissues of adult rats, J. Nutr., 86:369.

Dalen, N., and Olsson, K.E., 1974, Bone mineral content and physical activity, Acta Orthop. Scand., 45:170.

Daniels, J., and Oldridge, N., 1971, Changes in oxygen consumption of young boys during growth and running training, Med. Sci. Sports, 3:161.

Edgerton, V.R., 1976, Neuromuscular adaptation to power and endurance work, Can. J. Applied Sport Sci., 1:49.

Ekblom, B., 1969a, Effect of physical training on oxygen transport system in man, Acta Physiol. Scand., Suppl. 328.

Ekblom, B., 1969b, Effect of physical training in adolescent boys, J. Appl. Physiol., 27:350.

Eriksson, B.O., 1972, Physical training, oxygen supply and muscle metabolism in 11-13 year old boys, Acta Physiol. Scand., Suppl. 384.

Eriksson, B.O., Engstrom, I., Karlberg, P., Lundin, A., Saltin, B., and Thoren, C., 1978, Long-term effect of previous swim-training in girls. A ten-year follow-up of the "Girl Swimmers", Acta Paediat. Scand., 67:285.

Eriksson, B.O., Engstrom, I., Karlberg, P., Saltin, B., and Thoren, C., 1971, A physiological analysis of former girl swimmers, Acta Paediat. Scand., 67:285.

Eriksson, B.O., Gollnick, P.D., and Saltin, B., 1974, The effect of physical training on muscle enzyme activities and fiber composition in 11-year-old boys, Acta Paediat. Belg., 28:245.

Espenschade, A., 1960, The contributions of physical activity to growth, Res. Quart., 31:351.

Faust, M.S., 1977, Somatic development of adolescent girls, Monogr. Soc. Res. Child Dev., 42, no. 1.

Forbes, G.B., 1978, Body composition in adolescence, in: "Human Growth, 2, Postnatal Growth," F. Falkner and J.M. Tanner, eds., Plenum Press, New York.

Godin, P., 1920, "Growth during School Age," (translated by S. L. Eby), Gorham Press, Boston.

Goldspink, G., 1964, The combined effect of exercise and reduced food intake on skeletal muscle, J. Cell. Comp. Physiol., 63:209.

Goldspink, G., 1972, Postembryonic growth and differentiation of striated muscle, in: "The Structure and Function of Muscle (2nd ed.), Volume 1, Structure," G. H. Bourne, ed., Academic Press, New York.

Gollnick, P.D., Armstrong, R.B., Saltin, B., Saubert, C.W., Sembrowich, W.L., and Shepherd, R.E., 1973, Effect of training on enzyme activity and fiber composition of human skeletal muscle, J. Appl. Physiol., 34:107.

Greulich, W.W., and Pyle, S.I., 1959, "Radiographic Atlas of Skeletal Development of the Hand and Wrist" (2nd. ed.), Stanford University Press, Palo Alto, California.

Hager, A., 1977, Adipose cell size and number in relation to obesity, Postgrad. Med. J., 53 (suppl. 2): 101.

Hager, A., Sjöström, L., Arvidsson, B., Björntorp, P., and Smith, U., 1977, Body fat and adipose tissue cellularity in infants: a longitudinal study, Metab. Clin. Exper., 26:607.

Helander, E.A.S., 1961, Influence of exercise and restricted activity on the protein composition of skeletal muscle, Biochem. J., 78:478.

Hermansen, L., and Oseid, S., 1971, Direct and indirect estimation of maximal oxygen uptake in pre-pubertal boys, Acta Paediat. Scand., Suppl. 217:18.

Holloszy, J.O., 1967, Biochemical adaptations in muscle: effects of exercise on mitochondrial oxygen uptake and respiratory enzyme activity in skeletal muscle, J. Biol. Chem., 242:2278.

Holmer, I., and Astrand, P.-O., 1972, Swimming training and maximal oxygen uptake, J. Appl. Physiol., 33:510.

Howald, H., 1976, Ultrastructure and biochemical function of skeletal muscle in twins, Ann. Human Biol., 3:455.

Hubbard, R.W., Smoake, J.A., Matther, W.T., Linduska, J.D., and Bowers, W.S., 1974, The effects of growth and endurance training on the protein and DNA content of rat soleus, plantaris, and gastrocnemius muscles, Growth, 38:171.

Jeffress, R.N., and Peter, J.B., 1970, Adaptation of skeletal muscle to overloading -- a review, Bull. Los Angeles Neurol. Soc., 35:134.

Johnson, P.R., Stern, J., Gruen, R., Blanchett-Hirst, S., and Greenwood, M.R.C., 1976, Development of adipose depot cellularity, plasma insulin, pancreatic insulin release and insulin resistance in the Zucker obese female rat, Fed. Proc., 35:657.

Jones, H.H., Priest, J.D., Hayes, W.C., Tichenor, C.C., and Nagel, D.A., 1977, Humeral hypertrophy in response to exercise, J. Bone Joint Surg., 59A:204.

Kato, S., and Ishiko, T., 1966, Obstructed growth of children's bones due to excessive labor in remote corners, in: "Proceedings of International Congress of Sport Sciences," K. Kato (ed.), Japanese Union of Sports Sciences, Tokyo, p. 479.

Kiiskinen, A., 1977, Physical training and connective tissues in young mice -- physical properties of Achilles tendons and long bones, Growth, 41:123.

King, D.W., and Pengelly, R.G., 1973, Effect of running exercise on the density of rat tibias, Med. Sci. Sports, 5:68.

King, J.W., Grelsford, H.J., and Tullos, H.S., 1969, Analysis of the pitching arm of the professional baseball pitcher, Clin. Orthop., 67:116.

Klissouras, V., 1971, Heritability of adaptive variation, J. Appl. Physiol., 31:338.

Klissouras, V., 1972, Genetic limit of functional adaptability, Internat. Z. Angew. Physiol, Einsch. Arbeitsphysiol., 30:85.

Klissouras, V., Pirnay, F., and Petit, J.-M., 1973, Adaptation to maximal effort; genetics and age, J. Appl. Physiol., 35:288.

Knittle, J.L., 1972, Obesity in childhood: a problem in adipose tissue cellular development, J. Pediat., 81:1048.

Knittle, J.L., 1978, Adipose tissue development in man, in: "Human Growth, 2, Postnatal Growth," F. Falkner and J. M. Tanner (eds.), Plenum Press, New York, p. 295.

Knittle, J.L., Ginsberg-Fellner, F., and Brown, R.E., 1977, Adipose tissue development in man, Amer. J. Clin. Nutr., 30:762.

Komi, P.V., Klissouras, V., and Karvinen, E., 1973, Genetic variation in neuromuscular performance, Internat. Z. Angew. Physiol. Einsch. Arbeitsphysiol., 31:289.

Komi, P.V., Viitasalo, J.H.T., Havu, M., Thorstensson, A., Sjodin, B., and Karlsson, J., 1977, Skeletal muscle fibres and muscle enzyme activities in monozygous and dizygous twins of both sexes, Acta Physiol. Scand., 100:385.

Lamb, D.R., 1968, Influence of exercise on bone growth and metabolism, in: "Kinesiology Review, 1968," American Association for Health, Physical Education and Recreation, Washington D.C., p. 43.

Lamb, D.R., Van Huss, W.D., Carrow, R.E., Heusner, W.W., Weber, J.C., and Kertzer, R., 1969, Effects of prepubertal physical training on growth, voluntary exercise, cholesterol and basal metabolism in rats, Res. Quart., 40:123.

Leitch, A.G., 1976, Chemical control of breathing in identical twin athletes, Ann. Human Biol., 3:447.

Malina, R.M., 1969a, Exercise as an influence upon growth, Clin. Pediat., 8:16.

Malina, R.M., 1969b, Quantification of fat, muscle and bone in man, Clin. Orthop., 65:9.

Malina, R.M., 1975a, Exercise and growth, Na'Pao: Saskatchewan Anthrop. J., 5:3.

Malina, R.M., 1975b, Anthropometric correlates of strength and motor performance, Exercise Sport Sci. Rev., 3:249.

Malina, R.M., 1978a, Physical growth and maturity characteristics of young athletes, in: "Children in Sport: A Contemporary Anthology," R.A. Magill, M.J. Ash and F.L. Smoll (eds.), Human Kinetics Publishers, Champaign, Illinois, p. 79.

Malina, R.M., 1978b, Growth of muscle tissue and muscle mass, in: "Human Growth, 2, Postnatal Growth," F. Falkner and J.M. Tanner (eds.), Plenum Press, New York, p. 273.

Malina, R.M., 1979, Growth, strength and physical performance, in: "Encyclopedia of Physical Education, Volume 2," Addison-Wesley, Reading, Mass., in press.

Malina, R.M., and Rarick, G.L., 1973, Growth, physique and motor performance, in: "Physical Activity: Human Growth and Development," G.L. Rarick (ed.), Academic Press, New York, p. 125.

Malina, R.M., Spirduso, W.W., Tate, C., and Baylor, A.M., 1978, Age at menarche and selected menstrual charcteristics in athletes at different competitive levels, Med. Sci. Sports, 10:218.

Mashkara, K.I., 1969, Effects of physical labor on the structure of the bones of the upper extremities, Ark. Ana. Gistol. Embryol., 56:7.

McCafferty, W.B., and Horvath, S.M., 1977, Specificity of exercise and specificity of training: a subcellular review, Res. Quart., 48:358.

Milicer, H., and Denisiuk, L., 1964, The physical development of youth, in: "International Research in Sport and Physical Education," E. Jokl and E. Simon (eds.), C.C Thomas, Springfield, Illinois, p. 262.

Mocellin, R., 1975, Jugend und sport, Med. Klin., 70:1443.

Montgomery, R.D., 1962, Growth of human striated muscle, Nature, 195:194.

Nilsson, B.E., and Westlin, N.E., 1971, Bone density in athletes, Clin. Orthop., 77:179.

Norris, A.H., and Shock, N.W., 1974, Exercise in the adult years, in: "Science and Medicine of Exercise and Sport," W.R. Johnson and E.R. Buskirk (eds.), Harper and Row, New York, p. 346.

Oscai, L.B., 1973, The role of exercise in weight control, Exercise Sport Sci. Rev., 1:103.

Oscai, L.B., Babirak, S.P., McGarr, J.A., and Spirakis, C.N., 1974, Effect of exercise on adipose tissue cellularity, Fed. Proc., 33:1956.

Oscai, L.B., Spirakis, C.N., Wolff, C.A., and Beck, R.J., 1972, Effects of exercise and of food restriction on adipose tissue cellularity, J. Lipid Res., 13:588.

Pařízkova, J., 1963, Impact of age, diet, and exercise on man's body composition, Ann. N.Y. Acad. Sci., 110:661.

Pařízkova, J., 1968, Longitudinal study of the development of body composition and body build in boys of various physical activity, Human Biol., 40:212.

Pařízkova, J., 1970, Longitudinal study of the relationship between body composition and anthropometric characteristics in boys during growth and development, Glas. Antrop. Drust. Jugoslav., 7:33.

Pařízkova, J., 1973, Body composition and exercise during growth and development, in: "Physical Activity: Human Growth and Development," G.L. Rarick (ed.), Academic Press, New York, p. 97.

Pařízkova, J., 1974, Particularities of lean body mass and fat development in growing boys as related to their motor activity, Acta Paediat. Belgica, 28:233.

Pařízkova, J., 1975, Impact of daily work-load during pregnancy on the microstructure of the rat heart in male offspring, Eur. J. Appl. Physiol., 34:323.

Pařízková, J., 1978, The impact of daily work load during pregnancy and/or postnatal life on the heart microstructure of rat male offspring, Basic Res. Cardiol., 73:433.

Pařízková, J., and Carter, J.E.L., 1976, Influence of physical activity on stability of somatotypes in boys, Amer. J. Phys. Anthrop., 44:327.

Prives, M.G., 1960, Influence of labor and sport upon skeletal structure in man, Anat. Rec., 136:261.

Rarick, G.L., 1974, Exercise and growth, in: "Science and Medicine of Exercise and Sport," (2nd. ed.), W.R. Johnson and E.R. Buskirk (eds.), Harper and Row, New York, p. 306.

Saltin, B., and Grimby, G., 1968, Physiological analysis of middle-age and old former athletes: comparison with still active athletes of the same ages, Circulation, 38:1104.

Saville, P.D., and Smith, R., 1966, Bone density, breaking force and leg muscle mass as functions of weight in bipedal rats, Amer. J. Phys. Anthrop., 25:35.

Saville, P.D., and Whyte, M.P., 1969, Muscle and bone hypertrophy: positive effect of running exercise in the rat, Clin. Orthop., 65:81.

Scheuer, J., and Tipton, C.M., 1977, Cardiovascular adaptations to physical training, Ann. Rev. Physiol., 39:221.

Schmucker, B., and Hollmann, W., 1974, The aerobic capacity of trained athletes from 6 to 7 years of age on, Acta Paediat. Belgica, 28:92.

Schwartz, L., Britten, R.H., and Thompson, L.R., 1928, Studies in physical development and posture, 1, The effect of exercise on the physical condition and development of adolescent boys, Public Health Bull., No. 179, p. 1.

Simon, E., 1923, "Leibesubungen und Konstitution," Wurzgurg: Inaug. Diss.; as reported by E. Simon, 1964, Morphological development and functional efficiency, in: "International Research in Sport and Physical Education," E. Jokl and E. Simon (eds.), C.C Thomas, Springfield, Illinois, p. 225.

Sjodin, B., 1976, Lactate dehydrogenase in human skeletal muscle, Acta Physiol. Scand., Suppl. 436.

Skinner, J.S., 1968, Longevity, general health, and exercise, in: "Exercise Physiology," H.B. Falls (ed.), Academic Press, New York, p. 219.

Sprynarova, S., 1974, Longitudinal study of the influence of different physical activity programs on functional capacity of the boys from 11 to 18 years, Acta Paediat. Belgica, 28:204.

Steinhaus, A.H., 1933, Chronic effects of exercise, Physiol. Rev., 13:103.

Steinhaus, A.H., 1955, Strength from Morpugo to Muller -- a half century of research, J. Assoc. Phys. Mental Rehab., 9:147.

Stolz, H.R., and Stolz, L.M., 1951, "Somatic Development of Adolescent Boys," Macmillan, New York.

Takahashi, E., 1966, Growth and environmental factors in Japan, Human Biol., 38:112.

Tanner, J.M., 1952, The effect of weight-training on physique, Amer. J. Phys. Anthrop., 10:427.

Tanner, J.M., 1953, Growth and constitution, in: "Anthropology Today," A.L. Kroeber (ed.), University of Chicago Press, Chicago, p. 750.

Tanner, J.M., 1962, "Growth at Adolescence," (2nd. ed.), Blackwell, Oxford.

Tanner, J.M., 1965, Radiographic studies of body composition in children and adults, Symp. Soc. Study Human Biol., 7:211.

Thorstensson, A., 1976, Muscle strength, fibre types and enzyme activities in man, Acta Physiol. Scand., Suppl. 443.

Tipton, C.M., Matthes, R.D., and Maynard, J.A., 1972, Influence of chronic exercise on rat bones, Med. Sci. Sports, 4:55.

Tullos, H.S., and King, J.W., 1972, Lesions of the pitching arm in adolescents, J. Amer. Med. Assoc., 220: 264.

V. Döbeln, W., and Eriksson, B.O., 1972, Physical training, maximal oxygen uptake and dimensions of the oxygen transporting and metabolizing organs in boys 11-13 years of age, Acta Paediat. Scand., 61:653.

Van Huss, W.D., Heusner, W.W., and Mickelsen, O., 1969, Effects of prepubertal exercise on body composition, in: "Exercise and Fitness," D. Franks (ed.), Athletic Institute, Chicago, p. 201.

Watson, R.C., 1973, Bone growth and physical activity in young males, Unpublished doctoral dissertation, Madison: University of Wisconsin.

Weber, G., Kartodihardjo, W., and Klissouras, V., 1976, Growth and physical training with reference to heredity, J. Appl. Physiol., 40:211.

Wilmore, J.H., Girandola, R.N., and Moody, D.L., 1970, Validity of skinfold and girth assessment for predicting alterations in body composition, J. Appl. Physiol., 29:313.

18. SOCIOECONOMIC DIFFERENCES IN GROWTH PATTERNS

Charles Susanne

Free University Brussels
Pleinlaan 2, 1050 Brussels, Belgium

Much research by physical anthropologists is concerned with differences in anthropometric characters among socioeconomic groups. Genetic and environmental hypotheses have been proposed as possible reasons for this social distribution. The genetic hypothesis assumes genetic control of anthropometric parameters, i.e., a shifting effect similar to the relation between intelligence and height, and the selection of intelligence in relation to professional groups (Schreider, 1967). These genetic differences could be intensified by positive assortative mating.

The environmental hypothesis is based on the fact that human growth potential could be realized more fully in the most favorable living conditions. In this second hypothesis, the importance of genetic influences on growth and development is not denied. A decrease in anthropometric differentiation between social groups is expected with the environmental hypothesis, when the differences in living standards decrease between groups.

SOCIOECONOMIC EFFECTS ON BIRTHWEIGHT

Effects of nutrition on birthweight are unimportant; a growing fetus is protected against the effects of maternal deprivation (Thomson, 1978). The beneficial effect of increasing the dietary intakes of pregnant women in impoverished rural communities is too small to be noticeable in clinical practice, although it could be of considerable public health importance. An increased intake of 10,000 kcal per pregnancy in rural communities of Guatemala resulted in an increase of 28 to 80 g in birthweight (Lechtig et al., 1975). The severe Dutch famine of 1944-45 dramatically reduced

329

conception rate and there was no weight gain by the mother during pregnancy, but there was a decrease of only 9% in average birth-weight (Stein et al., 1975). These environmental effects are not drastic but they result in some social differences (Banerjee, 1969). In first-borns in Aberdeen (Scotland), the frequency of low birth-weight (<2.500 g) varies with social status (Thomson, 1963). Higher perinatal mortality rates occur in lower than in upper so-cioeconomic classes but when these rates are adjusted for birth-weight, the social differences disappear except perhaps for class V which is the lowest social class (Rush, 1974).

SOCIOECONOMIC EFFECTS ON GROWTH DURING CHILDHOOD

Young children are taller and heavier in upperclass, well-to-do families with high incomes and cultural advantages than in lower class, poor, underprivileged families. This is observed consis-tently in all populations. It is obvious that the occupational status of the father is only one of the determining variables although it is strongly correlated with other socioeconomic characters.

The status and rate of growth during childhood are among the most sensitive indicators of environmental influences. The ob-served height approximates the potential for growth when living conditions are favorable. The limits of this potential growth are determined by genetic factors.

Large socioeconomic differences have been observed in many studies in different parts of the world (e.g., Acheson and Hewitt, 1954; Douglas and Blomfield, 1958; Graffar et al., 1962; Goldstein, 1971; Chrzastek-Spruch, 1977). For instance, in U.S. children 6 to 11 years old examined in the U.S. Health Examination Survey, in-creasing trends of height and weight are observed as a function of an increase in annual income or educational level (Hamill et al., 1972). Whitelaw (1971) studied skinfold thicknesses at the triceps and scapula sites in children aged 5 to 15 years and observed a significant trend for increase with declining social class. This observation is related to the greater prevalence of obesity in adults of lower socioeconomic groups in Western societies (Moore et al., 1962; Silverstone et al., 1969). These differences are correlated with the consumption of more carbohydrates and less protein-rich foods by the lower socioeconomic classes. Douglas (1962) and Goldstein (1971) published similar results.

In African and Asiatic populations also, differences in growth between better-off versus poor groups have been observed often. The relationship between socioeconomic status and the prevalence of severe nutritional problems is evident in such populations (Chang et al., 1963; Ashcroft et al., 1966; Sabharwal et al., 1966;

Bailey, 1970; Rea, 1971; Raghavan et al., 1971; Amirhakimi, 1974;
Bogin and MacVean, 1978). Children with signs of protein-caloric
malnutrition have a significantly lower growth rate in height and
weight compared to apparently normal children or to those with
vitamin B complex deficiency (Rao and Satyanarayana, 1976).

Rea (1971) presented clear evidence of socioeconomic influences on the growth of children in Lagos under 5 years of age; these
children were studied in a short term longitudinal survey. Three
socioeconomic groups were included; at all ages and in both sexes
the differences for weight and height were in the directions to be
expected from the socioeconomic differences. There was a failure
of growth in all groups aged between 3 and 18 months. It is a
common finding that, in populations where malnutrition is widespread and where breastfeeding is customary, babies grow normally
during the first few months of life. Between 3 and 18 months,
however, a phase of nutritional inadequacy is observed. Breastfeeding may continue for a year or more but is not nutritionally
sufficient for the whole of this period. Consequently, mortality
and morbidity rates increase and protein and/or caloric malnutrition is more common, especially during the second year. The slowing of growth during this age range is less marked in higher socioeconomic groups. After 18 months of age, there is slight recovery
towards more normal growth.

Eveleth and Tanner (1976), reviewing data for children of low
or high socioeconomic level from many countries, concluded that
growth retardation usually begins at about 6 months of age. Using
the relationship log w-0,008 h = a-bc^{-kt} to describe the changes in
weight and height of children aged less than 2 years, El Lozy (1978)
showed the value of "a" decreases with worsening of socioeconomic
status. This corresponds with the observation that malnourished
children weigh less for the same height than well-nourished children. The value of "k" decreases also; this corresponds to a slowing of the rate of growth. The influence of nutrition on growth
is analysed in more detail in Chapter 19 by Johnston. The role of
infection in determining nutritional status is clear also (Rowland
et al., 1977; Chandra, 1979; Martorell, 1979).

SOCIOECONOMIC DIFFERENTIATION AND MATURATIONAL STATUS

The influence of nutrition on the rate of skeletal maturation
and on the age at menarche is obvious also. However, skeletal
maturation is retarded less than longitudinal growth in conditions
of unfavorable nutrition (Greulich, 1951; Acheson and Hewitt,
1954). As expected, a social differentiation of skeletal maturity
status has been observed (Dreizen et al., 1958; Acheson, 1960; Low
et al., 1964; Rea, 1971; Shakir and Zaini, 1974). Also, the timing
of pubescence is highly sensitive to environmental factors (Table 1).

Table 1.   Socioeconomic Differences in Menarcheal Age (Years)

	Population	High	Intermediate	Poor
GROUP A				
Kralj-Cercek, 1956	Slovenian	13.28	13.71	14.2
"	Susak	12.9	13.77	14.5
Burrell et al., 1961	South Africa Bantu	15.02	--	15.42
Lee et al., 1963	China	12.5	12.8	13.3
Sabharwal et al., 1966	Guatemala	12.8	--	14.5
Milicer, 1968	Wrocław	12.87	13.26	13.43
Aw and Tye, 1970	Singapore	12.4	12.66	12.98
Laska-Mierzejewska, 1970	Warsaw	13.90	14.27	14.45
"	Poland	13.77	14.04	14.30
Shakir, 1971	Baghdad	13.59	13.39	13.93
Bai & Vijayalakshmi, 1973	Andra Pradesh	13.11	13.27	13.35
Neyzi et al., 1975a	Istanbul	12.4	12.9 and 13.3	13.2
Singh and Roberts, 1975	South India	12.86	13.74	14.08
Roberts et al., 1977	India	12.65	13.53	13.69
Attalah, 1978	Cairo	12.59	13.09	13.89
Kark, 1956	South Africa	13.4	13.6	13.9
GROUP B -- INDIAN GIRLS				
Kantero and Widholm, 1971	Finland	13.07	13.25	13.22
Jéniček and Demirjian, 1974	Canada	13.43	13.03	13.12
Rona and Pereira, 1974	Santiago Chile	12.97	--	12.3
Wachholder and Cantraine, 1974	Belgium	12.75	12.71	12.8
Furu, 1976	Stockholm	13.05	13.14	13.04
Lindgren, 1976	Sweden	11.98	12.00	11.81

Note: The studies in GROUP B show socioeconomic associations that
        are not in the expected direction.

This sensitivity has been observed for age at menarche, age of
attainment of breast stages and of pubic hair and axillary hair
stages in girls and boys (Neyzi et al., 1975a,b). The reported
differences between rural and urban populations in the timing of
these events are probably related to environmental factors.   These

socioeconomic differences are probably related to nutritional differences. In addition to the above, an association with family size has been mentioned frequently (Roberts et al., 1971).

DISCUSSION

The social differentiation of physical size and of maturational status of the children is well-established. But most of the factors influencing the socioeconomic differences are interrelated and it is difficult to isolate the influence of any one factor. Direct or indirect environmental factors exerting an influence on nutrition or state of health are important. These factors include guaranteed minimum income, social care, transport, pure drinking water, sewerage, proper food preparation, good sanitary conditions, health care, national health insurance, immunization against childhood diseases, medical care and education, absence of heavy physical work by children and limitation of the number of children per family. The influence of emotional conditions and of maternal efficiency and care are evident, also.

Income and educational level are interrelated and interact in a complex manner. The complexity of rural and urban environmental differences during growth is obvious, too; these differences are related to sociological factors. Usually the per capita income is lower in rural than in urban areas. No discernible effect of urbanisation on height and weight is present in some countries after standardizing for race and income (Hamill et al., 1972).

Although social differences have been observed commonly, a considerable decrease in socioeconomic differences in the distributions of height and weight and of menarcheal age has occurred in most European countries. In these countries, nutrition and other environmental factors needed for an optimum physical development are generally available nowadays. This decrease in the differences in living standards between socioeconomic groups, associated with decreases in the previously observed anthropometric differences, favors an environmental hypothesis. In German children aged between 6 and 11 years of age, there are no significant differences between the various social groups nor between rural and urban groups (Walter et al., 1975). In German boys and girls aged 9.5 to 10.5 years of age, Walter (1977) showed that, although a slight increase of height and weight is observed with an increase in parental income, the correlation coefficients between income and height or weight are very low and nonsignificant. Similarly, Lindgren (1976) did not find significant socioeconomic differences in height, weight, or ages at peak height velocity, peak weight velocity or menarche, though the girls of the lower socioeconomic groups tended to have higher weights for height at all ages. In this study, the socioeconomic criteria were father's occupation and family income.

It appears that with improvements in living standards, a decrease occurs in menarcheal age and that major variations in age at
menarche in relation to socioeconomic status are less apparent in
industrial than in non-industrialised countries (Table 1). Many
reports show, indeed, the absence of social effects on menarcheal
age in modern industrial countries (Roberts et al., 1971, 1975;
Brundtland and Walløe, 1973; Lindgren, 1976; Furu, 1976; Jéniček
and Demirjian, 1974; Kantero and Widholm, 1971; Wachholder and
Cantraine, 1974). For skeletal maturity status also, no consistent pattern of rural-urban differences are present in the United
States, nor a relationship with family income or parental education (Roche et al., 1978). The gradual decrease in the differences
for height, weight and menarcheal age between poor and rich classes
should be correlated with the occurrence of secular changes in
industrial countries (Brundtland and Walløe, 1973; Dann and Roberts,
1973; Tanner, 1975; Walter et al., 1975).

This does not exclude the expectation that where there are
social differences, assortative mating will help maintain them.
Using data for stature, Schumacher and Knussmann (1978) compared
brothers and sisters when adult. Within each pair of siblings one
was upwardly mobile on the social scale but the other remained at
the level of the parents. Both members of each pair lived in the
same familial environment. There was a significantly greater
stature in the upward mobile siblings than in the others. This
could support a hypothesis that a genetic mechanism is operating.
Alternatively, the greater stature may be responsible for the
upward mobility.

CONCLUSION

The causes of the socioeconomic differences in growth seem to
be multiple. One major factor causing these differences is considered to be standard of living, especially nutrition. An increasing equality in living conditions between different socioeconomic
classes may have contributed to the diminishing disparity in growth
rates between groups of children in different socioeconomic strata.
However, in a large number of countries many environmental factors
needed for optimum growth and development are unavailable. The
existence of marked socioeconomic differences in the growth and
development of children in these countries allows the conclusion
that growth rate and level are very sensitive indicators of
environmental influences.

REFERENCES

Acheson, R. M., 1960, Effects of nutrition and disease on human
       growth, in: "Human Growth," vol. 3, J. M. Tanner, ed.,
       Pergamon Press, London.
Acheson, R. M., and Hewitt, D., 1954, The Oxford Child Health Sur-
       vey. Stature and skeletal maturation in the preschool-
       child, Brit. J. Prev. Soc. Med., 8:59.
Amirhakimi, G. H., 1974, Growth from birth to 2 years of rich urban
       and poor rural Iranian children compared with Western norms,
       Ann. Hum. Biol., 1:427.
Ashcroft, M. T., Heneage, P., and Lovell, H., 1966, Heights and
       weights of Jamaican schoolchildren of various ethnic groups,
       Am. J. Phys. Anthropol., 24:35.
Attalah, N. L., 1978, Age at menarche of schoolgirls in Egypt,
       Ann. Hum. Biol., 5:185.
Aw, E., and Tye, C. E., 1970, Age at menarche of a group of Singa-
       pore girls, Hum. Biol., 42:329.
Bai, K. I., and Vijayalakshmi, B., 1973, Sexual maturation of
       Indian girls in Andra Pradesh (South India), Hum. Biol., 45:
       695.
Bailey, K. V., 1970, A study of human growth in the framework of
       applied nutrition and public health nutrition programs in
       the Western Pacific region, Monogr. Soc. Res. Child Dev.,
       35:40.
Banerjee, P., 1969, Birth weight of the Bengali new born: effect
       of the economic position of the mother, Ann. Hum. Genet.,
       33:99.
Bogin, B. A., and MacVean, R. B., 1978, Growth in height and weight
       of urban Guatemalan primary school children of low and high
       socio-economic class, Hum. Biol., 50:477.
Brundtland, G. H., and Walløe, L., 1973, Menarcheal age in Norway:
       halt in the trend towards earlier maturation, Nature, 241:
       478.
Burrell, R., Healy, M., and Tanner, J. M., 1961, Age at menarche in
       South African Bantu schoolgirls living in the Transkei
       Reserve, Hum. Biol., 33:250.
Chandra, R. K., 1979, Interactions of nutrition, infection and
       immune response, Acta Paed. Scand., 68:137.
Chang, K., Lee, M., Low, M., and Kvan, E., 1963, Height and weight
       of Southern Chinese children, Am. J. Phys. Anthropol., 21:
       497.
Chrzastek-Spruch, H., 1977, Some genetic and environmental problems
       of physical growth and development of children aged 0-7
       years, in: "Growth and Development·Physique," O. Eiben, ed.,
       Akadémiai Kiadó, Budapest.
Dann, T. C., and Roberts, D. F., 1973, End of the trend? A 12 year
       study of age at menarche, Brit. Med. J., 3:265.
Douglas, J. W. B., 1962, The height of boys and girls and their
       home environment, Mod. Probl. Paediatr., 7:178.

Douglas, J. W. B., and Blomfield, J. M., 1958, "Children Under Five," Allen and Unwin, London.

Dreizen, S., Snodgrasse, R. M., Webb-Peploe, H., and Spies, T. D., 1958, The retarding effect of protracted undernutrition on the appearance of the postnatal ossification centers in the hand and wrist, Hum. Biol., 30:253.

El Lozy, M., 1978, Socio-economic influences on the weight-height relationship in pre-school children, Growth, 42:55.

Eveleth, P. B., and Tanner, J. M., 1976, "Worldwide Variation in Human Growth," Cambridge University Press, Cambridge.

Furu, M., 1976, Menarcheal age in Stockholm girls, 1967, Ann. Hum. Biol., 3:587.

Goldstein, H., 1971, Factors influencing the height of seven year old children. Results from the National Child Development Study, Hum. Biol., 43:92.

Graffar, M., Asiel, M., and Emery-Hauzem, C., 1962, La croissance de l'enfant normal jusqu'à trois ans, Acta Paed. Belg., 16:5.

Greulich, W. W., 1951, The growth and developmental status of Guamanian school-children in 1947, Am. J. Phys. Anthropol., 9:55.

Hamill, P. V. V., Johnston, F. E., and Lemeshow, S., 1972, Height and weight of children: socio-economic status, National Center for Health Statistics, 11:119.

Jéníček, M., and Demirjian, A., 1974, Age at menarche in French Canadian urban girls, Ann. Hum. Biol., 1:339.

Kantero, R. L., and Widholm, O., 1971, The age of menarche in Finnish girls in 1969, Acta Obstet. Gynecol. Scand., 50: Suppl. 14:7.

Kark, E., 1956, Puberty in South African girls. II. Social class in relation to the menarche, South Afr. J. Clin. Med., 2:84.

Kralj-Čerček, L., 1956, The influence of food, body build and social origin on the age at menarche, Hum. Biol., 28:393.

Laska-Mierzejewska, T., 1970, Effect of ecological and socio-economic factors on the age at menarche, body height and weight of rural girls in Poland, Hum. Biol., 42:284.

Lechtig, A., Delgado, H., Lasky, R., Yarbrough, C., Klein, R. E., Habicht, J.-P., and Béhar, M., 1975, Maternal nutrition and fetal growth in developing countries, Am. J. Dis. Child., 129:553.

Lee, M. M., Chang, K. S. F., and Chan, M. M. C., 1963, Sexual maturation of Chinese girls in Hong Kong, Pediatrics, 32:389.

Lindgren, G., 1976, Height, weight and menarche in Swedish urban school children in relation to socio-economic and regional factors, Ann. Hum. Biol., 3:501.

Low, W. D., Chan, S. T., Chang, K. S., and Lee, M. M., 1964, Skeletal maturation of Southern Chinese children, Child Dev., 35:1313.

Martorell, R., 1979, Nutrition-infection interactions and human growth, Paper, Human Biology Council, San Francisco.

Milicer, H., 1968, Age at menarche of girls in Wrocław, Poland, in 1966, Hum. Biol., 40:249.

Moore, M. E., Stunkard, A., and Srole, L., 1962, Obesity, social class and mental illness, JAMA, 181:962.

Neyzi, O., Alp, H., and Orhon, A., 1975a, Sexual maturation in Turkish girls, Ann. Hum. Biol., 2:49.

Neyzi, O., Alp, H., Yalcinday, A., Yakacikli, S., and Orhon, A., 1975b, Sexual maturation in Turkish boys, Ann. Hum. Biol., 2:251.

Raghavan, K. V., Singh, D., and Swaminathan, M. C., 1971, Heights and weights of well nourished Indian school children, Indian J. Med. Res., 59:648.

Rao, D. H., and Satyanarayana, K., 1976, Nutritional status of people of different socio-economic groups in a rural area with special reference to preschool children, Ecology of Food and Nutrition, 4:237.

Rea, J. N., 1971, Social and economic influences on the growth of pre-school children in Lagos, Hum. Biol., 43:46.

Roberts, D. F., Chinn, S., Girija, B., and Singh, H. D., 1977, A study of menarcheal age in India, Ann. Hum. Biol., 4:171.

Roberts, D. F., Rozner, L. M., and Swan, A. V., 1971, Age at menarche, physique and environment in industrial north east England, Acta Paediatr. Scand., 60:158.

Roberts, D. F., Danskin, M. J., and Chinn, S., 1975, Menarcheal age in Northumberland, Acta Paediatr. Scand., 64:1.

Roche, A. F., Roberts, J., and Hamill, P. V. V., 1978, Skeletal maturity of youth 12-17 years: racial, geographical area, and socio-economic differentials, National Center for Health Statistics, Series 11, No. 167.

Rona, R., and Pereira, G., 1974, Factors that influence age of menarche in girls in Santiago, Chile, J. Mammal., 55:33.

Rowland, M. G., Cole, T. J., and Whitehead, R. G., 1977, A quantitative study into the role of infection in determining nutritional status in Gambian village children, Br. J. Nutr., 37:441.

Rush, D., 1974, Perinatal mortality, race, social status and hospital of birth: The association with birthweight, in: "Congenital Defects. New Direction in Research,", D. T. Janerick, R. G. Skalko and I. H. Porter, eds., Academic Press, London.

Sabharwal, K. P., Morales, S., and Mendez, J., 1966, Body measurements and creatinine excretion among upper and lower socioeconomic groups of girls in Guatemala, Hum. Biol., 38:131.

Schreider, E., 1967, Un mécanisme sélectif possible de la différentation sociale des caractères biologiques, Biométrie humaine, 2:67.

Schumacher, A., and Knussmann, R., 1978, Soziale Körperhöhenunterscheide bei Geschwistern, Homo, 29:173.

Shakir, A., 1971, The age at menarche in girls attending schools in Baghdad, Hum. Biol., 43:265.

Shakir, A., and Zaini, S., 1974, Skeletal maturation of the hand
        and wrist of young children in Baghdad, Ann. Hum. Biol.,
        1:189.

Singh, M. D., and Roberts, D. F., 1975, Menarcheal age in South
        India, Am. J. Obstet. Gynecol., 122:537.

Silverstone, J. T., Gordon, R., and Stunkard, A. J., 1969, Social
        factors in obesity in London, Practitioner, 202:682.

Stein, Z., Susser, M., Saenger, G., and Morolla, F., 1975, "Famine
        and Human Development," Oxford University Press, New York.

Tanner, J. M., 1975, Trend towards earlier menarche in London,
        Oslo, Copenhagen, The Netherlands and Hungary, Nature, 243:
        95.

Thomson, A. M., 1963, Prematurity: Socio-economic and nutritional
        factors, Mod. Probl. Pediatr., 8:197.

Thomson, A. M., 1978, Clinical and environmental determinants of
        fetal growth, in: "Paediatrics and Growth," D. Barltrop,
        ed., Fellowship of Postgraduate Medicine, London.

Wachholder, A., and Cantraine, F., 1974, Etude de la puberté.
        Paramètres somatiques (taille - poids) et sociaux des 56
        filles de l'échantillon Belge. Centre International de
        l'enfance, compte-rendu, 64.

Walter, H., 1977, Socio-economic factors and human growth. Observa-
        tions on school children from Bremen, in: "Growth and Devel-
        opment.Physique," O. Eiben, ed., Akadémiai Kiadó, Budapest.

Walter, H., Fritz, M., and Welker, A., 1975, Untersuchungen zur
        sozialen Verteiling von Körperhöhe und Körpergewicht,
        Z. Morph. Anthrop., 67:6.

Whitelaw, A. G. L., 1971, The association of social class and
        sibling number with skinfold thickness in London school-
        boys, Hum. Biol., 43:414.

19. PSYCHOSOCIAL FACTORS IN HUMAN GROWTH

Deprivation and Failure to Thrive

Paolo Parisi[1] and Violetta de Martino[2]

[1]Department of Medical Genetics, University of Rome;
and The Mendel Institute, Rome
[2]Institute of Psychiatry, University of Rome

In a 13th century chronicle attributed to the Franciscan
Salimbene of Parma, the King of Sicily and then Holy Roman Emperor,
Frederick II von Hohenstaufen, is reported to have performed an
experiment "to find out what kind of speech . . . children would
have when they grew up, if they spoke to no one beforehand. So,
he bade foster mothers and nurses to suckle the children, to bathe
and to wash them, but in no way to prattle with them or to speak
to them . . . But -- the medieval historian concludes -- he labored
in vain, because the children all died. For they could not live
without the petting and the joyful faces and loving words of their
foster mothers."

Reasonable doubt can be cast on this possibly apocryphal
account concerning one of the most enlightened sovereigns of all
time. Yet, whatever its historical value, this account clearly
concurs with previous ones in indicating a rather profound concern
for the psychological needs of the infant dating back to the most
ancient times (cf. Patton and Gardner, 1962).

The tragic consequences of the lack of sufficient contact and
stimulation on the infant's growth and survival have, however,
become clearer and gradually accepted by scientifically oriented
minds only in relatively recent times. It was in 1941, at the
annual meeting of the American Pediatric Society, that Harry Bakwin
first suggested that the well-known failure to thrive observed in
infants hospitalized for relatively long periods of time might be
due to loneliness and emotional deprivation (Bakwin, 1942). Four
years later, moving the target from pediatricians to psychiatrists
and psychoanalysts, Rene Spitz extended the notion of what had
become known as "hospitalism" and indicated a very similar

condition in infants placed in institutions (Spitz, 1945) which he
later called "anaclitic depression" (Spitz, 1946b). There followed
a few papers in the forties and fifties and, after being described
in children confined in hospitals or institutions, the syndrome of
failure to thrive without an apparent organic basis was found also
in children living with their families, so that the new expression
"maternal deprivation" (Bowlby, 1951) soon became familiar among
pediatricians. In 1962, the increased awareness of the many psychological implications and complications involved in pediatric practice, largely the result of the dramatic changes that had already
come to characterize the so-called affluent society, prompted
Talbot to entitle his Borden Award Address to the American Academy
of Pediatrics with the following question: "Has psychological
malnutrition taken the place of rickets and scurvy in contemporary
pediatric practice?" (Talbot, 1963).

   An increasing number of case reports, follow-up, retrospective
and other studies have contributed much evidence in recent years,
and reviews have been published (Casler, 1961; Yarrow, 1961;
De Toni, 1972; Steinhausen, 1973). As a result, it is now recognized that a child may fail to thrive because of confinement,
emotional deprivation, and/or insufficient psychosocial stimulation, although a satisfactory interpretation has not yet been
reached and doubt remains that nutritional factors may sometimes
have been inadequately assessed. According to the factors stressed,
this condition has been variously called environmental retardation
(Gesell and Amatruda, 1941), hospitalism (Spitz, 1945), anaclitic
depression (Spitz, 1946b), emotional deprivation (Bakwin, 1949),
and maternal deprivation (Bowlby, 1951), etc., while in more
recent years expressions such as (nonorganic) failure to thrive or
psychosocial deprivation or psychosocial dwarfism have been
preferred.

FAILURE TO THRIVE AND PSYCHOSOCIAL DEPRIVATION: A REVIEW OF THE
EVIDENCE

Studies on Children Confined in Institutions

   "En la casa de niños expositos el nino se va poniendo triste
y muchos de ellos mueren de tristeza." (In the foundling home, the
children become sad and many of them die of sorrow.) Such was the
verdict of a Spanish bishop in 1760--a verdict that Spitz adopted
as an epigraph for his classic 1945 paper. It vividly expresses a
long-time awareness of the tragic problems related to the extremely
high mortality of homeless infants kept in foundling homes for
custodial care. As both Spitz and Bakwin recall, the subject was
extensively discussed at the 1915 annual meeting of the American
Pediatric Society, following Chapin's report according to which,

in all but one of ten infant asylums located in different cities of the United States, every child under two years of age died (Spitz, 1945; Bakwin, 1949). In more recent years, when mortality rates in institutions (at least in the United States and other developed countries) started to compare more favorably with the rates of mortality in the general population, institutionalized children almost invariably developed psychiatric and other disturbances, so that the role of the foundling home was rediscussed and a tendency developed to place homeless children in foster homes as early as possible.

Just about the time that failure to thrive of children confined in hospitals was being brought to the attention of pediatricians and attributed to emotional factors (Bakwin, 1942, 1949), the similarly evil effects of child confinement in institutions were stressed by a paper accordingly entitled "Hospitalism" and primarily directed to psychiatrists (Spitz, 1945), so that the foundling home came to be charged with responsibility for physical as well as mental growth impairment.

Spitz made a long-term investigation into the first year of life of confined infants, comparing two institutions: (1) a typical foundling home, and (2) the nursery of a penal institution in which delinquent girls were sequestered. The two institutions were strictly comparable in general housing, hygienic and nutritional conditions, as well as clothing, medical care, etc., which were all described in great detail as being of a high standard. In particular, food was reported to be "excellently prepared" in both institutions and to vary "according to the needs of the individual child at each age". The children in the nursery, however, had more toys, a richer visual radius, and possibly a higher radius of locomotion. Most important, they usually had the full-time care of their own mother, whereas in the foundling home many children had to be cared for by one nurse most of the time, so that "they lack all human contact for most of the day."

Figure 1 shows the evolution of the average Developmental Quotient during the first year of life in the children of the two institutions and in a matched control sample from the general population. The initial difference between the means for DQ was attributed to the poorer genetic status of the nursery children of delinquent minors. It can be seen that foundling home infants undergo a rapid and continuous decrease in their initially good mean DQ, while the opposite is true of nursery infants, who show a steady rise and do not significantly differ from their matched controls. By the age of 2 years, the mean DQ in the foundling home children had decreased to 45.

Moreover, "in spite of the fact that hygiene and precautions against contagion were impeccable," the foundling home children

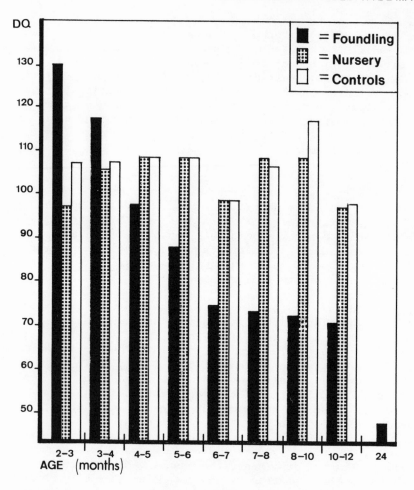

Fig. 1. Evolution of the average Developmental Quotient in Spitz's
         foundling home infants compared to nursery infants and
         controls. See text for explanations. (Redrawn after
         Spitz, 1945).

appeared highly susceptible to infection and, what is more, this
susceptibility was more marked in the older age groups, rather than
in the younger ones, as would be expected. The mortality rates
were impressively high. A follow-up study showed total mortality
in the foundling home had been over 37% in 2 years (Spitz, 1946a).
The children who could be reexamined were extraordinarily retarded,
both mentally and physically, and had heights and weights that were
about what would be expected for children half their age. By
contrast, the nursery children had developed normally and none of
them had died.

Another classic investigation was carried out in 1948 in occupied Germany by the British nutritionist Widdowson (1951). She studied the growth of two groups of war orphans aged 4 to 14 years in two closely comparable municipal orphanages: Bienenhaus and Vogelnest. Both groups had official rations only and the study was planned to evaluate the effect of additional food on growth patterns. Therefore, heights and weights of all children in the two groups, each composed of about 50 boys and girls, were measured every 2 weeks for a year. During the first 6 months, both groups had the official rations, whereas extra food was supplied in the second half of the year to the Vogelnest children, but not to the Bienenhaus children.

The results of the experiment, presented in Figure 2, were astonishing, to say the least. In the first 6 months of the study, although both groups were having exactly the same food, Bienenhaus children gained very little weight (< 0.5 kg) as compared to normal weight gain at Vogelnest (1.4 kg). In the second half of the year, however, irrespective of the extra food they were receiving, Vogelnest children gained less weight (~1.2 kg) than when they were on the basic rations. In contrast, Bienenhaus children, although they were having the same food as in the first 6 months, gained five times more weight (>2.5 kg). The same trend was seen

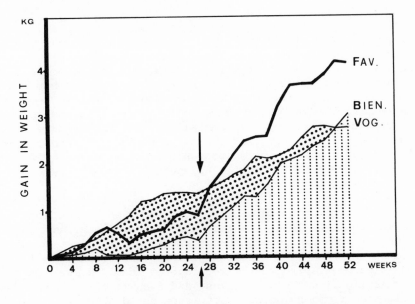

Fig. 2. Average weight gain (kg) in the war orphans at Bienenhaus (BIEN.) and Vogelnest (VOG.) and the favorites (FAV.) of the stern supervisor, reflecting the influence of emotional factors. See text for explanation. (Redrawn after Widdowson, 1951).

for height growth to a much less extent. Clearly, some other
factor was at work.

At the beginning of the study, the children at Vogelnest were
supervised by a nice happy young woman, while a very stern and
authoritarian woman, who had a small group of favorite children,
ruled the Bienenhaus home "with a rod of iron". Often meal times
were chosen to administer public rebukes, so that frequently the
children ate in a state of considerable agitation. Their very
poor growth in the first 6 months of the study was a clear reflec-
tion of this situation.

By a strange coincidence, just at the time when supply of
extra food at Vogelnest began, the authoritarian supervisor was
transferred from Bienenhaus to Vogelnest and she persuaded the
authorities to let her bring her favorites with her. When this
happened, as the right part of Figure 2 shows, the Bienenhaus
children, relieved of her stern discipline, gained considerably
more weight, although they continued to eat the same rations as
before. The Vogelnest children, instead, failed to benefit from
the extra food and, in fact, averaged a somewhat lower weight gain
than in the preceding 6 months. The favorites of the stern supervisor did benefit: Their weight gain was by far the greatest of
any.

Studies on Children Living with Families

Following the pioneering work of Bakwin, Spitz, and others in
the forties, the condition of infants in hospitals or other institutions came to be considered a real syndrome, with a well-defined
clinical picture: "The outstanding features are listlessness,
emaciation and pallor, relative immobility, quietness, unrespon-
siveness to stimuli . . . , indifferent appetite, failure to gain
weight . . . , frequent stools, poor sleep, an appearance of
unhappiness, proneness to febrile episodes, absence of sucking
habits." (Bakwin, 1949).

Somewhat similar features were soon observed in children
living with their families, so that the notion of confinement as
the origin of this failure to thrive was soon extended into that
of deprivation. Gesell and Amatruda (1941) had noted already that
the condition of "environmental retardation" could occur also in
children living with their families, and Senn (1945) had stressed
the influence of psychological factors on child nutrition, suggesting that an inadequate attitude by the mother might induce the
child to develop a distaste for food, leading to malnutrition and
failure to thrive. A correlation between growth failure and parental attitude was noted also, in passing, in an interesting
paper on excessive infant crying in relation to parent behavior

(Stewart, 1954). The theory of "maternal deprivation" was, however, developed by Bowlby, who stressed the dependency of a child's physical and psychological maturation on a satisfactory emotional relation with the mother (or mother substitute), particularly in the first 2 years of life (Bowlby, 1951, 1958). Ten years after its initial formulation, Bowlby's theory was reassessed by a World Health Organization study group (Ainsworth et al., 1962). The theory was criticized as being too simplistic and the notion of lack of sufficient psychosocial stimulation (e.g., visual, tactile, vestibular), as stressed in Casler's thorough review (1962), gradually came to be regarded as more important.

Case reports of children reared with their families but developmentally retarded, apparently due to insufficient psychosocial stimulation, parental deprivation, or overt abuse, occur in the literature of the sixties and seventies following a first, very detailed clinical study of two cases by Coleman and Provence in 1957 (Elmer, 1960; Patton and Gardner, 1962, 1963; Silver and Finkelstein, 1967). These reports included both white and black children and cases of twins and siblings (Leonard et al., 1966; Powell et al., 1967a; Siroky et al., 1971; Rayner and Rudd, 1973). However, family studies have usually failed to give any indication of possible genetic effects.

Whereas all the affected children show a severe growth retardation, usually associated with delayed skeletal maturation and other developmental problems, they do not all match the clinical picture originally described by Bakwin for children confined to hospitals or other institutions. In fact, rather than emaciation and pallor, they may have a healthy appearance. Their appetite, rather than being indifferent, is frequently described as voracious. The study of the family environment usually discloses a picture of child neglect or overt abuse, because of parental immaturity, marital strife, alcoholism, and the like.

Besides these numerous case reports, hospital records have been reviewed in some instances. Retrospective, follow-up, and other studies have thus been carried out, the results of which generally concur in pointing to emotional stress and lack of stimulation as the principal factors in possibly the majority of the cases of failure to thrive.

In 1947, Talbot and his associates reviewed the clinical records of more than 100 abnormally short children encountered at the Massachusetts General Hospital. They did not find an organic cause in about 50% of these, i.e., 28 boys and 23 girls aged 2.5 to 15 years. These patients were approximately as short as "pituitary dwarfs"; their skeletal age was also retarded and their subcutaneous tissue stores were scanty. Direct examination of parents and siblings failed to indicate any hereditary limitation

to growth potential. Therefore, extensive nutritional, endocrino-
logical, and psychological studies were carried out on 29 of these
patients. The results of these tests led to the general conclusion
that, although the dietary intakes, particularly of protein, were
basically adequate, dwarfism was probably due to a caloric malnutrition, and a resulting functional hypopituitarism, secondary to
emotional disturbances.

In more recent years, the records of the Boston Children's
Hospital were reviewed by Bullard et al. (1967). Out of 151
children admitted for a failure to thrive, 50 were found to have
no primary organic illness, but a frequent history of behavioral
disturbances. A follow-up study of 41 of these children 8 months
to 9 years after hospitalization revealed a high prevalence of
pathologic sequelae and emotional disturbances in close association
with family instability. In 35% of cases, and usually in relatively
stable families, there was no evidence of physical nor psychological disorder; a clear indication of the potential reversibility
of the condition.

Similar results were obtained by Shaheen et al. (1968) who
reviewed records at the Children's Hospital of Philadelphia and,
after excluding any case in which even slight evidence of a more
specific diagnosis was possible, identified 44 cases of pure
failure to thrive without an organic basis. A high prevalence of
psychological stress factors of various natures characterized the
patients' histories. Most of the children under 2 years of age
gained weight during hospitalization and most of these grew
normally 2 years after hospitalization.

In a retrospective study reviewing the records of 100 infants
admitted to the Boston Floating Hospital with a diagnosis of failure
to thrive, Hannaway (1970) found 51 cases without evidence of
organic illness; in 40 of these, abnormal maternal or environmental
relationships could be identified as the possible origin of the
condition.

The records of the Royal Alexandra Hospital for Children
(Sydney, Australia) were studied by Oates and Yu (1971) and 24 of
30 children with nonorganic failure to thrive were reviewed. A
history of family disruption was the usual finding; 10 families
were no longer intact and 3 children had been surrendered for
adoption. On further review of 21 of these 24 children at an
average of about 6 years after their initial presentation, Hufton
and Oates (1977) found persistent weight retardation in about 25%
of cases, while personality disorders and mental retardation were
common.

Sills (1978) reviewed the records of the Children's Hospital
of Buffalo and identified 185 cases of failure to thrive: 106 of

these did not have an organic etiology. When constitutional and
family causes as well as feeding and similar problems were accounted
for, pure psychosocial deprivation could be diagnosed in 92 cases.
However, because 45 more cases had an undetermined etiology and
because a clear organic etiology was found in only 18% of all the
children admitted with a failure to thrive (a percentage considerably lower than in previous studies), Sills suggested that the
tendency to look for organic causes, while searching with less dili-
gence for environmental factors, may frequently result in considerable bias.

FAILURE TO THRIVE AND PSYCHOSOCIAL DEPRIVATION: AN ANALYSIS OF
FACTORS AND TENTATIVE INTERPRETATIONS

Assessment of Nutritional Intake

     In view of these and similar reports of failure to thrive
without detectable organic basis, one cannot help asking the
obvious question: "But, did these children eat enough, in the
first place?" Because the case reports practically all refer to
children belonging to affluent populations, where even the poorest
people usually have enough to eat on account of developed social
welfare systems, the very possibility of underfeeding might have
been disregarded, or too rapidly dismissed. Yet, there may be
various reasons why a child should be underfed. First, food might
simply be lacking to the family, because of extreme poverty and/or
disorganization. Secondly, the child's nutritional intake might be
poor, in quantity and/or quality, because of parental neglect or
even without the parents being aware of it, out of ignorance or
lack of attention or of objective evaluation. Finally, the child
might refuse food, by not eating or spitting it or by subsequent
vomiting, out of anger, anxiety and overt struggle in the mother-
child relation, either in general or specifically at mealtimes.

     Because the information on nutrition will usually be supplied
by the mother, its reliability should be seriously questioned in
the absence of more thorough investigation. The mother might in
fact be reluctant to acknowledge lack of food in a society in which
poverty appears to be a fault. If food were available, she might
have feelings of guilt for proving incapable of coping with her
child's needs and not falling into the socially accepted mother's
stereotype. Alternatively, the mother might simply be unaware of
the possibility of her child's being underfed, out of ignorance or
on account of her own difficulties and personality troubles, as
frequently reported in the various studies and more extensively
discussed in the following section.

Is it possible, therefore, that underfeeding is probably the sole or major cause of the observed cases of nonorganic failure to thrive, and that the possible role of psychosocial factors on physical growth can be disregarded?

Whitten and associates (1969) have reported that, when fed an adequate diet, 11 of 13 maternally deprived infants gained weight during a 2-week hospitalization despite confinement, and that 7 of 7 continued to gain weight at home when fed by their mother under an observer's control. However, both the sample and the time of observation were too limited to yield final results. Moreover, the possible psychological and behavioral effects of the situational modifications were not controlled. The change in the feeding situation, from a conflicting relation with the mother to an even neutral relation with a nurse in the hospital may have been a positive experience for the child, at least in the short range. Also, a 2-week hospitalization may be too brief for an infant to physically resent the effects of confinement, especially if the previous relation with the family environment was unsatisfactory. Similarly, the presence of an observer at home at mealtimes, neutral as it may have been, may have not only influenced the mother's attitude (which the authors tended to dismiss), but also the infant's emotional response to it and to the feeding situation. The new environmental variable, the presence of an observer, may have attracted the attention and/or modified the perception of the infant, thus modifying the mother-child emotional relation and eventually improving the infant's psychological, behavioral, and physiological response to food.

In the classic studies on children confined to institutions, nutritional factors had been accounted for and dismissed as a possible cause of the observed growth retardation. It has been argued that what was controlled was the food given to the children, not what they actually ate. Specifically, it has been noted, for instance, that the orphans described by Widdowson as being "in a state of considerable agitation" as a result of their supervisor's public chastisements at mealtimes may not feel like eating all their food (Whitten et al., 1969). This seems reasonable, but anyone acquainted with similar institutions will find it questionable that orphanage children would have been allowed to leave food on their plates, especially in a postwar German orphanage ruled "with a rod of iron". On the other hand, Fried and Mayer (1948) had noted a striking correlation in institutionalized children between growth rate and emotional adjustment, observing that the correction of possible dietary inadequacies failed to result in normal growth unless the emotional stresses were removed.

More generally, it is difficult to see why the long-hospitalized children described by Bakwin and others should have been chronically underfed and have failed to thrive without nurses and doctors doing anything to improve their feeding. It is equally difficult to understand why the foundling home infants described by Spitz should have grown so poorly and shown such an incredibly high mortality and proneness to disease without any attempt being made to improve their feeding. In fact, Spitz reported the latter to be excellent and to vary "according to the needs of the individual child at each age". As for the possibility that underfeeding may have gone unnoticed, one should remember that each "Foundling Home is visited by the head physician and the medical staff at least once a day, often twice, and during these rounds the chart of each child is inspected as well as the child itself."

In a number of case reports and other clinical studies (starting with the classic observations by Talbot et al. in 1947 and those of Coleman and Provence in 1957) attempts are made to go beyond the cursory evaluation of socioeconomic conditions or a dismissing statement by the mother concerning the adequacy of diet. In these studies, in-depth nutritional histories are provided. Essentially these are derived from the mother, whose reliability remains questionable. The answers obtained from in-depth histories often differ from the casual statement by the mother and can elicit underfeeding, if present (Leonard et al., 1966; Bullard et al., 1967). When this is done accurately and cases of overt, or even suspected, underfeeding are excluded, many cases of failure to thrive still remain for which no explanation based on diet can be offered. Moreover, because a number of reports refer to school age children, it should be considered that, irrespective of the adequacy of the family environment, independent evaluations were possible and school dinners available to the children. In fact, and contrary to Bakwin's description of hospitalism and related anorexia, many of these children were "voracious", to the point of getting up at night to raid the pantry, of begging or stealing food from neighbors, nearby stores or school, of eating food from animal dishes or trash cans and doing all of these things without nausea or vomiting (Powell et al., 1967a; Frasier and Rallison, 1972; Rayner and Rudd, 1973). In conclusion, although underfeeding may be more common than usually assumed, it appears a non-organic failure to thrive may frequently occur with an adequate food intake.

Mothering and Infant Development

The one factor that really appears common to the children who fail to thrive without an organic basis is the deprivation and lack of environmental stimulation they experience as a result of physical and/or psychological confinement (whether in institutions or in their own families), inadequate relationships with adults, especially the mother or mother-substitute, child neglect or overt abuse. In the various clinical case reports, although the lack of

the father's active presence is occasionally stressed, it is the
mother who is usually reported to be inadequate to fulfill her
centrol role, either because of poverty, marital strife and related
environmental difficulties, or because of her individual personality
problems.

    Child growth and development are obviously very much related
to the adequacy of maternal care. In the Newcastle Survey of
Child Development, involving over 4,000 children, Neligan and
Purdham (1976) found the quality of the mother's care (assessed by
a health visitor in terms of food, clothing, supervision, affec-
tionate parental interest, etc.) during the child's first 3 years
of life was the most important factor, in addition to social class,
for the child's development. Somewhat similar results were obtained
by Moyes (1976) on St. Helena's schoolchildren population, although
the role of the biological mother was here obscured by the fact
that in this particular island most of the children live with a
mother-substitute, usually a grandmother. In a study of 3-year-
old children, Pollak (1979) found a number of developmental measures were not affected by the general housing conditions but were
very significantly related to adequacy of maternal care. It is
pertinent to mention that, in a prospective study, adopted children
were found to grow even better physically than their matched con-
trols--a clear indication of socioeconomic influences, but also
of more adequate mothering (Fisch et al., 1976).

    In a psychiatric study by Fischhoff et al. (1971), 10 out of
12 mothers who had deprived their children were found to have a
character disorder, showing disturbed childhood histories, poor
performance in current activities, desire for anaclitic relationships with intense need to be taken care of, and the use of denial
and isolation as the major defense mechanism. In another study
by Kerr et al. (1978), mothers of malnourished children, when
matched with mothers whose children were not malnourished despite
equally extreme poverty conditions, had more chronically disrupted
lives, reflecting disorganization in their housing conditions and
employment records, and showed narcissistic concerns that took
precedence over the needs of their children. In another study, a
high incidence of depression was found in the mothers of 32 under-
weight children (O'Callaghan and Hull, 1978). Mother-child relationships, particularly in the feeding situation, may be described
as characterized by continuous struggles in an atmosphere charged
with feelings of anger, anxiety, depression and frustration.
Frequently the mother is reported to be annoyed and frustrated at
the lack of professional opportunities or at her inadequacy or
inability to play with her child. Coleman and Provence's Case 2
mother, a college graduate, asked: "How does one play with a baby,
anyway?" Commenting on their finding that the mothers of these
children were commonly lacking in self-esteem, Leonard et al.
(1966) concluded that "each can be said to be failing to thrive

as a mother." And, in a general review of problems in growth, Olshin (1968) noted: "Although it is probably true that emotional deprivation and growth retardation are more commonly encountered among children of the depressed classes, it would be a mistake to discount the diagnosis in an infant from a family of affluence and education. Inadequate mothering crosses class lines . . ."

Primate Studies. According to the drive-reduction theory, the infant's attachment to the mother was thought to develop from the association between the mother's image and the alleviation of primary drive states, such as hunger and thirst. This theory was countered by the experiments of Harlow and Zimmerman (1959) who found contact comfort to be of critical importance in infant monkeys, with nursing and feeding playing a negligible role. Further experimental research on primates has shown even brief separation of infants from their mothers causes depression, withdrawal and other behavioral troubles, with a clinical picture strikingly similar to that of the anaclitic depression of psychologically deprived human infants (Mitchell et al., 1966; Kaufman and Rosenblum, 1969; Hinde and Spencer-Booth, 1971). Alterations of physical growth, however, were not observed in isolated infant monkeys fed an ad libitum diet (Kerr et al., 1969). If confirmed, the latter finding would suggest that failure of the human infant to thrive is more plausibly interpreted in terms of inadequate nutrition. Developmental stages in the monkey are simpler and are passed more quickly than in the human infant, and the nervous system, especially the higher centers that control emotional responses and interactions, are less complex. The fact that maternal deprivation induces gross, and sometimes permanent, behavioral abnormalities in infant monkeys may allow the inference that the same is true of the human infant. But the fact that associated effects on physical growth have not been elicited in infant monkeys may suggest that their faster development and simpler nervous systems make primates less prone to physical effects of psychological deprivation and stress.

Hormone Studies and Possible Mechanisms

Functional hypopituitarism was first identified in these patients by Talbot et al. (1947) and confirmed by later studies (Powell et al., 1967b; Krieger and Mellinger, 1971; Rayner and Rudd, 1973) but there are contrary reports (MacCarthy and Booth, 1971). The presence of hypopituitarism in nonorganic failure to thrive would appear to rule out interpretations based on diet inadequacy because growth hormone levels are higher than normal in severe malnutrition (Pimstone et al., 1968).

On the other hand, Talbot and his associates noted that normal growth was not necessarily resumed following correction of dietary

inadequacies, whereas the administration of methyl testosterone
appeared very efficient even in the absence of dietary changes.
Relative resistance to hormone treatment was indicated by some
later studies (Frasier and Rallison, 1972; Rayner and Rudd, 1973),
but usually the hormonal insufficiency was found to be reversible
with no treatment other than removing the patient from the emotion-
ally disturbed environment. When this was done, growth hormone
levels returned to normal and expected growth resumed (Powell et
al., 1967b; MacCarthy and Booth, 1971; Rayner and Rudd, 1973). It
has been reported, but not confirmed, that there is an increased
rate of cortisol secretion in these patients (Krieger and Good,
1970). Emotional stresses do stimulate adrenocortical functions.
However, these authors reported serum thyroxine levels were
decreased similarly in failure to thrive infants and in undernourished infants. This finding, perhaps with the occasional
absence of hypopituitarism (MacCarthy and Booth, 1971), calls for
a careful and critical evaluation of the nutritional history of
infants with failure to thrive.

As a whole, these observations support the hypothesis that
emotional factors play a role in failure to thrive and suggest that
the psychosomatic effects of stressful events are hormonally mediated. Patton and Gardner (1962) postulated a physiological pathway
whereby the impulses generated by the stressful events pass from
higher neural centers, particularly from the amygdaloid nuclei and
the limbic cortex, presumably the seat of emotional feelings, to
the hypothalamus, whence they would neurohumorally affect the
pituitary gland, resulting in a reduction of hormone-releasing
factors and, consequently, in a functional hypopituitarism. Another
tentative hypothesis concerning the possible mechanism is based on
the well-known effects of emotional states on intestinal mobility
and autonomic function, and postulates that stressful events may
result in an alteration of intestinal absorption. Most know from
personal experience that digestion can be impaired by emotional
disturbances but it is not clear that this could operate over a
long period.

As recalled by Widdowson (1951), "the effect of violent passion
on the digestive apparatus" was first elicited by Beaumont's observations, published in 1833, on a Canadian trapper suffering from a
gunshot wound which resulted in a gastric fistula. In more recent
times, another unique opportunity to study the relation between
digestion and emotional states arose when a feeding tube had to be
inserted into the stomach of an infant born with an underdeveloped
esophagus. For 15 months after birth, the mother carefully fed her
child by injecting a daily standard dosage of nutritional formula
into the tube, but never played with her nor cuddled her, fearing
to dislodge the tube. The child eventually had to be hospitalized
because of extreme depression and failure to thrive. Pepsin and
hydrochloric acid were found to be deficient and failed to respond

to histamine stimulation. Moreover, the hydrochloric acid secretion rate decreased when the child was depressed and withdrawn but it increased when she was angry, eating, or otherwise actively relating to external objects (Engel and Reichman, 1956; Engel et al., 1956).

CONCLUSION

Sills (1978) has suggested that most cases of failure to thrive are due to environmental deprivation, but that the clinician's bias in favor of organic etiology and the parents' reluctance to discuss psychosocial problems frequently result in lacking or faulty diagnoses. Of the 2,607 laboratory studies performed on the 185 patients he reviewed, none were useful without a specific indication from the history or physical examination. The obvious conclusion, in agreement with other studies, was that extensive laboratory investigations are unlikely to be effective and that nonorganic causes should be ruled out first in all cases of growth retardation.

A child may fail to thrive simply because he or she is underfed. This may be much more common than usually believed and be independent of the parents' education and socioeconomic status. Untenable as the tentative diagnosis may appear, it should not be dismissed without adequate information and control. A child's nutritional intake may be inadequate not only because of poverty, child neglect or overt abuse, but also because of parental ignorance and lack of attention or of an objective evaluation. The mother's reliability (or, for that matter, the reliability of the father) should be seriously questioned.

In some cases, however, nutrition may be adequate. If organic causes can be excluded, it is likely that these children suffer from some form of psychosocial confinement or lack of stimulation and that their failure to thrive is a psychosomatic response to the emotional stresses, isolation or deprivation to which they are exposed. The mechanism is unclear, but it is likely that hormonal factors and/or intestinal absorption are involved. In all these cases, the family environments, and especially the mother-child relationships and the mothers' personalities, should be the objects of close scrutiny.

A careful psychosocial history may be difficult to obtain from the usually reluctant parent and requires some independent control. However, it is essential for a correct diagnosis and treatment. Early diagnosis is very important because it can be difficult for these children to catch-up completely, both physically and mentally. Treatment necessarily involves a change in the environment, without which the child will frequently undergo repeated hospitalization and pathologic and behavioral sequelae.

REFERENCES

Ainsworth, M. D., Andry, R. G., Harlow, R. G., Lebovici, S., Mead, M., Prugh, D. G., and Woottoon, B., 1962, Deprivation of maternal care: A reassessment of its effects, WHO Public Health Papers, 14, Geneva.

Bakwin, H., 1942, Loneliness in infants, Am. J. Dis. Child., 63:30.

Bakwin, H., 1949, Emotional deprivation in infants, J. Pediatr., 35:512.

Bowlby, J., 1951, Maternal care and mental health, WHO Monogr. Ser., 2:67.

Bowlby, J., 1958, The nature of a child's ties to his mother, Int. J. Psychoanal., 39:350.

Bullard, D. M., Jr., Glaser, H. H., Heagarty, M. C., and Pivchik, E. C., 1967, Failure to thrive in the "neglected" child, Am. J. Orthopsychiatry, 37:680.

Casler, L., 1961, Maternal deprivation: A critical review of the current literature, Monogr. Soc. Res. Child Dev., 26, 2.

Coleman, R. W., and Provence, S., 1957, Environmental retardation (hospitalism) in infants living in families, Pediatrics, 19:285.

De Toni, G., 1972, Il ritardo dell'accrescimento somatico come conseguenza della privazione delle cure materne e di un' appropriata stimolazione emozionale, Minerva Pediatr., 24:2037.

Elmer, E., 1960, Failure to thrive - Role of the mother, Pediatrics, 25:717.

Engel, G. L., and Reichsman, F., 1956, Spontaneous and experimentally induced depression in infant with gastric fistula, J. Am. Psychoanal. Assoc., 4:428.

Engel, G. L., Reichsman, F., and Segal, H., 1956, A study of an infant with a gastric fistula. I. Behavior and the rate of total hydrochloric acid secretion, Psychosom. Med., 18:374.

Fisch, R. O., Bilek, M. S., Deinard, A. S., and Chang, P.-N., 1976, Growth, behavioral, and psychologic measurements of adopted children: The influences of genetic and socioeconomic factors in a prospective study, J. Pediatr., 89:494.

Fischhoff, J., Whitten, C. F., and Pettit, M. G., 1971, A psychiatric study of mothers of infants with growth failure secondary to maternal deprivation, J. Pediatr., 79:209.

Frasier, S. D., and Rallison, M. L., 1972, Growth retardation and emotional deprivation: Relative resistance to treatment with human growth hormone, J. Pediatr., 80:603.

Fried, R., and Mayer, M. F., 1948, Socio-emotional factors accounting for growth failure in children living in institution, J. Pediatr., 33:444.

Gesell, A., and Amatruda, C. S., 1941, "Developmental Diagnosis," Paul B. Hoeber, Medical Division of Harper and Row, New York.

Hannaway, P. J., 1970, Failure to thrive - A study of 100 infants and children, Clin. Pediatr., 9:96.

Harlow, H. F., and Zimmermann, R. R., 1959, Affectional responses
     in the infant monkey, Science, 130:421.
Hinde, R. A., and Spencer-Booth, Y., 1971, Effects of brief
     separation from mother on Rhesus monkeys, Science, 173:111.
Hufton, I. W., and Oates, R. K., 1977, Nonorganic failure to
     thrive: A long-term follow-up, Pediatrics, 59:73.
Kaufman, I. C., and Rosenblum, L. A., 1969, Effects of separation
     from mother on the emotional behavior of infant monkeys,
     Ann. N. Y. Acad. Sci., 159:681.
Kerr, G. R., Chamove, A. S., and Harlow, H. F., 1969, Environmental
     deprivation: Its effect on the growth of infant monkeys.
     J. Pediatr., 75:833.
Kerr, M. A. D., Bogues, J. L., and Kerr, D. S., 1978, Psychosocial
     functioning of mothers of malnourished children, Pediatrics,
     62:778.
Krieger, I., and Good, M. H., 1970, Adrenocortical and thyroid
     function in the deprivation syndrome. Comparison with
     growth failure due to undernutrition, congenital heart
     disease, or prenatal influences, Am. J. Dis. Child., 120:95.
Krieger, I., and Mellinger, R. C., 1971, Pituitary function in the
     deprivation syndrome, J. Pediatr., 79:216.
Leonard, M. F., Rhymes, J. P., and Solnit, A. J., 1966, Failure to
     thrive in infants, Am. J. Dis. Child., 111:600.
MacCarthy, D., and Booth, E. M., 1971, Parental rejection and
     stunting of growth, J. Psychosom. Res., 14:259.
Mitchell, G. D., Raymond, E. J., Ruppenthal, G. C., and Harlow,
     H. F., 1966, Long-term effects of total social isolation
     upon behavior of Rhesus monkeys, Psychol. Rep., 18:567.
Moyes, C. D., 1976, Adverse factors affecting growth of school-
     children in St. Helena, Arch. Dis. Childh., 51:435.
Neligan, G. A., and Prudham, D., 1976, Family factors affecting
     child development, Arch. Dis. Childh., 51:853.
Oates, R. K., and Yu, J. S., 1971, Children with non-organic
     failure to thrive: A community problem, Med. J. Aust., 2:199.
O'Callaghan, M. J., and Hull, D., 1978, Failure to thrive or
     failure to rear?, Arch. Dis. Childh., 53:788.
Olshin, I. J., 1968, Problems in growth, Pediatr. Clin. North Am.,
     15:433.
Patton, R. G., and Gardner, L. I., 1962, Influence of family
     environment on growth: The syndrome of "maternal deprivation",
     Pediatrics, 30:957.
Patton, R. G., and Gardner, L. I., 1963, "Growth Failure in Maternal
     Deprivation," Charles C Thomas, Springfield.
Pimstone, B. L., Barbezat, G., Hansen, J. D., and Murray, P., 1968,
     Studies on growth hormone secretion in protein-calorie mal-
     nutrition, Am. J. Clin. Nutr., 21:482.
Pollak, M., 1979, Housing and mothering, Arch. Dis. Childh., 54:54.

Powell, G. F., Brasel, J. A., and Blizzard, R. M., 1967a, Emotional
     deprivation and growth retardation simulating idiopathic
     hypopituitarism. I. Clinical evaluation of the syndrome,
     N. Engl. J. Med., 276:1271.

Powell, G. F., Brasel, J. A., Raiti, S., and Blizzard, R. M.,
     1967b, Emotional deprivation and growth retardation simulat-
     ing idiopathic hypopituitarism. II. Endocrinologic evalua-
     tion of the syndrome, N. Engl. J. Med., 276:1279.

Rayner, P. H. W., and Rudd, B. T., 1973, Emotional deprivation in
     three siblings associated with functional pituitary growth
     hormone deficiency, Aust. Paediatr. J., 9:79.

Senn, M. J. E., 1945, Influence of psychological factors on the
     nutrition of children, Am. J. Public Health, 35:212.

Shaheen, E., Alexander, D., Truskowsky, M., and Barbero, G. J.,
     1968, Failure to thrive - A retrospective profile, Clin.
     Pediatr., 7:255.

Sills, R. H., 1978, Failure to thrive - The role of clinical and
     laboratory evaluation, Am. J. Dis. Child., 132:967.

Silver, H. K., and Finkelstein, M., 1967, Deprivation dwarfism,
     J. Pediatr., 70:317.

Siroky, J., Pelikan, L., Farkova, H., Mores, A., and Koluchova, J.,
     1971, Schweres Deprivationssyndrom bei einem Zwillingspaar
     nach langdauernder sozialer Isolation, Folia Phoniatr.,
     23:355.

Spitz, R. A., 1945, Hospitalism - An inquiry into the genesis of
     psychiatric conditions in early childhood, Psychoanal. Stud.
     Child., 1:53.

Spitz, R. A., 1946a, Hospitalism - A follow-up investigation
     described in volume I, 1945, Psychoanal. Stud. Child., 2:113.

Spitz, R. A., 1946b, Anaclitic depression, Psychoanal. Stud. Child.,
     2:313.

Steinhausen, H.-Ch., 1973, Psychologische Merkmale verschiedener
     Formen des Minderwuchses, Acta Paedopsychiatr., 39:278.

Stewart, A. H., 1954, Excessive infant crying (colic) in relation
     to parent behavior, Am. J. Psychiatry, 110:687.

Talbot, N. B., Sobel, E. H., Burke, B. S., Lindemann, E., and
     Kaufman, S. B., 1947, Dwarfism in healthy children: Its
     possible relation to emotional, nutritional and endocrine
     disturbances, N. Engl. J. Med., 236:783.

Talbot, N. B., 1963, Has psychologic malnutrition taken the place
     of rickets and scurvy in contemporary pediatric practice?,
     Pediatrics, 31:909.

Yarrow, L., 1961, Maternal deprivation: Toward an empirical and
     conceptual re-evaluation, Psychol. Bull., 58:459.

Whitten, C. F., Pettit, M. G., and Fischhoff, J., 1969, Evidence
     that growth failure from maternal deprivation is secondary
     to undereating, J. Am. Med. Assoc., 209:1675.

Widdowson, E. M., 1951, Mental contentment and physical growth,
     Lancet, 260:1316.